Cultural-Existential Psychology

Cultural psychology and experimental existential psychology are two of the fastest-growing movements in social psychology. In this book Daniel Sullivan combines both perspectives to present a groundbreaking analysis of culture's role in shaping the psychology of threat experience. The first part of the book presents a new theoretical framework guided by three central principles: that humans are in a unique existential situation because we possess symbolic consciousness and culture; that culture provides psychological protection against threatening experiences, but also helps to create them; and that interdisciplinary methods are vital to understanding the link between culture and threat. In the second part of the book, Sullivan presents a novel program of research guided by these principles. Focusing on a case study of a traditionalist group of Mennonites in the Midwestern United States, Sullivan examines the relationships between religion, community, guilt, anxiety, and the experience of natural disaster.

DANIEL SULLIVAN is an Assistant Professor in the Psychology Department at the University of Arizona in Tucson. He is the author of several articles and book chapters on topics in experimental existential psychology, including terror management theory, enemyship and conspiracy theories, and interpretations of suffering and victimhood. He has also written on film and literature, and with Jeff Greenberg was the coeditor of *Death in Classic and Contemporary Film: Fade to Black* (2013).

Cultural-Existential Psychology

The Role of Culture in Suffering and Threat

Daniel Sullivan
University of Arizona

CAMBRIDGE
UNIVERSITY PRESS

CAMBRIDGE
UNIVERSITY PRESS

University Printing House, Cambridge CB2 8BS, United Kingdom

Cambridge University Press is part of the University of Cambridge.

It furthers the University's mission by disseminating knowledge in the pursuit of education, learning and research at the highest international levels of excellence.

www.cambridge.org
Information on this title: www.cambridge.org/9781107096868

First published 2016

A catalogue record for this publication is available from the British Library

Library of Congress Cataloguing in Publication data
Sullivan, Daniel, 1940–
Cultural-existential psychology : the role of culture in suffering and threat / Daniel Sullivan.
New York : Cambridge University Press, 2016.
LCCN 2015044941 | ISBN 9781107096868 (hardback)
LCSH: Psychology – Social aspects. | Existential psychology. | Culture – Psychological aspects.
LCC BF57 .S885 2016 | DDC 150.19/2–dc23
LC record available at http://lccn.loc.gov/2015044941

ISBN 978-1-107-09686-8 Hardback

To Leah and Beckett

One of the ultimate concerns of the modern worldview can be thus characterized. Man has always been aware of certain realities and values, certain objects of belief and validities, for which there is no room in his seemingly strictly circumscribed space . . . At first he expresses the certainty of this awareness in that he consolidates all such things in separate existences outside of life. He beholds them in the sharply separated beyond and lets them react back from there onto life . . . Against this naiveté arises critical enlightenment, which recognizes nothing "beyond" the subject; it throws back everything located in the beyond within the bounds of subjective immediacy, and thus declares as illusion whatever tends to persist nevertheless in independent confrontation. This is the first step of the great tendency in intellectual history: to place back into life itself, by means of a mighty revolution, everything that had been established outside of life in its own existence and which came to life from beyond. But since at this point life is conceived as absolute immanence, everything remains in a subjectivization . . . a denial of the form of the beyond, and one fails to notice that with this delimitation of the subject he has in fact made himself dependent on the idea of the beyond, and that it is only in and from this beyond that the boundary could take shape in which life was caught and busied itself in the unbreakable circle of the self.

– Georg Simmel (1918/2010, p. 17)

When the auratic traces of the sacred have been lost and the products of a synthetic, world-picturing power of imagination have vanished, the form of understanding, now fully differentiated in its validity basis, becomes so transparent that the communicative practice of everyday life no longer affords any niches for the structural violence of ideologies . . . In place of the positive task of meeting a certain need for interpretation by ideological means, we have the negative requirement of preventing holistic interpretations from coming into existence . . . The desired equivalent for no-longer-available ideologies might simply consist in the fact that everyday knowledge . . . remains diffuse, or at least never attains that level of articulation at which alone knowledge can be accepted as valid according to the standards of cultural modernity. *Everyday consciousness* is robbed of its power to synthesize; it becomes *fragmented.*

– Jürgen Habermas (1987, pp. 354–355; emphasis in original)

Contents

Figures

Tables

Preface

This book attempts to be interdisciplinary, and to draw on a considerable body of literature that has amassed in the social sciences and philosophy in the past 200 years. Its format is somewhat unusual: Part I of the book presents a new theoretical perspective, cultural-existential psychology, while Part II reports original research that I conducted as an initial demonstration of the fruitfulness of this perspective.

For these reasons, readers from different disciplines may find some parts of the book more difficult to process than others. The aim of this preface is to state clearly the intentions of the book and each individual chapter, as a kind of guide for the reader.

Chapter 1 is an introduction to the research traditions that preceded and contribute to cultural-existential psychology. It begins with summaries of the recent experimental existential and cultural movements in social psychology, and discusses the need to combine these two perspectives to provide a comprehensive scientific account of how people in diverse settings differentially experience and react to suffering and threat. It then reviews some of the precursors of a combined cultural-existential perspective in the history of the social sciences.

Chapter 2 lays out the three "fundamental principles" of cultural-existential psychology. The first is that humans are unique animals by virtue of our capacity for symbolic consciousness. The second is that culture is both a defense against and a source of the problems of theodicy and nihilism. In other words, cultural systems provide "threat orientations" – they predispose us to experience certain kinds of events as threatening, while also simultaneously providing characteristic means of interpreting and defending against those threats. The third principle is that multiple, interdisciplinary methods are required to fully understand how the individual's experience of threat and suffering is shaped by culture.

Chapter 3 offers a new integrative model of the types of threats that all humans are capable of experiencing, derived from existential philosophy. In line with terror management theory, the cultural-existential perspective posits that death is the ultimate threat in human experience, and that death awareness is the ultimate source of all other threats. However, because people invest in symbolic structures that protect them from awareness of death – such as religion and self-esteem – they often experience threat not as death angst, but rather as an infringement on one of these protective structures.

The chapter distinguishes between three general levels of threat experience that are hierarchically related to the ultimate threat of death angst. At the lowest level of threat experience, people often undergo everyday feelings of either *anxiety* or *guilt*. Anxiety broadly encompasses feelings of uncertainty about how to act in the world, the probability of certain desired or undesired outcomes, or the meaningfulness of one's daily activities. Guilt broadly refers to feelings of inadequacy, immorality, or low self-esteem that individuals experience after a behavior that violates internalized standards for proper and worthy conduct.

If these lower-level threats are not resolved, they can become more serious, and the individual may feel that higher-order symbolic structures – such as their basic conviction that they are a worthy person – have come under threat. At this stage, individuals undergo the second-level threat of *angst*. Unresolved angst can bring the individual to the rare third-level threat of *nihilism*: the lack of any belief that life is worth living. The chapter distinguishes between *nihilistic disorientation* – the belief that there are no meaningful goals or values worth achieving – and *nihilistic despair* – the belief that I, as an individual, am completely incapable of achieving the goals or values that I consider meaningful.

Chapter 4 presents a novel, comprehensive model of cultural differences. Cultures vary on two primary dimensions. On the dimension of *social orientation*, some cultures are *collectivist* – people have a group-centric worldview, and they see themselves as interdependent with others. Other cultures are *individualist* – people have an egocentric worldview, and they experience themselves as independent from others. On the dimension of *social control*, some cultures are characterized by *visible control* – strong moral norms are reinforced by relative intolerance of deviant behavior. Other cultures practice *invisible control* – norms are primarily un-formalized and deviance is widely tolerated. Bringing these two dimensions together yields a model of four cultural "ideal types." The chapter concludes by discussing these types.

Chapter 5 concludes the theoretical portion of the book by integrating Chapter 3's model of existential threat with Chapter 4's model of cultural variation. Different cultural patterns provide different *threat orientations*, directing the individual toward certain kinds of threat experience and away from others. Two broad types of cultural threat orientation are presented. *Disorientation-avoidant* cultures prioritize the avoidance of nihilistic disorientation – the beliefs and practices of such cultures protect the sacred nature of local values, but at the cost of orienting individuals toward experiences of lower-level guilt. A fundamentalist sect, for example, is disorientation-avoidant: strict religious beliefs shield members from any threat of meaninglessness, but feelings of guilt are inevitable when members fall short of their faith's high standards. *Despair-avoidant* cultures emphasize the avoidance of nihilistic despair – individuals are socialized to protect their sense of self-esteem and uniqueness, at the cost of predisposing them to lower-level anxiety. Secular members of middle-class and affluent US society are immersed in a despair-avoidant culture: when individuals in this setting encounter threats to their self-esteem, they invoke a variety of defenses to protect their self-worth, but these defenses often involve seeing the world as hostile and uncertain, creating potential anxiety. While collectivist/visibly controlled cultures (e.g., feudal Japan) foster a disorientation-avoidant threat orientation, individualist/invisibly controlled cultures (e.g., the contemporary United States) breed despair avoidance.

Part II presents a program of previously unpublished research, which serves as a case study demonstrating how the framework described in Part I may be used to generate novel hypotheses and insights. In particular, in three studies using multiple methods, I show how cultural-existential theory can illuminate the particular ways in which one cultural subgroup – traditionalist, rural Mennonites in the United States – experiences a variety of threats.

Chapter 6 presents the first of these studies. Archival survey data for this study were collected in 1980 from rural Mennonites born between 1898 and 1940. During the lifetimes of the participants, this particular group of Mennonites assimilated to mainstream US culture. I am therefore able to use these archival data to examine how processes of cultural change influence people's interpretations of negative events. Specifically, I present generational analyses showing that as the Mennonite community assimilated to mainstream values over time, their cultural values became intertwined with mainstream interpretations of suffering.

Chapter 7 presents a cultural-comparative study quantitatively assessing threat experiences in different subcultures. In this and the following chapter, I offer the results of a collaboration with a minority Mennonite group that has resisted assimilation, namely Church of God in Christ or "Holdeman" Mennonites. In terms of the cultural model presented in Chapter 4, Holdeman Mennonites represent a *collectivist/visibly controlled* culture. I administered a survey regarding experiences of existential threat to these Mennonites, as well as individualist Unitarian Universalists and a standard sample of university undergraduates. The strongly collectivist Mennonites displayed a threat pattern characteristic of *disorientation avoidance*: they scored higher than the other two groups on measures of guilt, but lower on measures of anxiety and concerns about meaninglessness. By contrast, the other two, more individualist groups (undergraduates and Unitarian Universalists) displayed patterns more characteristic of *despair avoidance*: they scored comparatively higher on measures of anxiety and lower on measures of guilt.

Chapter 8 completes the empirical portion by examining in detail the subjective experience of actual threat in particular Mennonite individuals. Specifically, I describe results from in-depth interviews with members of a Holdeman congregation who survived the devastating Greensburg, Kansas, tornado of 2007. The entire population of Greensburg was reduced to half after the storm because many people lacked the financial means and support to rebuild their lost homes. However, the small Holdeman community had a swift and nearly full recovery. I found that the community-oriented, orthodox Holdemans interpreted the storm in light of their religious beliefs, and did not see the experience as threatening their meaning system. Furthermore, because of their communal social structure and practical knowledge, the congregation was able to quickly rebuild.

Finally, **Chapter 9** reflects on the ideas and findings presented throughout the book, probing and problematizing them in the hope of generating future research efforts. The book concludes with consideration of major existential problems faced in contemporary society by people from diverse cultures.

A few notes may help readers from different disciplinary backgrounds approach this work in ways that are best suited to their interests. First, in presenting a novel and interdisciplinary perspective, I have found it necessary to create many new terms or use terms that might not be familiar to those outside of a given discipline. I have therefore provided a short glossary of frequently used terms at the end of the book (Appendix A). Second, I have attempted to present the quantitative research in Chapters 6 and 7 in a nontechnical way that would be readily interpretable for readers unfamiliar with psychological research methods. For those interested in details of the study methods and statistical analyses, full information can be found in Appendices B–D.

For those readers who are primarily interested in the research reported in Part II, Chapters 3 and 4 are the most essential theoretical chapters for interpreting the results. The other theoretical chapters may be skimmed. Other readers may be more interested in the overall framework of cultural-existential psychology than in the specific case studies of US Mennonites, in which case the first five chapters stand as an independent whole.

Acknowledgments

A work like this is the product of many years of interaction with scholars, friends, and family, both living and dead.

The research section (particularly Chapter 7) is based on my doctoral dissertation conducted at the University of Kansas. It is substantively revised. Nevertheless, my dissertation committee had a definite positive impact on this work. I would like to thank Mark Landau, John Janzen, Glenn Adams, Nyla Branscombe, and Chris Crandall for serving on my committee.

Over the years two mentors have guided the spirit of my intellectual efforts. The first is Jeff Greenberg; were it not for him, I would probably not be a psychologist. I learned from him the importance of defending good ideas, despite the fact that they are frequently unpopular. The second is Mark Landau. Mark was an extremely patient and supportive mentor throughout my graduate career, and this book would not have been possible without him.

Many others have been invaluable sources of intellectual inspiration, guidance, or comradeship. The following are people who have all had a lasting impact on my ideas and approach to research: Bob Antonio, Glenn Adams, Zachary Rothschild, Lucas Keefer, Sheridan Stewart, Roman Palitsky, Kirk J. Schneider, Achim Stephan, and Leah Kapa.

I owe a special debt to people and institutions which made the original research reported here possible. The following people shared with me their current knowledge or past data regarding Mennonites in Kansas: John M. Janzen, William R. Bowerman, Michael H. Crawford, Jeffrey Longhoffer, Daniel Liechty, and Doug Penner. Sheridan A. Stewart and Joseph Diefendorf were more than research assistants – they contributed ideas and went well beyond the call of duty in collecting data from people throughout Kansas. The Mennonite Library and Archives at Bethel College was a tremendous resource. The bierocks at Lincoln Perk coffee shop in Hesston fueled my long drives across the state.

I have received instructive and encouraging feedback on the research presented in this book from various groups of scholars. In particular,

I thank Lynn Davidman's qualitative methods seminar and the Cultural Psychology Research Group at the University of Kansas. I also thank Athena Aktipis and the 2015 Needs-Based Transfers and Disaster Recovery Workshop at the Decision Center for a Desert City in Phoenix. I thank Peter Foley and the Institute for the Study of Religion and Culture at the University of Arizona.

I received funding for this book or the research reported from the National Science Foundation, Grant DGE-0907996, and from the Provost's Author Support Award at the University of Arizona. Becky Taylor at Cambridge University Press initially supported the book. Collaborative writings with Tom Pyszczynski and Aaron Kay shaped some of the ideas. I received helpful comments from Shigehiro Oishi and Michele J. Gelfand, although I take responsibility for any shortcomings of the product. Roman Palitsky did an invaluable service by preparing the references and index, while also contributing substantially to the ideas presented.

Of course, the research would not have been possible without the collaboration of two Holdeman Mennonite congregations and one Unitarian Universalist congregation in Kansas. I wish to express deep appreciation for the ministers and congregation members who facilitated my studies. I also thank the undergraduates who have participated in my studies over the years.

One cannot undertake a work of this sort without substantial emotional and material support from family. I deeply thank: Brian and Elizabeth Sullivan; Keith and Justin Sullivan; Milt and Judy Kapa; Laura, Ken, Dean, and Simone Gottschalk; and Mitch and Owen Kapa. The love, humor, and wisdom of Leah Kapa and Beckett Sullivan could see me through anything.

Part I

Theory

1 Theoretical roots of cultural-existential psychology

As Edgar Allan Poe wrote, "Misery is manifold. The wretchedness of earth is multiform." It is a reality of the human situation that we are both embodied and symbolically conscious – aware of ourselves as existing through time – and while this is the source of our greatest potentialities, it also makes us subject to intense experiences of adversity. Like any other organism, our bodies are vulnerable in countless ways – to bacteria, toxins, accidents – and are continually undergoing processes of decay that will eventually result in death. Yet, unlike any other organism, we also experience the ineffable vulnerability of our sense of self: we fear the uncertain future, feel regret or mourn the irretrievable past, and are often discontented with the present state of our lives. We encounter negative information about ourselves, unexpected disasters and illnesses, belief systems radically different from our own, and pangs of separation from other people who are important in our lives, and, after a certain point in our mental development, most of us become perennially aware of the looming fact that we will die.

In short, one of the problems that has plagued psychology throughout its history is the seemingly endless capacity for humans to undergo diverse forms of suffering and threat. Unlike any other animal, perfectly mentally sound humans can be almost paralyzed by fear of things that *are not present in the moment* and which *might not even be real.* Surely all of us remember a childhood terror of monsters or ghosts. Yet, many of us still know all too well what it is like to worry about the disapproval of a god, the possibility that a friend is betraying us behind our back, or the potential death of a loved one who is gone on a trip. Because we humans can be threatened by imagined or nonempirical entities and events, there is a staggering malleability to the sources of our suffering, such that we cannot even agree as a species about what real evil is. Indeed, what is *terrifying* to one person might seem laughable to another.

Consider the possibility that another person might make your genitalia disappear by touching you. This possibility might not rank high on the list of fears that keep the readers of this book awake at night. And yet within the cultural context of certain parts of West Africa at certain times, this fear has made a great deal of sense and been a source of real anxiety for people (Adams & Dzokoto, 2007). On the other hand, consider the possibility that humankind may be destroying the planet through our unremitting use of fossil fuels and production of greenhouse gases. Although rather difficult to grasp mentally, this fear ranks high among the concerns of many contemporary US citizens, yet it would hardly make any sense to most people in most cultures through most of history, who would likely shrug it off as nonsense.

Remarkable in the human experience is not only the diversity of real and symbolic concerns from which people suffer – from poverty to debilitating pain to neurotic disorders – but also the sometimes unfathomable resilience and creativity demonstrated by people in their attempts to cope with suffering, and to live every day with the bitter knowledge of death. How is this so? How is it that we humans consistently find the means – as André Malraux put it – "to deny our nothingness"? (qtd. in Friedman, 1967). Part of the answer is that we live largely in a symbolic world – a world of language, culture, art, and religion. Although this world can be complicated and even cruel, it is vastly preferable to the indifferent, destructive world of *decaying physical matter* in which we also live. We are not helpless in a world of physical and symbolic dangers, of threats to our bodies and our sense of significance. Rather, we employ those same cognitive capabilities that made us recognize our mortal limits to convince ourselves that we are powerful and immortal. Yet, we do not all live in the same symbolic world, and humans have devised an array of imaginative strategies for denying the same biological realities that have haunted and will haunt every person on earth.

This book provides a comprehensive, interdisciplinary framework, rooted in social psychology, for synthesizing the plethora of data and theories relevant to human suffering and coping. Research in social psychology suggests that people typically rely on psychological coping mechanisms for dealing with physical and symbolic threats, and that they derive these buffering mechanisms from the local *cultural worldview* in which they are immersed as a function of being connected to a particular social group. Research also suggests that these cultural worldviews are radically diverse. Yet, prior investigations have not generally integrated these two insights. Correcting this gap, the present study is an exercise in *cultural-existential psychology*: an investigation of the ways in which different cultural patterns orient individuals toward certain categories of suffering and coping. It explores the central thesis that *culture filters all aspects of the experience of existential threat and defense*. People in certain cultures are predisposed to see certain kinds of information and events as threatening to their sense of meaning or self-esteem, even though similar information and events might not be threatening at all to people in certain other cultures. Furthermore, culture also orients us toward certain psychological defenses and means of coping when we are confronted with events we see as threatening.

Since the inception of the modern social sciences little more than a century ago, scholars have amassed a great deal of data and theoretical perspectives pertaining to the human capacity for suffering. The present volume draws on this vast body of information, as well as my recent, modest empirical studies to present a novel theoretical and methodological lens through which to view human experience. This lens – cultural-existential psychology – incorporates ideas from across the history of the social sciences to understand how people think about and react to adverse events. This perspective is concerned both with the *existential* realities of suffering and death that all humans face, and with the striking *cultural* differences in how groups of people around the world process and respond to these realities.

This perspective offers the theoretical and methodological tools to answer questions such as these: Why do members of traditional Jewish communities respond to death by burying the dead quickly, tearing their garments, and refraining from celebrations for a long period, while members of the contemporary Asante nation engage in lavish funerary celebrations to display their family's wealth? Why did the threat of being buried alive terrify nineteenth-century Americans, but has been considered a great honor reserved for priests among the Dinka of South Sudan? When different cults in the United States and Japan, both believing that the world was going to end at a certain time, were confronted with the reality that the world *did not* end, why did the US cult's members cling even more rigidly to their beliefs, while the leader of the Japanese cult attempted suicide in dishonor? And why do North American children fear monsters, while Vietnamese children fear the disappointment of their parents?

A cultural-existential perspective will help scholars across disciplines answer countless such questions pertaining to the ways in which cultural patterns shape our reactions to unfortunate or unexpected events. But this synthetic framework offers more than a solid basis for interdisciplinary research. It also sheds light on a number of areas of considerable importance for our collective well-being in contemporary society. Understanding how cultural beliefs shape our experience of threat reveals why there are such tremendous political divides in the United States and elsewhere – conflict is bound to occur if members of different political parties literally *see* completely different threats in the world (e.g., global climate change versus the immorality of abortion). This synthetic understanding can also provide practitioners with much-needed tools for translating the large body of research on coping with trauma or disorder (primarily conducted among North American populations) to diverse communities in other parts of the world, who also need assistance recovering from disaster or treating mental illness. And finally, the cultural-existential view helps clinicians reconsider many prevalent contemporary ailments – from sleep disorders to anxiety about one's workplace status – as stemming from cultural factors endemic to contemporary capitalist society.

I believe that it is an important moment to articulate interdisciplinary perspectives such as cultural-existential psychology. The opening epigraph from Jürgen Habermas has in this regard a twofold significance. One the one hand, as I hope to show in later chapters of this book, most of its readers will likely hail from a culture which creates a "fragmented consciousness" because the breakdown of binding meaning systems (under individualization and modernization) has predisposed us to anxiety and self-doubt. For the self-understanding and improvement of individuals from such cultures, an exploration of the roots of our fragmented consciousness will be essential. Furthermore, insofar as these proclivities to anxiety and our defensive reactions to them are heightening political discord, illuminating their cultural origin may permit our societies to move forward on major problems. Yet, at the same time, the fragmented consciousness to which Habermas refers has a more insidious effect within the academy, which is perhaps preventing it from serving its social function. In the cultural collapse of "grand narratives," people are hesitant to embrace totalizing, cross-disciplinary perspectives, for fear of doing violence to some corner of reality. One can pose the question: Would not the greater violence be to allow human reality to destroy itself?

This introductory chapter aims to summarize the interdisciplinary background of the proposed cultural-existential psychology. As mentioned, scholars across the human sciences have at different times presented models and data relevant to understanding cultural diversity in the experience of threat and defense. I begin my presentation of the current framework with an overview of these important past efforts, beginning with more recent trends in social psychology and moving backward to earlier approaches in the other human sciences. In Chapter 2, I will then present the foundational principles of cultural-existential psychology, before turning in subsequent chapters to detailed theoretical consideration of existential threat experience, cultural diversity, and their intersection.

Theoretical roots in social psychology

My research background is in social psychology, and I believe this field is well positioned (in terms of methods and theoretical approach) to serve as a starting place for investigation of culture's influence on adversity. While sociology tends to focus on structural variables and macro-level demographics, and anthropology and ethnography focus on the localized experiences of particular groups of people, social psychology straddles the line between these areas of focus, illuminating how subjective, local experiences influence and are influenced by broader social trends. The positioning of cultural-existential psychology within this particular niche thus offers several advantages. Methodologically, the framework is centered at the intersection of subjective experience and immediate contextual factors, which can be explored through experiments and cross-cultural comparisons. However, methodological moves can easily be made from this starting point in either direction, whether "upward" toward the examination and classification of more macro-level, social structural factors, or "downward" toward more detailed, person-centered explorations of subjective experience.

As a framework grounded in social psychology, cultural-existential psychology draws most immediately on two subfields that have emerged in this discipline over the past three decades. The first is experimental existential psychology (XXP; Greenberg, Koole, & Pyszczynski, 2004), which seeks to understand human experiences of threat, defense, and flourishing by testing the ideas of existentialism using contemporary experimental methods. The other is cultural psychology (Markus & Kitayama, 1991; Shweder, 1995; Triandis, 1989), which uses a variety of methods to demonstrate (1) the complex interrelationship between culture and psyche and (2) the resulting diversity in motivational, cognitive, and attitudinal processes – once assumed to be fairly universal by social psychologists – as a function of variation in cultural and social organizational factors. One simple way of summarizing the aims of cultural-existential psychology is to view it as an attempt to bridge these two subfields, which I will now consider in some detail.

Experimental existential psychology. This research area was inaugurated three decades ago with the emergence of terror management theory (Greenberg, Pyszczynski, & Solomon, 1986), which proposes that people are motivated to maintain the symbolic resources of self-esteem and a meaningful cultural worldview in order to protect themselves from the haunting awareness of their mortality. Terror management research highlights the largely nonconscious role of death awareness in the creation and maintenance of human culture, as well as in the everyday motivations of individuals. This role of death angst has long been acknowledged by existentialists such as Heidegger (1962), but is generally unacknowledged in most accounts of social life and individual psychology (Hankiss, 2001). Indeed, the major breakthrough of experimental existential researchers has been to take such ideas – once deemed the special province of philosophy – and devise a variety of means for testing them with current methods and statistics.

For example, hundreds of psychological studies carried out in dozens of countries have shown that reminding people temporarily of their own death increases their investment in cultural beliefs or markers of their personal value – to the point that they will aggress against others who endorse opposing political views, or show willingness to engage in risky and even suicidal behaviors to demonstrate their personal worth (for a review, see Greenberg, Solomon, & Arndt, 2008). Importantly, these compensatory behaviors do not bear any logical relation to the problem of death; being an ardent Democrat or a Republican is not likely to make one live longer. Instead, these studies demonstrate that humans rely on specifically *symbolic* resources to maintain equanimity in the face of death awareness. Among organisms, only we are fully aware of the devastating fact that we will inevitably die, and only we must convince ourselves that we are so special that we will be immortal: in an afterlife, in the memory of others, or by belonging to a group that transcends our individual existence.

Starting from the initial contribution of terror management theory, XXP has provided the most comprehensive and compelling account to date of how individuals are motivated by the need to protect themselves from basic anxieties. In general, XXP research builds off of and empirically supports the six central themes of existential philosophy (Barrett, 1962; Cooper, 1990; Cumming, 1980; Guignon & Pereboom, 1995; May, 1983; Schrag, 1961; Tillich, 1959): (1) the uniqueness of humans as a species, and the unique nature of each individual existence; (2) the psychological importance of personally meaningful experiences of concrete situations; (3) the reality of human embodiment, which implies the psychological unity of motivation, cognition, and affect; (4) the importance of will and symbolic cognition for humans; (5) the importance of both existential threat *and* existential freedom in psychological experience; and (6) the dialectical nature of human psychological processes. I will briefly review how XXP research has substantiated these existential claims, acknowledging that some issues have received greater attention than others.

Perspectives such as terror management theory emphasize the unique aspects of human psychology, such as our capacity for symbolic cognition and our awareness of personal finitude. These unique species-wide attributes are central to cultural-existential psychology, and they will be discussed in detail in Chapter 2. Some contemporary perspectives in psychology that claim to be resonant with an existential perspective (such as the meaning maintenance model; Proulx & Inzlicht, 2012) do not actually fit within the boundaries of XXP because they largely ignore those aspects of human psychology that make us unique. Perspectives such as these attempt to reduce human experiences of meaning and threat to functional patterns observable in other species that lack symbolic cognition, an untenable reduction from an existentialist vantage.

Due to its methodological roots in social psychology, XXP possesses a natural focus on the significance of situational factors in human thinking and behavior, as well as the importance of the ways people differentially construe situations based on internalized motivations and cognitive patterns (Ross & Nisbett, 2011). Research has demonstrated the psychological impact of subtle (but existentially relevant) situational variables, such as standing by a cemetery (Jonas, Fritsche, & Greenberg, 2005) or feeling excluded by strangers with whom one is playing a simple online game (Zadro, Williams, & Richardson, 2004). XXP studies also attest to the important role that individual interpretations of events (such as traumatic experiences; Janoff-Bulman & Yopyk, 2004) play in subsequent motivation and experience.

However, while some theories in XXP maintain a proper awareness of human species uniqueness, and all recognize the importance of situational factors, most (because of their grounding in a broadly empiricist approach to science) do not pay adequate attention to *individual* uniqueness (e.g., Sharpless, 2013), particularly as it manifests in the concrete, situated experiences of the existing individual (Schneider, 2013). Nevertheless, some promising ground in this direction has been covered by the study of individual "life stories" in narrative-based psychologies (Hammack, 2010; McAdams, Josselson, & Lieblich, 2006). It will be argued in Chapter 2 that qualitative research is an important antidote to the bias against studying idiosyncratic individual experience in XXP.

Although it assumes certain existential givens that differentiate humans from other species, XXP also strives to retain an awareness that humans are embodied animals. This implies that the framework both is broadly consistent with evolutionary theory and traces a large portion of human suffering back to the conflict between biological limitations and symbolic consciousness (Pyszczynski, Sullivan, & Greenberg, 2015). Like much contemporary research in social psychology, XXP studies underline the existential theme of unity among psychological processes. Humans are not rational processors, comparable to computers, who occasionally experience emotions; rather, we are flesh-and-blood beings guided by symbolic, long-term goals. The conditions of our bodies at any moment in time influence how we cognize our environment; for example, feeling physically warm makes us more likely to perceive strangers as friendly (Williams & Bargh, 2008). Being exposed to a physically disgusting smell or sight makes us more likely to condemn moral transgressors (Schnall, Haidt, Clore, & Jordan, 2008). The reverse is also true – our symbolically mediated thoughts and perceptions can influence our relationship to our physical bodies. Feeling guilty about an action makes it more likely that we will take a bath or wash our hands, for instance (Rothschild, Landau, Keefer, & Sullivan, 2015). We are constantly monitoring our environments for information about whether we are proceeding toward our goals and whether the world is operating as we believe it should; even very slight disturbances in our conviction that these things are true can produce negative emotion, often on an unconscious level (e.g., Holbrook, Sousa, & Hahn-Holbrook, 2011). A variety of threats to habitual psychological experience, ranging from subtle anomalies such as a surrealist painting to more severe examples such as thoughts of death, arouse states of aversive affect and alter the way people evaluate others and perceive the world, even prompting them to find illusory but comforting patterns in random arrays of information (for review, see Jonas et al., 2014). In short, although psychologists have historically compartmentalized human motivation, perception, cognition, and emotion, XXP research is at the forefront of modern perspectives arguing for their indissoluble unity.

At the same time that XXP acknowledges the physical nature of human existence, it also recognizes the importance of human willing and our capacity for abstract, imaginative thought. Contemporary research has shown that humans have needs for ultimate meaning and purpose: we need to see our actions as contributing to something greater than the satisfaction of our immediate biological needs, and we need to believe that unexpected and unfortunate events nevertheless are sensible in light of some pattern of higher meaning (Wong, 2006). In other words, people do not only want to do things to survive; they want to do things that will make them immortal, and this is only possible by participating in a collective web of symbolic meaning. Yet, immortality does not only come from being part of something greater than oneself. A large branch of contemporary existential research has been spurred by self-determination theory (Ryan & Deci, 2000), which holds that people have a fundamental need to see their actions as autonomously driven, and will experience a variety of psychological setbacks if they lack this sense of intrinsic motivation. In short, as terror management theory holds, people desire not only a clear sense of socially shared meaning, but also a sense of their own personal value as individuals, including the conviction that they can act efficaciously in the world to bring about their own desires.

Our cognitive capabilities and will to bring our imagined possibilities into existence is the source of our potential for freedom and transcendence. Yet, the uniquely human combination of embodiment and symbolic culture is a double-edged sword. One of the most important contributions of XXP is the construct of *existential threat* and its crucial role in human motivation and behavior. While this construct and its various manifestations will be discussed in great detail in Chapter 3, for now I provisionally define the term as an experience of negative (conscious or unconscious) affect resulting from an infringement on the person's symbolic defenses against death, that is, their sense of meaning or personal value. The vast majority of research in XXP has been dedicated to demonstrations of the multiplicity of ways in which individuals psychologically defend against various existential threats – including meaninglessness, guilt, ostracism, uncertainty, and death awareness. These studies generally evince the importance of a process referred to as fluid compensation (Proulx, 2012): people often "fluidly compensate" for threats by affirming alternate meaning structures or goals that may have nothing to do with the immediately experienced threat. A child who has been ridiculed at school may seek psychological reassurance by having a tea party with an imaginary friend, and an adult who has received a negative evaluation at work may repair their ego by engaging in a sexual conquest or watching a favorite sports team.

The last major theme of existential philosophy is the dialectical nature of human psychological processes. Humans have conflicting needs, for freedom and security, autonomy and integration, novelty and familiarity, and so on. Generally, the satisfaction of one of these needs leads to a deficit in the relative satisfaction of the opposing need, generating dialectical motivation to reorient toward the other need. This dialectical aspect of human motivation is central to existential philosophy, and will be discussed at length in Chapter 3. To date, it has not received significant empirical testing, although it is implied by some XXP perspectives, including terror management theory (e.g., Pyszczynski, Greenberg, & Goldenberg, 2003).

Clearly, the six central themes of existentialism are framed in a universalistic way – they are assumed to apply to all persons in all contexts. Although XXP acknowledges the fundamental importance of culture for human psychology, it is predicated on a functional conception of culture – cultural worldviews provide standards for individuals to meet in order to attain self-esteem and the conviction that they are objects of ultimate value in a meaningful universe (Becker, 1973; Hallowell, 1967;

Pyszczynski et al., 2015). However, research in this area has tended to ignore the role of culture in shaping the experience of threat, focusing instead on the presumably universal role of existential threat in generating attachment to culture. This is partly the case because existentialism itself emerged in response to a particular cultural background, namely trends toward individualism and the breakdown of traditional meaning structures in nineteenth-century Europe (May, 1983). Thus, while XXP makes a major contribution to cultural-existential psychology by highlighting universal aspects of human threat experience, it is only one side of the current story.

Cultural psychology. One of the major aims of the present book is to overcome the universalizing limitations of XXP by connecting research in this area to another rising subfield of social psychology, namely cultural psychology. This is a diverse subfield whose practitioners tend to focus less on motivational givens and more on contextual variation in human behavior and thinking styles (e.g., Nisbett, Peng, Choi, & Norenzayan, 2001; Triandis, 1989; Vygotsky, 1978). Cultural psychology offers a compelling social psychological perspective on how individual motivations are shaped by local beliefs and social ecology.

In this approach, *culture* refers to the sum total of patterns of behavior, beliefs, and humanly influenced objects in which an individual is immersed by virtue of connection to a particular social group (Adams & Markus, 2004). Importantly, the cultural patterns that individuals draw upon, enact, and modify are sometimes explicit (i.e., discursively symbolic) and sometimes implicit, meaning they can have the character of nonconscious *habitus* (Bourdieu, 1977). These implicit patterns are often maintained and reinforced by elements of local, historically shaped ecologies or "intentional worlds" (Gelfand et al., 2011; Shweder, 1995) and constitute aspects of system integration, or the functioning of societies on a mass level outside the immediate awareness of individual actors (Giddens, 1984). For example, technological and economic factors make a massive contribution to the way individuals experience time and space (Giddens, 1984); however, this aspect of experience is not typically consciously recognized, nor is it always symbolically represented in a given cultural context.

One of the guiding dictums of cultural psychology is the notion of mutual constitution (Markus & Kitayama, 2010), that culture and mind "make each other up" in a reciprocal process. Utilizing the concept of mutual constitution involves adopting a transactional (Heft, 2012; Pepper, 1942) or reciprocal interactionist (Mischel & Shoda, 1995) view of human-environment interplay. The idea is essentially a recapitulation of Giddens' (1986) resolution to the problem of agency and structure:

> Structure [read: culture] is both the medium and the outcome of the human activities which it recursively organizes. By the recursive character of social life I mean that social activity in respect of its structural properties exists in and through the use of the resources which agents make in constituting their action, which at the same time reconstitutes those structural properties as qualities of the system in question. (p. 533)

While this framing of the issue focuses on the classic social-psychological boundary between the individual agent and the surrounding social structure, the same idea is expressed differently by Shweder (1995). Shweder invokes the more anthropological boundary between the mind of a particular person and the culture that the person both draws upon and enacts:

> Psyche and culture are ... seamlessly interconnected. A person's psychic organization is largely made possible by, and is largely expressive of, a conception of itself, society, and nature; while one of the very best ways to understand cultural conceptions of self, society, and nature is to examine the way those conceptions organize and function in the subjective life of intending individuals ... Cultural psychology aims to develop a principle of intentionality – action responsive to and directed at mental objects or representations – by which culturally constituted realities (intentional worlds) and reality-constructing psyches (intentional persons) continually and continuously make each other up, perturbing and disturbing each other, interpenetrating each other's identity, reciprocally conditioning each other's existence. (p. 71)

This principle of *intentionality* stands in stark contrast to standard theorizing in psychology, which tends to assume a material, nonsubjective reality in which humans are immersed and which they more or less accurately process through universal mechanisms of cognition and perception. But this principle is very much in line with existential and phenomenological theorizing (e.g., Husserl, 2000; Schrag, 1961), which holds that all human perception of the environment is colored by intention (in the form of motivation, goal-directedness, and emotion), and that human embeddedness in culture yields an ecology which is deeply permeated by the record of past and present intentions (Binswanger, 1958). It is echoed by the psychologist James Gibson's (1979) notion of *affordances* – that human perception is structured according to the relevance of various objects in the field of vision for the individual's current projects.

Just as Shweder suggests, the intentionality that people instill in their environments has causal bearing on the intentionality of those people. Cultural psychologists have conducted hundreds of studies over the past

25 years showing that many psychological processes once assumed to be fairly universal – including aspects of motivation, behavior, cognition, perception, and belief – actually are quite variable across culturally shaped environments. Research in this area has demonstrated, for example, that in some cultures people are more individualistic (they think of themselves in terms of personal identities and prioritize personal goals) while in others they are more collectivistic (they think of themselves in terms of relational attachments and prioritize the well-being of others; Markus & Kitayama, 1991; Triandis, 1995), and these differences are reflected in the products that individuals produce and the environments they build (e.g., Miyamoto, Nisbett, & Masuda, 2006; Morling & Lamoreaux, 2008). Such cultural variability stems from a variety of sources: there are differences in the way rural and urban people evaluate the attractiveness of others (Anderson, Adams, & Plaut, 2008), in the level of empathy displayed by people with high versus low socioeconomic status (Kraus, Piff, & Keltner, 2011), and in the preference for familiar stimuli displayed by people who are residentially mobile versus those who are not (Oishi, 2014). Dozens of such differences, and their consequences for a variety of psychological phenomena, have been documented in the literature.

Cultural psychology has proven a fruitful perspective for research, not only because it documents psychological diversity, but perhaps primarily because in the process it serves to "denaturalize" conventional psychology. Not only does psychology – with its common emphasis on behaviorist or computer processor models of cognition and action – often ignore key aspects of human experience such as intentionality and embodiment, but it also tends to assume that it can reveal "constant" or "biologically determined" *truths* about human behavior. Certainly, there are undeniable aspects of human biology that contribute to the universal potentialities of our experience, but the field of human symbolism and intentionality makes the manifestation of these potentialities extremely malleable. Therefore, any data gathered on "universal" or "normative" psychological processes in a lab are unlikely to generalize across all, or even many, settings, because they are themselves the product of a particular cultural situation (e.g., Gergen, 1973).

Despite its rich potential and theoretical contributions, cultural psychology has not always lived up to its promise. Indeed, research in this area has tended to perseverate on the description of variable patterns rather than the explication of processes: in short, the opposite problem of that evidenced by XXP's preoccupation with universal processes. Despite the encouragements of scholars like Shweder, who emphasize the mutual intentionality of psyche and culture, in the end most cultural psychological research has a reductionist flair, categorizing those cultural differences that are most straightforwardly described and largely ignoring the role of individual motivation in the perpetuation of those differences.

By bringing together two research fields that have been previously separated in the literature – XXP and cultural psychology – the present framework of cultural-existential psychology hopes to overcome some of the limitations of each by capitalizing on their respective strengths. Some of the best thinkers in the history of the social sciences have agreed that any comprehensive theory of humanity should incorporate both a framework for understanding human motivation and development (rooted in awareness of our special biology) *and* a framework for understanding the organization and change of cultures and social structures (Gillin, 1954b; Sherif, 1977). While XXP provides the former, cultural psychology offers a path toward the latter. More immediately germane to the objectives of this book, by bridging these subfields, cultural-existential psychology is uniquely poised to provide a comprehensive understanding of the multifarious ways in which people experience, conceptualize, and cope with adversity. Drawing on experimental existential research, this perspective highlights how people nonconsciously spend much of their lives trying to avoid unpleasant thoughts about finitude, meaninglessness, or inadequacy, and how they rely on culturally conditioned defenses when these thoughts become unavoidable. But integrating insights from cultural psychology, it further accounts for systematic diversity in the kinds of information and events that different people perceive to be threatening, and the characteristic tactics they employ for handling these threats.

In sum, cultural-existential psychology can be viewed as an immediate development from the trends of XXP and cultural approaches in social psychology. However, the broad goal of this perspective – to understand variation in human threat experience – has been approached before in other disciplines. Before presenting the theoretical and methodological principles of cultural-existential psychology in Chapter 2, it will be instructive to review other traditions from across the human sciences that anticipated and exert an influence on the framework.

Theoretical roots in anthropology and sociology

Philosophical anthropology. By building off of XXP, cultural-existential psychology grounds its understanding of personal experience in philosophy and biology. The connections between existential philosophy and modern biology were explored by philosophical anthropology, a mid-twentieth-century German movement that sought an understanding of human nature based on the emerging picture contributed by Darwinian science and the modern synthesis. Gehlen (1980) was perhaps the most prominent member of this movement, although contributions were also made by Mitscherlich (1970) and Binswanger (1958). Here I will touch not only on the specific contributions of this perspective to cultural-existential psychology, but more generally on the important points of intersection between a biological and an existential view of the human condition.

Many thinkers have highlighted the counterintuitive similarities between existential philosophy and contemporary biological theory (e.g., Barash, 2000). For example, both Darwinian theory and existentialism attempted to overturn centuries of Western thought positing immutable essences or "perfect forms" in nature (Jonas, 1966). In this, both worldviews oppose finitude and change to the principles of immortality and stasis that dominated religious thinking in the cultural "West" and elsewhere (Bloch & Parry, 1982; Gauchet, 1997; Giddens, 1983; Volk, 2002). The perspectives share a common emphasis on the *immanence* or singularity of existence. Rather than positing separate planes of existence – one transcendent/metaphysical and one material (as do most religious systems) – or a dualistic distinction between "Nature" and "Humanity," matter and mind, evolutionary and existential perspectives propose that there is one domain of material, animal existence, of which humans are a part (Phillips, 2000). Even religious existential viewpoints – such as Kierkegaard's – stress the unrepeatable development of the individual in a specific time and place. Note that an insistence on the materialist immanence of human life does not imply a deterministic view of human action – indeed, both existentialism and sophisticated philosophical biology place importance on human choice, behavioral flexibility, and responsibility (Dennett, 1984; de Sousa, 2010). Rather, existentialism is compatible with modern biology insofar as both reject the priority of broad, essentialist categories, and instead focus on situation-specific processes of change in individual organisms that are both products of and influences on their environments.

This brings us to a second major point of convergence between evolutionary biology and existentialism, namely a view of organisms as syntheses of contingency and necessity (de Sousa, 2010; Jonas, 1966). Existentialism's dialectical view of human nature (elaborated in Chapter 3) is also biologically based. Jonas (1966) explicates how evolutionary theory presents all sentient organisms as possessing characteristics of possibility and necessity. First, capacities evolved by organisms that increase their "freedom" in certain respects also become new forms of limitation and necessity. Metabolism is a prime example: this basic capacity permits organisms' movement in and influence upon their environments, yet it also exerts a demand on organisms – they *must* metabolize to persist. Organisms demonstrate the necessity-contingency dualism on another level: the perennial conflict between their egocentric desires and their capacity for relationship with – indeed, their dependence upon – objects and organisms in the environment, which are sometimes inhibitory, sometimes facilitative of those desires. This conflict is the source of *feeling* in organisms – the effortless ability to evaluate events in terms of their positive or negative consequences for the self. Feeling is the organism's internal representation of its relationship with the environment. In seemingly many species, feeling manifests in some form, alternating at the most basic level between *exogenous* feelings (of being acted upon by external forces) and *autogenous* feelings (of acting in the self's present interest; Langer, 1988; see also Innis, 2009). This distinction is critical for psychology and has been recapitulated in many theories, as in Angyal's (1941) proposed autonomous and heteronomous forces in the determination of motivation.

XXP is interested in how these processes play out uniquely in the human species. Drawing from evolutionary perspectives, XXP asserts that complex processes are scaffolded onto more basic processes, both phylogenetically across the evolutionary span leading up to the emergence of contemporary humans and ontogenetically in the development of each individual. These arguments will be explored in Chapter 2, but for now it is sufficient to say that XXP views humans as developing capacities for symbolic and metaphor-based cognition that build upon nonsymbolic processes of perception and cognition observable in other animals (Hallowell, 1965; Mead, 1934; Nelson, 2007). Philosophical anthropologists proposed that this symbolic scaffolding is able to occur largely because humans have an extended period of neoteny or pre-reproductive development (Bjorklund, 1997; Keller & Kärtner, 2013; Konner, 2007; Ratner, 2013). Gehlen (1980) influentially argued that because humans undergo considerable psychological and physical development postnatally, we have remarkable flexibility in our relatedness to the environment. This means, however, that early in development we are less readily adapted to our environments than most other organisms. We rely on flexible capabilities for learning and neural development rather than evolved instincts. The fact that considerable human cognitive and physical development occurs after birth, combined with the human capacity for symbolic self-awareness, means that human behavior patterns are largely open-ended and require external guidance. Culture "institutionalizes" behavior patterns, providing guidance and continual feedback on our actions (Gehlen, 1980).

Psychological anthropology. By virtue of its grounding in contemporary existential psychology, the cultural-existential perspective shares with philosophical anthropology an emphasis on biological universals. At the same time, its equal footing in contemporary cultural psychology implies theoretical roots in anthropology, most directly in psychological anthropology or the "culture and personality" school of the 1940s to 1960s. Although psychological anthropologists have been primarily interested in documenting psychological dynamics in diverse settings, their theoretical perspective has been broadly similar to that of social psychology. Both fields share an emphasis on the importance of situational factors for individual attitudes and behavior, and on the ability to scientifically compare and contrast the relative influence of different situational factors for psychological outcomes (Hsu, 1961; Shweder, 1984). Though not necessarily forming a coherent "school" in the sense of sharing a definitive set of theoretical or methodological principles, workers in early psychological anthropology made three common assumptions according to R. A. LeVine (2001):

> (a) All adult behavior is "culturally patterned," just as all adult speech is patterned by a particular language; (b) childhood experience, also culturally patterned, has a long-term influence on adult personality; (c) adult personality characteristics prevalent in a community have an influence on its culture. (p. 808)

These assumptions are similarly shared by cultural-existential psychology; for instance, (a) and (c) restate the "mutual constitution" view of the self-culture relationship. Psychological anthropology stressed a variant of this idea which LeVine (1973) referred to as the "personality mediation" perspective. In this view, culture may be divided into "primary" or social structural patterns/institutions that operate largely outside of conscious awareness (economic patterns, aspects of human geography, etc.) and "secondary" or expressive patterns that individuals discursively and ritualistically enact and create. The socialized individual operates as the mediating unit between these two general forms of culture, drawing them together by endorsing and enacting expressive patterns that maintain and legitimize historically derived structural patterns. Whiting and Child's (1953) comparative study of how socialization patterns in different cultures affect the prevalence of adult defense mechanisms and interpretations of illness is a classic study supporting the role of personality mediation.

Another framing of the personality mediation concept comes from Spiro (1961), who argued that, rather than attempting to understand how particular cultural institutions function in relation to others in a society, scholars should seek out relationships of "functional congruence" between the needs of the individual and patterns hospitable to the transmission of the culture (Inkeles & Levinson, 1954). In other words, for societies to maintain integration and for cultural beliefs to be heritable, practices that insure integration and associated legitimizing beliefs must also meet the psychological needs of individuals.

This led Spiro (1961; 1965) to the influential concept of culturally constituted defense mechanisms. Cultural systems persist largely to the extent that they provide approved outlets for individuals to defend themselves against psychologically problematic events and cognitions. Approaching the issue from a psychodynamic perspective, Spiro focused on how institutions provide individuals with cognitive tools for reinterpreting and channeling their selfish or antisocial desires, so as to prevent any disruption to social harmony. For example, attributing misfortune to malevolent spirits seemed to allow Burmese villagers to harmlessly vent aggression that they would normally feel toward their neighbors and family (Spiro, 1967).

While Spiro proposed that culture offers routes for the sublimation of problematic individual desires, Hallowell (1967) suggested another way in which culture relates to the psychological experience of threat. Specifically, he pointed out that local beliefs influence the way different groups of people interpret the same physical or biological (negative) event, and also the way individuals respond to the event. He used the example of the Ojibwe people of the Northern United States and Canada, who (he contended) traditionally interpreted illnesses as the result of deviant behavior, and felt that public confession of deviance to one's family or community was the best cure for illness. In Hallowell's view, culture does not only provide means for reconciling conflict between the individual and her culture; it also capitalizes on anxiety-inducing situations (such as severe disease) by offering interpretations of those situations that are culturally reinforcing. Indeed, Siegel (1955) – another psychological anthropologist – went so far as to contend that certain cultural beliefs actually evolve to *induce* anxiety in their adherents, in order to maintain a high level of social integration. He proposed that insular groups such as the Anabaptist Hutterites persist by making strong psychological demands on the individual and offering ingroup-relevant symbols and practices as the only form of relief from anxiety (while forbidding other possibilities, such as drugs). In this way, cultural beliefs are continually strengthened in a reciprocal process, whereby the beliefs induce anxiety, to which group members respond by increasing psychological investment in the same beliefs (Gabriel, 1983).

In a framework that draws together these different perspectives, the anthropologist John Gillin argued that culture predisposes individuals to perceive certain events and information as threatening, and to employ certain defenses for coping with or repressing those threats (Gillin, 1967;

Gillin & Nicholson, 1951). Quite simply, Gillin (1967) wrote: "cultures ... may be regarded as systems which produce a balance between the threats and anxieties of life as seen through the local cultural screen, on the one hand, and means and methods available for 'handling' such threats" (p. 139). From this viewpoint, there is a threat-culture mutual constitution cycle: cultural patterns orient individuals toward interpretations of and responses to threatening events that attach them even more deeply to those patterns (Berger & Luckmann, 1966; O'Dea, 1966).

Existential sociology. While philosophical anthropology emphasizes the unique aspects of humanity as a biological species, and psychological anthropology highlights the interaction between cultural patterns and individual existential needs, existential sociology imported existentialism's focus on the person's unique experience into social scientific research. This movement draws on the *Verstehen* tradition in sociology, which examines existence not by reducing it to operational, quantifiable categories, but rather by empathizing with and adopting the perspective of human subjects (Fontana, 1984; Tiryakian, 1962). It shares with symbolic interactionism (e.g., Blumer, 1969) and ethnomethodology (e.g., Garfinkel, 1972) a common source of influence in the phenomenological writings of Husserl, Merleau-Ponty, and Schutz, who sought to understand consciousness and social interaction as they are directly experienced by the conscious, interacting subject.

Building off of Tiryakian's (1962) attempt to integrate existential philosophy with sociological inquiry, Lyman and Scott (1970) proposed a "sociology of the absurd" that would take seriously the contention that all beliefs and discourses are socially positioned and potentially fallible. This implies there is no hope of obtaining a systematic set of "objective" axioms about the workings of human society. However, existential sociology does not respond to the reality of social constructionism with a "hermeneutics of suspicion" (Ricoeur, 1970) which undermines all beliefs by reducing them to psychological motivations or the machinations of social power. Rather, it investigates how people's beliefs meet their existential needs for a sense of ultimate meaning and personal value. From the point of view of existential sociology, then, people can be seen as enacting an endless string of structurally interchangeable "dramas" or "games" (e.g., Duncan, 1968; Lyman & Scott, 1970), the objects of which are to maintain a mutually determined view of reality as meaningful and to compete with others for feelings of worth and empowerment.

J. Douglas and Johnson (1977) developed a qualitative, ethnographic methodological basis for existential sociology. This methodology employs case study, participant observation, interview, and content analytic approaches to reconstructing individuals' *lifeworlds*: their fundamental assumptions about the physical operation of reality, the nature of social relationships, and the meaning of their activities (see Habermas, 1987). As an example, Kotarba (1977) engaged in participant observation and informal interviews with several individuals suffering from chronic pain while they were attending acupunctural treatment sessions. The researcher gained an understanding of how the person's private, embodied battle with chronic pain creates a rift between them and the world of their families and colleagues, who are accustomed to pain and illness being temporary conditions. By eschewing traditional demographic methods and theoretical categories, Kotarba (1977) achieved an existential perspective on the isolating phenomenological experience of chronic pain for the patients.

Research in existential sociology draws extensively on the concept of the self. Proponents of this field have argued that the existential self is (1) embodied, (2) becoming, (3) situational, and (4) reflexive (Kotarba, 1979). The first two points fit well with the tenets of existentialism. Existential sociology's emphasis on embodiment implies a prioritization of affective processes in human experience. Its focus on *becoming* resonates with existentialism's acknowledgment of human willing and freedom, and it contrasts sharply with the search for stable, bounded categories of behavior and motivation in mainstream social science. The fact that the human self is constantly becoming implies that personal experience is continually in flux and development, and meaning for the individual is perennially negotiated. When considering interpretations of threat and suffering, for example, we cannot assume that individuals will rely on a certain interpretation of an event once and for all; rather, the meaning of the event for the person may change dramatically over the course of days or decades. This theme also brings to bear the existentialist insight that human experience is often one of symbolic threat – meanings are enacted and fragile, rather than given and stable, which leads to individuals' frequent need to search for or defend meaning (contradicting mainstream social science perspectives that see meaning as immersive and effortless; Lester, 1984). The situational element of the self is in line with a broad social psychological perspective; personal meaning and motivation cannot be understood without reference to the (social) situation in which the individual finds herself. In recent writings (Kotarba & Johnson, 2002), existential sociologists have especially highlighted how the self often encounters situations of conflict between personal desires and perceptions, on the one hand, and the categories and machinations of society on the other. Thus, the self is often a site of tension (Lyman & Scott, 1970).

The reflexivity of the self is a theme of considerable importance for cultural-existential psychology, as will be discussed in Chapter 5. Briefly, reflexivity refers to the individual's capacity to be critically aware and develop a body of knowledge of their own motivations, beliefs, and historical background. In contrast to the "personality mediation" view of psychological anthropology, and the "fish in water" view of most cultural psychologists (e.g., Markus & Conner, 2013), the self's reflexivity suggests that people can become aware of their embeddedness in culture, and choose to reject or creatively alter traditional cultural beliefs and practices. Although acknowledgment of reflexivity is a crucial corrective to more determinist views of cultural, social, and situational influence, it should also be noted that reflexivity is itself socioculturally situated, and some cultures promote reflexivity to a greater degree than others (a theme explored in Chapter 5). In its ignorance of the extent to which factors such as reflexivity are culturally conditioned, existential sociology evinces the strongly individualistic bias it shares with existential philosophy.

Existential anthropology. Michael Jackson's (2005; 2013) recently proposed existential anthropology is a fourth originary source for cultural-existential psychology. In a similar vein to the present framework, Jackson argues that there are existential universals (needs, motives, biological boundaries) for humans, which nevertheless manifest or are satisfied differently across cultural contexts. In order to adequately understand the unfolding of existential motives in specified spatiotemporal contexts, Jackson proposes two major guidelines. First, existential anthropology should be an "anthropology of events" (Jackson, 2005; pp. xxv–xxviii); by focusing on the creation or enactment of meaning in reaction to concrete events in the world (e.g., a marriage, an illness, a natural disaster), we gain insight into how people's symbolic beliefs shape and are shaped by historical experience. Second, rather than highlighting the relative importance of either the acting subject or the mediating culture, studies should focus on the "in-between" – the elusive space in which the individual's cognitive-motivational structure reciprocally interacts with the social and physical worlds. As Jackson (2005) writes: "Bypassing both the individual subject and culture as *sui generis* phenomena, we seek to explore the space of appearances – where that which is *in potentia* becomes *in presentia* – disclosed, drawn out, brought forth, given presence or embodied" (p. xiv).

This space of the "subjective in-between" dissolves gradually, at one end, into the realm of intersubjectivity and the microsocial, generally the province of anthropology and sociology, while at the other end it blurs with the intrapsychic (Jackson, 2013). This understanding of experience has roots in the Heideggerian notion of being-in-the-world, and highlights how individual action and meaning-making is always already positioned in a matrix of personal and cultural history, environmental relationships, and socially constructed significance (Binswanger, 1958; Schrag, 1961). At the same time, it also connects to Heideggerian (see Dreyfus, 1991) and Sartrean (1948; cf. Ratcliffe & Broome, 2012) concepts of "possibility" and "exigence": culturally supported or personally typical acts and interpretations are *potentially but not necessarily* enacted in any particular context (recall philosophical anthropology's necessity-contingency dialectic).

Further drawing on Sartre, Jackson (2005) discusses how the subjective in-between is built up in response to concrete events through the interaction of "sense" and "signification." Here Jackson has especially in mind events that challenge our taken-for-granted sense of the stability of self and world, unexpected or threatening occurrences that resist ready assimilation – what Jaspers (1970) referred to as "limit situations." In response to such events, *sense* is the personally experienced "overflow of meaning," the rush of experiential data that momentarily eludes symbolic mediation. In the space of the subjective in-between, such raw experience is partially met by *signification* – publically available, communicable forms of meaning that are intersubjectively negotiated. In the wake of an experience of severe trauma, for example, a deeply isolating and partially incommunicable event is often gradually shared with others and reinterpreted through socially afforded narratives and schemas (Daniel, 1994; Herman, 1997).

Jackson advocates for this kind of understanding of experience and its application to an anthropology of events in order to overcome the limits of much prior social scientific work, which sees individuals either as passively determined by biology, institutions, and culture, or as virtually unlimited in their capacity for subjective interpretation and self-authorship. His ideas resonate with many other important conceptualizations of culture, such as those that view culture as a broad pattern of "affordances" that orient the individual toward functional possibilities, particularly when the affordances resonate with individual intentionality (Heft, 2005). Similarly, Giddens' (1986) structuration theory suggests that culture is best conceptualized as an ever-modifiable network of possibilities, like a language:

> Structural features of language do not exist as patterns situated in time and space, like patterns of social relationships; they consist of relations of absences and presences embedded in instantiation of language, in speech or in text. Structure here presumes the idea of an absent totality . . . It is a parallel idea of structure (as an absent totality) which I hold to be important for the social sciences . . . The

problem with conceptualizing structure as a set of relations of presences is that structure then appears as a constraint which is "external" to action. (pp. 532–533)

By approaching social structure and culture in this way, we can avoid the limitations of both psychological and sociological reductionism.

How does Jackson propose that researchers actually examine the compelling but vague hypothesized space of the subjective in-between? The theoretical basis of existential anthropology has four methodological implications (Jackson, 2013). First, fieldwork is absolutely essential; researchers must work closely with individual research participants to understand their lifeworld and contextualized patterns of meaning-making. Second, despite the importance of detailed case studies, Jackson equally advocates for cross-cultural comparison. We cannot understand the interplay between existential universals and cultural variation unless we compare data obtained in multiple disparate contexts. Building off of the first two implications, an interdisciplinary approach is also required. As mentioned, the subjective in-between represents the interactive fusion of highly subjective elements with widely shared, institutionally rooted symbols and practices. A single disciplinary perspective is not sufficient to even approach comprehension of this multilevel phenomenon. Finally, like any sound methodologist, Jackson stresses the importance of continual critical reflection on one's ideas and repeated retesting. When dealing with the exigencies of culture and human creativity, it is always possible to encounter situations that belie one's theoretical expectations or prior data, and call for the revision of theory.

Conclusion

These four prior traditions in anthropology and sociology have not been dominant in their respective fields. Nevertheless, they demonstrate that groundbreaking interdisciplinary work has been done in the recent past – and continues to be done today – to understand the phenomenological experience of human suffering from a holistic standpoint, incorporating social scientific, biological, and humanistic approaches simultaneously. With the increasing specialization of psychology, sociology, and anthropology in the past half-century, these holistic perspectives have fallen increasingly out of favor. By proposing a cultural-existential psychology, I hope to seize on the contemporary moment, in which both cultural and existential views are once again flourishing in psychology, but are not yet communicating with one another. By building a bridge between these current research areas, I hope to also remind researchers of a time only a few decades past when the social sciences generally engaged in much more fruitful cross-pollination. The suggested unification of cultural and existential psychological perspectives directs our attention to similar endeavors undertaken in the past.

From philosophical anthropology, cultural-existential psychology inherits an understanding of humanity's unique biological situation, and its importance in psychology. Psychological anthropology contributes an imperative for cross-cultural comparison in order to understand the role of institutionalized patterns and practices in sculpting personal experience. Existential sociology makes an important case for the freedom and subjective potentialities of the individual actor, while Jackson's existential anthropology ties together many of these strands. In the following chapter, I outline the fundamental principles of a cultural-existential psychology that would draw upon and expand these prior contributions.

2 Fundamental principles of cultural-existential psychology

Cultural-existential psychology is a framework for organizing data on the link between cultural variation and interpretations of suffering and threat, and for drawing out the correspondences between the functional-motivational conceptions of culture in XXP and cultural psychology. Its special province would be the role of cultural variables in orienting individuals toward particular experiences of and responses to adverse occurrences. While the tenets of this framework are not new, it attempts to translate into contemporary social psychology an insight long recognized but often ignored, namely *that neither cultural meaning nor human suffering can be adequately understood without reference to the other.* It is not a coincidence that several of the most important thinkers for the social sciences – notably Nietzsche, Weber, Durkheim, Georg Simmel, Otto Rank, and Karl Jaspers – wrestled both with the realities of human suffering and the contingencies of cultural-historical variation.

The purpose of this chapter is to provide a broad overview of what a cultural-existential psychology would entail. Drawing substantially on the prior frameworks and endeavors discussed in Chapter 1, I propose three fundamental and guiding principles for a cultural-existential psychology. These principles undergird the theory and research that I will present in the remainder of this volume. The first two principles are primarily theoretical, and the third primarily methodological.

Humans are unique animals by virtue of their capacity for symbolic consciousness

The symbolic nature of human consciousness has several implications which play a pivotal role in cultural-existential psychology. Our symbolic consciousness emerged as a result of a multifaceted evolutionary process referred to by Susanne Langer (1988) as the "great shift" from nonhuman to human psychology. This shift involved the scaffolding of symbolically mediated motives and experiences onto more biologically ubiquitous, evolutionarily inherited processes.

According to Langer (1988), nonhuman animals (especially higher mammals) exist in a unidimensional phenomenological environment, what she refers to as the "animal ambient." Cognition and perception in the animal ambient are highly "episodic" (Donald, 2012). The experience of the animal ambient is one of transient, intense emotional reactions to immediately present stimuli that either impede or facilitate internally motivated acts. There is very limited ability for nonhuman animals to conceive of stimuli or events outside of the immediate periphery, and there is no linguistic (i.e., symbolically mediated) communication between animals (Deacon, 1998) nor any truly imitative learning or mimesis (Tomasello, 1999). This is not to say that the animal ambient or motivational range is impoverished; rather, the nonhuman animal exists in relation to an immediate phenomenological environment, which it typically acts upon as a function of innate and experientially acquired behavior patterns.

The *symbol* itself is the key to the evolutionary transition from the animal to the human ambient (Langer, 1988). The ability to think through symbols allowed humans to cognitively "fix" objects from the swirling chaos of perceptual input. True speech and mimetic cognition became possible as symbols were fixed and publically shared as words (Donald, 2012; Langer, 1988), allowing for the emergence of a social environment consisting of other symbolically endowed beings. In addition, symbolic thought permitted reflexivity and the isolation of particular goals from the ongoing flux of internally generated, incipient impulses. Symbolically mediated goals, subject to mental rehearsal and visualization, were scaffolded onto the situationally bounded goals characteristic of nonhuman animals (Boesch, 1991).

Speech and the growing abstractness of motivation facilitated another key transformation, namely the addition of long-term, self-referential memory and autobiographical time as a dimension of phenomenological experience. Extended temporal self-awareness is a defining aspect of human consciousness (Deacon, 1998; Suddendorf & Corballis, 1997; Wheeler, Stuss, & Tulving, 1997). As Minkowski (1970) proposed, the human experience of time is characterized by the experience of *élan vital*: "being toward" an open future in the pursuit of projects. Since the dawn of culture, humans have possessed at least a vague awareness of the reality of the life cycle and inevitable personal mortality. We are partly defined by our capacity to potentially adopt a long-term, symbolic perspective on the self and its projects. As a result, nearly all cultural practices may be partly characterized as providing the individual with what Gehlen (1980) called institutionalizations – guidelines for behavior that symbolically anchor an extended temporal perspective to ordered sequences of meaningful activity in the present. Symbolic self-awareness makes human life a long-term project, but culture has the capacity to embed self-awareness in recursive practices that provide immediate reassurance about the self's abilities and prospects.

Because the sense of self is embedded in an intergenerationally transmitted, symbolic web of culture, human experience is shaped far more dramatically by processes of cultural than of biological evolution. As Tomasello (1999) indicates, human socialization is characterized by the "ratchet effect" – cultural advances are ratcheted up from prior advances, through processes of both vertical and horizontal transmission of ideas, so that human experiences between generations may be radically different. Humans born in the age of the Internet and personal computers entered a rather different world than the one their parents were born into; nevertheless, because of our cognitive flexibility and extended neoteny, we are perennially capable of adapting into the ever-changing environments that we create for ourselves.

To summarize the foregoing, psychological experience across the life span is influenced by what are assumed to be four uniquely human attributes (Langer, 1988): (1) the capacity for symbolic consciousness and language; (2) a keen sense of self-awareness and capacity for self-reflection contingent on (1); (3) an awareness of personal mortality and perennial finitude (i.e., extended temporal self-consciousness) contingent on (2); and (4) an embeddedness in culture that results from the three prior givens and also grounds our experience of them.

A major consequence of the "great shift" to the human ambient is the transition from dwelling in a single environment to simultaneous dwelling in multiple phenomenological "worlds." There is a remarkable yet heretofore unacknowledged convergence across social scientific thinkers on a common model of human experience, which holds that human individuals exist in three primary phenomenological worlds (Pyszczynski et al., 2015).

Binswanger (1958) argued that, in addition to dwelling in a culturally mediated natural world or *Umwelt*, humans also live in the social world of other beings with whom they can symbolically communicate, the *Mitwelt*. A third distinguishable world is the private realm of inner experience and self-narrative, the *Eigenwelt*. Many important consequences follow from distinguishing between these phenomenological worlds that will influence our considerations throughout this book; here, only a few preliminary examples of their analytic utility will be mentioned.

Some current perspectives in neuroscience (Fuchs, 2011; Thompson & Varela, 2001) have found it critical to distinguish between three simultaneous levels of neurocognitive functioning in human experience: an ongoing state of self-awareness and -regulation (*Eigenwelt*-consciousness); the perpetual experience of self-environment relationship mediated by the brain (*Umwelt*-consciousness); and the unique neuronal pathways and developmental trajectory of intersubjective awareness (*Mitwelt*-consciousness). At a different level of analysis, contemporary social psychology suggests that people primarily experience security and insecurity in relation to epistemic meaning (a primary resource of the *Umwelt*), feelings of attachment and belongingness (primarily relating to the *Mitwelt*), and their sense of self-esteem (the primary resource of the *Eigenwelt*; Hart, 2014). Building on the thought of Vygotsky, Michael Cole (1998) argues that in the process of human development, the social world of culture occupies a mediational space between the biological organism (i.e., the developing individual) and the natural environment. Making a highly comparable distinction between the *objective*, *social*, and *subjective* worlds, Habermas (1985) argued that people in different cultures make different validity claims and have different expectations regarding these worlds. For instance, to establish a law characterizing some aspect of the objective world, Western scientists must demonstrate its potential observability by all individuals, but the subjective perspectives of Western artists are not held up to this standard. We expect a fellow being in the *Mitwelt* to treat us according to certain norms of reciprocity that we do not expect from an object in the *Umwelt*, and so on.

Binswanger's analysis of the three worlds is rooted in Heideggerian thought, and assumes a fairly universal structure of experience that is only slightly variable for each individual. From a cultural-existential vantage, however, it is useful to consider how the *Umwelt*, *Mitwelt*, and *Eigenwelt* may be differentially shaped across cultural settings. Heidegger himself distinguished between the level of *Existenziale* – universal structural aspects of human existence – and the level of *Existenzielle* – concrete manifestations and interpretations of human existence in localized spatial-temporal and symbolic contexts (see Schrag, 1961). If the natural/objective, social, and subjective worlds are *existenzial* features of universal experience, we should further develop conceptual tools for considering how they manifest as *Existenzielle* in varied settings.

Such tools were provided by Hallowell (1967) in his essay "The Self and Its Behavioral Environment." Hallowell describes how culture provides the individual with five foundational orientations for self-understanding and behavior, and thereby creates an environment affording particular actions and interpretations over others. Hallowell's concept of cultural orientations can be linked to Binswanger's existential-phenomenological analysis to provide an understanding of cultural variation in the experience of *Umwelt*,

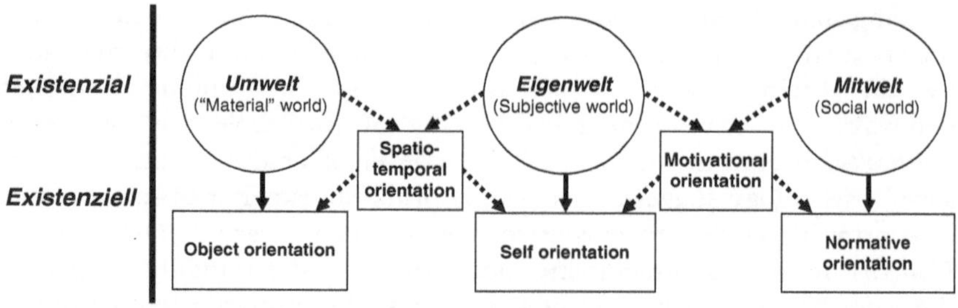

Figure 2.1. Three phenomenological worlds and five cultural orientations.

Mitwelt, and *Eigenwelt*. A graphical overview of the integration of the two schemes is presented in Figure 2.1.

Hallowell proposed that culture offers the individual an *object orientation* – an understanding of the laws of causality and physics that structures their experience of the *Umwelt*. Research (Nisbett et al., 2001; Norenzayan & Lee, 2010) shows that object orientations can be quite variable across cultures. Culture also provides a *normative orientation* – a shared understanding of the boundaries and expectations for appropriate and role-required behavior that shapes the *Mitwelt*. Normative orientations have been shown to be extremely important determinants of behavior and extremely diverse (Elias, 1969; Gelfand et al., 2011). Furthermore, culture provides a *self-orientation* – linguistic and symbolic concepts that mediate the *Eigenwelt* and through which one establishes an independent identity. Although existentialists typically insist on the idiosyncratic nature of self-knowledge, understandings of what it means to be a self are culturally variable (Markus & Kitayama, 1991). This is not to imply that individuals do not all possess unique life histories and perspectives – rather, the claim is that these unique self-narratives are developed in constant collaboration with locally afforded symbols, self-concepts, practices, and technologies. For instance, the type of self that can exist in a cultural environment where there are no computers nor any means of writing is very different from the type of self that exists in an environment pervaded by these tools (Clark & Chalmers, 1998; Ong, 1982).

Hallowell further named two "bridging" orientations that operate as the social-psychological glue binding the *existenzial* worlds together. First, we must conceive of the *Eigenwelt* as mediating between the *Umwelt* and the *Mitwelt*, as represented in Figure 2.1. This conception is prominent in many social scientific perspectives; for instance, phenomenological

(Jackson, 1996) and social ecological (Heft, 2005) views tend to treat the individual as the unit in which "objective" conditions of embodied, material existence and the symbolic elements of social life and cultural reproduction meet and are integrated. Once this conception is in place, what Hallowell calls the *spatiotemporal orientation* becomes the mediating *Existenziell* that bridges the *Umwelt* and *Eigenwelt*, and provides a foundation for object and self-orientation. Since all experience occurs within the dimensions of time and space, differential ways of being within these dimensions link the person's embodied-cognitive experience to ongoing processes in the material world around them. Individuals construct their own relationships to particular spaces across the life span (Tuan, 1977) and experience the self as unfolding continually through time (Minkowski, 1970). Distortions in spatiotemporal orientation are often associated with severe disorders of the self (Ellenberger, 1958; Fuchs, 2013). The spatiotemporal bridge between self-experience and experience of the natural world is not constructed in the same way across cultures, however. Research in sociology and anthropology has long and convincingly documented remarkable variety in forms of spatiotemporal cognition in different settings, as well as variation in the ways societies differentially organize everyday space-time routines (Giddens, 1990; Palitsky, Sullivan, Keefer, & Stewart, in press; Sullivan, Keefer, Stewart, & Palitsky, in press a).

Finally, a *motivational orientation* bridges the *Eigenwelt* and the *Mitwelt*, providing the psychological energy for enactment and development of the self's potentialities and adjustment of the self to the normative orientation in one's culture (see also Spiro, 1961). According to terror management theory (Greenberg et al., 1986), motivation is primarily directed toward shoring up the psychological resources of self-esteem (relevant to the self orientation) and the cultural worldview (largely constituted by the normative orientation). Self-determination theory (Ryan & Deci, 2000) similarly views motivation as determined through a blending of autonomous, self-originating impulses and extrinsic, socially shaped goals. Over the life course, the individual often internalizes motives derived from their society's normative orientation, increasingly connecting these motives to their own self-orientation. In Boesch's (1991) theory, culture provides possibilities for action – the normative orientation is a "zone of tolerance" for acceptable behavior, from which the individual selects certain goals and motives through which to channel and formulate their self-orientation (a similar conception is provided by Kitayama, Park, Sevincer, Karasawa, & Uskul, 2009, in their "cultural task analysis").

Although these basic categories of *Existenziale* and *Existenzielle* are present in all cultural contexts, their expression is not uniform. Indeed, cultures can be partly differentiated on the basis of, say, the relative emphasis that their motivational orientation places on the *Eigenwelt* as opposed to the *Mitwelt*. Another point of distinction between cultures is the extent to which the *Mitwelt* and the *Umwelt* are viewed as wholly separate worlds (Habermas, 1985). While modern post-Enlightenment cultures tend to draw sharply defined lines between the objective and social world, this tendency is far from typical when we consider the blending of object and normative orientations that has occurred in many settings throughout history (Gauchet, 1997; Sahlins, 2008). Some of these cultural differences in experience of the phenomenological worlds will be further considered in Chapters 4 and 5.

Prior XXP research has stressed the universal function of culture for humans – protecting them from threats of mortality, uncertainty, and meaninglessness – and admitting of cultural diversity only insofar as it acknowledges that the specific content of the culturally derived anxiety buffer varies by context. In other words, XXP – like most mainstream psychology – has primarily been in pursuit of *existenzial* structures. However, there is a great deal of patterned variation in the contextually afforded manifestations of human threat experience that has been glossed over by existential psychologists but which lends itself to systematic exploration. This exploration of human *Existenzielle* is a primary goal of cultural-existential psychology.

Indeed, it is perhaps only possible to acquire a thorough understanding of the *Existenziale* and *Existenzielle* of humanity by examining their relation to one another. As Schrag (1961) writes: "The content of the concrete existential commitment [i.e., the *Existenzielle*] is in no way determined by man's ontological and universal possibilities [i.e., the *Existenzial*], but the concrete existential commitment has its conceptual clarification within the horizon of these universal possibilities" (p. 19).

Culture is both a solution to and a source of the problems of nihilism and theodicy

Different scholars across disciplines in the social sciences have long argued that people have a deep-seated motive to understand suffering. These scholars have pointed to different reasons for the presence of this motive, providing mutually reinforcing and compatible explanations. Many thinkers (e.g., Becker, 1969; Douglas, 1966) observe that people are motivated to understand suffering for pragmatic reasons related to the need to behave efficaciously in the world. Understanding the causes of suffering typically facilitates future effective action by providing routes to avoid calamity in the pursuit of goals. Elaborating on this idea, Lerner

(1980) is a major proponent in social psychology of the notion that people need to understand instances of seemingly random misfortune in such a way that their basic sense of personal efficacy remains intact. Several theorists (e.g., Berger & Luckmann, 1966; Janoff-Bulman, 1992; Jaspers, 1970; Nietzsche, 1967) have further proposed that suffering interpreted as meaningless thrusts people into a "marginal" situation, calling into question their basic understanding of reality and sense of ontological security. If the fabric of perceived reality and existing belief systems is not repaired in such instances, nihilism might result.

For all these reasons, people are motivated to make sense of their own and others' suffering. This is especially the case for *traumatic* or potentially traumatic suffering (Herman, 1997), that is, suffering that does not fit within the everyday frame of experience and therefore prompts individuals to question their basic assumptions about the world. As Nietzsche and Weber both argued, the explanation and meaningful interpretation of suffering is a primary function of culture (Sullivan, 2013). In other words, culture solves the problem of theodicy (i.e., of unexplained or potentially meaningless suffering) and therefore circumvents nihilism.

Given the universal cultural function of theodicy and nihilism avoidance, there is a great deal of variation in the content of the belief systems that different cultures contain to perform this function (Shweder, Much, Mahapatra, & Park, 1997; Spiro, 1967). Cultures both filter what forms of suffering register as threatening to individuals, and provide normative interpretations of and responses to these forms (Gillin, 1967; Gillin & Nicholson, 1951).

In proposing the threat-culture constitution cycle as a summary of much work in psychological anthropology, Gillin and colleagues identified many interesting implications of the fact that culture filters psychological threat and defense, implications which will concern us throughout this book. One implication is that cultures recognize some "threats" that may not actually be literal threats to individuals in any meaningful sense, but nevertheless generate extreme anxiety because of their incorporation into local *Existenzielle*; conversely, it is by no means the case that cultures accurately identify all objective threats to their existence. Largely because culture plays such a significant role in grounding threat interpretation, it can be quite difficult to distinguish between "objective" and "imagined" threats; however, some tentative examples can serve to make the point. A percentage of Orthodox Jews become pathologically preoccupied with the inevitable possibility that they will violate one of the 613 mitzvot held sacred by their religion (Huppert, Siev, & Kushner, 2007). Since the majority of these laws concerning diet and the timing of practices would be considered arbitrary by members of other religions, what is a very real anxiety for the sufferers would be seen as nonsensical and groundless by non-Jews. Yet to take another example, many citizens of the United States and Western Europe do not currently consider global warming to be a significant threat to their well-being, yet it is quite possible that the effects of this "invisible" threat will result in countless deaths in the coming decades (Langford, 2002; Morton, 2013).

Thus, culture is both a source of potential existential threats *and* a solution to such threats. This dual-edged nature of culture was observed in the foundational theoretical work of modern anthropology. Malinowski emphasized how religious rituals in premodern cultures neutralize anxiety, while Radcliffe-Brown pointed out that the taboos set by culture and the possibility that rites may be improperly performed or laws not upheld actually generates stress. In an integrative statement drawing on these perspectives, Homans (1941) proposed that cultures provide beliefs and rituals that alleviate some threats, and yet create opportunities for new threats once they have been objectified by members of the culture (see Berger & Luckmann, 1966; Gabriel, 1983). As Nietzsche observed, cultural beliefs can even have the ironic and unintended consequence of generating the potential for nihilism – the absence of a conviction that life is worth living (Reginster, 2009; these points will be further elaborated in Chapters 3 and 5).

Ultimately, variations in suffering interpretations are related to the functioning of societies: worldviews tend to provide interpretations of suffering that reinforce the existing social order. Suffering interpretations sustain societies, just as they sustain the individual who is encountering problematic suffering (Spiro, 1967). Sometimes, cultural beliefs orient the individual toward acts that are beneficial for society but which cause suffering that would be unbearable in the absence of those beliefs. Other times, beliefs that suffering will result from certain antisocial actions prevent people from performing those actions. Generally, the implication of these observations is that it is possible to predict variation in suffering interpretation in light of cultural and social structural variables. This will be largely the theme of Chapter 5 and Part II of the present volume.

A few additional remarks should be made here concerning the important relationship between culture and individual experiences of threat or suffering. First, there are clear differences in the broad forms of suffering that culture helps us interpret. For example, there are differences between individual and collective experiences of suffering; normative interpretations of these two types of suffering may be similar or different in various circumstances (e.g., Wolfenstein, 1957). As another example, in many instances, the same cultural interpretations are drawn on to interpret both one's own and others' suffering. However, there are also many circumstances under which there may be important differences between the types of explanation people typically give for their own suffering versus the comparable suffering of another person (e.g., Perloff, 1987). Worldviews may sometimes encourage similar interpretations of both "everyday" and traumatic suffering, yet in other instances the severity of an incidence of suffering may have a major influence on its likely interpretation (Douglas, 1966; Kotarba, 1977). Some forms of extreme or shockingly novel suffering – such as the first use of atomic bombs in combat, or surviving intensive and prolonged torture – may actually resist all forms of cultural interpretation, dramatically unmooring the *Eigenwelt* from the other phenomenological worlds and allowing the individual no way to communicate their pain. Yet, if individuals can bear such terrible experiences, they are often eventually able to draw on cultural resources to reconstruct their understanding of the world and interpret their trauma, though this new understanding will never match their pre-trauma orientations (Daniel, 1994; Lifton, 1968).

It is worth noting that our experiences of threat largely define the contours of what we consider to be good and normal in our societies (Douglas, 1966). The entire subdiscipline of ethnomethodology was founded on the insight that social norms can best be illuminated by observing the limit points at which behavior transitions from acceptable to deviant (Garfinkel, 1972). Thus, any understanding of what a given cultural group considers to be the "good life" – those ultimate goals and sources of meaning that people typically consider the most important aspects of their life and motivation – necessitates an understanding of what the same group considers to be evil, undesirable, inhuman, or unbearable (Hallowell, 1967).

At the same time, it is also clear that exposure to theodicy problems is not always purely problematic for the individual. A major theme of existentialism is the notion that individuals can personally grow or become authentic only when they attain a realistic understanding of the disturbing realities of life – such as the promise of death – and when they accept responsibility for their own existence and values (Mikulincer & Florian, 1997). Perhaps most eloquently, Jaspers expressed this view in his treatment of existential threats as "limit-situations" – border experiences where the immanent, mundanely familiar structures of our lives threaten to rupture, and to reveal possibilities for transcendence and dizzying new horizons (Bornemark, 2006). There is an important element of terror in awe (Keltner & Haidt, 2003; Otto, 1958), and often those experiences we hold most sacred or meaningful contain elements of pain.

Mixed, interdisciplinary methods are essential for understanding the individual's aversive experiences in a cultural context

The third fundamental principle underscores cultural-existential psychology's stance as an interdisciplinary approach to social science. From existentially informed perspectives, this approach recognizes the importance of *truly* individual experience and meaning-making, and that these processes can never be fully captured through demographic or survey data and statistical analysis. Yet, in order to examine what is universal and distinct in the experiences of different culturally positioned groups – a major goal of the approach – methods and standards for cross-cultural comparison are required. For these reasons, cultural-existential psychology endorses a variety of methods from anthropology, sociology, and experimental psychology.

There is a long history in the social sciences of a largely false dichotomy between quantitative and qualitative sources of data (Hammersley, 1992). To reduce a great deal of sophisticated but often nonproductive argumentation, quantitative researchers sometimes claim that qualitative work is not ultimately useful because its generalizability is questionable and the conclusions drawn by researchers (particularly regarding causality) cannot be subject to rigorous tests. Aside from the obvious positivist bias inherent in such a perspective (cf. Kincaid, Dupré, & Wylie, 2007), this view is based on an inflated sense of the power of hypothesis testing (Cumming, 2014) and on the "objective" nature of statistics. Statistics are a technique, and, like any technique, their employment is influenced by the subjectivity of the user (Abelson, 1995), not to mention sundry other factors such as developments in technology. This is why R. A. Fisher himself saw statistics as a mode of "reasoned argument" rather akin to the case made by a defense lawyer in an attempt to obtain "rigorously specified uncertainty" (see Marks, 2003). Operationalizing variables and statistically analyzing their relationships is as much a means of interpreting the world as the ethnographer's musing over their experiences with a small group: these are simply different forms of interpretation. The differences in these forms are important, but they do not imply the inadequacy of the other and are not mutually exclusive.

At the opposite end of the spectrum, qualitative researchers sometimes accuse quantitative research of (primarily hidden) bias (Glaser & Strauss, 1967; Harding, 1993), or of an inability to address certain questions pertaining to meaning and phenomenology. Quantitative research certainly contains bias, but the same is true of qualitative research, and a particular concern is the methods qualitative researchers have available for reducing that bias (bias reduction is a focal issue in quantitative research, whether it is achieved in practice or not). As for claims that certain questions are only amenable to qualitative examination (such as the meaning of a deeply personal experience), the history of social science shows that any question or subject can be quantified, and in any event "qualitative" researchers often make quantitative claims that simply go untested (for instance, saying that someone "suffered severely" or "had a very meaningful experience" is an implicit quantification of their experience; Hammersley, 1992). In reality, a variety of quantitative and qualitative approaches can be employed to address nearly any research question and can be fruitfully used in parallel or sequence to reinforce one another (Campbell, 1961; Firestone, 1987; Jahoda, Lazarsfeld, & Zeisel, 1971; Mingers, 2001; Teddlie & Tashakkori, 2006). Nevertheless, there are meaningful general distinctions between qualitative and quantitative approaches that suggest their relative utility for addressing different kinds of research questions within the purview of cultural-existential psychology.

Generalizability versus validity. Quantitative researchers often claim that their approach achieves maximum generalizability *and* validity. Such claims cannot ultimately stand – careful reflection reveals that while generalizability is typically increased through quantitative approaches, qualitative work generally provides greater validity. Greater generalizability occurs through quantitative work as a sheer result of the greater number of participants that can be meaningfully included in such studies (Hammersley, 1992), as well as the possibilities of cross-sample comparison and statistical inference that similar results would be obtained in repeated samples (especially when bootstrapping or permutation techniques are employed; Thompson, 1989). Yet, qualitative methods generally provide greater validity for two reasons. First, qualitative case studies allow for extended, detailed examination of the life situations and personal history of individuals and small groups, generating a nuanced picture of a social psychological context that is at best approximated in surveys or experiments (Hammersley, 1992; Nasby & Read, 1997). Second, although the fact is routinely forgotten, quantitative studies often occur in contextually specific, highly unique environments (such as psychology laboratories) and involve highly unique and artificial tasks (such as completing Likert-style survey questions; Adams & Stocks, 2008; Reis, 2012; Webb, Campbell, Schwartz, & Sechrest, 2000). Findings in laboratories and surveys provide useful arguments about what is *likely* to occur in settings beyond those of data collection, but they cannot offer the rich documentation of actual, historically situated occurrence that is collected in case study research (see Gergen, 1973). This capacity for documenting a complex, culturally situated set of events is of course precisely the reason why findings from qualitative research are typically less generalizable. But this should not be taken to imply that one *cannot* generalize from qualitative research, nor that qualitative researchers should try to defend their work by resisting attempts at generalization (Gomm, Hammersley, & Foster, 2000). Any research worthy of the name implies a context of generalization and comparison.

Naturally, many readers (particularly social psychologists) will object to the claim that qualitative research is more valid, because they are likely accustomed to a definition of validity stemming from Campbell (1957) that prioritizes quantitative, experimental data from the outset. That is, many researchers assert that validity is primarily a question of *internal validity* or conviction about causality (Carlsmith, Ellsworth, & Aronson, 1976), and that experiments are the best means of achieving this. Of course, one can define validity in a number of ways, and one's definition can ultimately predetermine which methods are preferred. Hence, qualitative researchers have questioned the value of empirical validity standards altogether (Gergen, 2015; Kvale, 1995). Rather than straying too far down this road, I will simply define validity as achieving an accurate representation of reality, and assert that qualitative methods – when practiced well and comprehensively – almost inevitably achieve this to a greater degree.

It is true that experiments make an important contribution to establishing internal validity, insofar as techniques of random assignment and experimental control can be utilized to increase one's conviction that an isolated independent variable has causal impact on a dependent variable. However, experimental results are rarely conclusive about whether one has successfully operationalized the causal variable(s) of interest, or whether one has identified the most important variable in a causal process. In addition, causality can be assessed in ethnographic research, including through qualitative experiments (Robinson & Mendelson, 2012). Ultimately, internal and external validity are best assessed through the use of multi-trait, multi-method approaches, including the creative blending of quantitative and qualitative findings (Campbell & Fiske, 1959; Webb et al., 2000).

The rule that qualitative research is more valid should also be qualified with reference to the study of processes that are inherently difficult or impossible for individuals to directly observe, such as neural activity or nonconscious processes. Here, quantitative techniques may have ultimate validity. Some of these situations will be considered presently.

Communication versus representation. Social science is often conceived as a systematic attempt to generate what Kvale (1995) – invoking the theorizing of Habermas (1985) – called communicative validity claims: statements subject to reasoned, dialogic argument about the relationship between processes in the natural world (*Umwelt*) and the common goals or beliefs of societies (*Mitwelt*). If this is indeed the goal of social science, then quantitative studies are preferable over most qualitative methods. Regardless of whether the quantitative methods and statistics employed by a given researcher accurately describe natural processes, there is at least a system and set of standards in place for evaluating and communicating conclusions (e.g., all researchers understand, or can come to understand, the meaning of descriptive statistics and observed *p*-values). By appealing to these agreed-upon standards (however subjectively determined they might be), quantitative researchers can arbitrate disputes about the relative validity of different claims (Hull, 1988). The validity of qualitative research is ultimately a function of the methodology and capabilities of the individual researcher, which makes appeal to common standards far more difficult (although naturally this problem can be mitigated by the use of qualitative research teams and checks by other researchers; Carspecken, 1996; Taylor & Bogdan, 1998). Indeed, methodologies in qualitative research are quite diverse and hybridized (Denzin & Lincoln, 2008; Saldaña, 2009), and the individual researcher is often described as a fundamental, irreplaceable "tool" in the research process (Clarke, 2005). This means that appeals to subjective experience and personal conviction often act as "conversation-stoppers" (Rorty, 1999) in the area of qualitative inquiry. If another scholar disagrees with the ethnographer's conclusion, the latter can always claim privileged access to the data and the individuals or cultural group under investigation, or – as is common since the emergence of postmodernism – that their interpretation is only one among dozens of possible interpretations. It is difficult to find agreed-upon standards to which qualitative researchers can appeal to resolve disputed communicative validity claims (Miles & Huberman, 1994).

However, well-founded arguments can be made that the purpose of scientific inquiry is not only to communicate and arbitrate disputable claims about the realities of the natural or social worlds (Carspecken, 1996). A long tradition suggests that social science in particular also has a duty to accurately *represent* people's subjective experience of reality – and thus to approximate a recording and interpretation of the Other's (or even the Self's) *Eigenwelt* (Dilthey, 1961). In short, social science must also represent the *subjective validity claims* (Carspecken, 1996) of particular social groups and individuals (especially those who are conventionally underrepresented), and not merely engage in a communicative dialogue between empowered scientists and policy-makers. This is certainly the case for cultural-existential psychology, which draws partly on an existentialist conviction in the autonomy and idiosyncrasy of all individual perspectives (Sharpless, 2013). By conveying in rich detail the narratives of personalized meaning endorsed by participants, qualitative research is better suited than quantitative research to represent the participants' subjective experience and unique position (Neimeyer & Hogan, 2001).

Communicative validity claims and generalizability are critical goals for social science research, but these goals can be very difficult to realize in practice when one is conducting cross-cultural research. Standard methods for arbitrating validity claims are developed in a (typically Western) context, and these methods (tests, surveys, experimental manipulations) do not readily translate across diverse contexts (Greenfield, 1997). Cross-cultural qualitative inquiry, which can develop a "grounded theory" based on spontaneous engagement with field data and not on predefined standards, methods, and hypotheses (Glaser & Strauss, 1967), is a useful means of shedding reflective light back on the hidden assumptions built in to the standard methodology and theory underlying quantitative research (e.g., McKinnon, 2005).

A further insight of cultural-existential psychology is that some of the most important life experiences can be those of extreme terror, trauma, or loss that are very difficult to represent (Daniel, 1994). It is probably facile and absurd to consider asking a victim of severe torture to rate their experience on a scale of 1 to 7. But interviews, participant observation, text analysis, and other forms of qualitative inquiry can approximate a representation of even the most radical experiences.

Conscious versus nonconscious processes. Existential sociology highlighted the fact that people's interpretations of their experience – however illusory and arbitrary they might be – are nevertheless important as crystallizations of meaning in their lives. Recognition of this fact should not blind us to the importance of *nonconscious* forces. Both from a psychoanalytic and a Marxist sociological perspective, we can recognize that people's subjective validity claims are often defensive, and that people's behavior and attitudes are largely a function of contextual and institutional factors of which they are not consciously aware. A great deal of research in psychology (Bargh, 1997; Kihlstrom, 1990; Nisbett & Wilson, 1977; Westen, 1998) and sociology (Bensman & Lilienfeld, 1991; Schooler, 1996) provides support for this general contention. The majority of this research is quantitative. It is possible to investigate defensive and nonconscious processes through qualitative research (e.g., Adorno, 2010; Willis, 1977), for example, by engaging in interrogative or challenging interview techniques with participants, or if the researcher has training in therapy (Frosh & Saville Young, 2008). Such cases notwithstanding, investigating nonconscious processes is difficult in qualitative research, where ultimately the researcher must interpret the meaning and origin of participants' explicit statements. Since there is often no objective record of information against which the researcher can appeal to check the validity of participants' statements, the qualitative researcher's ultimate concern should be to accurately represent their participants' experience, and too much non-verifiable depth interpretation can subvert that goal.

By contrast, quantitative research is inherently well suited to the investigation of nonconscious or defensive processes because it shifts the balance of power and interpretative control in the researcher's direction by providing some objective record (however reductive) against which various claims on the part of the participant can be precisely compared (Corbin & Morse, 2003). Hypotheses can be tested – of which participants are completely unaware – through the use of experimental manipulations and the calculation of correlations between measures that may seem quite separate in the participant's mind. For example, most research participants would not likely endorse the idea that their level of self-esteem has any relation to their ability to repress death-related anxiety. Investigating such a hypothesis qualitatively would be challenging and would likely require a fair degree of speculation on the researcher's part. However, a negative correlation between measures of self-esteem and death-anxiety – including *implicit* measures that are nearly impossible for participants to consciously bias – can be readily calculated. Experimental and quantitative methods have ultimately emerged as more amenable to the testing of nonconscious defense mechanisms, while qualitative methods are far better suited for accurately representing the conscious experience of individuals.

Cultural-existential psychology recognizes that all of these scientific aims and social psychological processes are vital and worthy of pursuit. Therefore, to provide a thorough understanding of the relation between culture and threat experience in any particular group, this approach draws on at least three levels of methodology presented schematically in Figure 2.2. This multi-method perspective recognizes that different disciplines and related tools of inquiry provide types of data that range from concrete to abstract, from "close-to-the-ground" to interpretative, and these different forms of data range in their suitability for addressing different aspects of the threat-culture relationship (Gillin, 1954a).

To understand how members of a particular group experience threat and defense, we must first have some understanding of the social structural and socio-ecological setting in which the group is embedded, as research in psychological anthropology has made clear. Cultural patterns have their origin largely in such institutional and human geographic

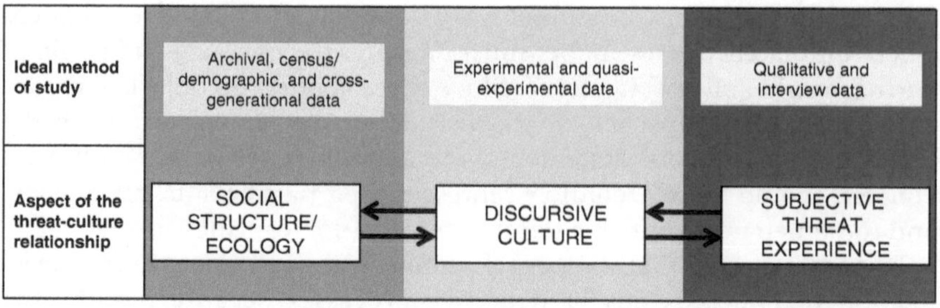

Figure 2.2. Multiple methods of study for understanding the relationship between culture and people's experience of suffering and threat.

factors, including but far from limited to the relative mobility of individuals in the setting, population density, technologies utilized in the setting, historical patterns of belief and behavior, and local modes for organizing and constructing space and time. Such structural aspects of a cultural setting can be profitably investigated using various forms of quantitative, non-obtrusive data, such as demographic and archival records, behavior setting surveys or human geographic records, and/or longitudinal data that can be used to trace changes in social structure or belief patterns across time. These methods provide a great deal of foundational information about the *Umwelt* in which members of a cultural group dwell. The majority of research in cultural and experimental existential psychology operates at a second level of analysis – namely investigation of the motivational and normative orientations provided by a particular *Mitwelt*. The study of discursive culture – the beliefs, attitudes, and norms that can be accessed and articulated by most members of the culture (Giddens, 1984) – can be accomplished through the use of experimental methods or quasi-experimental and correlational surveys. By collecting quantitative self-report or behavioral data from many individuals within a culture, we obtain a broad view of the meaning systems and practices that individuals draw upon and reproduce in daily life. Further, these quantitative approaches allow us to systematically compare different *Mitwelten*, the primary goal of cultural psychology. Yet, an analysis of the threat-culture relationship that only employs these sociological and psychological methods is incomplete, because it does not capture the crucial personal experience and subjective interpretation of threat (as critiques from existential sociology and existential anthropology have shown). Full comprehension of the ways in which the individual's *Eigenwelt* is torn and repaired through the painful dialogue of meaning and suffering is best obtained through ethnographic or interview studies, which force the researcher to confront the concrete realities of a person's unique experience. Clearly, it should be understood that these idiosyncratic subjective interpretations are not formulated in an existential void, but rather are grounded in historical, structural forces (*Umwelt*) and socially constructed (*Mitwelt*). Hence the necessity of mixed methods.

Some past research programs have admirably demonstrated the fruitfulness of a multi-method approach such as the one presented here. Notable examples include the work of the Frankfurt School on unemployment at Marienthal and the authoritarian personality in the 1950s United States, or Gelfand and colleagues' (2011) multilevel mapping of the construct of cultural tightness-looseness. However, such examples are sadly few in the social scientific literature. Part II of the present volume will present my own attempt to flesh out this third methodological principle in my research on threat experiences with various Mennonite groups in Kansas.

Having traced the proximal and more distal social scientific roots of cultural-existential psychology, and presented its three fundamental principles, I will now shift the discussion toward a more detailed consideration of the key constructs of threat (Chapter 3) and culture (Chapter 4) in the present theory. A final methodological note is required before I proceed. An assumption shared by all the research traditions considered in this and the foregoing chapter is that human (especially psychological) experience is grossly misrepresented when investigated through a lens of biological or neurological reductionism (see Miller, 2010). Despite the vital necessity of recognizing the importance of evolutionary continuity in human life, our existence is characterized by symbolic and technological forces which far outstrip the Being of any other species. This is nowhere more obvious than in the case of human threat and suffering experience. Although many aspects of our biological and mental reactions to threat evince a deep similarity to those of other animals, our unique capacity for experiencing symbolic threats – and resolving them through symbolic resources – cries out for non-reductionist analysis closer to the level of lived experience (Geertz, 1975). It is this sort of analysis I will be attempting in the following pages.

3 A model of existential threat

The first two chapters laid the groundwork for a cultural-existential psychology by surveying its theoretical roots in prior social scientific movements and presenting its three guiding principles. The remainder of Part I will be devoted to the conceptual "heavy lifting" of the framework. In particular, I will explicate the two primary constructs around which all cultural-existential theory revolves: *threat* (Chapter 3) and *culture* (Chapter 4). The last chapter of Part I will bring these two constructs together in a model of cultural variation in threat orientation.

To understand *existenziell* variation in how people of different cultural backgrounds concretely encounter threats, we must first establish a framework for discussing the *existenzial* or universally valid structure of human threat experience. In particular, we should specify what is meant by the term "existential threat," and outline a taxonomy of qualitative and quantitative variation in types of threat. I will do so in this chapter by expanding on a prior typology of existential threat developed by myself and my colleagues (Sullivan, Landau, & Kay, 2012a). This typology is theoretically grounded in the work of the existentialists, but is also supported by empirical evidence from contemporary social psychology.

The nature of existential threat

> Anxiety is the existential awareness of nonbeing.
>
> – Tillich (1952, p. 35)

Tillich's simple sentence contains a complete, elegant definition of existential threat. In particular, this sentence highlights four key aspects of existential threat: *anxiety, awareness, nonbeing*, and *existential.* I will consider each in turn.

Anxiety refers to the fact that, during an experience of existential threat, the individual senses (at least initially) a loss of clear direction to guide her actions and the absence of a concrete object on which to focus her fear or negative affect (Tillich, 1952). As the experience of existential threat begins, it initially launches the individual into a state of cognitive confusion. In a true state of *fear*, the individual appraises a concrete object in the world that induces terror and revulsion. The individual acts in response to this object, and typically is immediately aware of how she should respond to it (for instance, by fleeing the scene). By contrast, in a state of existential threat, the individual experiences a surge of welling negative affect, but struggles – at first in vain – to find an object to which she can attach the emotion. According to Tillich, all anxiety strives to become fear; the normative individual cannot bear to remain in a state of objectless anxiety for long. Thus, an initial state of anxiety, if it does not dissipate or fade as a result of some change in the individual's immediate circumstances, will eventually become concretized and attached to some object. This desire to concretize initially objectless anxiety is partly the reason why there are different varieties of existential threat: the individual will experience her anxiety differently depending on the object to which it is eventually attached. This understanding of the role of generalized anxiety in threat experience has been supported by neurological and experimental research (carried out from a variety of theoretical perspectives), which demonstrates that individuals respond to threat in a two-step process of initial hypervigilance and avoidance motivation followed by compensatory approach motivation (Jonas et al., 2014).

Awareness suggests that existential threat inherently involves some experience of self-consciousness on the part of the individual. In one of their initial expositions of the nature of existential threat, the cocreators of terror management theory pointed out that self-awareness is inherently linked to the potential for debilitating anxiety (Pyszczynski, Greenberg, Solomon, & Hamilton, 1990). Existential threat always involves an initial sense either that the self may be deviating from cultural standards designed to protect it from anxiety, or that the external standards which uphold the self are in question. As Sartre would put it, this means that existential threat thrusts the individual from *en-soi* (i.e., non-self-aware) consciousness into *pour-soi* (i.e., self-aware) consciousness (see Hayim, 2007, p. 14). In the framework of objective self-awareness theory (Duval & Wicklund, 1972), existential threat involves a sudden transition from subjective to objective self-awareness; and from the perspectives of cybernetic self-regulation (Carver & Scheier, 1981) and action identification theory (Vallacher & Wegner, 1987), there is a simultaneous shift in the individual's goal orientation, such that she becomes more aware of the abstract goals for ultimate value and meaning she is pursuing, and which have now come under threat. Hence, existential threat shares an affinity with the self-conscious emotions (generally understood to be guilt, shame, pride, and embarrassment) widely researched in social psychology (Tracy & Robins, 2007). It also can be understood in terms of Lazarus'

(1991) appraisal theory of emotion: existential threat involves a negative affective state resulting from an appraisal of an object or event as incongruent with the self's goals. In a state of existential threat, there is some recognition on the part of the individual (occurring either consciously or nonconsciously) that broad goals for personal value and meaning are coming under attack. Existential threat is not cognitively localized, as in the case of more routine, nonexistential threats, but rather involves the spreading activation of a negatively valenced associational network, through which an experienced discrepancy between an ideal and an actual state has the potential to become more global, possibly leading to an ultimate discrepancy between the individual's desire for being and awareness of nonbeing (Pyszczynski et al., 1990; Westen, 1985).

Nonbeing is thus that of which the self is aware during the experience of existential threat. Nonbeing is a fundamental but often-overlooked element of human symbolic consciousness. On the existentialist view (especially in Sartre's writings), negation and lack are key elements of human cognition and motivation (Cooper, 1990; Martin, 2002). We are organisms who desire the permanence of certain concrete (buildings, photographs, loved ones) and abstract (values, memories) objects. This dialectically connotes that we also significantly and painfully recognize the destruction, disappearance, or mere absence of important objects.

As mentioned, existential threat encounters involve a heightened sense of self-awareness. When the self becomes an object for its own awareness, the potential nonbeing of the self is immediately implied, even if this potential is only registered outside of immediate consciousness (Silvia, 2001). For Tillich, then, all threat encounters point toward nonbeing, and all threats are ultimately grounded in the individual's awareness of her impending mortality. All temporary losses of self in experiences of partial nonbeing (i.e., experiences which call into question one's sense of meaning or personal value) would not be threatening in the absence of the guaranteed total and irreversible state of nonbeing we all approach.

Thus, when the individual is aware of her nonbeing, she has become aware of the potential for her sense of personal existence in reality to be lost or partly lost: in short, for her personal existence to become decoupled from the external reality in which it is immersed. In this context, it is critical to remember (as discussed in Chapter 2) that humans have multiple modes of "Being" – ontological, physical being (*Umwelt*), but also shared/cultural (*Mitwelt*) and personal/moral being (*Eigenwelt*). Thus, in addition to physical survival needs, individuals have needs for a sense of ultimate meaning rooted in social identity, and a sense of positive personal moral value and self-esteem. Awareness of nonbeing can involve a direct focus on the self's physical limits, but it often rather involves a mediated awareness of the fragility of these symbolic modes of being.

Finally, the person experiences awareness of nonbeing in an *existential* fashion. As Tillich uses it, the modifier *existential* has two primary implications. First, it suggests that existential threat is part of the normal range of experience of the average person within a culture (i.e., at lower levels of severity, existential threat is not pathological; Tillich, 1952). Second, it means that existential threat involves awareness of *one's own* potential (and imminent) nonbeing specifically.

To summarize, existential threat entails the individual becoming aware of the tenuous nature of her own, unique existence – the fragility of her meaning systems and sense of self-value – in such a way that she is initially unable (or unwilling) to precisely pinpoint the source of the threat. An initial state of free-floating negative affect in consciousness (or the activated potential for negative affect outside of consciousness; see Johnston & Malabou, 2013; Westen, 1985) arises as the individual senses that the structures that maintain her unique convictions of value and meaning are under threat. Existential threat implies a deviation from the normal, taken-for-granted relationship between the self and the world – a deviation sharp enough for the self to intuit that her working understanding of herself or the world may be entirely called into question (Berger & Luckmann, 1966; Jaspers, 1970).

To label a threat *existential* (as opposed to nonexistential) implies that the threat is experienced (consciously or nonconsciously) as an attack on the person's ego, that is, their symbolic structures of meaning and value. Nonexistential threats do not involve the level of self-awareness that is activated in a state of existential threat. Frustrations in the performance of simple tasks or even physical attacks on the self should not be considered existential threats unless they activate a network of negative associations representing the potential dismantling of the individual's symbolic defenses against nonbeing. The awareness Tillich refers to as inhering in a state of existential threat does not necessarily imply full conscious awareness of the threat; as will be discussed in more detail, defenses acquired through socialization can "short-circuit" or modify existential threats before they enter full consciousness (Johnston & Malabou, 2013; Lazarus, 1991). The important point is that a degree of *self*-awareness or -consciousness is active during existential threat; a discrepancy between one's sense of how the world should be and the reality of a situation activates the potential for deeper (generally repressed) anxieties connected, ultimately, to the self's awareness of its mortal condition. We may encounter many threats (often with greater realistic potential for causing us physical harm) on a more or less regular basis that are either processed in a more automatic fashion (as when we swing aside to avoid an incoming fist outside a barroom) or for which we have more ready responses (as when we adjust our strategy in the course of an increasingly difficult game) than in the case of existential threat. If we cope with such practical threats and they do not activate a spreading network of associations connected to broader insecurities, then they should not be labeled existential.

Existential threat is a unique category of phenomenological experience, heavily symbolically mediated, that humans do not seem to share with other animals. In these situations, the individual is suddenly acutely aware of the separation and potential discord between two or more of the worlds in which she lives: the *Eigenwelt* feels suddenly cut off or unmoored from the *Mitwelt* or *Umwelt*. True existential threat involves the activation of a spreading associational network, such that higher-order, abstract defenses against death are infringed upon, and the potential for death thought accessibility occurs outside conscious awareness.

Death – the ultimate form of nonbeing

Existential perspectives hold that death (and, critically, death awareness) is at the root of all existential threat encounters, because death is the asymptotic limit of all experienced finitude and the ultimate threat to ontic, physical existence, which also implies the annihilation of symbolic, psychological affirmation on the cultural and personal value dimensions (Tillich, 1952). Drawing on this existential tradition, Bauman (1992) has outlined the profound philosophical and sociological significance of human death awareness. The idea of one's own death is the concept of nothingness, *par excellence*. Consciousness is oriented toward stability, consistency, presence, activity – and death is the denial of all these constructs. The death of others, however painful and destructive for the individual, can nevertheless be assimilated to cultural patterns of interpretation like any other datum of experience. But one's own death is the final site of the body's betrayal of culture's promise: that which cannot be experienced by the self *cannot* have meaning. All other experiences of liminality, ambiguity, transitoriness, chaos, and terror approximate but never surpass the individual's death, which can only be culturally redeemed by survivors (Douglas, 1966; Kristeva, 1982). This gives personal death supreme psychological status as *unthinkable* and *unacceptable*, despite its unforgiving ontological status as *unavoidable*. As Bauman (1992) states: "Death is the archetypal *contradiction in terms*. The non-being of matter is difficult, if not impossible, to *imagine*; to imagine the non-existence of mind is downright impossible. Such a non-being may be thought only in its denial. The very act of thinking death is already its denial" (p. 15; italics in original). And as Nagel (1993) writes:

> Observed from without, human beings obviously have a natural lifespan and cannot live much longer than a hundred years. A man's sense of his own experience, on the other hand, does not embody this idea of a natural limit. His existence defines for him an essentially open-ended possible future, containing the usual mixture of goods and evils that he has found so tolerable in the past . . . Viewed in this way, death, no matter how inevitable, is an abrupt cancellation of indefinitely extensive possible goods. (p. 69)

This unacceptability of death for human consciousness has inestimably important consequences for human cultural production, as Bauman, Becker (1973), Brown (1959), Nietzsche (1874/1997), and Rank (1930/1998) have pointed out in exhaustive detail. Humans create histories and cultural value systems largely to cover the unacceptable experience of physical transitoriness with the appealing illusion of permanence. Our religious beliefs, secular commitments, moral principles – all those beliefs we consider fundamental to our cultural identities and personal lives – have the generally implicit goal of offering us symbolic immortality (Lifton, 1968). In an ironic but important consequence demonstrative of the threat-culture cycle discussed in Chapter 1, this state of affairs has resulted in the striking elaboration of the threat of nonbeing in human experience. Because humans oppose their symbolic being (their cultural beliefs and felt personal value) to the unacceptable threat of physical nonbeing, threats to their symbolic being acquire similarly intolerable gravity.

There are many metaphors through which humans have attempted to grasp the painful riddle of death (Macho, 1987). Yet as the ultimate symbol and incarnation of nonbeing, death evades all interpretation and threatens meaning and identity from all angles. Indeed, the idea of personal mortality is only the abstract (but ultimate) limit of a series of concrete, threatening reminders of finitude that the individual encounters throughout the life span, every day. As children, we realize the inadequacies of our physical bodies in their often-powerless attempts to navigate an intimidating adult world (Bettelheim, 1976). As young adults, we often feel confused, enslaved, or disgusted by the bodily changes induced by puberty, sexual desire, and pregnancy (e.g., Johnston-Robledo & Chrisler, 2011). As we grow older, various symptoms of bodily decay, the gradual rise of illness and fatigue, and a general loss of the physical and mental vivacity of youth all remind us of steadily encroaching death (Featherstone & Hepworth, 1991). Throughout the life span, we are periodically horrified by experiences where our bodies fail and constrain our symbolic selves in dramatic ways: we break limbs, vomit to the point of dehydration in the midst of fever, are beset by attacks of bloody, liquid stool, and so on. Such experiences of corporeality are obviously uncomfortable on an embodied level, but they also have psychological impact. As implied by the existential perspective discussed in Chapter 1, humans seek to exist on a symbolic, rather than a physical, plane – we want to believe that our selves and souls transcend their physical, animal, finite casings. This suggests that a very important way in which humans experience the threat of death is as the threat of *animality* or *creatureliness* (Becker, 1975).

From the perspective of cultural-existential psychology, just as human capacities for symbolic consciousness make us uniquely aware of our animal, mortal nature, and instill in us a unique desire to escape this fate, so too do these capacities provide us with the psychological resources on which we rely to repress these fundamental anxieties. As mentioned in Chapter 1, terror management theory (Greenberg et al., 1986) has generated a large body of research documenting the ways in which individuals protect themselves from death-related thoughts by shoring up symbolic resources – their faith in cultural meaning systems (the fabric of the *Mitwelt*), and their sense of positive self-esteem (the valence of the *Eigenwelt*). Specifically, the majority of terror management studies test the hypothesis that if a psychological structure provides protection from death anxiety, then reminders of death should increase cognitive and behavioral striving to bolster that structure.

This hypothesis was initially tested in a classic study (Rosenblatt, Greenberg, Solomon, Pyszczynski, & Lyon, 1989). Municipal court judges completed some personality measures as well as hypothetical measures relating to their professional activities. Embedded in the "personality" measures for half the participants were questions reminding the judges that they would eventually die. After responding to either these questions or neutral prompts, judges were asked to set bond for a hypothetical prostitute. Whereas judges in the control condition recommended an average bond of $55, those who had been reminded of mortality recommended a $450 bond on average. Follow-up studies have shown that death reminders lead to harsher judgments across a wide range of moral transgressions (e.g., Florian & Mikulincer, 1997), and also increase the amount of reward given to individuals who uphold, rather than transgress, cultural standards for valued behavior.

In another classic study (Greenberg et al., 1990), Christians rated other persons who were described as highly similar but differing in their religious background (Christian vs. Jewish), either after being reminded of their death or not. In the control condition there were no differences in participants' evaluations of the targets; however, a death reminder elicited increased affection for the fellow Christian target and exaggerated hostility toward the Jewish target. Similarly, American college students primed with mortality or a control topic evaluated essays written by other students that either praised or condemned the American way of life (Greenberg et al., 1990). Control-primed participants rated the author of the pro-US essay more favorably than the author of the anti-US essay, but this tendency was exacerbated among participants reminded of mortality, who showed more positive and negative reactions to pro- and anti-US authors, respectively.

Since these early investigations, reminders of mortality have been shown to affect a broad range of behaviors that entail maintaining faith in one's worldview, self-esteem, and also a sense of attachment to close others, including altruism, aggression, attributions, achievement striving, aesthetic judgments, conformity, disgust, health-related behavior, political preferences, religious belief, self-serving biases, sexuality, structure seeking, and symptoms of psychopathology (for reviews, see Greenberg et al., 2008; Greenberg & Arndt, 2012). Furthermore, these effects have been observed using a variety of operationalizations of death reminders, ranging from video footage of disturbing accidents to subliminal primes of the word "death," from administration of questionnaires outside a cemetery versus a grocery store to the presence versus absence of a death-related poem on a classroom chalkboard. A meta-analysis of these studies concluded that the effect of mortality reminders was one of the most robust in psychology (Burke, Martens, & Faucher, 2010).

Research has also revealed a unique time course for the emergence of these effects. Unlike most other priming effects that fade as a function of increased time between the administration of the prime and measure of the outcome (e.g., Martens, Burke, Schimel, & Faucher, 2011; Förster, Liberman, & Friedman, 2007), effects of death reminders emerge not immediately after priming but only after a delay and distraction. Defensive investment in one's worldview and self-esteem occur when the accessibility of death-related thoughts is elevated, but not when such thoughts are the current focus of conscious attention. On the basis of these findings, terror management theory posits a dual-mode model of the repression of death anxiety. Initially, when thoughts of death enter consciousness, individuals employ a *proximal mode* of defense, entailing direct responses that either deny one's vulnerability to death (e.g., vowing to exercise harder or quit smoking, or taking comfort in religious beliefs about literal immortality) or push death-related thoughts from conscious attention (e.g., distracting the self from such thoughts by focusing on more positive life aspects). Later, when thoughts of death are accessible but outside of conscious awareness (Greenberg et al., 2003), individuals engage the *distal mode* of defense, which involves bolstering the symbolic resources that convince the self of its specialness and immortality. The empirical identification of this time course for the effects of death reminders has important implications, which have also been supported by this body of research. First, it is not the mere experience of conscious negative affect that is driving these effects – there is something significant about death thoughts, as posited by existential theory. Studies have shown unique effects of death reminders compared to a variety of other aversive states, including reminders of isolation, intense physical pain, meaninglessness, and uncertainty. Second, participants in these studies do not consciously perceive any connection between their thoughts of death and subsequent defensiveness, and of course these acts of defensiveness do nothing to actually address the participants' problem of mortality. Rather, these are nonconscious processes of repressive psychological compensation.

As terror management research attests, death is the ultimate ontological and symbolic threat in human experience. The understanding of personal mortality undermines all the culturally derived orientations, as well as the three phenomenological worlds. People fear death because it eliminates the possibility of reaching important personal goals (*Eigenwelt*), it separates them from loved ones and implies the transience of their cultural group (*Mitwelt*), and it is an uncertain event that threatens their sense of the stability, constancy, and integrity of their being in the material world (*Umwelt*; Florian & Kravetz, 1983). Accordingly, research shows that threatening any of these symbolic resources (i.e., one's self-esteem, sense of attachment to others, or one's cultural worldview) elevates thoughts of death outside of consciousness (Hayes, Schimel, Arndt, & Faucher, 2010). In line with the aforementioned thesis about the connection of death fear to fear of animality, research also shows that reminding individuals of their animal nature (e.g., by showing them pictures of feces or mucus) elevates the nonconscious accessibility of death-related thought (Cox, Goldenberg, Pyszczynski, & Weise, 2007).

Existentialism's threat dialectic theory

Although physical death is the ultimate source of finitude and hence threat in human experience, because cultural beliefs typically convince individuals of their literal or symbolic immortality, existential threat is only rarely experienced as conscious, unrepressed death fear. Rather, nonbeing is often experienced indirectly in relation to our symbolic defenses against mortality awareness. Since existential threats can take the form of infringements on different aspects of our being (disharmony in the *Umwelt, Mitwelt*, or *Eigenwelt*), it is necessary to establish a categorical scheme for distinguishing between different threat experiences. Such a scheme will ultimately allow us to analyze the prototypic ways in which threat manifests differentially in various cultural settings. A first step toward this scheme lies in returning to the foundational work of the existentialists. As Tillich found, examination of the work of the existentialists reveals a remarkable unity in their analyses (see also Cooper, 1990). In particular, their analyses converged on the types of existential threat which humans experience. This convergence can be summarized as existentialism's *threat dialectic theory* (Sullivan et al., 2012a).

According to this theory, people oscillate on a fairly regular basis between two opposing "poles" of threat (Schneider, 1999). At a very basic level, we can conceptualize these poles as threat that can occur *prior to* action in the world, and threat that can occur *following* action in the world. The former is usually discussed in terms of *abstractness* and the experience of uncertainty or anxiety, while the latter is usually discussed in terms of *concreteness* and the experience of inadequacy or guilt. In the theory, these two types of threat are interrelated and people generally shift from one form to the other in dialectic fashion as they engage in and subsequently reflect upon action. As philosophical anthropology indicates, this dialectical movement between the abstract uncertainty of the future, the moment of choice, and the concrete irreversibility of the past is rooted in the reality of human biology and temporality. Each choice we make, and the alternatives that we forsake, become part of our organism. As Langer (1988) wrote,

> Whenever an act is induced by a change in the vital situation, such as the life process itself constantly engenders . . . it is likely that not only the impulse of that act, but also one or more conflicting impulses or alternative potential acts are formed, which are doomed to speedy abrogation. This play of impulses forms the dynamic matrix of life . . . the life comprises also all the potential acts which exist only for milliseconds or less. (p. 116)

Thus, threat dialectic theory is rooted in the assumption – common to all existentialists (Guignon & Pereboom, 1995) – that individual identity and consciousness at any given moment is a problematic mixture of an irreversible personal history and an openness to an unknown but imagined future.

In one of the earliest formulations of these ideas, Kierkegaard (1844/1981) proposed that humans' symbolic self-awareness leads them to realize that their actions are not determined by necessity, and that every act is a selection out of a nearly infinite array of possible behaviors. This awareness causes uncertainty about how to act and has the potential to generate intense anxiety, experienced as a kind of "dizziness" at the multifarious paths to action lying before the individual (Marino, 1998). The individual is impelled to action in an attempt to overcome this uncertainty, but the same level of self-awareness that allows the individual to see her actions as undetermined often causes her to question her actions after they have been performed. In Kierkegaard's terminology, there is a sense of having sinned or a potential feeling of guilt connected with nearly all human action. Self-awareness and the capacity for abstract, counterfactual thinking prompt the individual to compare her actual actions and life circumstances to her imagined possibilities. This comparison often generates depressive sentiments of inadequacy or remorse. In a later formulation, Kierkegaard (1849/2004) described the two poles of existential threat as *possibility's despair* and *necessity's despair*, and indeed argued that selfhood inheres in a synthesis of these two experiences. Humans oscillate between despair connected with the perception that action is infinitely undefined and arbitrary (i.e., possibility in the absence of necessity), and despair connected with the contradictory perception that actions and abilities are, in fact, finite and limited (i.e., necessity in the absence of possibility). Naturally, this conflict arises from the unique human situation of embodied symbolic consciousness.

Drawing on the ideas of Kierkegaard as well as Husserl, Sartre (1943/2001) reformulated the threat dialectic, giving it a more promotion-focused orientation. Specifically, Sartre asserted that humans are defined by *facticity* (unchangeable aspects of identity, embodiment, and historical circumstance), but aware of their potential for and motivated toward *transcendence* (put simply, altering or overcoming facticity by asserting free will). In Sartre's system, the conditions of both facticity and transcendence that make up the self can provide comfort or strength but can also be seen as threatening. The self's agency is threatened by the limiting, potentially inadequate nature of its facticity, but the self can also be overwhelmed by the burden of responsibility it bears for its uncertain transcendence, the realization that it always has an alternate choice in any situation. Accordingly, Sartre (2001) proposes that the self often defensively "flies" from conscious awareness of the reality of its constitution, seeking refuge in a denial of existing circumstances in a process Sartre calls "bad faith."

There are multiple forms of defensive bad faith described in Sartre's writings (Hayim, 2007), which can be summarily classified as the flight from transcendence and the flight from facticity (Martin, 2002). In the former, individuals attempt to deny the inescapability of choice and uncertainty, immersing themselves uncritically in social roles and conventions and behaving as if they lacked any agency to alter their circumstances. In the latter, they seek abstract refuge from feelings of limitation and inadequacy by convincing themselves that they stand above normative influence and accidents of birth; flying into transcendence, they cling to the fantasy that their lives are endlessly malleable. As in Kierkegaard's system, Sartre holds that individuals fluctuate between these forms of bad faith, alternately flying from transcendence into facticity, and then from facticity back into transcendence.

The writings of the existential philosophers concerning the experience of threat have influenced a number of psychologists, who have commonly reframed the threat-dialectic theory in terms of the experience of two opposing *existential emotions*: anxiety and guilt. Slightly prior to Sartre's publication of his ideas, the psychoanalyst Otto Rank was drawing on Nietzsche as well as Freud to develop a theory of human emotions rooted in the experience of existential threat. For Rank (1996), the psychological experience of threat is grounded in the biological reality of death, which manifests for the individual as an instinctive fear of separation (beginning with the original traumatic separation from the mother at birth). For the individual who acquires an understanding of personal mortality, two forms of negative emotion develop out of this rudimentary fear: anxiety, a "separating" emotion experienced as the potential loss of selfhood (*Eigenwelt*) and driving the individual toward individuation; and guilt, a "binding" emotion experienced as the potential loss of the Other (the loved one, deity, or broader community; *Mitwelt*) and driving the individual toward re-immersion in or re-identification with the Other (Young, Sullivan, Stewart, & Palitsky, unpublished data). In some of his writings, Rank (1947) referred to the threats underlying these dialectical emotions as two different manifestations of fear: "death fear" (the fear of loss of self, eliciting anxiety) and "life fear" (the fear of individuation, eliciting guilt).

Following Rank, Kierkegaard, and Tillich, the existential therapist Rollo May (1983) also discusses anxiety and guilt as the two types of emotional experience that can arise in response to the self's momentary awareness of its nonbeing. May characterizes anxiety as a dizzying sense of uncertainty connected with a new potentiality for selfhood, some option for self-expansion or growth that threatens the sense of security derived from routine habit. Guilt, alternately, is the emotion that besets the individual who fails to fulfill such potentialities. Drawing on the threat-dialectic theorists, Lazarus and Lazarus (1994) used the overarching term "existential emotions" to describe the two self-conscious emotions of anxiety and guilt experienced when one's sense of meaning or value comes under threat. In addition, they classified shame as a third existential emotion, noting its similarity to guilt but distinguishing it therefrom by defining shame as arising from threats to the ego-ideal or internalized standards of self-value, and guilt as arising from superego-induced threats to one's sense of the self as moral.

In sum, multiple theorists have triangulated on the notion that existential threat alternately takes the form of uncertainty about how to engage with the world and feelings of inadequacy connected with one's attempts to engage the world. The former can be conceived as epistemic threats, generally experienced as the existential emotion of uncertainty-related anxiety, whereas the latter are threats to personal value generally experienced as the existential emotion of guilt (Hart, 2014; Lazarus & Lazarus, 1994; Sullivan et al., 2012a). However, the analysis up to this juncture has been largely qualitative, distinguishing between broad *types* of threat experience. A complete model of existential threat must also account for the obvious fact that threats have a quantitative dimension, meaning they range in severity as a function of the extent to which they infringe on the self's symbolic resources (and hence the extent to which they connote the self's ultimate finitude). Accordingly, in the following integrative model, I will distinguish between both types and *levels* of existential threat.

Levels and types of existential threat: an integrative model

Existential threats can manifest at both "relative" and "absolute" levels (Sullivan et al., 2012a; Tillich, 1952). At the first level – relative threat – the individual senses (fully consciously or not) that one of their modes of being has been (potentially) compromised in a concrete situation. The individual typically has an array of culturally conditioned defenses that can be employed to neutralize the threat. If these defenses are ineffective, however, the threat becomes absolute, meaning that the person experiences an overwhelming dread as their ultimate sense of meaning or personal value is called into question. Such absolute threat experiences, if sustained, result in nihilism or profound absurdity: the perceived loss of any legitimation for one's existence (Camus, 1955/1991; Nietzsche, 1887/1967).

Thus, I will distinguish between three levels of existential threat. I will connote the first level of threat with the terms *anxiety* and *guilt*, referring to emotional experiences of either prospective uncertainty or retrospective regret in concrete situations. Following Heidegger (1962), I will broadly use the term *angst* to designate threat experiences at the second level. Drawing further on Heidegger and on Tillich (1952), I will distinguish between *meaninglessness angst* – the second-level form of anxiety – and *condemnation angst* – the second-level form of guilt. Finally, I will use the term *nihilism* to designate the complete loss of a mode of being, which only occurs in extreme and pathological instances.

Before discussing each of these levels and types of threat in detail, it will be useful to make a few general remarks about the important psychological distinctions between the three levels of threat experience. Experiences of first-level anxiety and guilt are less severe than experiences of angst as I use the term. This is partly because first-level threats are experienced *dialectically* (Schrag, 1961; Tillich, 1952). Building off of threat dialectic theory, this means that when a person experiences a first-level threat, they are habitually prompted to gravitate away from the threat in the opposite psychological direction. In other words, when a person experiences anxiety – which is essentially the threat of the abstract, of too much ambiguity in a situation – they flee (in dialectical fashion) toward the concrete, toward clear and unambiguous identities, definitions, and objects. On the other hand, when a person experiences guilt – essentially the threat of inadequacy through attachment to an undesirable concrete identity – they flee (again dialectically) toward the opposite pole, now toward abstraction, away from concrete identities and the facticity of the past. In short, we have a psychological anxiety-buffering system that is designed to cope with first-level threat experiences. Research (reviewed below) has shown that when information suggests we are tipping too far in one direction – either toward groundlessness and uncertainty, or toward stifling, certain groundedness – we enact compensatory tactics that give us a reassuring sense of movement in the opposing direction.

Experiences of second-level angst, however, are *non-dialectical* (Schrag, 1961; Tillich, 1952). When we are caught in the grip of meaninglessness or condemnation angst, the threat is overwhelming and we are unable to mobilize our habitual defenses. Indeed, we often enter states of angst when our typical tactics for compensatory dialectical movement have (for whatever reason) failed to re-center our sense of being in response to a first-level experience of anxiety or guilt. Lost in dizzying uncertainty, we cannot find any concrete resource or identity at hand in which to seek refuge; or weighted down by a deep sense of inadequacy, we cannot escape the undesired reality of our concrete situation. In experiences of angst, all possibilities seem temporarily blocked, our standard, culturally derived defenses fail us, and we non-dialectically stagnate in a state of too much abstraction or too much concreteness.

Finally, the third level of existential threat – that of true nihilism – is a rare and pathological condition. As we will see, Nietzsche proposed that nihilism inheres in the strong conviction either that there is nothing worth doing in the world, or that we as individuals will never be able to achieve the things that are worth doing (Reginster, 2009). Thus, a major difference between third-level nihilism, on the one hand, and first-level threat and second-level angst, on the other, is that the latter experiences are generally not long-lasting and often primarily affective. The experience of nihilism is primarily a cognitive or symbolic threat, although it has devastating physical and emotional consequences. Nihilism is the human threat experience *par excellence* – the fully cognizant, self-aware conviction that life is not worth living (Camus, 1955/1991). No other organism seems capable of arriving – after a series of complex symbolic operations – at the conclusion that it might just as well terminate itself. The possibility of nihilism is the reason why some scholars argue that consciousness was an evolutionary maladaptation (Zapffe, 1933/2004), and it is the extreme threat to the functionality of culture (Ligotti, 2012). Because embodied existence draws the individual instinctively toward self-preservation, however, people rarely succumb to nihilism. Thus, it is generally more useful to speak of nihilistic beliefs or cultural orientations, rather than nihilism as a psychological state. Nihilism is the "upper bound" or limit of threat experience, an ideal type that rarely manifests in human lives (although it can, with crushing results).

In the remainder of this chapter, I will discuss the three main levels and two broad types of existential threat in detail, drawing on the empirical and philosophical literature to elucidate them. A pictorial overview of the model is presented in Figure 3.1. Throughout the discussion, it is important to bear in mind (as Figure 3.1 indicates) that behind the first- and second-level experiences of threat and angst lurk the originary threats of nihilism and death awareness – the conviction that we might as well do nothing, and the knowledge that we will one day *be* nothing.

First-level, dialectical threats

A great deal of empirical work in psychology has examined variations of the two broad types of dialectical threat – uncertainty or anxiety on the one hand, and inadequacy or guilt on the other – although typically these threats have been studied independently of one another.

An important distinction between the two primary forms of lower-level, dialectical threat lies in their standard relation to temporality (Schrag, 1961; 1969). Experiences of anxiety prototypically have a prospective relation to time because individuals' concerns with meaning relate to their level of certainty about how to act in the future, whereas guilt experiences prototypically have a retrospective relation to time because individuals' self-esteem concerns relate to the value of actions that they have already performed (or failed to perform).

Fuchs (2013) expands on this temporal analysis of anxiety and guilt. He points to the importance of considering not only the individual's time orientation in existential threat experiences, but also how the latter

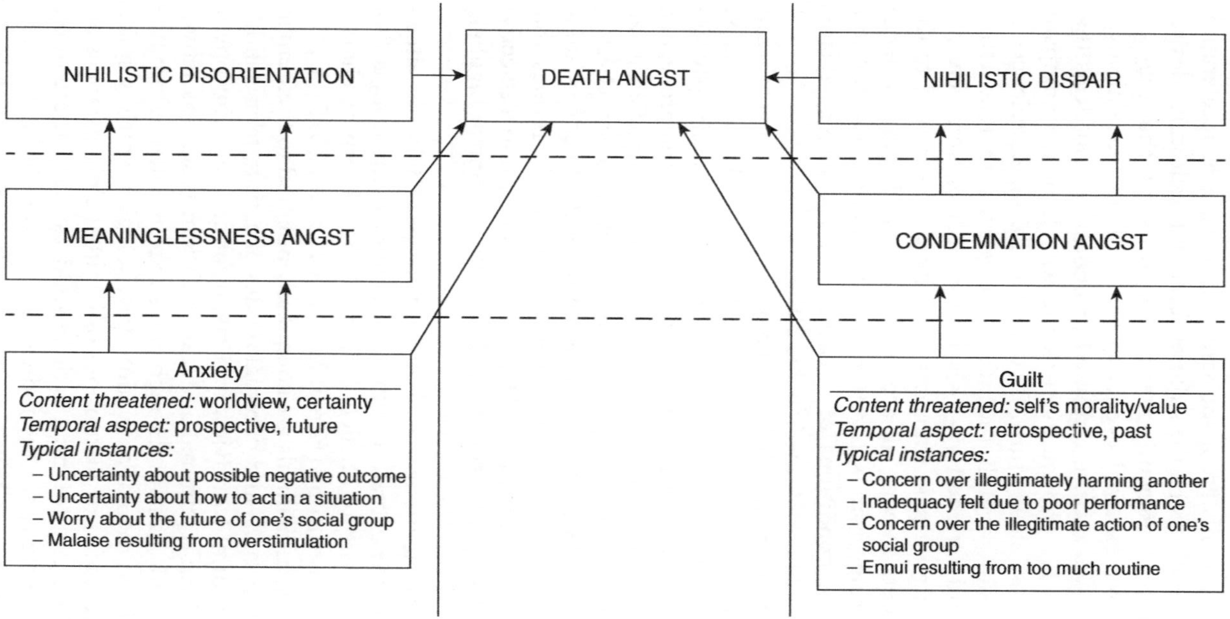

Figure 3.1. The proposed integrative model of existential threat experiences.

desynchronize the individual's relation to intersubjective or social time constructs. Specifically, Fuchs (2013) argues that experiences of agitation, anxiety, and mania are associated with a sense of acceleration vis-à-vis the lived time of others: the sufferer feels that their inner desires and goals are not being sufficiently met by a slow world, that they are moving too quickly for external events to satisfy them. An employee waiting to hear if he will receive a desired promotion or not feels that time cannot pass quickly enough even as the wheels of the company decision-making process slowly turn. By contrast, during experiences of time pressure, depression, or guilt, the individual feels that their own time is desynchronized and retarded vis-à-vis intersubjective time: she has fallen behind; fixated on a past transgression, she cannot return to the present world of others moving all around her. Neurological evidence from patients suffering from schizophrenia and depression bolsters the case that extreme conditions of existential precariousness distort time experience in these directions (Fuchs, 2013).

Beyond the general temporal distinction between the first-level threats of anxiety and guilt, there are many other differences between these prototypic threat experiences that have been documented in the psychological literature. Interestingly, research on these threats has proceeded largely independently, partly because guilt tends to be classified as an emotion (and hence has been the province of "emotions researchers"), whereas anxiety has a somewhat ambiguous status as an affective state in the literature. However, an existential perspective clearly reveals that these threats are dialectically related. Hence, as I now turn to a selective review of the literature on anxiety and guilt, I will attempt to highlight points of contrast between these threats.

Anxiety. Anxiety is experienced as a sense of creeping doubt or uncertainty connected with the perceived significance, implementation, and/or validity of one's endeavors and beliefs (Tillich, 1952). It can be characterized as psychological entropy (Hirsh, Mar, & Peterson, 2012). Under normal circumstances, individuals are adequately oriented to their environments through clear goals and habitual modes of action, their validity sanctioned by the cultural worldview and taken for granted. Entropy in the psychological system is minimal under such circumstances, as activity is channeled into goal pursuit through an environmental affordance eliciting strong, isolated mental activation. Psychological entropy spikes when unexpected obstacles or disruptions of habitual circumstances are encountered and different potential actions suddenly vie for attention, leaving no dominant motive for the individual (Sartre, 1965). At a very basic level, anxiety manifests in instances of frustration, of uncertainty about how to act in a particular situation. For example, studies on people's understanding of their own actions (e.g., Vallacher & Wegner, 1987) have examined mild forms of anxiety by asking participants to perform routine tasks in unconventional and difficult ways (e.g., eating chips with chopsticks).

Once anxiety is understood as psychological entropy, we can distinguish between its two major points of origin (Block, 2002). On the one hand, anxiety can be externally induced when input to the cognitive-sensory system overwhelms extant schemas and sense-making capacities, but anxiety can also be internally generated when inner drives or motives fail to find situational outlets for satisfaction. In either instance, the flow of action in a typically harmonious individual-environment exchange is disrupted.

In much of the literature, anxiety is operationalized in the first sense as the overwhelming of cognitive capacities by environmental factors, generating feelings of uncertainty and expectancy violations. For instance, studies derived from the meaning maintenance model (Proulx & Heine, 2008; 2010) have operationalized anxiety as the uncanny violation of expected routines. Other studies have examined anxiety in the form of environmentally induced uncertainty about one's values or the worth of one's goals, a threat shown to elicit compensatory affirmation of meaning sources (e.g., political attitudes) and reactive approach motivation (e.g., Hogg, Adelman, & Blagg, 2010; McGregor, 2006; Nash, McGregor, & Prentice, 2011). The terror management literature (e.g., Hayes et al., 2010) has yielded an impressive number of studies demonstrating the effects of anxiety in the form of threats to the validity of one's cultural worldview posed by members of an alternate worldview.

Anxiety can also manifest in the second sense, when the environment fails to provide a clear outlet for motivation. In these instances, anxiety is experienced as a profound sense of boredom or indifference to life, what Tillich (1952) called "emptiness." In light of Klapp's (1986) theory of boredom, we can state that anxiety arises in situations where the individual is overcome by *noise boredom*, which results from sensory overload and an abundance of potential sources of entertainment or courses of action, none of which emerge as compelling. As Klapp, Schwartz (2005), and a number of other psychologists have argued, anxiety resulting from an entropic overabundance of choice and stimuli is a common variation of existential threat in modern consumer cultures.

In all of these diverse research programs on anxiety, it has been established that individuals respond to various gradations of this type of threat by defensively over-investing in existing meaning structures, whether it be through reconceptualizing action in narrower terms, bolstering group identities, defending cultural values, or seeking out clear goals to reduce psychological entropy. Summarizing this work, research suggests that low-level anxiety is invariably accompanied by a compensatory psychological "approach" motivation toward a clear or familiar object or goal (Jonas et al., 2014). In Sartre's (2001) terminology, individuals in a state of anxiety fly from transcendence toward the bad faith of facticity: they deny the realities of uncertainty and possibility in their lives by seeking stable guides and standards for action. The social psychologist Muzafer Sherif (Sherif & Harvey, 1952) summarized his work on compensatory defensiveness against anxiety in a highly compatible fashion:

> Anxiety in its milder or neurotic form expresses a state of ego-tension which is the by-product of experienced threats or uncertainties ... which are felt as directed at our personal goals, personal values ... under critical circumstances, the stability of our physical and social bearings are disrupted with the subsequent experience of not being anywhere definitely, of being torn from social ties of belongingness, or when nothing but a future of uncertainty or blockages is experienced as our lot ... The individual tossing in such a state of anxiety or insecurity flounders all over in his craze to establish for himself some stable anchorages ... the result is an increased degree of suggestibility. (pp. 280–281)

Thus, several decades of social psychological research have established that circumstances of uncertainty and perceived potential meaninglessness prompt individuals to defensively seek and adhere to entitative social identities, clear goals, and rigid, narrow patterns of behavior.

Guilt. The element most basic to a guilt-inducing situation is the perception that one's behavior is discrepant from an internalized moral or social standard, prescribed role in a given social context, or goal (e.g., Higgins, 1987; Kelly, 1955; Kugler & Jones, 1992; Lewis, 1997). Implicit here is the notion that attribution of personal responsibility – deciding that one had control over a negative outcome – is the foundation of any guilt feeling (McGraw, 1987). Research has established that individuals need to feel a sense of control or responsibility for a particular action in order to experience guilt in connection with that action. This highlights one key aspect of the distinction between guilt and anxiety. While the latter often involves the threat of lack of control or uncertainty in a situation, the former is characterized by the perception that one had control over one's actions, and performed an action discrepant with one's standards.

This standard psychological understanding of guilt is perfectly compatible with an existential view; however, the latter has some additional connotations. For example, the existential view indicates that one's self-esteem and sense of moral value are closely connected, an insight largely unrecognized in the psychological literatures on these two phenomena. Historically, psychology has separated these constructs by positing that a self-esteem threat is a more cognitive or motivational experience directed at one's sense of competence or intelligence, while guilt is an emotion that arises not from threatened ability but rather moral violations. Of course, operational distinctions between self-esteem threats and guilt inductions are certainly meaningful and may be necessary to conduct certain types of research. But an existential view suggests that the vast body of research on self-esteem threat and defense within social psychology (e.g., Steele, 1988; Tesser, 1988) should be further integrated with research on guilt and shame. In the current model, any experience of the self's deviation from internalized standards – be it a deviation from one's sense of personal competence or one's perceived moral value – is felt as some form of guilt or potential guilt.

The connection between self-esteem threat and feelings of guilt has roots in the human desire to deny animality. As discussed, the fear of death often manifests in human experience as a fear of creatureliness, concretely encountered in such biological processes as excretion, menstruation, sexuality, physical illness, and so on. There is a symbolically mediated connection in human experience between disgust elicited by such "animalistic" bodily stimuli and moral disgust elicited by transgressions (Ricoeur, 1967; Rozin, Lowery, Imada, & Haidt, 1999). Hence, experiences of inadequacy on the symbolic planes of both personal morality and competence have their origin in feelings of physical powerlessness or impurity. This deep psychological connection between symbolic and bodily impurity explains a number of research findings, such as the desire to hide the body during experiences of shame (Tangney & Dearing, 2002), or the guilt-reducing impact of an experimentally manipulated opportunity to wash one's hands after a transgression (Zhong & Liljenquist, 2006). It also explains why reminders of death – the ultimate creaturely limit – increase feelings of guilt in the wake of deviant actions (Arndt, Greenberg, Solomon, Pyszczynski, & Schimel, 1999).

Beyond implying a closer connection between self-esteem threats and guilt feelings, an existential perspective further suggests that standard definitions of guilt may require some reconsideration. Guilt is almost universally viewed in social psychology as an interpersonal phenomenon – it is typically defined as a feeling of remorse arising from recognition that one has done illegitimate harm to *another person* (Baumeister, Stillwell, & Heatherton, 1994). While this form of guilt may be the most common, it is not the only way in which individuals experience guilt. Drawing on the existential psychological tradition, May (1983) argued that guilt should be reconceived as a feeling of debt or indebtedness, and that the quality of any guilt experience depends on the entity toward which the guilty individual feels indebted. Specifically, people can feel guilt in connection with the *Mitwelt* – the interpersonal guilt commonly recognized in psychology – but they can also feel guilt in relation to the *Eigenwelt*, toward the self. This is especially the case when the individual reflects on their unlived lives or lost possible selves; for instance, having made a choice to prosper in a stable career, a person may feel a sense of guilt toward the part of themselves that always wanted to live recklessly and travel the world.

As in the case of anxiety, guilt may also be conceptualized in terms of certain experiences of boredom. Returning to Klapp's (1986) theory of boredom, guilt or inadequacy feelings are associated with *banality boredom* – a sense of being bogged down by routine and non-stimulating environments, activities, and information. As many theorists have noted (e.g., Cohen & Taylor, 1978), individuals often experience guilt not in connection with any particular discrepant action, or even as a global attribution of the self's unworthiness. Instead, such feelings can sometimes arise as a global attribution about the unworthiness or unattractiveness of the self's routine behaviors. The person feels restless and unfulfilled by their habitual patterns, and longs for novelty.

Regardless of the exact manifestation of guilt feelings, they are aversive, and individuals respond to first-level guilt with ready psychological defenses. Tillich (1952) proposes that individuals defend against guilt in one of two primary ways. In many instances, people respond to guilt by compensatorily attempting to adhere more closely to moral standards in the future, or by boosting the self's value in a different domain, responses that have been empirically observed (Steele, 1988; Tangney & Dearing, 2002). Another variant on this form of defense is the desire to make amends to others, repairing the damaged social bond over which guilt has been experienced (Estrada-Hollenbeck & Heatherton, 1997; Tangney & Dearing, 2002). Rank (1996) generally referred to this category of guilt responses as identification: the desire to reconnect the inadequate self with the world, to win back the approval of the social world by reaffirming one's ability to comply with its standards or get along with others (see Young et al., unpublished data).

However, Tillich also notes an interesting second class of defensive responses: namely, individuals will sometimes deny the validity of the rule they have violated, or the information threatening their self-esteem, as a means of preserving the self's value at the expense of certainty about culturally determined standards. This strategy has also been documented in various empirical studies (e.g., Landau, Greenberg, & Sullivan, 2009). In extreme instances, individuals may even deny the general legitimacy of the social world itself, in order to avoid accepting guilt for failure within that world (Sullivan, Landau, Young, & Stewart, 2014). In line with threat dialectic theory, concrete experiences of guilt and inadequacy prompt the individual to flee toward the abstract: toward distancing of the self from moral norms, cultural standards, binding relationships, or concrete commitments, in order to absolve the self of its failing.

Much of the social psychological research relevant to guilt has focused on the distinction between guilt and shame as negative self-conscious emotions. Tangney and colleagues (e.g., Tangney & Dearing, 2002; Tracy & Robins, 2007) hold that guilt is related to isolated *behaviors* perceived as wrong ("I shouldn't have done that"), while shame is related to global attributions of unworthiness to the *self* ("I'm a terrible person"). From the perspective of the present model, shame distinguished from guilt in this way may be compared to condemnation angst, a more extreme experience of non-dialectical threat. Experiences of angst will be discussed in the following section. While guilt arises in connection with a particular act that is discrepant with internalized standards, it can be transformed into condemnation angst (i.e., shame) if this discrepancy is interpreted as a representation of the self's global deviation from internalized standards.

The dialectical relationship between anxiety and guilt. In sum, many scholars have argued that first-level, "dialectical" threat takes two forms – uncertainty about how to act given nearly endless possibilities for action, and inadequacy experienced in connection with the self or its actions. Defensive compensations for one type of threat often orient the individual toward an experience of the other type. If we feel anxious uncertainty, if our convictions about how to act in the world are temporarily threatened, we compensatorily invest in our worldview and concrete identities. On the other hand, if we feel the sting of guilt, we readjust by abstracting away from that concrete sense of inadequacy, either looking toward the future for reparative self-affirmations or distancing ourselves from demanding cultural standards altogether.

Having reviewed the empirical literature on anxiety and guilt, we can form a cohesive model of this threat-dialectical experience. Such a model is presented in Figure 3.2. On the order of first-level threats, anxiety aroused in a given situation induces a sense of psychological rootlessness, which elevates needs for certainty or control over one's situation. People often satisfy these needs by investing in concrete defense mechanisms: clear and familiar identities, relationships, goals, and so on. If such a concrete defense mechanism is available, certainty and control is at least temporarily restored. However, over time, an individual's investment in a particular concrete defense may eventually generate a nascent feeling of

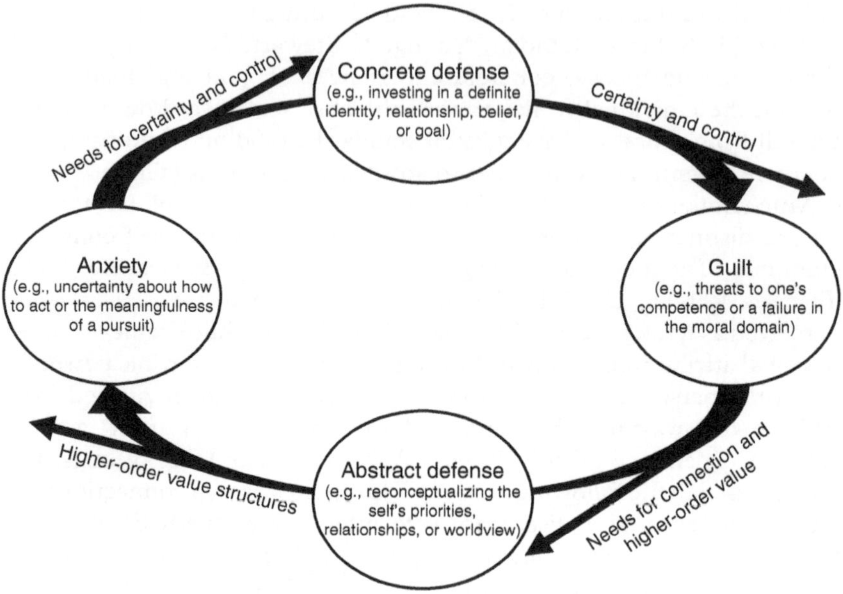

Figure 3.2. A dialectical relationship between anxiety and guilt.

guilt, because by definition guilt feelings are more likely to occur when feelings of control and certainty (and therefore responsibility) are high. For example, an individual feeling anxious about the significance of their life may invest more time in their career; this will make them feel more certain about their purpose (i.e., to be successful), but opens the door for guilt pangs (e.g., perhaps they really should be spending more time with their family). If concrete feelings of guilt are aroused, they activate new needs for a sense of connection and investment in a higher-order value structure that transcends the self, pushing the individual toward more abstract defense mechanisms. Continuing the example, the individual may reconceptualize their career as ultimately unimportant, a cognition that justifies spending more time with family. Although such abstract defenses can be consoling, and offer the individual a path out of the dialectical circle, they might alternatively (over time) start the chain over again. In the example, the individual may become anxious while they are sitting with their family, wondering whether they are really doing a good enough job at work, prompting them to reinvest in their career again.

Initial empirical examination of these processes has been carried out by myself and my colleagues (Rothschild, Landau, Sullivan, & Keefer,

2012). Specifically, we examined the defensive process of scapegoating as a result of either anxiety or guilt. In our studies, we found that people will scapegoat outgroups for contributing to harmful climate change when they are exposed to information emphasizing either their own (the participants') inability to understand or cope with climate change (a control threat, inducing anxiety), or their personal culpability for the problem (a guilt threat). The effect of the anxiety prime on increased scapegoating was statistically mediated by diminished personal control, while the effect of a moral value threat on scapegoating was mediated by increased feelings of guilt.

More importantly for present purposes, these data also demonstrated a dialectical relationship between these threats. In one study, participants who were induced to feel guilty about climate change and then given the opportunity to engage in defensive scapegoating subsequently showed not only lowered guilt, but also diminished perceptions of personal control. In other words, guilt-ridden participants made an external attribution to dissolve the threat, claiming that agents beyond their influence (in this case, greedy oil companies) are actually responsible for climate change. This abstract defense, however, forced them to yield up some of their own sense of control and certainty; they denied their personal control over world events in order to escape the burden of guilt. This temporarily diminished sense of personal control might serve a protective function as it absolves the self of guilt, but it also could lead to a sense of anxiety about the self's inability to take efficacious action in the world.

Angst – second-level, non-dialectical threats

As the previous section has shown, first-level threats provoke a variety of dialectical defenses internalized through successful socialization. However, at times these defenses fail us; the threat to our worldview, or to ourselves, will not succumb to symbolic dialectics. In these unfortunate circumstances, we are plunged into more severe experiences of *angst*.

The reason why we cannot marshal habitual defenses to overcome angst as we can in cases of first-level threat is that while the latter experiences are contextualized and limited, the encounter with angst explodes out of context and triggers conscious awareness that our foundational defenses against nonbeing – our worldview and sense of a valuable self – have been compromised. Normally, we manage threats by psychologically containing them at the first level of anxiety or guilt – we trace the threat back to some identifiable source, such as an enemy other who has questioned our worldview, or a concrete incident in which we violated a cultural norm. But during angst, a spreading network of cognitive associations prevents us from containing the threat. It is no longer a single person, idea, or action that infringes on our secure belief system or self-esteem; rather, those resources in their entirety have become insecure.

Heidegger (1962) described angst as the revelation of nothingness at the foundation of our existence in the world. In the lifeworld of taken-for-granted, everyday concerns, we effortlessly convince ourselves that we have a stable identity and exist in a "real" society full of meaningful symbols, goals, and values. Despite this, the physical reality of our being is that we are fleshy matter arisen out of prior formlessness; we are steadily decomposing, and our matter may be completely transformed, such that we lose all semblance of "our being," at any moment (Phillips, 2000; Volk, 2002). While being hit by a bus may physically do this to us, angst hurls us toward this reality psychologically by undermining the symbolic resources that normally keep us sure that things are otherwise.

While the dialectical threats of anxiety and guilt are experienced as discrete, intentional emotion states, accompanied by specific appraisals (Lazarus & Lazarus, 1994), experiences of angst do not involve emotions per se but rather *existential feelings* (Ratcliffe, 2008; Stephan, 2012). Existential feelings are not comprised of particular motivational or attributional components; rather, they are atmospheric background orientations that underlie our more specific motivations, cognitions, and emotions at any point in time, or "ways of finding ourselves in the world" (Ratcliffe, 2012, p. 24). At certain times, we feel generally "at ease" in the world, we have a basic sense of ontological security, whereas at other times – even in the absence of a clear triggering cause – we feel uncomfortable and insecure, vaguely threatened, as if we suddenly cannot trust and do not truly know the world, others, and ourselves (Laing, 1960; Stephan, 2012). Experiences of angst are negative existential feelings, which overcome us when our worldview or self-esteem is substantially compromised.

These experiences of angst involve the withdrawal of possibilities from one's intentional purview (Ratcliffe, 2012). Under normal circumstances, the intentional structure of human consciousness and our embeddedness in culture insure that we see the environment around us as a landscape of familiar possibilities. Objects and individuals reveal themselves to us as enticing tools or compatriots in the pursuit of desired activities. Experiences of angst involve a radical cutting-off of these taken-for-granted possibilities. Supporting this analysis, personal accounts of individuals suffering from schizophrenia suggest that everyday possibilities are lost when the mind lacks a sense of bodily integrity or organized temporality, or when the stability of the world is disturbed by hallucinations (Ratcliffe, 2012; Ratcliffe & Broome, 2012).

Following threat dialectic theory, we can distinguish between two broad forms of angst. If first-level anxiety is unresolved, it can escalate into *meaninglessness angst*, a felt loss of possibilities offered by the world. We begin to experience the world as an uncertain and chaotic place, where no goals may be worth pursuing and the outcome of any personal action cannot be predicted. By contrast, if first-level guilt is not successfully defended against, we may experience *condemnation angst* – the loss of possibilities for expressing or asserting the self and pursuing its value. We feel that the self is unreliable and unworthy, we feel uncomfortable in our bodies, we feel cut off from the potential for approval and communion with others.

The existentialists were committed to a largely individualist worldview, often prioritizing the unique perspective and experience of the individual over the norms and ideologies of the masses (see Chapter 1). Part of the existentialist project of promoting individualism involved an analysis of existential threat experiences as individuating and revelatory of the individual's isolation in an inhospitable world (e.g., Hankiss, 2001). Hence, post-Heideggerian analyses often suggest that angst involves a realization of the self's profound isolation. In Heidegger's philosophy, *Angst* inheres in the realization that the culturally mediated world in which the self is immersed is completely arbitrary, a historical accident and social construction, with the result that local values no longer seem binding or meaningful (Dreyfus, 1991; Elkholy, 2011). Such meaninglessness angst might be considered an experienced reduction or collapse of the *Umwelt* to the *Eigenwelt* – the self realizes that its relation to the world is arbitrary and contingent, rather than necessary and secure. By contrast, in Heideggerian analyses, truly existential guilt (or condemnation angst) involves the realization that the self is fundamentally fallen and guilty – the self is alone and completely responsible for its own fate and construction, despite the fact that it seeks protective immersion in contingent cultural values and ideologies (Dreyfus, 1991; Elkholy, 2011). Condemnation angst could then be considered a reduction or collapse of *Mitwelt* to *Eigenwelt* – one is not ultimately responsible to others, as in instances of "superficial" guilt arising from passing transgressions, but rather fundamentally responsible to and for *oneself*.

These existential analyses of angst imply the possibility of radical disjuncture between the self and the world (either the physical or social worlds, or both). They suggest that there is a bio-phenomenological level of individual experience that exists prior to or beneath historically contingent cultural influence, and that this level can be suddenly exposed in angst. Moreover, Heideggerian analyses often imply that this level of individual experience is in some sense more authentic than everyday existence in the culturally filtered world (Elkholy, 2011). Cultural-existential psychology shares with these analyses the notion that second-level threat experiences involve pervasive, negative existential feelings and an extreme felt loss of the self's possibilities. However, it deviates from the classic existential view that the self can be reduced to an a-cultural, "authentic" level.

Even experiences of angst are filtered by cultural orientations, *despite* the fact that they can involve a profound sense of disruption of typical cultural categories. A great deal of evidence from a variety of settings strongly suggests that although there are *existenzial* universals in the experience of major episodes of existential threat – such as the fundamental experiences of psychosis or depression – the exact symptomology and expression of these second-level threats is culturally mediated and bespeaks *existenziell* variation.

For example, cultural orientations shape the exact content of the terror and loss of meaning experienced during episodes of meaninglessness angst. The content of psychotic delusions and hallucinations has been shown to vary across settings in relation to cultural content. Suhail and Cochrane (2002) compared schizophrenic delusional content among Pakistani patients living in Pakistan, Pakistani patients living in Britain, and British White patients. The researchers found that the content of delusions varied by culture, and interestingly the current environment had a greater influence than shared genetic or cultural background, as the British Pakistani group was more similar to the British White than the native Pakistani group. While the former groups expressed more delusions related to the desire for personal control and the intrusion on mental thought of electronic devices (e.g., radio waves), the latter group expressed relatively more delusions involving ghosts or black magic, in line with Pakistani traditional beliefs.

Furthermore, meaninglessness angst does not universally involve the highly cognitively mediated experience of a breakdown in abstract meaning systems or an identity crisis, despite the prevalence of such ideas in existentialist writing and reports from Western patients. Indeed, a large body of research suggests that various forms of somatization of psychological problems and anxiety disorders are more common than cognitive meaning loss in many cultures, particularly in East Asia (Hoge et al., 2006; Hwang, Myers, Abe-Kim, & Ting, 2008). This may reflect the fact that symbolic order and meaning are closely connected to a sense of mind-body and person-environment harmony, as well as physical cleanliness and order, in many Asian cultures such as Japan (Namihira, 1987; Ohnuki-Tierney, 1984). Where cultural meaning is more deeply embedded in the body and the surrounding environment, the loss of meaning is also more likely to take the form of an embodied threat.

Culture influences the expression not only of threatened meaning loss, but also of concerns with the self's ultimate value. There is evidence that experiences of condemnation angst are also culturally variable. For example, Kimura (1965; 1967; see also Draguns, 1980; Jilek, 1971) observed that depression in Japan involved a strong orientation toward the *Mitwelt*, with fears and feelings of regret centering around a general sense that the self has disappointed or been an undue burden on others, while depression in individualistic Germany involved more of a retreat into the *Eigenwelt*, accompanied by feelings of isolation and an obsessive focus with particular personal failings. This finding matches up with other research conducted in Western settings suggesting that depression there often involves a spiral of introspective negative self-focus (Pyszczynski & Greenberg, 1992). Marsella (1980) has argued that these differences in depression experience are partly a result of the highly reflexive, agentic culture afforded in modernized, Western settings (the concept of reflexivity will receive extended discussion in Chapter 5). In such settings, there is considerable abstract, linguistic mediation of identity and reality, leading to a more cognitive experience of self-condemnation and isolation, compared to the more embodied and interpersonal experience of depression prevalent in less reflexive (e.g., East Asian) contexts.

Beyond these and many other synchronous cultural differences in experiences of meaninglessness and condemnation angst which could be highlighted, we may also consider diachronic developments in the labeling, treatment, and experience of these non-dialectical threats. Categories like *trauma* and *depression* are relatively recent inventions in post-Enlightenment, Eurocentric culture, having been used in their modern sense for only about a century (Ehrenberg, 2010; Luckhurst, 2008). Historians of emotion and psychology have argued that these diagnostic concepts only emerged with a growing probabilistic orientation toward risk in modernized societies, and with a heightened sense of the individual as a unique, atomized entity that could also be divided against itself (in the unconscious). These cultural transformations permitted the emergence of the concept of trauma not as the result of possession or sin, but rather as the result of a radical alteration of subjectivity precipitated by some external event. Ehrenberg (2010) argues that the experience and public understanding of depression changed dramatically in Western societies over the course of the twentieth century. As forces of cultural individualism, competition, and status anxiety became increasingly prominent, expectations that the person be both successful and authentic overwhelmed many individuals, generating a chronic underlying state of condemnation angst that has been normalized through the rapidly growing diagnosis of depression.

To conclude this discussion of angst, it is certainly the case that people in all cultures have the capacity to suffer from an overwhelming sense of meaninglessness and loss of ground, on the one hand, or from a sense of the self's failure, inadequacy, or dishonor, on the other. Nevertheless, the experience of these two forms of non-dialectical threat is subject to more cultural variation than classic existential accounts would suggest. While the existentialists emphasize the deeply individual experience of these threats, it is in fact the case that even the manifestation of seemingly extreme or biologically rooted phenomena such as schizophrenia, depression, and trauma varies across settings. For example, while angst and mental disorder are often connected to cognition and subjectivity in Western, individualist contexts, they are more often associated with embodied problems and moral or interpersonal categories in many other areas.

I will return to the cultural shaping of angst in Chapter 9; for now, this preliminary discussion was necessary as a corrective to the somewhat individualistic focus of the existentialist model. I conclude my presentation of the existential threat model by discussing the two forms of nihilism that can result from sustained, unresolved experiences of angst.

Nihilism

Anticipating terror management theory and XXP, Nietzsche believed that cultural worldviews give our lives meaning by providing us with goals. He accordingly defined nihilism as the complete loss of motivation to pursue goals. Nietzsche (1964) argues that such extreme goal loss can take the form of a negation either of *our values* or of *ourselves*. Reginster (2009) categorizes these two forms of nihilism as *disorientation* and *despair*, respectively:

> According to Nietzsche, a goal has the ability to inspire (and so to give life meaning) only if two conditions are met: the agent estimates that the goal has *value*, and that it is *realizable*. In nihilism as disorientation, the first condition is not met: the values in terms of which the worth of a goal could be estimated are devaluated. In nihilism as despair, by contrast, it is the second condition that is not fulfilled: our most valuable goals, our highest ideals, prove to be unrealizable. (p. 33; italics in original)

Disorientation is the form of nihilism that can result from uncertainty about the value of one's goals and the stability of one's worldview; in other words, from sustained anxiety and meaninglessness angst. Despair is the form of nihilism that can result from an inability to achieve one's culturally sanctioned goals: in other words, from chronic experiences of guilt and condemnation angst. Put simply, nihilistic disorientation results when the individual's worldview is no longer seen as valid or compelling, and they lose all guides for further action, whereas nihilistic despair results when the individual feels utterly inadequate and condemned by the standards of their worldview.

As stated earlier in this chapter, nihilism is rarely experienced by the individual, who typically remains enmeshed in a self-sustaining framework of cultural meaning. Culture provides a variety of habitual defenses against the dialectical threats of anxiety and guilt, and even ultimate threats of meaninglessness or condemnation angst are to some extent contained or filtered by the individual's worldview. In a certain sense, the categories of nihilism are ideal limits on two dark horizons that stretch toward the asymptote of death. They are better conceptualized as cultural-level as opposed to individual-level constructs (Fischer, 2009): cultures are oriented toward or away from the two types of nihilism, with implications for the types of lower-level threats that individuals within a culture tend to experience. Thus, I will not elaborate on the constructs of nihilistic disorientation and despair here. Rather, these constructs will primarily serve to link the existential model of individual-level threat experiences to a model of culture that will be presented in the next chapter.

As discussed in Chapter 2, a fundamental principle of cultural-existential psychology is that culture both alleviates and facilitates problems of theodicy and nihilism. This principle will be leveraged in Chapter 5 when I distinguish between two major forms of cultural threat orientation, by which I refer to the standard mode in which a culture orients its members toward some threat experiences and away from others. This will be accomplished by showing how cultures differ in whether they are primarily structured to minimize the risk of either nihilistic disorientation or nihilistic despair.

Summing up the model of existential threat presented here, the relationships between the different levels and types of threats can be seen in overview in Figure 3.1. To clarify the overall model, let me give a concrete example of how an individual might progress through these threat levels. If I were uncertain about what concrete steps to take to write and format my doctoral dissertation in social psychology, and began to procrastinate and avoid working on the document, I would likely experience anxiety. If this anxiety were sustained over several weeks in unpleasant rumination, I may begin to question whether

I even want to become a social psychologist, and whether this profession has any value, and ultimately whether academia itself is a viable enterprise – at this stage, I would be experiencing meaninglessness angst. Imagining further that my defense date passes, I fail, drop out of graduate school, and do not seek further academic employment, unable to resolve the ultimate questions about the value of this profession – I may become convinced that there is no viable path to value in my society, and experience nihilistic disorientation. At this stage, it is likely that I would contemplate suicide.

An alternate sequence is possible whereby I (1) experience guilt over my inability to write a good dissertation; (2) fail my defense, become convinced that I am a terrible academic, and experience condemnation angst; and (3) drop out of graduate school, and – finding no other means of employment – decide that I am a valueless person while in the thrall of nihilistic despair. The important differences between these two sequences are (1) my prospective focus in the case of the anxiety path versus my retrospective focus in the case of the guilt path and (2) the fact that as I proceed along the path toward nihilistic disorientation, *my worldview* is increasingly divested of any value or coherence, whereas while I proceed along the path of despair it is *myself* that is thus divested.

Additional considerations

A few observations and caveats should be made explicit regarding the current classification of threats. Nihilistic disorientation, meaninglessness angst, and anxiety, on the one hand, and nihilistic despair, condemnation angst, and guilt, on the other, are far from orthogonal constructs. Consider that nihilistic disorientation is the ultimate threat to one's cultural worldview, while nihilistic despair is the ultimate threat to one's self-esteem. XXP researchers have long argued that self-esteem and the cultural worldview are deeply intertwined: individuals derive self-esteem by meeting the standards of the worldview (e.g., Greenberg et al., 1986). Thus, levels of self-esteem and perceived meaning are often correlated, and threats to one resource will often infringe upon the other (hence, guilt and anxiety may often co-occur). However, it is possible and useful to distinguish between these two general types of threat for several reasons. Most relevant for the present project is that we can distinguish between cultures on the basis of whether they primarily protect individuals against nihilistic disorientation, and thereby orient them toward experiences of guilt, or whether they primarily protect individuals against nihilistic despair, and thereby orient them toward anxiety.

One might wonder whether the current model – focusing on derivatives of nihilistic disorientation and despair, ultimately traceable to originary death angst – is overly restrictive. Are there not many instances of experienced threats and existential problems in life that do not seem to fit readily into this framework and the research reviewed here? For example, what about threats to personal control? What about experiences of sadness, mourning, and loss? What about rejection and isolation? And finally, what about extreme experiences of trauma and suffering, both physical and psychological – are these not, in some ways, the ultimate existential threats? Where do all such experiences fit into the current model?

People's experiences of these various kinds of threats are often compatible with the model, meaning that the model can often be used to understand them. However, they are not explicitly represented in the same manner as the threats of anxiety, guilt, and death angst (and their correlates). This is so for the following reasons. First of all, many less severe experiences of such other threats are heavily culturally mediated and accepted as normative, if not beneficial, for the individual. For example, many societies have extensive mourning rituals. This is not to say that the loss of a loved one cannot take on dimensions of existential threat. But often, the loss of other individuals, particularly in certain cultural settings, is considered to be such a routine part of life that it does not imply a fundamental infringement on the self's sources of value and meaning (again, a key element of *existential* threat). Indeed, emotions such as sadness are often considered part of a healthy life. This is not true of the emotions connected with anxiety and guilt, which are generally considered undesirable and potentially avoidable in most cultures.

Second, more severe instances of the kinds of threats listed above are often characteristic of pathological experiences of mental or personality disorder. For instance, the lack of control experienced in schizophrenia, or the profound feeling of alienation present in depression certainly have the characteristics of an existential threat. However, the foregoing model is *primarily* intended to capture experiences of threat and defense within the normative bounds of experience for the average individual. This is another meaning of the term *existential* – that these threats belong to the province of "normal," as opposed to pathological, experience. This is not to say that a cultural-existential psychology perspective, and the foregoing model, is irrelevant to understanding pathology. The categories of angst are particularly effective at illuminating experiences such as depression or depersonalization, as I will consider again in Chapter 9. Nevertheless, since the focus of the model is foremost on nonclinical populations, elements of trauma are not as explicitly captured here.

Third, many instances of these threats can be readily assimilated to the categories of the model. Consider the case of social isolation. This has been recently argued to take two negative forms – loneliness (Cacioppo & Patrick, 2008), which involves a sense that one has not achieved a desired level of social connectedness, and which is associated with low self-esteem; and existential isolation (Pinel & Long, 2012), characterized by the perception that one's worldview and perspective are not shared by others. These alternate experiences of negative isolation can be readily understood as instantiations of condemnation angst (loneliness) and meaninglessness angst (existential isolation). Consider also the case of losing a loved one. Grief in this context has been shown to be associated with both fear and guilt (Bonanno, Goorin, & Coifman, 2008). Many bereaved individuals have difficulty adjusting because they feel like life has lost its meaning, or they lack the capacity or knowledge for acting in the world now that their close other is gone; such instances can be understood in terms of meaninglessness angst. Bereaved individuals who primarily experience guilt in connection with their loved one obviously fall more under the category of condemnation angst.

Fourth, there is a common element running through all of the threats listed above, namely that of loss, separation, and impermanence (of or from control, a loved one, social connection). This makes it clear that, understood in light of existential theory, all of these experiences and their associated negative emotions are more proximal experiences of death angst. Husserl's phenomenology demonstrates that true suffering must always be understood as a revelation to the suffering individual of their finitude (see Geniusas, 2013). And Winnicott's and Kristeva's psychoanalytic discussions of trauma indicate that this experience is characterized by the acquisition of an embodied understanding of mortality (see Alford, 2014; Beardsworth, 2004; also Herman, 1997). This observation does not mean that these experiences are not worth understanding in their own right; all of them present somewhat unique difficulties, and have phenomenologically distinct constellations. However, they take on their *existential* significance in light of their connection to the ultimate threat of death angst, and hence in a very important way are in fact represented in the current model.

In contrast to these *threats of loss*, existentialism holds that the fundamental categories of anxiety and guilt, while ultimately traceable to death angst, are not wholly reducible to the latter because they are related to the dialectical structure of human experience: world and self, transcendence and facticity, future and past. Especially relevant for the purposes of this book are the ways in which different cultures orient individuals toward different poles of these dialectical structures to interpret all manner of threats primarily in terms of guilt or anxiety. To make these kinds of distinctions, however, we must move beyond the individual, existential level to develop a model of broad cultural differences. In the following chapter, I undertake the presentation of such a model.

4 Cultural variation as patterns of social orientation and control

The present chapter offers a two-variable model of cultural differences. In Chapter 5, this model will be connected to the foregoing typology of existential threats, in order to understand how different cultures offer the individuals within them broadly different types of threat orientation (ways of interpreting and defending against threats). Although in the present context the primary purpose of this cultural model is to explain existential threat processes, it has considerably broader implications and could be applied to make predictions regarding any culturally fluid phenomenon.

Since Tonnies' (1971) influential *Gemeinschaft/Gesellschaft* distinction, cultural psychology has been dominated by binary thinking about cultural differences (individualism vs. collectivism, tight vs. loose cultures, residentially mobile vs. residentially stable settings, etc.). However, beginning even with the writings of Durkheim, there is also a tradition in the social sciences of representing cultural variation using a two-variable approach, combinatorially resulting in four broad cultural types. Generally, these two-variable models classify cultures along the dimensions of *social orientation* – how the self is related to others within a culture – and *social control* – how the self's behavior is regulated within a culture. My goal in this chapter is to synthesize these prior two-variable models in a new, integrative framework. Despite the tremendous predictive power of the predominant binary systems, the present discussion aims to demonstrate the historical importance and contemporary relevance of two-variable, "quaternary" approaches. In particular, despite the fact that social orientation and social control are often conflated in theoretical dichotomies (Koltko-Rivera, 2004), my approach suggests these are related but meaningfully independent dimensions.

Prior two-variable models of cultural variation

The current model builds on prior prominent two-variable approaches to cultural variation in the social sciences. These are, in sociology,

Durkheim's model of social structure; in symbolic anthropology, Douglas' grid-group theory; and in social psychology, dimensional individualism-collectivism, as well as the prospect of a closely related model combining the variables of tightness-looseness and individualism-collectivism. These models are presented in overview in Table 4.1. In cognitive anthropology, Fiske's relational models theory, while not strictly a two-variable model, bears similarities to these others. Before outlining the current approach, I will briefly review and highlight the limitations of each of these prior models.

Sociology: Durkheim's model. In *Le Suicide* (1897/2007), Durkheim presented the outline of a two-variable cultural typology, with the aim of identifying different forms of culturally afforded suicide (Jankélévitch, 2008). His two cultural variables were (1) *integration* – the extent to which the individual is integrated into a broader community, and therefore the extent to which the person's psychology is dominated by the *collective* as opposed to the *individual consciousness*; and (2) *regulation* – the extent to which the individual's behavior is guided and limited by external social rules and fear of possible sanctions. Durkheim believed that the range of people's cognitive, behavioral, and emotional experience was limited by *social facts* – comprehensive aspects of the society in which they live, possessing qualities of externality and constraint (Giddens, 1971). The integration variable is composed of those social facts having more to do with externality, that is, with the ways in which reality is socially defined for the individual in the context of their interpersonal relationships. Culture provides interpretive representations for classifying entities and dimensions encountered in the world (e.g., animals, time) that reinforce local understandings of human sociality (Durkheim & Mauss, 1903/2009). Regulation consists of social facts involving a greater element of constraint – the practical, legal, and moral rules of a society that the individual must either uphold or violate with every behavior.

Durkheim's approach has had a profound influence on the social sciences, and it essentially sets the stage for all later two-variable models. However, it was insufficient because Durkheim did not distinguish very clearly between integration and regulation and sometimes used the terms interchangeably, despite the fact that later scholarship supports the distinctive functionality of these two dimensions (Thorlindsson & Bjarnason, 1998).

Symbolic anthropology: grid-group theory. Mary Douglas' (1970; 1978) model begins with the Durkheimian variable of integration (i.e., degree of collective consciousness), which she labeled "group," and adds an additional variable intended to mark the level of social control in a society (i.e., the extent of freedom of behavior), which she labeled

Table 4.1. *Overview of prior two-variable models of culture in sociology, anthropology, and psychology.*

	Durkheimian theory	Douglas' grid-group theory	Dimensional individualism-collectivism	*Revised* dimensional individualism-collectivism
Variable 1: Social orientation	**Integration** Predominance of collective over individual consciousness	**Group** Degree of attachment to and immersion in a collective	**Individualism-collectivism** Predominance of group over personal motivation/ orientation	**Individualism-collectivism** Predominance of group over personal motivation/orientation
Variable 2: Social control	**Regulation** Degree to which behavior is constrained by legal/ moral rules	**Grid** Degree to which behavior is externally constrained and regulated	**Horizontality-verticality** Predominance of differentiated versus equivalent relations/ statuses	**Tightness-looseness** Degree to which behavior is normatively regulated and deviance sanctioned

"grid" (Douglas, 1970). The resulting "grid-group" theory combined the "grand dichotomies" of nineteenth-century social science (which contrasted industrial individualism against preindustrial collectivism; Ostrander, 1982) with Basil Bernstein's (1990) theory of social control.

Crossing grid and group yields four ideal cultural types: high group & grid "hierarchical" cultures, with strong deference to group authority, norms, and goals; high group + low grid "egalitarian" cultures, with strong solidarity but little regulation of behavior; low group & grid "individualist" cultures, where self-reliant individuals compete with one another for access to resources; and low group + high grid "fatalist" cultures, consisting of disenfranchised individuals who are controlled by society and unable to achieve solidarity in group formations (e.g., the modern proletariat or precariat; see Lupton, 2013). Douglas utilized this scheme in discussions of how different cultural groups process and perceive a wide range of phenomena, from the body (1970) to food and illness (1978). Most influentially, the theory has been used to understand variations in the perception of risk and danger (Douglas & Wildavsky, 1982). For example, people in high grid/high group cultures tend to see illness and misfortune as stemming from deviant behavior, while those in low grid/low group settings conceptualize risk in terms of probabilistic calculations and insurance mechanisms. Hindmoor (2010) utilized the theory to categorize different accounts of 2008's Great Recession: hierarchicalists trace the Recession to moral failures of under-regulation, egalitarians to the greed of individual financiers, individualists to the blundering interventionism of governments, and fatalists to inexorable unforeseen circumstances. Grid-group theory's predictions regarding interpretations of suffering have also been profitably applied to the study of cultural differences in perceptions of crime and punishment (Vaughan, 2002).

Despite its wide application, grid-group theory has some limitations that prevent it from being an ideal model. Douglas was rather inconsistent in her presentation of the theory, leaving the precise operationalization of the grid and group variables ambiguous. In particular, the definition of the low group + high grid quadrant was often unclear and rather restrictive. Most consistently, Douglas (1994) defined this quadrant as consisting only of the Foucauldian "criminal class" of individuals existing in total institutions (e.g., asylums, prisons) within modern society. Because this group is better understood as a subculture than an independent cultural type, this aspect of the model is disadvantageous. Additionally, like Durkheim's regulation variable, social control (grid) is understood in the model as a "more-or-less" quantitative continuum. As I will discuss in more detail presently, this is an untenable assumption, because all societies must have some prominent form of social control to function.

Cognitive anthropology: relational models theory. Although it shares a "quadriform" structure with the other frameworks discussed here, relational models theory (Fiske, 1991) is not an attempt to organize cultural differences according to two dimensions. Rather, it outlines four primary cognitive schema or models that individuals universally apply to relationships and other diverse aspects of social life. Specifically, Fiske (1991) proposed that people conceptualize relationships and other life domains according to one of four models: "communal sharing," which sees people and objects as essentially equivalent and inseparable (e.g., motivation and decisions are collectively, rather than individually, determined); "authority ranking," which sees people and objects as unequal and clearly related to one another by relationships of rank and responsibility; "equality matching," which sees people and objects as separate, unique entities between which relations of equality should hold; and "market pricing," which sees people and objects as isolated units ranging in value and functional worth. This scheme has been applied in a wide variety of research areas, primarily examining how people think about different relationships and the origins of interpersonal conflict in the application of conflicting models (for a review, see Haslam, 2004). For instance, Rai and Fiske (2011) argued that these models provide the cognitive underpinnings of different moral frameworks: communal sharing gives rise to the moral prioritization of unity and loyalty, authority ranking to the moralization of hierarchy maintenance, equality matching to ideals of fairness and reciprocity, and market pricing to the idealization of proportionality and deservedness.

The theory does not argue that these models arise from particular cultural dimensions, but rather that they are general descriptions of the ways people universally understand different aspects of social life (e.g., people tend to view their families in a communal sharing mode, and their governments in an authority ranking or equality matching mode; Fiske, 2004). Nevertheless, there is considerable cultural, historical, and intra-individual developmental variation in the predominance of the models, particularly when it comes to understanding fundamental features of social life (Fiske, 1991). Most germane to the present discussion, the four models map very well onto the four cultural categories yielded by most two-variable typologies, especially dimensional individualism-collectivism.

Social psychology: dimensional individualism-collectivism. In social psychology, an explosion of research on cultural differences, drawing on the work of psychological anthropologists and cross-cultural psychologists, was instigated by Triandis' early writings (e.g., 1989) on collectivism and individualism as different value orientations, as well as Markus and Kitayama's (1991) more social cognitive perspective on the difference between independent and interdependent self-construals. Triandis and coauthors (e.g., 1995; 1998) attempted to organize the burgeoning literature with a two-variable model that crossed individualism-collectivism with a *verticality* dimension, taking into account the relationship of individuals to status and authority in society.

Triandis (1995) proposes that cultural variation in the magnitude of status differences can be understood at a more basic level in terms of how the self is seen in comparison to others: are others the same as the self (i.e., no status differences), or are others inherently seen in terms of difference from the self (i.e., prominent status differences)? These two modes of normative social comparison are symptomatic of broader cultural tendencies to either value equality (horizontal) or hierarchy (vertical; Shavitt, Torelli, & Riemer, 2011). The model combining verticality with individualism-collectivism yields four possible cultural types: *horizontal individualist*, which prizes uniqueness and individuality but sees all people as deserving equal treatment (e.g., social democracy, as in Scandinavian countries); *vertical individualist*, which follows a "free market" model and fosters competition and differential rewards between unique individuals (e.g., market democracies such as the United States); *horizontal collectivist*, which strives for equality between group members who see themselves as highly similar to and in strong solidarity with all others (e.g., an Israeli kibbutz); and *vertical collectivist*, marked by strong hierarchy, rigid norms, and social solidarity (e.g., traditional Korea, Japan, and India).

Triandis and colleagues have made comparisons between their typology and relational models theory, most of which have received some empirical substantiation (see Shavitt et al., 2011). Roughly, people in horizontal individualist cultures prioritize the equality matching model; in vertical individualist, market pricing; in horizontal collectivist, communal sharing; and in vertical collectivist, authority ranking.

As a model, dimensional individualism-collectivism has one major flaw: the verticality dimension is simply not a very well delineated construct. The interconnections between ideas about authority and ideas about the self's similarity to or difference from others are not clarified by the theory. Although the four cultural types are reasonably well explained in the model, and seem to map a great deal of cross-cultural variation, it is rather unclear what the sources of verticality are in a society, and whether or not verticality manifests similarly in individualist versus collectivist societies. For example, it seems strange to claim that in both horizontal individualist and horizontal collectivist societies, the self is seen as "the same" as others; most research would suggest that horizontal individualist societies promote an independent self-construal, which would involve seeing the self as a unique, separate entity. Also, the ideals of egalitarianism that are alleged to characterize both horizontal individualist and horizontal collectivist cultures seem to be rarely actualized in practice (e.g., Sidanius & Pratto, 2001), making the presence of status differences alone a somewhat unsuitable dimension for broadly classifying cultures.

Some of the problems of the dimensional individualism-collectivism approach might be overcome by integrating two major perspectives in contemporary social psychology, namely individualism-collectivism and tightness-looseness (Gelfand, Nishii, & Raver, 2006; Gelfand et al., 2011). Pelto (1968) attempted to synthesize earlier anthropological uses of the terms "tight" and "loose" by defining tightness in highly social structural terms. Specifically, Pelto argued that greater tightness inhered in (1) communal ownership of economic resources; (2) corporacy (integration) of the group; and (3) presence of hierarchy. In their revised model, Gelfand and colleagues (2006) provide a simple definition of tightness, with only two components: the strength and clarity of social norms, and the strength and clarity of sanctions. These researchers have taken pains to point out that tightness – like the verticality dimension – varies independently of individualism-collectivism.

Although it has not yet been attempted in the contemporary literature, fleshing out the dimensional individualism-collectivism model by replacing the verticality dimension with tightness-looseness seems to yield a great deal of predictive power in classifying different cultures. Both tightness-looseness and individualism-collectivism are well-defined and extensively researched constructs. The resulting model would seem to mirror grid-group theory in many respects. In tight collectivist cultures, hierarchy and strong social norms would reign. In tight individualist cultures, individuals would see themselves as unique, but their behavior would be highly regulated. In loose collectivist cultures, group members would be bound by solidarity and belongingness feelings, but definitions for acceptable behavior would be constantly in flux. And in loose individualist cultures, individuals pursuing their own personal goals would be left to their own devices, their behavior unconstrained. This model improves on both grid-group theory and dimensional individualism-collectivism by clearly defining the vertical dimension.

Despite the advantages of this model, there is a lingering problem also present in grid-group theory. Social control – here, tightness-looseness – is conceived as starting at a zero point and increasing. But social control is not set at "zero" in any society; there are simply more manifest and more latent forms of social control. Taking a different tack, my model builds upon and advances beyond prior approaches by positing that societies around the world have different primary patterns of social orientation and social control, that these two variables can be meaningfully dichotomized, and that cultures may be classified into one of four major types based on the interaction between these two variables.

An integrative model

Like prior two-variable models, the present model crosses differences in social orientation with differences in social control. It is based on a processual conception of culture (Adams & Markus, 2004; Berger, 1967; Giddens, 1984). Specifically, my approach should be distinguished from other models (including some of those reviewed above) that emphasize a "subjectivist" concept of culture consisting primarily of norms, attitudes, and values. Instead, the current model emphasizes the idea of culture as patterns of mutually constituted mental and material elements. It assumes that there are more "explicit" and more "implicit" aspects of culture (Adams & Markus, 2004). Explicit forms are accessible to what Giddens (1984) calls "discursive consciousness." They are those aspects of culture that individuals could articulate if asked (e.g., consciously held beliefs, values, and so on). Implicit forms, on the other hand, have more to do with the nonconscious *habitus* of a culture: characteristic patterns of behavior and unspoken knowledge that individuals have been socialized to endorse but might not be able to articulate if pressed to do so.

Figure 4.1 presents an overview of the variables of social orientation and social control as they are conceived in this model. The different primary aspects of each dimension are arranged according to their degree of explicitness. Here, I elaborate on each of these aspects.

Patterns of social orientation: collectivism versus individualism

In keeping with prior approaches, the current model posits as one dimension the degree of integration into the social group. Individuals are socially oriented by their culture either toward their relationships with others and their embeddedness in the collective, or inward and away from such relationships. Importantly, there are relatively more explicit and relatively more implicit aspects of individualism-collectivism.

Value orientations: sociocentric versus egocentric worldview. At the most explicit level are the value orientations typically studied in the context of a "subjectivist" understanding of culture. In a collectivist culture, the worldview internalized by the individual is sociocentric and

		Social orientation			Social control	
		Collectivism	Individualism		Visible	Invisible
Explicit ↑	*Value orientation*	Sociocentric worldview	Egocentric worldview	*Norms*	Injunctive	Descriptive
↕	*Self-construal*	Interdependent	Independent	*Sanctioning*	Intolerance of deviance	Tolerance of deviance
↓ Implicit	*Phenomenological situation*	Embedded relatedness	Abstracted independence	*Surveillance*	Concentrated	Diffuse

Figure 4.1. Cultural patterns of social orientation and social control and their components, arranged by degree of explicitness.

largely shared with others in the culture, whereas in an individualist culture the person tends to internalize a more personal, hybridized, egocentric worldview (see Pyszczynski et al., 2003). Shweder et al. (1997) classified these different worldviews in terms of the ethics of community and divinity (common in collectivist settings) versus the ethic of autonomy (common in individualist settings). These distinctions can be summarized by stating that in collectivist social orientation, the *Mitwelt* is prioritized in people's explicit values, goals, and meaning structures, while the *Eigenwelt* takes precedence under conditions of individualist social orientation.

Reviews of the cross-cultural (Oyserman, Coon, & Kemmelmeier, 2002) and priming (Oyserman & Lee, 2008) literatures on cultural differences suggest that cultural collectivism is associated with valuing group membership and group processes, whereas individualism is associated with valuing independence and uniqueness. Priming collectivism increases felt obligation to help others (Gardner, Gabriel, & Lee, 1999) and social obligations in general (Gardner, Gabriel, & Dean, 2004). Comparative survey research (Miller, 1997) among children and adults in the United States and a Hindu Indian population shows that the latter possess a more sociocentric morality. This morality consists of relatively stricter and more widespread feelings of interpersonal obligation, greater value placed on selflessness and self-sacrifice, and a tendency to make moral decisions on the basis of contextual specifics as opposed to an abstract, "principle"-based model.

These worldviews differentially translate into the individual's structuring of her life history and goal pursuit. Weber (1951), in his essay on Puritanism and Confucianism, argued that while individualists strive for self-consistency across all life domains, collectivists value flexibly adjusting the self to the world and a diversity of social roles. He traces this difference to the attitude of "mastery of the world" in individualism, as compared to one of "adjustment to the world" in collectivism. This difference in egocentric and sociocentric worldviews, and its implications for behavior and differing forms of self-consistency, has been documented in a number of ways. Morelli and Rothbaum (2007) argue that individualists have an intraindividual and collectivists an extraindividual concept of coherence. In descriptions of the self in both actual roles (Suh, 2000) and hypothetical situations (Suh, 2002), Americans show greater consistency of their self-view than do Koreans. Spencer-Rodgers, Peng, Wang, and Hou (2004) found that mainland Chinese and Asian Americans are less concerned with reducing inconsistencies in descriptions of the self across different role contexts. English, Chen, and Swann (2008) argue that while the motive for self-verification is universal, evidence suggests that Westerners prefer people to verify self-concepts, whereas East Asianers may prefer verification of "collective self-concepts" or situation-specific selves.

In a similar vein, research shows that the behavior of collectivists is best predicted from the norms and goals of the group; in other words, the personal goals of collectivists tend to overlap with those of the group (Singelis, Triandis, Bhawuk, & Gelfand, 1995). The behavior of individualists, on the other hand, is best predicted based on personal goals (which may conflict with group goals) and attitudes. Individualism-primed participants are more oriented toward self-relevant goals, while collectivism-primed participants are more oriented toward group goals (Gardner et al., 2004). In sum, a great deal of evidence suggests that collectivist cultures foster sociocentric, and individualist cultures egocentric worldviews.

Self-construal: interdependent versus independent. Markus and Kitayama (1991) laid the groundwork for much subsequent study of cultural differences by introducing the concepts of the interdependent self-construal (afforded by collectivist culture) and the independent self-construal (afforded by individualist culture). These characteristic modes of conceiving of the self in relation to others and the environment are related to the value orientations just discussed, but contain elements that are more implicit. More explicit aspects of self-construal include the tendency to experience more other-focused (interdependent) or more ego-focused (independent) emotions, or defining the self in relation to others (interdependent) versus evaluating the self in comparison to others (independent). However, there are also elements of self-construal that are less consciously accessible. For example, understandings of selfhood itself are often implicit within a culture and shaped by patterns of social organization. Here, Landrine's (1995) distinction between the *referential* and the *indexical* self-concept is useful. Individualist cultures propagate an understanding of the self as referential:

> The self is presumed to be an entity; a bounded, unique, singular, encapsulated, noncorporeal, ghostlike, and godly entity somewhere within the body. The self is seen as contiguous with but not synonymous with the body ... The self is presumed to be a cognitive and emotional universe, the center of awareness, emotion, judgment, and action. (p. 747)

Collectivist cultures, by contrast, promote an understanding of the self as indexical:

> The indexical self has no enduring, trans-situational characteristics, no traits or desires or needs of its own in isolation from its relationships and contexts ... The self and the roles it occupies are unconsciously presumed

to be synonymous ... [sometimes] the self is understood as a mere vessel for immaterial forces and entities. (pp. 752–757)

As Sampson (1988) points out, these differences in self-construal have their roots in social structure. The "fluid" self-other boundaries of an interdependent self-construal function within a context where social harmony is maintained through links of obligation, deference, and interpersonal sanction, whereas the "firm" self-other boundaries assumed by an independent self-construal are functional in a capitalistic context that operates by extracting productivity from individuals subject to identification and evaluation. From a different angle, Charles Taylor's (2007) analysis emphasizes the religious-cosmological aspect of this distinction: the embodied and socially embedded experience of an interdependent self is commonly linked to a sense of the self as *porous* on a metaphysical plane. To give an example, Taylor discusses how medieval European peasants – bound to one another through collectivist ties in a rigidly stratified social system – lived in an *Umwelt* populated by spirits, Satanic entities, and mysterious forces that were believed capable of impeding upon or possessing the self without warning. This state of affairs differs sharply from the contemporary sense of the self in secular cultures as *bounded*: a self-possessed entity moving through a knowable natural world, against which it can be protected by scientific, medical, and legal means.

The firm, bounded self therefore has its origins in contemporary, post-Enlightenment institutions that reorganize social control and interpersonal relations according to the logic of an egocentric worldview (Shweder & Bourne, 1984). Institutions and ideologies functioning to secure such goals as privacy and human rights create a social world in which each person is assumed to be a supreme value in and of themselves, unique and integral independent of the vagaries of historical or geographic context (what Esposito, 2013, calls "immunizing" institutions; see Chapter 5). This kind of *Mitwelt* is very different from that experienced in collectivist settings, where individuals are interdependently defined in terms of their social role and obligation to their family or community. In such settings, the individual must be understood indexically, with reference to context (Shweder & Bourne, 1984).

This schematization of the self as context-dependent or -independent is a prototypic example of the different forms of cognition afforded by collectivist versus individualist social orientations (Varnum, Grossmann, Kitayama, & Nisbett, 2010). Differences in cognitive processes are one of the more implicit elements associated with variation in self-construal (Markus & Kitayama, 1991). Specifically, the interdependent self has a holistic cognitive style, while the independent self has an analytic cognitive style (Nisbett et al., 2001; Shweder & Bourne, 1984). The former mode of thought takes the larger perceptual field into account and understands entities in terms of context and relationships, while the latter breaks objects out of context by fixing them in terms of category membership and distinct properties.

Phenomenological situation: embedded relatedness versus abstracted independence. At the most implicit level of social orientation, we find cultural differences in the individual's phenomenological situation vis-à-vis others, which underlie more discursively accessible differences. Specifically, persons in collectivist cultures experience themselves as embedded in an inescapable network of a priori relationships, whereas persons in individualist cultures experience themselves as free-floating, bounded entities in a sea of potentially dissoluble relationships that are largely constructed post hoc.

These phenomenological situations arise as a function of fundamental differences in the cultural construction of space and time, which I cannot review in detail here (for a detailed discussion, see Palitsky et al., in press; Sullivan et al., in press a). To summarize, collectivism is afforded by environments where space and time are not clearly differentiated but rather bound up with one another through symbolically mediated, embedded practices. In preindustrial or more rural contexts, time and space are typically less commoditized, and time is often not understood as a separate dimension outside the boundaries of habitual activities enacted in routine locales (Evans-Pritchard, 1939; Giddens, 1990; TenHouten, 2005). By contrast, in industrialized or urbanized settings – the institutions of which are generally more conducive to individualism – time and space are separated and commodified as distinct dimensions. The individual sees time and space as "empty" resources to be "filled" through freely chosen activities carried out for profit.

Associated with these temporal-spatial differences is variability in the embeddedness of practices. For instance, individualism can be predicted by the degree of geographic and job mobility in a society (Oishi & Kisling, 2009). More mobile individuals who carry out activities across extended swaths of time-space (via technological mediation) develop a more context-independent sense of the self and its goals and relationships. By contrast, individuals who are more residentially stable display a collectivistic preference for familiar locales and family or ingroup members. Individualists under conditions of abstracted independence become accustomed to the idea that social ties can be broad but shallow: North Americans report both larger social networks and greater proclivities for loneliness compared to West Africans (from a more collectivist culture;

Adams & Plaut, 2003). A hallmark of individualist social orientation is thus the phenomenological situation of navigating a broad network of geographic locations and social ties, whereas the situation in conditions of collectivist social orientation tends to be one of continuous "face-to-face" interaction with familiar individuals in stable surroundings (Schutz, 1970).

Patterns of social control: visible social control versus invisible social control

The second dimension in the current model represents (in line with past models) the more regulatory, rather than the orienting, aspects of culture. These aspects are generally subsumed under the umbrella construct of social control, which can be difficult to define (Spierenburg, 2004). As Meier (1982) points out, in early sociological theorizing, social control connoted the broad conditions of social organization; however, research and theory transitioned in the 1940s and 1950s to a more restricted understanding of social control as the mechanisms whereby deviance was contained and compliance with social norms enforced. More recently, beginning with the post-Foucauldian work of Stanley Cohen (1985), and drawing on H. S. Becker's (1963) labeling theory of deviance, theorists began to think about social control as a more insidious and pervasive process, through which experts, researchers, and other representatives of "mainstream" social institutions maintained power differences in society.

Following Horwitz (1990), I adopt a normative understanding of social control for which the concept of deviance is paramount. However, my definition of social control is somewhat broader than Horwitz', which focuses on retrospective reactions to deviance. In contrast to this narrow focus, my definition includes aspects of other prior models, notably Douglas' grid dimension and the tightness-looseness construct. Specifically, I consider social control to encompass both formal (i.e., state- or authority-enforced) and informal (i.e., locally or family-enforced) processes and belief systems (consciously or unconsciously) designed to preempt or retrospectively sanction deviance. Importantly, social control mechanisms include therapies and pedagogies, as well as state/local authorities and the propensity of community members to react to deviance with moral outrage.

In line with the work of Basil Bernstein (1990), I propose that there are visible (manifest) and invisible (latent) forms of social control. As in the case of social orientations, patterns of social control range in their degree of explicitness. The more explicit aspects of social control are those that have been integrated into prior models and studied extensively: the relative presence and type of behavior-governing norms, and the strength of sanctioning of deviant behavior (e.g., Gelfand et al., 2011). A related but more implicit, social structural factor largely missing from prior cultural models is the type of surveillance practiced to uphold the social order. Although in all cultures social control processes operate in both more explicit and more implicit forms, it is important to note that, overall, social control processes are more explicit in some cultures than others – hence the labels "visible" and "invisible" social control. Indeed, as grid-group theory suggests, identifying the degree of explicitness of social control in a society is a key tactic for distinguishing between cultures.

Norms: injunctive versus descriptive. Cialdini, Reno, and Kallgren (1990) distinguish between injunctive norms, which refer to what *ought* to be done and are obeyed in awareness of the possibility of moral sanction, and descriptive norms, which simply comprise information about what typically *is* done in a given situation. In cultures dominated by visible patterns of social control, norms are typically formulated in religious, political, or moral codes, and they are seen as injunctive (Bernstein, 1990). Members of these cultures typically have discursive access not only to the norms themselves, but to the moral or metaphysical justifications for them. In cultures governed by invisible patterns of social control, by contrast, norms are less likely to be formulated in explicit moral codes. Members of these cultures tend to see norms as descriptive: to the extent that they believe they are following norms, they believe that they do so simply because this is what is done.

It is also important to recognize the tightness aspect of norms. In visibly controlled cultures, where norms are viewed as injunctive, individuals are "narrowly" socialized to have a more complex and integrated "cognitive map" of the connection between particular contexts and the correct (normative) behavior in that context (Bernstein, 1990; Tambiah, 1973). In this sense, visibly controlled cultures are relatively "tight" (Gelfand et al., 2011), whereas invisibly controlled cultures are relatively "loose" and individuals in such cultures may not know exactly how to behave in each new situation.

Cultural representations of group differences and degree of hierarchy are also important aspects of the normative element of social control. There tends to be an association between visible social control and the explicit, injunctive formulation of status and group differences in a society (Gelfand, Lim, & Raver, 2004). Norms for behavior tend to be more moralized in settings where individuals need to be mindful of their relative rank or status vis-à-vis others (see Shweder et al., 1997). However, visible control structures can also be utilized to enforce equality of representation and opportunity between groups who are considered to have different fundamental properties or backgrounds (as typically occurs when visible control is combined with an individualist social orientation).

An important aspect of invisibly controlled culture is the "outsourcing" of norms to the structure of environments (Bernstein, 1990; see also Weber's 1946 discussion of bureaucratization). Invisible control operates largely by assuring individuals of their agency at the same time that their behavior is actually being subtly manipulated by situational forces. So, for example, the classrooms of modern, upper-class children in the United States and Europe foster a seeming environment of creativity where the pupils appear to be choosing their own activities and directing the course of the class. In reality, however, instructors have access to a complex array of pedagogical theories and are indirectly socializing their students based on current conceptions of development (Bernstein, 1990). Indeed, social psychology as a discipline contributes to the modern maintenance of invisible control systems – many popular theories, such as self-determination theory or norm focus theory itself, have been translated into workplace environment interventions that companies can use to subtly manipulate the behavior of their employees.

"Big data" approaches to advertising and consumer activity are another key means through which invisible control is achieved in modern cultural settings (Morozov, 2013a). Online companies such as Amazon and Google amass considerable amounts of data regarding their users, which they share with other companies and use to direct the purchasing power of consumers. Again, in such instances, individuals tend to have the subjective experience of agency and choice (after all, I am the one who clicks to buy a new ebook), but in reality their behavior has been influenced by a considerable amount of descriptive normative information (e.g., about how many other individuals have "liked" the book), tailored through "invisible" forces to appeal to their individual preference structure.

Sanctioning: intolerance versus tolerance of deviance. There are at least three reasons why deviant behavior is generally less tolerated in visibly than in invisibly controlled cultures. The first is that, in the latter where norms are more descriptive and less codified, the range of behaviors that obviously qualify as deviant is more restricted (Gelfand et al., 2004). The second, closely related reason involves the content of the norms that are violated by deviance in visible as opposed to invisible control cultures. Durkheim (1899/1978) argued for distinguishing between what might be called "symbolic" and "human" forms of criminality. Symbolic criminality involves deviant acts that are seen as violating some transcendent (superhuman) principle, such as a religious or humanist moral dictate. Human criminality, by contrast, consists of crimes that are simply viewed as infringements of one person on another. Because norms are typically seen as injunctive in visible control cultures, the violation of norms in such cultures often qualifies as symbolic criminality, and is more likely to receive harsh sanction.

The third reason stems from the different forms of social structure that tend to encourage visible as opposed to invisible patterns. Visible control cultures only tend to arise in settings where an infrastructure for actively punishing deviance exists (Horwitz, 1990), such as greater number of police per capita and more autocratic forms of government (Gelfand et al., 2011), and where the boundaries of group membership or citizenship are clear and require enforcement (Douglas, 1970). Visibly controlled cultures often promote, in addition to an elaborate system of injunctive norms, associated beliefs regarding the contaminating potential of deviant individuals for the group as a whole (Hiebert, 1973; Taylor, 2007), and these beliefs in turn promote active punishment or reform of deviants. Invisibly controlled cultures function according to a model of more relaxed sanctions, either because they lack the societal stratification that is a prerequisite for active sanctioning, or because they have less vested interest in reforming and reincorporating deviant individuals (who can, alternatively, simply be expelled).

Visibly and invisibly controlled cultures differ not only in the overall severity of sanctions for deviance; they also differ in the means through which potentially deviant actions are regulated and channeled. Pitts (1961) identified three primary mechanisms through which societies regulate deviant behavior. The most obvious is overt, ritualized sanctioning of counter-normative activity. Following Foucault's (1977) analysis, the major distinction here is that visibly controlled cultures tend to exert direct, visible punishment on criminals, while invisibly controlled cultures tend to isolate them through confinement or expulsion. A dramatic example would be public execution (in visibly controlled, totalitarian states) versus prison sentencing (in more democratic states), but an equally apt illustration might be found in the reintegrative shaming processes characteristic of many tight subcultures (Braithwaite, 1989). In some religions, norm-breakers are subjected to shunning behavior within the confines of the community – they are considered defiled and so must eat separate meals, sit in separate sections of the house of worship, and so on. But they are not completely removed from the community, and the hope is that this visible sanction will eventually reform the wayward individual.

The second form of control highlighted by Pitts (1961) are various means of tension reduction provided by culture to reduce the motivation for deviance in the first place. Here we might make a distinction between the Freudian defense mechanisms of sublimation and displacement. Visibly controlled cultures tend to socialize their members to sublimate antisocial or selfish desires that might otherwise result in deviance; often, these sublimation mechanisms are couched in theological terms (Cohen, Kim, & Hudson, 2014). For example, a belief in an afterlife psychologically rewards individuals for foregoing deviant activity by convincing them that they will eventually achieve paradise. By contrast, invisibly controlled cultures tend to reduce motivational tension by displacing it through various media of entertainment (Simmel, 1982). Sexually deviant acts, for example, can be simulated through virtual pornography.

Finally, Pitts (1961) indicates the significance of processes of labeling and acting toward deviant members within a society. This aspect of social control yields an important but counterintuitive distinction between visibly and invisibly controlled cultures. In the former, deviance is less tolerated because it is clearly defined through injunctive norms. However, in such settings *intolerance* of deviant *acts* is often accompanied by *tolerance* of deviant *individuals*, because the latter are symbolically integrated into society. Many traditional religious communities view deformity or mental disorder with a mixture of fear and awe, and see those at the margins of the community as simultaneously occupying an integral place within its symbolic order (Deardorff, 2009; Douglas, 1966; Gauchet & Swain, 1999). For example, the Maasai of Kenya are reported to believe that physical impairment may be caused by an ancestral sin, but impaired individuals are fully cared for by family members and integrated into the economic life of the community (Talle, 1995). Similarly, Nicolaisen (1995) observes that the Punan Bah of Malaysia – who maintain visible control by behaving at all times in accordance with the perceived dictates of their ancestors – consider childless individuals to be subhuman, but family members traditionally compensate for this status by presenting one of their children to the disabled individual as a gift.

By contrast, in invisibly controlled cultures, deviant acts are tolerated to a greater degree because norms are less explicit. Yet, the very lack of clear symbolization of deviant *action* in the culture ironically produces *less* tolerance for those *individuals* who are defined as deviant. Invisibly controlled cultures do not maintain explicit demarcations between groups of individuals who are hierarchically ranked within the society – rather, in principle, all individuals stand on equal footing with one another. This results in deviant or disabled individuals being defined with reference to an ideal of what the "normal" or "able" person in the culture is believed to be, and rather than such individuals being clearly integrated into the society, their care tends to be outsourced to institutions, rendering them invisible (Foucault, 1977; Stiker, 1999). Hence, stigma tends to arise around those considered abnormal in invisible control cultures (Gauchet & Swain, 1999; Goffman, 1963). Such individuals become problems to be managed, isolated, or "rehabilitated" in accordance with ideals of normality, rather than to be integrated or symbolically represented in terms of their difference.

Surveillance: concentrated versus diffuse. In visibly controlled cultures, implicit patterns of surveillance are concentrated: individuals are closely observed by others, including authority figures, in their everyday environments, and are generally aware of these patterns of mutual observation. This is particularly true in rural, relationally embedded contexts. Durkheim (1893/2014) stressed the idea that simply being in close proximity to others about whom one is knowledgeable and with whom one shares beliefs reinforces conformity to norms. This is evident from experimental research conducted in residentially stable cultures showing that the mere presence of observing "eyes" in the room activates internalized standards (Imada & Kitayama, 2010). In correlational research, residential stability is positively associated with informal social control (i.e., the perception that neighbors will intervene if negative events, such as violence or deviance, occur; Sampson, Raudenbush, & Earls, 1997). People in visibly controlled cultures are directly aware of the sources of authority and accountability within their society (Gelfand et al., 2004).

Contrasting with concentrated surveillance, two variations of diffuse surveillance exist or have existed in some cultures. Broadly defined, diffuse surveillance involves the experience of being perpetually surveyed by intangible others or institutions to which the self has only limited access. The earliest form of diffuse surveillance, prominent in ancient cultures and still present in some cultures today, inheres in belief systems promoting the idea that ancestors or spirits are constantly watching one's individual actions and are prepared to mete out punishment if one transgresses norms (Johnson & Bering, 2006; Spiro, 1967). The connection between belief in a watchful god or gods and a sense of being under surveillance has been substantiated in experimental research and is referred to as the "supernatural monitoring" effect (Gervais & Norenzayan, 2012).

The diversity of world religious beliefs is important for the contrast between concentrated and diffuse surveillance. Generally speaking, belief in a "high god" or monotheism is representative of concentrated surveillance, whereas belief in a number of different gods, spirits, or ancestors who can intervene in daily life is representative of diffuse surveillance. This distinction hinges on the crucial factor of perceived *access* to the surveying figure(s). As Gauchet (1997) has discussed at length, transcendent, high gods are seen as otherworldly and yet simultaneously more accessible to the individual's prayers and understanding, whereas a coterie of "lesser" deities or spirits exist closer to the plane of everyday human affairs, and yet are paradoxically less accessible and more difficult to understand, because they are associated with a primal, originary event to which humans have no mode of mediated connection. Importantly, Swanson (1964; see also Peregrine, 1996) determined, through cross-cultural correlational research, that a greater number of sovereign groups (i.e., more complex political hierarchy) predicts greater belief in a high god. Similar research by Roes and Raymond (2003) suggests that greater society size overall is positively associated with belief in a transcendent, moralizing God. In short, concentrated surveillance in the religious sense of a transcendent God who intervenes morally in human affairs is more associated with political hierarchy and complexity in a society.

A second, very different form of diffuse surveillance operates in some postindustrialized societies, such as the United States. This "modern" form of diffuse surveillance involves two primary aspects, elucidated by Giddens (1983):

> By "surveillance" I refer to two connected phenomena. First, to the accumulation of information – symbolic materials that can be stored by an agency or collectivity. Second, to the supervision of the activities of subordinates by their superiors within any collectivity ... Surveillance in each sense only becomes of major importance with the advent of capitalism. (pp. 169–170)

Capitalism and the centralization of power in the nation-state encourage the first form of diffuse surveillance (information storing), but they also encourage fusion of both forms of surveillance in phenomena of sequestration, "self-surveillance," the "monastic cell," and "technical control" (Edwards, 1979; Foucault, 1977; Giddens, 1983). Modern social control is characterized by its rigorous automaticity (often being performed by or with considerable assistance from machines), its depth in invading or utilizing the body (e.g., random drug screens, fingerprint records), and its breadth in permeating many public and private areas (Staples, 2003). In contrast to the concentrated surveillance documented in Sampson et al.'s (1997) research on inner-city neighborhoods, the ideal of diffuse surveillance is not an environment where people feel certain that others would punish them if they committed a crime, but rather an environment which is pre-designed to invisibly prevent any crime from being committed in the first place.

Algorithmic methods based on big data again become important for the maintenance of diffuse surveillance in contemporary, high-socioeconomic status settings. For instance, big data has been used by police in US cities to predict crimes and even intervene in them as they are happening: with recording devices installed in nearly every corner of modern metropolises, algorithms can be run to predict crimes based on past causal sequences (e.g., if the sound of glass shattering is statistically likely to be followed by a crime, police will be instantly alerted by computer when glass shatters in a particular neighborhood; Morozov, 2013a). Potential criminals even supply society with the data needed to apprehend them prior to any crime – Facebook (which legally requires no warrant) uses database scanning technology to alert authorities to likely pedophiles based on their posts and uploads (Morozov, 2013a).

As Bernstein (1990) pointed out, a paradox of invisibly controlled systems is that they extract more information from individuals than visibly controlled systems as a necessary part of their operation – they provide the illusion of privacy while actually reducing it. Individuals in contemporary democratic and technologically literate societies *feel* as if they are in complete control of their own actions and decision-making processes, and that they possess private, "true" identities to which society at large has no access (Savani, Markus, Naidu, Kumar, & Berlia, 2010; Stephens, Hamedani, Markus, Bergsieker, & Eloul, 2009). However, media such as Facebook and Amazon insure that more information is permanently recorded in a public space about such individuals than was the case at any other time in history (Ma & Agarwal, 2007). The egocentric worldview and independent self-construal characteristic of individualist culture combine with social technology to foster the recording of individual lives (e.g., through the construction and maintenance of "profiles"), and this ongoing source of "personal" data about the self in turn becomes part of the "invisible barbed wire" of contemporary, information-based control systems (Morozov, 2013b).

One key conceptual tool for distinguishing between concentrated and diffuse modes of surveillance is to examine the role played by debt in social control within different societies. Specifically, visible control cultures employ systems of *finite debt*, while invisible control cultures possess systems of *infinite debt* (Lazzarato, 2011). In tight, monotheistic religious cultures, for example, people owe finite debts for particular transgressions to the religious community and the deity, and these debts can be paid through rituals of atonement (Brown, 1959). Similarly, in early developments of the money economy, exchanges of credit and debt involved a considerable degree of trust between individuals or organizations that were well known to one another (Simmel, 1982). By contrast, under modern capitalism, individualist desires for self-creation and instant gratification may be "infinitely" satisfied through the incurring of debt via a dizzying array of possible loans, credit cards, and other mechanisms. This considerable expansion of the role of debt in everyday life under contemporary capitalism is a testament to the invisible nature of modern mechanisms of social control. Individuals and nations have the experience of asserting agency in the present by acquiring possessions or achieving goals that might otherwise be beyond their reach; yet, ultimately, the incurrence of debt means that they have only outsourced social control to the future, where their possibilities for free action are becoming increasingly constrained (Lazzarato, 2011).

The recent scandal over the revelation that the US National Security Agency has been partnering with cell phone companies to monitor citizens' calls testifies to the close connection in US culture between cultural individualism, relative wealth per capita, and mechanisms of invisible control. Individualist societies and democracies can only be maintained through policing and direction of behavior outside of the awareness of individuals. Individualists from higher-SES backgrounds are socialized in an environment that feels secure, where their rights are protected and they are free to make whatever choices they want under conditions of maximum privacy. In reality, however, the behavior of people in individualist societies is increasingly documented and regulated through the Internet and other diffuse surveillance technologies. When people become aware of this (as during the NSA scandal), the situation seems to clash with their individualist ideals. But in reality individualism and diffuse surveillance often go hand in hand.

Overview of cultural types

As discussed thus far, the present model builds on prior models by proposing that the overarching constructs of social orientation and social control may each be dichotomized in order to meaningfully classify cultures. Broadly speaking, cultures differ in their patterns of social orientation by being either generally more collectivist or more individualist, and they possess either more visible or invisible means of social control. Examining the interaction between these two dichotomous variables yields four ideal cultural types, presented schematically in Figure 4.2.

Contrasting cultures on the social orientation and control dimensions gives us a sense of the broad structural differences between the types. However, to better understand the lifeworld or phenomenological experience of individuals within these different cultures, it will also be useful to discuss how these cultural patterns are translated to individual consciousness and daily life using the framework presented in Chapter 2.

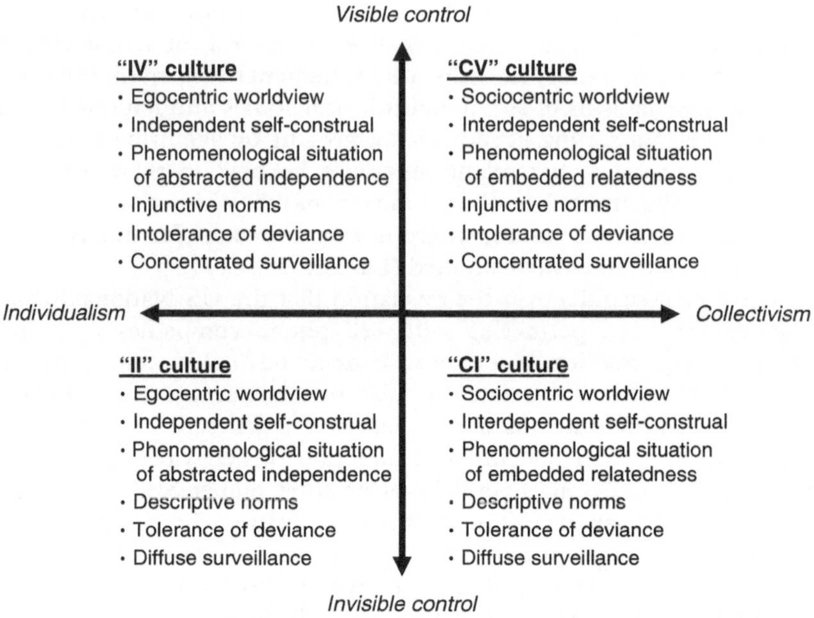

Figure 4.2. Four cultural types and their characteristic patterns generated by the current two-variable model.

Specifically, Hallowell's (1967) approach – which identifies five *Existenzielle* or orientations provided to the individual by their culture (see Figure 2.1, p. 30) – can be leveraged to understand the social psychological enactment of these patterns within individual (sub)cultures. Table 4.2 presents an overview of how the five orientations typically guide cognitions, attitudes, and behavior across the four cultural types, drawing on previous research primarily conducted according to the prior theoretical models discussed at the beginning of this chapter.

To conclude, I will briefly discuss each of the ideal cultural types in light of Hallowell's orientational perspective. A few caveats are in order. First, while the orientation/control model is useful for generalizing from the mass of facts regarding cultural differences that have been gathered across the social sciences, and follows in what is perhaps the most prominent tradition of cultural theory in those disciplines (the two-variable approach), it is of course the case that no particular (sub)culture will conform exactly to one of the types presented here. Most societies (particularly in globalized modernity) are stratified by numerous subgroups and subject to manifold extraneous influences, insuring that any given

Table 4.2. *Cultural orientations within each of the four primary types.*

	CI (Collectivist, invisible control)	CV (Collectivist, visible control)	IV (Individualist, visible control)	II (Individualist, invisible control)
Self-orientation	Defined in relation to ancestry, kin, and neighbor relationships (*F; S*)	Defined in terms of rank, duties, or place in hierarchy (*F; S*)	Defined as separate but in solidarity with others (*F*), and through possession of individual rights (*S*)	Defined in terms of social status or occupational role (*F; S*)
Normative orientation	Traditional legitimacy and altruism (*F*); loyalty/betrayal and sanctity/degradation (*H*)	Charismatic legitimacy and obedience (*F*); authority/subversion and sanctity/degradation (*H*)	Rational legitimacy and substantive equality (*F*); harm/care and fairness/cheating (*H*)	Legitimacy of deservingness and self-sufficiency (*F*); fairness/cheating and liberty/oppression (*H*)
Motivational orientation	For intimacy and interdependence with others and the environment (*F; S*)	For power and rank (*F*); to uphold duties and obligations (*S*)	For personal identity and self-reliance (*F; S*)	For achievement, power, and status (*F; S*)
Object orientation	Fetishes and relics denote identity and control (*F*); nature and culture bound with good/evil, pure/impure dimensions (*D*)	Objects denote rank (*F*); nature and culture divided into sacred/transcendent realms (*D*)	Appropriated symbols of identity and solidarity (*F*); nature romanticized as pure (*D*)	Commodities (*F*); nature can be calculated and controlled (*D*)
Spatial-temporal orientation	Corporate/ancestral land; eternal relationships with ancestors (*F*); patterned-cyclical time (*T*)	Sovereign land of the ingroup/ruler; time hierarchically ordered (*F*); episodic-futural time (*T*)	Individuals have equal rights to private space and time (*F*); immediate-participatory time (*T*)	Time and space are emptied and commodified (*F*); ordinary-linear time (*T*)

Note. Parenthetical letters indicate the following supporting references:
D – Douglas (1978); *F* – Fiske (1991); *H* – Haidt (2013); *S* – Shavitt et al. (2011); *T* – TenHouten (2005).

culture will likely contain blended elements of two or more of these ideal types, or at the very least contain subgroups conforming to different types. Although for my purposes I will primarily utilize the model to contrast different cultures, I have no intention of suggesting that there are hard-and-fast lines insuring the conformity of all individuals in a culture to a particular archetype. Naturally, there is variation within any culture in the extent to which individuals display typical traits or behavior patterns. Individuals may also gravitate from one subculture to another as a function of life events, as when a person converts to a fundamentalist religion (Sales, 1972). Furthermore, cultures are dynamic; historical events, or trends of modernization, can cause them to shift away from one pattern and toward another (Kay & Sullivan, 2013).

Recognizing these complexities of social life and individual variation, the comparative aims of cultural-existential psychology (see Chapter 2) nevertheless require some model for formulating hypotheses and organizing data relevant to the differences between (sub)cultures. I therefore present the cultural types while fully admitting that generalization is a necessary evil.

Collectivist/invisible control (CI). Individuals in CI cultures define themselves primarily in terms of relational connections. Depending on the relative isolation of a CI culture, the boundaries of group membership may be tentative, leading to intensive social identity maintenance processes, such as symbolic reinforcement of group characteristics and redefinition of deviant group members (Douglas, 1970). Relative equality among group members and only a few variables of social stratification are characteristic of these cultures (Fiske, 1991). Despite a strong sense of interdependency and relational self-definition, a general relative lack of explicitness about norms and tolerance for deviant behavior can result in a certain degree of self-reliance and independent behavior among group members (Hallowell, 1967; Woodburn, 1982). The ethic of community is strong in CI cultures (Shweder et al., 1997). These cultures tend to be smaller-scale, nomadic or subsistence-based groups (Gauchet, 1997; Henrich et al., 2010a).

In terms of Hallowell's cultural orientations, the self-orientation provided by CI culture primarily defines the self as "fluidly" or "porously" linked to those living in proximity with the self, usually including kin (often both living and dead). The CI normative orientation involves strong adherence to traditional patterns of behavior, although these are often not explicitly framed in injunctive, moralized terms. Utilizing Haidt's (2013) vocabulary, the primary moral foundations of CI culture are *loyalty/betrayal* and *sanctity/degradation*: the world is divided into ingroup/outgroup members, and polarities of good and evil, pure and impure. The CI motivational orientation is distinguished by strong pressures to maintain affiliation with the group.

The *Mitwelt* and *Eigenwelt* tend to be conflated in these cultures (Habermas, 1985), reinforcing the "naturalness" of group membership and responsibilities. Everything connected to the group, its members, and their local environment is considered good and natural in an objective sense; everything that lies beyond the group, or threatens it from within, is considered evil and objectively unnatural. As a result of this conflation, members of CI cultures typically experience space and time as symbolically laden and socially relevant dimensions. In the religions of many nomadic-pastoral cultures, land is considered hallowed by links to ancestors. Time in such cultures is experienced as "patterned-cyclical" (TenHouten, 2005): communal rituals and oral traditions continually renew a posited past time of societal origin, linking the present to the past (see also Bloch & Parry, 1982).

Collectivist/visible control (CV). Individuals in CV cultures define themselves largely in terms of relational connections and collective identities. CV cultures are marked by the presence of an intricate and morally imperative system of norms. The boundaries of membership in the collective are typically clear and secure (Douglas, 1970). Hierarchy and power distance are often prominent features of these societies (Fiske, 1991). The ethics of community and divinity are strong in such settings (Shweder et al., 1997). Such cultures tend to be larger, collectivist societies with a fairly developed form of political hierarchy and infrastructure, such as the modern nation-state of China (Gauchet, 1997). However, this need not always be the case. Certain smaller, more enclosed or isolated communities may develop strong systems of visible control alongside a strong sense of group solidarity. Examples of such cultures in the United States might be the Hutterites (Pelto, 1968) or certain conservative Mennonite groups (Hiebert, 1973).

The self-orientation provided by CV culture is typically a definition of the self with relation to sacred or communal duties, specified by one's place in a moralized hierarchy of possible ranks. CV normative orientation often involves considerable deference toward charismatic leaders. With respect to Haidt's (2013) model, it links the dimension of *sanctity/degradation* to that of *authority/subversion*: in CV culture, obedience to injunctive norms and their interpretation by religious or political leaders is paramount, and deviation from these dictates can make the self unclean or disgraced. In some CV cultures, improper modes of contact between members of different ranks within the society can also be a source of degradation. Within CV organizational cultures – such as most militaries – a primary motivation is the desire to gain greater status and thereby power. However, many CV cultures do not encourage social mobility, meaning that the majority of their members have a motivational orientation toward duty and obedience to their superiors or sacred laws.

In the religious belief systems associated with CV culture, there is often a sharp differentiation between a transcendent "true" or supernatural world and the profane, natural or "false" world of the everyday (Dalferth, 2012). Thus, the *Umwelt* is split into a holy realm, typically associated with a high God, and the world of human affairs. This idea of transcendence facilitates the maintenance of visible control, as in the Judeo-Christian tradition, because individuals adjust to suffering and self-sacrifice through a theodicy that promises redemption in the other, transcendent realm. Furthermore, individuals forego selfish pursuits for fear of retribution from the transcendent power. The division between transcendence and immanence has implications for temporal-spatial experience. Time is often hierarchically and/or cyclically structured in CV culture, with various layers of cosmological time (including more profane and more sacred levels) intersecting (Taylor, 2007; Thapar, 2002). In contrast to the patterned-cyclical time of CI culture, which tends to blur past and present, CV cultures often afford an episodic-futural orientation (TenHouten, 2005): the idea of the infinite becomes prominent along with the idea of transcendence, and members of CV culture look to the future for the promise of personal or group immortality. CV cultures characteristically interpret "home"-land as representative of the group, and some variants also foster religious ancestor worship comparable to that found in much CI culture.

Individualist/visible control (IV). Individuals in IV cultures tend to define themselves in terms of unique, expressive personal identities. The ethic of autonomy is fairly strong in most of these cultures (Shweder et al., 1997), yet social control is also explicit and exchanges between atomized individuals are significantly regulated. IV culture represents the ideal of the Western Enlightenment: a society where unique individuals agree to live together for their common good, united by their shared respect for the basic rights of each person. In this variant of individualism, the possible excesses of self-involvement are (ideally) tempered by a conviction that individuals share a common humanity, which should be protected through an equal distribution of social resources. This cultural type is best manifested in the social democratic society, such as modern Scandinavian nations (Triandis & Gelfand, 1998), in which individualist culture is predominant but the government has characteristics of socialism, including regulation of the economy and other forms of visible social control. Indeed, IV culture is only possible where infrastructures and forums exist for individuals to come together in communal dialogue and receive equal representation, and where regulations are placed on wealth and power channels.

IV culture is dominated by the form of individualism that Simmel (1971) referred to as "quantitative," that is, individualism based on equality and a common recognition of human essence and entitlement. This has also been referred to as expressive individualism (Bellah, Madsen, Sullivan, Swidler, & Tipton, 1985; Tipton, 2002). Here individualism takes the form of a valorization and defense of the right of each individual to develop their unique potentialities and enjoy substantive equality of opportunity. In terms of Haidt's (2013) theory, IV culture is rooted in the moral foundations of *fairness/cheating* and *harm/care*: the individual and their protection is the supreme moral ideal in this culture (Durkheim, 1893/2014; Taylor, 2007). This sense of moral commitment to the individual is grounded in a universalistic morality, which posits that all persons, even those outside the ingroup, should be treated fairly and even with reverence (Janoff-Bulman & Carnes, 2013).

As in CV culture, IV culture upholds a dualistic separation between the realms of nature and culture. However, because IV culture tends to arise in more pluralistic, secular societies (Schluchter, 1981), this does not imply the religious transcendence/immanence distinction. Rather, in Rousseauian fashion, IV culture characteristically associates human essence with an idealized version of nature, and sees society and institutional forces as responsible for inequality and violence in the world. Thus, a romanticized "Nature" is often viewed as redemptive and regenerative, as well as worthy of protection. The natural world is considered both the precious source of society's resources and as a wild space analogous to the untamed depths of the creative individual (Watson, 2006). In TenHouten's (2005) theory, IV culture promotes an immediate-participatory form of time consciousness: individuals are encouraged to focus on and revel in the present, to attempt to achieve states of "flow" (Csikszentmihalyi, 1991) and "mindfulness" (Brown, Ryan, & Creswell, 2007). This focus on present experiences arises partly from a secular rejection of religious future orientation and from an individualistic imperative to develop the self and pay heed to its needs and desires.

Individualist/invisible control (II). Individuals in II cultures conceive of themselves in terms of unique personal identities. The ethic of autonomy reigns in this type of culture (Shweder et al., 1997). Hierarchy and status differences are a prominent feature in such societies insofar as the largely unregulated pursuit of personal benefit leads to fierce competition for material and symbolic resources (Douglas, 1970). Ideas of market fundamentalism and nonintervention tend to be prominent in

II cultures (Fiske, 1991). Such cultures are generally larger societies with an individualist ethos and a fairly developed form of political hierarchy and infrastructure, such as the contemporary United States. Generally, II culture thrives in settings where people live more isolated lives and there are few checks on differential access to and maintenance of resources (Fiske, 1991).

II culture is representative of what Simmel (1971) called "qualitative" individualism, an individualism of difference that assumes innate variations in skills, traits, and status between persons. This has also been called "utilitarian" individualism (Bellah et al., 1985; Tipton, 2002). It is characterized by social atomism and a "free market" ethos. In II culture, individuals use folk Darwinian-selectionist metaphors to understand the workings of economy and society, despite their conceptual inappropriateness (Rosenberg, 2000). Such understandings paint society as a place of constant uncertainty and competition, in which the only fundamental value is that of noninterference in the activities of all persons. Proponents of II culture insist on deregulation of social life so that individuals may pursue their best interests and succeed or fail according to their merits (Langevoort, 2011). As Haidt (2013) would put it, II culture observes the moral foundations of *liberty/oppression* and *fairness/cheating*. Deservingness is the primary moral axis, and self-esteem the primary psychological resource in II culture. Individuals are primarily motivated for status and achievement, not only to secure access to pragmatically important resources but also to buffer their self-esteem, often in the absence of unambiguous, overarching meaning systems and a sense of community.

II cultures in the modern world are inevitably secular and even characterized by a kind of "banal" nihilism – a general skepticism toward ideology and human political endeavors (Diken, 2009). In the cosmology of II culture, space and time are devoid of any major symbolic content; these dimensions have been commodified, "emptied" of predetermined content so that they might be "filled" with profitable activities and investments. Nature provides resources that may be exploited by society. In general, people are oriented to time via an "ordinary-linear" time consciousness (TenHouten, 2005): they see time as a series of passing moments stretching backward and forward from the present.

Conclusion

Having built a model of cultural differences from the work of noted theorists in sociology, anthropology, and social psychology, it is now possible to put together the major pieces of the cultural-existential puzzle.

This will be the task of the final chapter in the "Theory" section of this book. The four cultural types identified here partly function by orienting their members to interpret certain kinds of information and events as threatening, and to experience and defend against those threats in particular ways. In Chapter 3, I proposed that all cultural meaning systems are in some way designed to defend against the two primary forms of nihilism – disorientation and despair – with the ultimate aim of quelling the human potential for death angst. Using the current cultural model, in the following pages I will argue that some patterns of social orientation and control primarily protect the individual from one form of nihilism rather than the other.

5 Cultural threat orientations: disorientation avoidance and despair avoidance

Different cultural worldviews tend to prioritize the avoidance of one form of nihilism over the other. Having outlined the different levels and types of existential threat in Chapter 3, and the different general patterns of culture in Chapter 4, it is now possible to link these analyses by postulating the existence of two general threat orientations that are prominent at the cultural level.

Although it is possible for an individual to experience nihilism, as discussed in Chapter 3, this extreme form of existential threat is only likely to be found among clinical or unusual populations. Therefore, it is more apt to use the term "nihilism" when discussing the threat orientation of an entire culture. Specifically, cultures can be classified on the basis of the type of nihilism against which they primarily inoculate their members (Sullivan, 2013). Some cultures may be called *disorientation-avoidant* (DISA), meaning that the beliefs and socialization processes within the culture operate to maintain the sacrosanct nature of a comprehensive view of reality and to neutralize the threat of meaninglessness angst. In DISA cultures, the primary concern is to maintain the sacred nature of cultural values. Values can be drawn into question in a number of ways: through exposure of their origin (in the psychological needs of individuals); through the realization in the world of a critical level of human suffering that they seem ill equipped to explain or provide solace from; through exposure to alternative value systems that construe the world, its purpose, and the valued personal identity in fundamentally different ways; and so on. DISA cultures instruct their members to prevent the emergence of nihilistic disorientation as a result of these factors at all costs, and equip them with various means of doing so.

By contrast, other cultures are *despair-avoidant* (DESA) – the primary function of shared beliefs and socialization is to protect the value of the individual and neutralize the threat of condemnation angst. DESA cultures focus on the avoidance of personalized feelings of despair among the particular members of the culture. Nihilistic despair – the sense that one is personally incapable of achieving one's highest values – can arise from a variety of sources, and is typically experienced as either a sense of low self-esteem, depression, and/or chronic guilt, or as alienation, the feeling that one's "authentic" self is not given adequate expression in one's social role and daily labors. DESA cultures instruct their members that such despair is always to be avoided, and they also equip them with a variety of strategies for avoiding or navigating nihilistic despair.

Importantly, I propose that cultural values and beliefs are often such that by primarily protecting individuals from one form of nihilism, they orient individuals toward lower-level threat experiences of the opposite form, meaning that DISA cultures tend to orient individuals toward guilt and condemnation angst, while DESA cultures tend to orient them toward anxiety and meaninglessness angst.

It is useful to consider these cultural orientations in terms of prototypic examples. Here the classic case involves the distinction between collectivist, orthodoxly religious cultures, on the one hand, and individualist, more secularized cultures on the other. Although the religious-secular and collectivist-individualist continua are far from perfectly correlated, a great deal of theory and evidence indicates that, historically, devout religiosity and collectivist social orientation were normative in most human societies, and the rise of individualism tends to be associated with a move toward secularity or a less rigid form of religiosity (e.g., Bellah, 1964; Durkheim, 1972; Gauchet, 1997; Norris & Inglehart, 2012; Watson, 2014). Without straying too far into the realm of the contested secularization thesis, it is necessary to note that the connection between rising individualism and secularization is especially clear when we define secularism in a sociologically valid way. This means we should understand "secularity" not as the complete absence of religion but rather as the emergence of a culture in which religion appears to be a lifestyle or choice that may be invalid, rather than an inherently given mode of being (Casanova, 2012; Taylor, 2007).

Accepting the validity of the individualism-secularism association at the most general level, it is clear that collectivist, orthodoxly religious cultures are paradigmatically DISA in at least three ways: (1) a set of integrated beliefs make all aspects of life seem interconnected and meaningful, sheltering the individual from meaninglessness angst; (2) the need to maintain group harmony is satisfied by providing individuals with clear goals and standards for behavior, which preempt anxiety and uncertainty; and (3) in many religious traditions and collectivist cultures, suffering is commonly explained as resulting from deviant behavior, thus orienting individuals toward guilt and condemnation angst and away from nihilistic disorientation (Sullivan, Landau, Kay, & Rothschild, 2012b). It should also be clear that in terms of the foregoing cultural model (Chapter 4), collectivist, orthodoxly religious cultures are prototypically CV cultures; hence, DISA threat orientations are most likely to manifest purely in CV settings.

By contrast, individualist, primarily secular cultures are paradigmatically DESA in at least three ways: (1) the presence of norms and values prioritizing individual worth and success equip the individual with a variety of self-serving biases, and hence protection against condemnation angst (Cross, Hardin, & Gercek-Swing, 2011); (2) the focus on personal, rather than group-centric, goal striving, as well as increased tolerance for idiosyncratic behavior, relieves individuals of felt obligation to most of the people around them and reduces the likelihood of guilt; and (3) since secularism and individualism are often associated with a more skeptical attitude toward reality and a diminished sense of social support, individuals in such cultures are oriented toward anxiety and meaninglessness angst even as they eschew nihilistic despair (Sullivan et al., 2014). Referring to the cultural model, individualist, secular cultures are prototypically II cultures, highlighting the fact that DESA threat orientations are most likely to be found in II settings.

As discussed in Chapter 2, even as cultures tend to orient individuals away from one class of existential threats and toward another, they also provide a defensive infrastructure or belief system that ameliorates those threats (Gillin, 1967). For instance, CV cultures often encourage interpretations of misfortune that stress personal guilt; however, they also provide means to routinely process and reduce guilt, such as rituals of religious atonement or reparation toward community members. II cultures orient individuals to experience misfortune in terms of uncertainty and anxiety about a chaotic world, yet at the same time they promote beliefs that convince individuals that they personally will be able to navigate the uncertain world, even if others cannot.

Beyond the association between DISA/DESA threat orientations and particular cultural patterns, there are also socio-ecological aspects that tend to coincide with these distinct existential approaches. Broadly speaking, DISA cultures tend to arise in environments that do not afford ready means of coping with unpredictable hazards and instability. Where one's life is precarious and the social order threatened by potential collapse, DISA beliefs develop to inoculate the worldview from those forces that threaten to undermine its validity. This notion is supported by the "existential security" hypothesis for religious belief – namely, that orthodox religiosity is stronger in regions with greater poverty, violence, and general hardship – which has received considerable empirical (Norris & Inglehart, 2012) and theoretical (Watson, 2014) support. DESA cultures, on the other hand, tend to develop in environments where ready techniques for controlling uncertain hazard and maintaining individual and collective life appear available. In environments where the worldview (and in particular those rationalized structures that sustain the worldview, such as the nation-state, science, and the economy) appears to have gained a certain autonomy from and mastery over the natural environment – meaning random hazards and fluctuations external to the cultural system seem less threatening to it – the protection and maintenance of cultural values tends to have secondary importance. Instead, individuals come to see maintenance of a personal sense of ultimate value – and avoidance of nihilistic despair – as a primary goal, in the service of which aspects of the worldview may be questioned, altered, and even completely sacrificed.

While Nietzsche provided the fundamental nihilistic categories of disorientation and despair, the work of three other social theorists – Peter L. Berger, Marcel Gauchet, and Roberto Esposito – contains rich portraits of the DISA/DESA cultural threat orientations. These thinkers have reconceptualized classic sociological theories of modernization, secularization, and rationalization – which have, in various ways, traced the shift from prototypic CV to II cultures – in order to show the fundamental existential operations at work in these cultural transformations.

Gauchet (1997) begins his analysis with the observations presented in Chapter 3: humans are, by virtue of their biological makeup, torn between the axes of guilt and anxiety, between a sense of obligation to and embeddedness in the past and a sense of uncertainty about and openness to the future. He contends that the history of human culture is a history of prioritizing one over the other of these modes of being, through the shaping of our orientations toward the *Umwelt*, *Mitwelt*, and *Eigenwelt*. Gauchet proposes that cultural history was inaugurated with an orientation toward the past and a sense of indebtedness to the social and natural world, but that over time human societies have increasingly shifted toward the opposite pole and embraced a sense of individual and social agency:

> Everything takes place as if the human species has chosen to favor in turn one or the other of these temporal dispositions: either a bias in favor of the priority of the world and the law of things; or one in favor of the priority of humans and their creative activity: either submission to an order received in toto, determined before and outside our will; or responsibility for an order accepted as originating in the will of individuals who themselves are supposed to exist prior to the bond holding them together. (p. 11)

Esposito (2013) uses the concepts of *communitas* and *immunitas* to encapsulate these two general orientations. These terms represent opposing ends of a continuum centering around the sense of social obligation – those belonging to the *communitas* are obligated, bound, indebted, through mutual interdependence and the demands of prescribed social roles, whereas those in a state of *immunitas* are immune, exempt, protected from obligation to any entity other than themselves. While individuals in a state of *communitas* perennially sacrifice their potential agency and subjectivity to laws of visible control binding individuals together, those under conditions of *immunitas* feel a strong sense of self-determination, guaranteed and undergirded by institutions of invisible control.

Community exposes each person to a contact with, and also to a contagion by, an other that is potentially dangerous. In the face of precisely such a threat … modernity activates a process of immunization, following the paradigmatic clash between *communitas* and *immunitas*. If the former binds individuals to something that pushes them beyond themselves, then the latter reconstructs their identity by protecting them from a risky contiguity with the other, relieving them of every obligation toward the other and enclosing them once again in the shell of their own subjectivity. Whereas *communitas* opens, exposes, and turns individuals inside out, freeing them to their exteriority, *immunitas* returns individuals to themselves, encloses them once again in their own skin. *Immunitas* brings the outside inside, eliminating whatever part of the individual lies outside. (Esposito, 2013, p. 49)

Connecting these analyses to the previously presented model of cultural differences (Chapter 4), it should be clear that *communitas* is most purely incarnated in CV cultures, while *immunitas* captures the ideal-typical condition of II cultures. In the following sections, I will unpack the abstract concepts of these analyses, supplementing them with the classic ideas of the modernization theorists (such as Berger). In particular, I will endeavor to show how the state of *communitas* in CV culture affords a DISA threat orientation: individuals typically possess an unshakeable foundation of meaning, but are susceptible to experiences of guilt. By contrast, the state of *immunitas* in II culture affords a DESA threat orientation: individual self-esteem is kept immune, at the expense of exposing individuals to anxiety.

It is critical to note at the outset that the analyses of Berger, Esposito, and Gauchet are framed in diachronic terms: they focus on a historical transition from CV to II culture, and from DISA to DESA threat orientation, over the course of human history. Their causal accounts of this transition differ, and they variously emphasize such important sociohistorical factors as the rise of nation-states, the emergence of individualistic religions after the Axial Age, the Protestant Reformation, the Enlightenment, capitalism, globalization, and the growth of the middle class. I will sketch in overview a composite version of their diachronic account, because it is useful for understanding the distinction between DISA and DESA cultures, and, indeed, there is considerable evidence that II culture and the DESA threat orientation have become much more prominent in the last 300 years (for a similar account, see Sullivan, 2013). However, it should be kept in mind that from the perspective of cultural-existential psychology, these threat orientations represent universally present possibilities of human cultural experience. I am not ultimately as interested in tracing the historical forces that have precipitated shifts in threat orientations, as I am in developing ideal-typical categories that may be applied to the synchronic comparison of contemporary cultural groups (in line with the principles of Chapter 2). Thus, the reader should be aware that while many of the following remarks appear to suggest an irreversible trend away from DISA and toward DESA culture, these processes are anything but the historically linear developments that this necessarily abstract and simplified treatment suggests. Within any society at any point in history, groups of individuals have differentially oriented themselves away from either disorientation or despair. Even in today's capitalistic, globalized world, pockets of CV, DISA culture continue to flourish, as the research in Part II will show.

DISA culture: dispossession, *communitas*, and guilt

Berger (1967) contends that the primary cultural difference between preindustrial religious societies and modernized secular societies is that, in the former, people lack an awareness of the socially constructed nature of human belief systems. Such cultures encourage an epistemological collapse of the *Mitwelt* and *Umwelt* – products of human thought and culture, such as religious beliefs and posited gods, are perceived to be "objective," natural elements of the world (Radin, 1927). Such a situation tends also to produce a less sharply delineated *Eigenwelt*: if humans are embedded in reality, rather than constructively contributing to it, it seems unreasonable to assume that each person has a totally unique perspective on the world (Habermas, 1985).

As Berger (1967) argues, religion is the ultimate source of meaning creation and defense against the anomie of potential meaninglessness. Hence, early, pantheistic cultures – where religion suffused social life and indeed was indistinguishable from it – eliminated nearly all possibility of nihilistic disorientation. All contingency was transformed to certainty, all chaos reinterpreted as fate through a religious cosmology. Gauchet (1997) suggests that "primeval" religion of this sort was perfectly DISA because it located the originary source of all meaning in the activities of ancestors carried out in a foundational, sacred time and place (such as the

"Dream Time" of Indigenous Australians; see TenHouten, 2005). This created a phenomenological situation of absolute servitude to the perceived past, and an impossibility that such foundational meaning could ever be called into question. By contrast, with the rise of dualistic monotheism (e.g., the Judeo-Christian tradition), the cultural strategy of avoiding disorientation through the merger of *Mitwelt* and *Umwelt* is transformed into a strategy of sharp division, with a posited transcendent "true world" beyond the immanent "false world" of contingent reality (Berger, 1967; Nietzsche, 1889/1997).

Such DISA cultures may be described as *alienated* in terms of the existential situation of their members (Berger, 1967), because their belief systems deny the role of human will and activity in the construction and direction of society. In Gauchet's (1997) terms, the maintenance of DISA culture is an ongoing process of *dispossession*, whereby individuals disavow their capacity to transform their *Umwelt*, convincing themselves instead that they are immersed in a static and unchanging natural world (or, in the dualistic faiths, that they are merely "visiting" the earthly plane before returning to a timeless transcendent dimension).

In a sociological sense, Esposito (2013) proposes that such belief systems develop in social groups bound by the logic of *communitas*, by a deep sense of obligation to and dependence on others concretized in clear social roles and practices of communal sharing and gift-giving. While Gauchet and Habermas emphasize the epistemological coterminance of *Umwelt* and *Mitwelt* in DISA culture, Esposito points instead to the fluidity of the membrane between *Eigenwelt* and *Mitwelt*. The self is radically exteriorized and open to the social world in such settings; indeed, the state of *communitas* could be defined by the lack of an individual subject. Rather than firmly anchored in one's body and perception, the self is diffused through the *Mitwelt* in binds of obligation and social connection. This state of indebtedness was and is corporealized quite literally in acts of sacrifice and violent initiation rites throughout pantheistic or tribal cultures (Langer, 1982; Trompf, 1994), and in the repressive sanctions and public punishments meted to criminals in early states (Durkheim, 1893/2014; Foucault, 1977). Clastres (1974/1987), summarizing the extensive data on excruciatingly painful rites that are willingly undergone in scores of smaller-scale societies, vividly argues that these render material the individual's boundedness to the community: "The law they come to know in pain is … *You are worth no more than anyone else; you are worth no less than anyone else*. The law, inscribed on bodies … cruelly taught, is a prohibition of inequality that each person will remember" (p. 186).

Indeed, DISA culture functions according to the "law of community" (Esposito, 2013), which keeps the individual in a perennial state of culpability and debt to others and society at large. DISA cultures possess a deep understanding of human finitude and the limits of human potentiality; they distribute their existential awareness of these limits as a shared sense of guilt between their members (Brown, 1959). This communal sense of inadequacy translates in DISA religions to the formula "theodicy is anthropodicy" (Berger, 1967): evil is explained as the result of human failings on the immanent plane. Seeing human culpability and moral deviation as the source of suffering preserves the "flow" (Esposito, 2013) and "indebtedness" of meaning (Gauchet, 1997) within cultures of *communitas*.

Thus, the DISA orientation involves not only a fundamental denial of the human capacity to alter the world and events within it. Beyond this, individuals within DISA culture see themselves as perennially indebted to the (social) world. At the same time, they consider that indebtedness to be both shared and finite (see the discussion of debt in relation to visible and invisible forms of social control in Chapter 4).

DESA culture: reflexivity, *immunitas*, and anomie

According to the diachronic account we are tracing, how is it that DISA culture – which was apparently quite predominant in early human cultural history – was eventually transformed into DESA culture? Berger (1967) argues for the historical importance of the emergence of profound forms of *reflexivity*. I dealt briefly with the notion of reflexivity in my discussion of existential sociology (Chapter 1). As I use the term, reflexivity arises from, but goes beyond, the human capacity for *reflection* – that is, to mentally isolate events and actions in time and reflect back on them (Giddens, 1983; for further discussion of these terms, see Sandywell, 1996). Reflexivity operates at both individual and cultural levels. At the individual/ psychological level, reflexivity refers to people's ability to reflect on the socially constructed, subjectivist nature of their beliefs. At the cultural/ societal level, reflexivity refers to a culture's capacity to build a store of knowledge about the origins and history of its institutions and guiding beliefs, with the aim of willfully shaping the further development of those institutions. In cultures where reflexivity is not very advanced, socialization tends to be relatively "symmetric": individuals more or less unquestioningly adopt the norms, values, and beliefs of the preceding generation (Berger & Luckmann, 1966). When cultures develop a certain degree of reflexivity, socialization becomes increasingly "asymmetric": individual consciousness is no longer a replica of the collective consciousness.

To be more specific, individuals who experience primarily reflexive enculturation often engage in highly self-aware reflection on the nature, origins, and ultimate purpose of their actions, while persons who are non-reflexively enculturated engage in such monitoring to a much lesser extent, and tend to experience their particular actions as spontaneous, their range of possible actions as predetermined, and their actions in general as "natural." In other words, reflexively socialized individuals tend to see any particular action, pursuit, or role they undertake as only one possible means of engagement with the world among many alternatives, while non-reflexively socialized individuals have a greater tendency to consider their given actions, pursuits, and roles the only proper or available means of world engagement (Bernstein & Henderson, 1973). At the limit, greater reflexivity affords the individual the prospect of rejecting all current social roles, or devising new ones, at least on an intellectual level; at the very least, it affords the individual considerable flexibility in how they execute social roles (and thus plays a direct part in the development of egocentric worldviews; see Chapter 4).

Clearly, reflexive socialization can only occur to the extent that a given culture contains a diverse, critical, and independent knowledge base regarding the nature of activities performed within that culture (Giddens, 1990). Ascribing the existence of a freestanding knowledge base about cultural activity to certain cultures does not imply that more reflexive cultures possess greater total knowledge about their normative practices. Rather, in reflexive cultures, a substantial percentage of all beliefs and information about the nature of cultural practices is not bound up with their immediate performance, but is rather consolidated somehow at a distance from them (literacy, as opposed to orality, enormously facilitates this process; Ong 1982). With reflexivity, the individual is offered certain ideas about the world and ways of being in it that have an independent existence from the many available actions, goals, and pursuits through which they may be concretized. Alternatively, less reflexive enculturation leads to a greater sense of unity between cultural practices and the knowledge that justifies them. The individual's ideas about the world and how to be in it cannot be readily separated from the specific actions, goals, and pursuits of her daily life; she conceives of only one way, or a limited few ways of being, and finds her actions readily dictated by such with little call for independent reflection.

The diachronic emergence of cultural reflexivity was made possible by the growth of nation-states and broad forms of government-level, diffuse surveillance (Gauchet, 1997; Giddens, 1983), as well as "secondary" (Gehlen, 1980) and "immunizing" (Esposito, 2013) institutions. These institutions included laws guaranteeing personal rights (most importantly rights of private property), and Enlightenment-based ideologies of personal freedom. Nation-states and immunizing institutions extended their reach as societies developed greater technical capabilities to store information about their normative practices in some (text-based) manner separately from the enactment of those practices (Dreyfus & Rabinow, 1983). What is more, in European culture, post-Renaissance scientific ideals ensured that this knowledge base became increasingly critical and revisionary with regard to cultural practices. In this connection, the ideals of empiricism and historicity characteristic of the European Enlightenment were major factors in the acceleration of the reflexivity of modernity. As Giddens (1990) writes,

> With the advent of modernity, reflexivity ... is introduced into the very basis of system reproduction, such that thought and action are constantly refracted back upon one another. The routinization of daily life has no intrinsic connections with the past ... To sanction a practice because it is traditional will not do; tradition can be justified, but only in light of knowledge which is not itself authenticated by tradition ... [Cultural reflexivity] consists in the fact that social practices are constantly examined and reformed in light of incoming information about those very practices, thus constitutively altering their character. (p. 38)

We can trace in greater detail the process through which cultural reflexivity has led to the increasing preponderance of reflexive consciousness at the individual level, and simultaneously to the emergence and spread of DESA culture. Wittrock (2012) argues that reflexive cultures possess four key historically recent attributes. These elements have been gradually assimilated into the fabric of modern cultural institutions in the manner described by Giddens, to the point where individuals are now socialized in ways that are inherently encouraging of reflexive consciousness.

First, cultural reflexivity is associated with the rise of *historical consciousness* in a society. Critical historical consciousness inheres in the epistemological assumption that history is a developing causal sequence of identifiable, interrelated, and temporally linear events; in other words, history is a series of facts that can be empirically known (Langer, 1957). This kind of empirical historical consciousness encourages the collection and preservation of information by a society about that society (Dreyfus & Rabinow, 1983), ultimately laying the groundwork for questioning the origins and validity of social beliefs and practices (Nietzsche, 1874/1997).

Second, cultural reflexivity is associated with a transformation in the cosmology that is typical of premodern or non-reflexive cultures (Wittrock, 2012), a transformation Habermas (1987) refers to as a "rationalization of the worldview" via a process of "linguistification of the sacred." Religious norms and worldviews, which originally required no justification beyond their ritual enactment and transmission via oral socialization, were gradually transcribed and stored in various texts and files. The text-based storage of information implies the notion of an authoritative source that can be contested, which in turn leads to further processes of textual exegesis, apologetics, and rational legitimization. Cultural reflexivity involves . . .

> an *articulation* and *interpretation* of . . . cosmologies in terms of their oral mediation as well as their textual *inscription*, and the emergence of a set of rules for the authoritative interpretation of such texts. Such processes of codification and standardization . . . set the stage not only for the articulation and diffusion of orthodoxy but also for heterodox challenges. (Wittrock, 2012, p. 109)

During the Axial Age (circa 800 BC–200 BC; Bellah & Joas, 2012), the seeds of reflexivity were planted when intellectuals began to conceive of religious beliefs and cultural values as somehow existing outside of the natural world, as added to or enforced upon it, as stored somewhere else (i.e., the *Mitwelt* began to clearly separate from the *Umwelt*). Again, non-reflexive cultures do not enforce a sharp distinction between what is "cultural/artificial" and what is "natural." In this situation, it is cognitively difficult to engage in substantial reflection on one's practices, because it is in no sense clear that one's practices could easily be different. One might as well reflect on the possibility that one could be a fish. Symbolic thinking is such that humans have always engaged in such abstract reflection, but until the *Umwelt*/*Mitwelt* distinction is clearly made, cultural reflexivity is severely blocked. The spread of record-keeping and justification of history and cultural practices in textual sources greatly facilitated this conceptual separation.

Third, growing cultural reflexivity involved changes in conceptualizations of and experience within society. Habermas (1987) refers to this process as the "universalization of law and morality" via a "generalization of values." The rise of nation-states and markets created situations in which diverse, geographically separated cultural and ethnic groups began to be forcibly united under common political-legal structures (Gauchet, 1997; Watson, 2006). This forced cultural values – which were originally closely tied to the concrete rituals and practices of localized groups – to become increasingly abstract to accommodate a variety of local beliefs and customs under a common symbolic umbrella (Durkheim, 1893/2014). The historical transition from pantheism to monotheism is a primary example of this phenomenon (Norenzayan, 2013). The development of scientific rationality is another example of a universally applicable approach to navigating the natural and social worlds, with the potential for breaking down extant cultural barriers (Parsons, 1971). Rather than being closely identified with ingroup members bound to one another in a spatiotemporally restricted area of *communitas*, people developed the conceptual ability to think of themselves as members of an overarching empire or even human race. In addition to such abstract ideologies, the solidification and centralization of power and resources in the nation-state allowed for the enforcement and maintenance of universalized legal and moral values (Gauchet, 1997; Giddens, 1983). States began to use information as power, reflexively organizing the development of society by marshaling communal resources in a way that was impossible at more communitarian levels of social organization.

Fourth, and most important where the emergence of DESA culture is concerned, cultural reflexivity involved changing ideas of human agency, which Habermas (1987) summarily called the transition to modern individualism. Wittrock (2012) proposes that reflexivity partly consists in "increasing awareness of the *malleability* of human existence, of the potentials of *human action* and human agentiality within the bounds of human mundane temporality" (p. 109; emphases in original). Protective conditions of *immunitas* arose through (among other factors) the institutionalization of: textual sources of commonly accessible cultural information; personal rights guaranteed through universalized legal-moral structures; critical and scientific attitudes toward the natural world and inherited beliefs; and the economic and technological conditions necessary to foster individual job and residential mobility. Whereas non-reflexive *communitas* keeps individuals in an alienated state of felt dependence on external power sources, cultural reflexivity sharpens the boundary line between *Eigenwelt* and *Mitwelt*, carving an ideological space of freedom for individual expression and movement.

Thus – building on the foregoing analysis – reflexivity and DESA culture develop through a dual process of re-appropriation of human potential, a sociological and psychological phenomenon that Gauchet (1997) calls the *reduction of Otherness* and the *increase of interiority*. At the cultural level, immunizing institutions – such as the nation-state and political institutions, science and technology, and modern economic structures – "reduce Otherness" by restoring to society its capacity for mastering and intervening in the natural environment (a capacity originally denied through cultural beliefs). The external environment no longer appears to be a set of transcendent and immovable forces, but rather becomes a more or less pliant stage and resource base for the enactment of human projects. Simultaneously, at the individual level, reflexive consciousness "increases interiority" by more clearly delineating the *Eigenwelt* and transfiguring the self into a source of transcendent meaning, assuming the position once held by God(s) or the world. The modern individual experiences a rich inner world and can feel a strong sense of isolation and independence from the social world around her. As beliefs and institutions increasingly reinforce the agency of both the individual and society at large, people are liberated from the alienation characteristic of DISA culture.

There is a price paid, however, for this immunization and liberation of the individual. Recall the entropy model of uncertainty discussed in connection with the threat of anxiety (Chapter 3). DISA cultures orient individuals away from anxiety by maintaining a perpetual state of low psychological entropy – certain concrete goals are nearly always salient, and there are a relatively small number of culturally sanctioned paths for achieving personal value. By contrast, reflexive, DESA culture offers a proliferating range of possible paths for achieving self-worth, which generates a considerably greater degree of psychological entropy.

Thus, the immunizing institutions of DESA culture operate as a double-edged sword. On the one hand, freedom from the alienation of a binding *communitas* and sociocentric worldview offers the individual great latitude to create their own sense of meaning and to escape feelings of guilt or condemnation angst. In a high-entropy environment, personal setbacks and failures can be perennially attributed to a perceived hostile world or to the probabilistic vagaries of risk. The orientation toward anxiety and uncertainty provided by DESA culture gives the individual the psychological advantage of outsourcing threat to the environment, thereby avoiding any sense of culpability. If the self experiences an accident, it can blame the incident not on its own ineptitude, but rather on an unpredictable world of hazards.

This immunitary logic of self-serving biases and external attributions is crucial in an individualistic culture where personal self-esteem is the ultimate existential resource. However, just as biological immunity is achieved at the cost of temporary exposure to a virus and hence involves a dangerous element, so too can the small doses of psychological entropy perennially encountered in DESA culture create a situation of long-term psychological fragility. These momentary dialectical defenses against the threat of guilt may over time cause the self to lose all conviction that there are values worth pursuing or that the world is navigable and safe, opening the door to meaninglessness angst. In Berger's (1967) terms, DESA culture frees the self from alienation but exposes it to *anomie*. As Esposito (2011) writes:

> The body defeats a poison not by expelling it outside the organism, but by making it somehow part of the body ... the immunitary logic is based more on a

non-negation, on the negation of a negation, than on an affirmation. The negative not only survives its cure, it constitutes the condition of effectiveness. It is as if it were doubled into two halves, one of which is required for the containment of the other: the lesser of two evils is intended to block the greater evil, but in the same language . . . [The individual] must incorporate a fragment of the nothingness that it seeks to prevent, simply by deferring it . . . the immunitary process . . . can prolong life, but only by continuously giving it a taste of death. (pp. 8–9)

Prior research supporting the DISA/DESA distinction

A variety of studies and theoretical perspectives in psychology and sociology support the general DISA/DESA distinction, although no single perspective has comprehensively considered the relationship of cultural worldviews to existential threat in the same manner. Here, I will provide a brief overview of the extant supporting empirical evidence; in Part II of this book, I present some of my own initial studies derived from this framework.

A few major studies have identified dual worldviews that closely parallel the DISA/DESA dualism. One such distinction in sociology arose from decades of longitudinal data (beginning in 1981) collected from nearly one hundred countries through the World Values Survey (Inglehart, 1997; Norris & Inglehart, 2012). This is the distinction between the *survival* values of "traditional" societies existing in a steady-state economy and general existential insecurity (i.e., perceived vulnerability to threats to physical safety), and the *self-expression* or *well-being* values of "post-materialist" societies existing in a largely stable, financialized economy and general existential security (i.e., lack of concern with threats to physical safety). The cross-country, cross-temporal data suggest that as societies become economically secure and technologically advanced (some complicated historically determined variation aside), they tend to de-emphasize obedience to communal and religious authority, and to prioritize the life satisfaction and creativity of individuals. Although these data do not permit much detailed exploration of existential threat concerns, they do support the notion that a shift from CI or CV culture toward IV or II culture is associated with a shift from prioritizing the cultural worldview toward prioritizing self-esteem as an existential resource.

A social-level analysis more attuned to the issue of threat interpretation, but which has remained primarily at the stages of theory and historical exegesis, can be found in Ulrich Beck's (1992) notion of a "risk society," Giddens' (1990) discussion of premodern versus modern "environments of risk," and Mary Douglas' (e.g., Douglas & Wildavsky, 1982) later work on the cultural construction of risk categories. There are certainly important differences between these analyses that I cannot adequately discuss here (for discussions, see Lupton, 2013; Scott, 2000; Wilkinson, 2009). Nevertheless, they broadly converge on the notion that premodern, preindustrial, religious, and/or collectivist cultures tend to orient the individual toward bio-natural threats (disasters, diseases), direct aggression from other humans, or feelings of personal culpability, whereas postmodern, postindustrial, secular, and/or individualist cultures tend to orient the individual toward random technological hazards (car accidents, chemical spills), obscure long-term threats (global warming), or feelings of meaninglessness and diffuse anxiety. These perspectives build on the World Values Survey data by suggesting that traditionalist survival values are accompanied by an orientation toward guilt and shame concerns, while post-materialist self-expression values are accompanied by an orientation toward anxiety and calculable risk.

In psychology, a similar worldview distinction has been made and evaluated at the level of individual (rather than country) data, namely Tomkins' distinction between normativistic and humanistic worldviews (Nilsson, 2014; unpublished data). A normativistic worldview posits that the world exists prior to human interpretation, and that there are values transcendent of humanity "built into" this external world, while a humanistic worldview posits that value is largely a human construction, and humans themselves are the ultimate objects of value. The normativistic worldview has a DISA threat orientation – the ultimate form of nihilism would be disorientation, the disruption of transcendent values – whereas humanism is associated with a DESA orientation and the preservation of individual value. Importantly, built into this theory is the assumption that most individuals do not possess a fully articulated cognitive map of their worldview, but rather experience normativism or humanism as a preponderance of "ideo-affective" or emotional reactions to events (de St. Aubin, 1996). Accordingly, survey data show that these worldviews are inversely related not on more political or epistemological dimensions, but rather with relation to affectively charged domains (Nilsson, 2014). Specifically, normativists tend to believe that humans are inherently flawed and require discipline and emotional control in order to preserve order and meaning, while humanists tend to believe that humans are unconditionally good, and emotional expression and creativity even in defiance of normative structures should be encouraged.

The social constructionist emphasis of the humanist worldview echoes the centrality of reflexivity in DESA orientations. Within social psychology, Baumeister (1999) has highlighted the importance of reflexive consciousness for human experience, and pointed out that a great deal of social psychological research has investigated the pursuits for self-verification, self-esteem, and the escape of self-awareness that are brought about by this psychological capacity. Baumeister (1986; 1987) has also followed in the tradition of the social theorists discussed here by insisting that the problem of reflexivity is especially prominent in those cultures designated Western and (post)modern, where individualism is prominent and the issue of the self's identity and valuation is paramount. The high prevalence of self-serving biases in individualist cultures (which tend to be reduced or less related to personal value in collectivist cultures; Heine & Hamamura, 2007) is a testament to the fact that they afford a DESA orientation.

An interesting question for psychology is how DISA and DESA orientations at the cultural level are translated into everyday psychological experience. Drawing on the foregoing models of existential threat (Chapter 3) and cultural patterns (Chapter 4), the present account suggests that the variables of social orientation and control that underlie DISA versus DESA orientations also predispose the individual to preferentially interpret threatening anomalies in terms of either guilt or anxiety. This general explanation is supported by a considerable body of psychological anthropological research overviewed in Chapter 1. Social psychological studies also provide scattered support for this explanation. Table 5.1 summarizes several relevant studies, each of which provides support for one of the following four hypotheses that can be derived from the DISA/DESA framework (see also Sullivan, 2013):

- Individuals in more collectivist (vs. individualist) cultures should experience less anxiety
- Individuals in more collectivist (vs. individualist) cultures should experience more guilt
- Individuals who are more religious (vs. secular) should experience less anxiety
- Individuals who are more religious (vs. secular) should experience more guilt

Crucially, although the studies presented in Table 5.1 are not numerous, they have operationalized the relevant variables in a variety of divergent ways, strongly implying convergent support for these hypotheses.

But what are the exact social psychological mechanisms through which collectivism and (visibly controlled) religion foster guilt, and individualism/secularity foster anxiety? To a considerable extent, these are questions for future research. The initial step – which I take up in Part II – is to establish the descriptive and predictive value of the DISA/DESA dualism. But two tentative suggestions

Table 5.1. *Extant evidence supporting central hypotheses derived from the DISA/DESA perspective.*

Publication	Summary of findings	Hypothesis supported
Eaton and Weil (1955)	Communitarian Hutterite (compared to non-Hutterite US) patients with mental health difficulties manifest depression and self-blame rather than anxiety	*Religiosity → +Guilt* *Religiosity → −Anxiety*
Leichty (1961)	US (compared to Vietnamese) children more likely to list external events/ forces as greatest fear; Vietnamese (compared to US) children more likely to list offending parents as greatest fear	*Individualism → +Anxiety* *Collectivism → +Guilt*
Gillin (1967)	Individualist Latinos (compared to collectivist Indigenous people) in San Carlos demonstrate greater anxiety and aggression; Indigenous people (compared to Latinos) demonstrate greater negative emotion when they offend others	*Individualism → +Anxiety* *Collectivism → +Guilt*
Dick (1983)	Traditionalist Mennonites (compared to non-Mennonite US citizens) show greater guilt	*Religiosity → +Guilt*
Richards (1991)	Devout (compared to nontraditionally) religious US students showed higher guilt proneness	*Collectivism → +Guilt*
Bierbrauer (1992)	Lebanese and Kurdish (compared to Germans) report greater collectivism and expectation of guilt and shame as a result of norm violations	*Collectivism → +Guilt*
De St. Aubin (1996)	In a US sample, higher scores on a humanistic worldview (related to individualism) measure associated with life narratives featuring distress and fear; higher scores on a normativistic (collectivist) measure associated with low levels of fear	*Individualism → +Anxiety* *Collectivism → −Anxiety*
Singelis, Bond, Sharkey, and Lai (1999)	In samples of Hong Kong, Hawaiian, and mainland US students, more collectivist samples showed higher embarrassability, and independent self-construal was negatively related to embarrassability	*Collectivism → +Guilt* *Individualism → −Guilt*
Twenge (2000)	Meta-analytic reviews of 170 samples of college students and 99 samples of children demonstrate that Americans have become more anxious since the 1950s, likely due to decreases in social connections	*Individualism → +Anxiety*

Table 5.1. (*cont.*)

Publication	Summary of findings	Hypothesis supported
Eid and Diener (2001)	Chinese (compared to Taiwanese, US, and Australian) participants rate guilt as more desirable	*Collectivism → +Guilt*
Abdel-Khalek (2002)	In a large sample of Kuwaiti adolescents, religiosity is associated with lower anxiety	*Religiosity → −Anxiety*
Young and Morris (2004)	Christian Americans report greater anxiety about life decisions (compared to Hindu Indians)	*Individualism → +Anxiety*
Shreve-Neiger and Edelstein (2004)	Review of ten studies demonstrating that greater religiosity (e.g., more frequent church attendance) is associated with lower anxiety	*Religiosity → −Anxiety*
Bedford (2004)	Mandarin (compared to English) speakers make more distinctions between varieties of guilt and shame	*Collectivism → +Guilt*
Hofstede and Hofstede (2005)	In a sample of world countries, more vertically collectivist countries score higher on uncertainty avoidance	*Collectivism → −Anxiety*
Walinga, Corveleyn, and van Saane (2006)	Dutch Christians (compared to Dutch nonreligious citizens) show greater guilt	*Religiosity → +Guilt*
Albertsen, O'Connor, and Berry (2006)	Asian (compared to European and Latin) Americans show higher guilt; Catholics and Protestants (compared to secular people) show higher guilt	*Collectivism → +Guilt* *Religiosity → +Guilt*
Billig (2006)	Secular (compared to religious) Jewish Israelis living in Gaza perceive the region to be more dangerous	*Secularism → +Anxiety*
Sorrentino et al. (2008)	Canadians (compared to Japanese) demonstrate greater uncertainty orientation	*Individualism → +Anxiety*
Bear, Uribe-Zarain, Manning, and Shiomi (2009)	Japanese (compared to US) children report greater guilt and shame and are less likely to externalize blame in connection with transgressions	*Collectivism → +Guilt*
Furukawa, Tangney, and Higashibara (2012)	In large samples of elementary school children, Japanese scored highest on shame, Koreans highest on guilt, and US children highest on pride	*Collectivism → +Guilt* *Individualism → −Guilt*
Norris and Inglehart (2012)	Based on the World Values Survey, individuals in more secularized countries are more likely to report questioning the meaning of life	*Secularism → +Anxiety*
Inozu, Karanci, and Clark (2012)	Highly (compared to less) religious Canadian Christians and Turkish Muslims show greater guilt	*Religiosity → +Guilt*

Table 5.1. (*cont.*)

Publication	Summary of findings	Hypothesis supported
Kesebir and Kesebir (2012)	In a sample of 5 million US books, the frequency of the word "conscience" declined from 1901 to 2000	*Individualism* → −*Guilt* *Secularism* → −*Guilt*
Savani, Morris, and Naidu (2012)	Indian (compared to US) participants express greater guilt when primed with an authority figure after making choices contradicting that figure's wish	*Collectivism* → +*Guilt*
Boiger, Mesquita, Uchida, and Feldman Barrett (2013)	Japanese (compared to US) participants see shame-inducing situations as more common, and experience greater shame in connection with personal, public offenses	*Collectivism* → +*Guilt*
Cheng, Cheung, Chio, and Chan (2013)	In a sample of eighteen countries, external locus of control is more strongly associated with anxiety in individualist (vs. collectivist) nations	*Individualism* → +*Anxiety*
Scheff (2015)	Use of the word "shame" declined, 1800–2000, in English, French, Spanish, and German books	*Individualism* → −*Guilt* *Secularism* → −*Guilt*

regarding process drawn from prior psychological research can be offered here.

An intriguing suggestion made but underdeveloped by Freud is that the individual can experience unconscious emotions that, through processes of culturally conditioned cognitive distortion, can be filtered into consciousness and phenomenologically experienced as alternate emotions. Contemporary neuroscience and emotions research indicates that this may indeed be the case (Johnston & Malabou, 2013; Lazarus, 1991), and that guilt and anxiety in particular may be likely candidate emotions for such defensive processes. Specifically, it has been hypothesized that an individual experiencing what might be a sense of guilt at an unconscious level could be socialized to consciously experience this emotion as anxiety (Mowrer, 1950), and, vice versa, a potentially anxiety-inducing event could be consciously reinterpreted as a source of guilt (Becker, 1973, pp. 213–214). Thus, one possibility is that individuals in DISA cultures are socialized to translate much nonconscious potential for anxiety into conscious guilt, while the opposite is true for individuals in DESA cultures.

A second, complementary mechanism involves how individuals interact with those who are in a threatening or anomalous situation. The interpretations that others form of a person's misfortune are culturally biased and likely influence the person's own interpretation. Consider the case of potentially embarrassing, counter-normative or incompetent actions. Goffman (1959; 1967) astutely revealed how the norms of interpersonal interaction in IV and II cultures are largely built around the preservation of face, the avoidance of any potential for embarrassment on the offender's part. Such reactions on the part of interlocutors are critical to maintaining a DESA orientation – if others constantly respond to our potentially deviant acts by attempting to preserve our self-esteem, then we will likely be successful in inoculating this resource. Consider, however, the many examples of CI and CV cultures that routinely engage in processes of what has been called "reintegrative shaming" (Braithwaite, 1989). Among individuals such as the Kaluli of Papua New Guinea (Schieffelin, 1983), or several more traditionalist Mennonite groups (Rubin, 2000), even fairly minor deviant acts are seized as opportunities for shaming the individual, in the broader interest of maintaining social control. In such settings, maintaining shared values takes precedence over preserving a fragile sense of self-esteem.

Theodicies of self and world

We can summarize and reflect on the foregoing by connecting Esposito's *communitas/immunitas* distinction to the ideas of Hans Jonas. Jonas (1966) contends that, at the outset of human cultural history, people living in a state of *communitas* saw life everywhere around them. They believed in living ancestors, spirits, volitional inanimate objects, and animals with whom they shared a common essence. In this world where *Umwelt*, *Mitwelt*, and *Eigenwelt* blended together in a constant stream of pulsating being, mortality emerged as the primary problem for human consciousness (Langer, 1988). The *communitas* of DISA culture assumes immortality and transcendent meaning as the given background of existence, and is preoccupied with the identification and purgation of death and evil: hence the complex human-centered moral systems, the elaborate schemas connecting physical to ritual impurity and sin, the vivid cosmology and cautionary habitus regarding devils and witches, the rites of purification and expulsion surrounding the guilty, deformed, and corrupt that characterize DISA culture. DISA theodicy is a *theodicy of the world*, one that seeks to control and explain forces of misfortune and death in the world even at the cost of containing personal agency, desire, and esteem – wherein, indeed, it tends to locate the forces of evil. Meaning and life are sheltered against mortality, contingency, and the biological limits of human nature at every turn.

By contrast, Jonas argues that with the rise of reflexivity and modern immunizing institutions, the situation is reversed: the *immunitas* of DESA culture recognizes death and chaos everywhere, and prioritizes the control and protection of individual life at all costs. Modern science reveals a hostile, indifferent, and violent universe, one that is constantly subject to radical change and transmutation. Modern medicine reveals pathogens all around and within us; modern economics holds us in perennial competition with one another for our selfish interests. Yet, despite the chaos and death that haunt our television screens and risk statistics, we continue to see ourselves as immune, because the self has become the new interiorized zone of transcendence, an abstract ideal that eludes all concrete definition and hence escapes the evil and inadequacy of the world. In contrast to the causal categories of DISA culture, the self in DESA culture is never held to account for suffering and misfortune – these problems are calculable, natural elements in a rationally understood yet ever-contingent world. In a dramatic reversal of Berger's formula, anthropodicy has once again become theodicy, or, in other words, DESA culture offers a *theodicy of the self*, a repartee of ideologies and defense mechanisms that preserve the self's abstract value and authenticity by tracing all evil to sources of contagion, risk, and persecution outside the individual.

In this chapter, I have outlined in broad theoretical strokes a world-historical diachronic transition from predominantly DISA to DESA culture. This line of analysis suggests that the DESA threat orientation has become more common as a number of cultures have shifted from a collectivist to an individualist social orientation, and from visible forms of alienating social control to more invisible forms. However, as noted earlier, the primary aim of the last two chapters has not been to provide a new modernization theory or social-historical research; rather, I have drawn on historical analyses to illuminate the social structural origins of cultural ideal types, which can be utilized in comparative research (as will be demonstrated in Part II). All four cultural types identified in Chapter 4 continue to exist in the contemporary world, although no culture conforms perfectly to a particular type, and most blend elements of the different forms of social orientation and control. And DISA and DESA threat orientations persist in diverse settings as cultural options for equipping individuals with modes of threat interpretation and defense. Cultural evolution proceeds at a rapid clip (Tomasello, 1999), and in the modern era of globalization and volatile financial capitalism, unexpected events and cultural exchanges can quickly set cultures on a new trajectory or initiate a period of value conflict. Cultural types have never been stable and contained, but in recent centuries it has become increasingly common for cultures to undergo rapid shifts from one primary form of organization to another, or to experience hybridization. I will explore the implications of this contemporary complexity in the concluding chapter.

Part II

Research

6 Modernization and changes in attitudes toward suffering among Kansas Mennonites

The second part of this book reports a program of research I have conducted as a proof of concept of cultural-existential psychology. It focuses on the experiences of a cultural subgroup in the United States, namely traditionalist Mennonites in Kansas. By examining the role of their culture in the reactions of these individuals to different forms of suffering and threat, using a variety of methods, I hope to demonstrate how one might carry out studies inspired by the perspective presented in Part I.

Following the methodological approach outlined in Chapter 2, I begin my study of the Mennonites by using historical and archival data to examine the broader socio-ecological context of this culture and how it changed over the course of the twentieth century (present chapter). In the subsequent chapters, I turn to a focused examination of one denominational subgroup within the Mennonite family that has retained a traditional CV cultural structure despite ongoing pressures to embrace mainstream US II culture. Chapter 7 uses cultural-comparative survey methods to situate the threat-relevant attitudes of this group in relation to those of other cultural subgroups. Finally, Chapter 8 presents a qualitative investigation of the particular ways in which one congregation within this denomination experienced the existential threat of a highly destructive tornado.

The present chapter contains a historical analysis of how Mennonites in Kansas – a somewhat isolated and culturally intact subgroup at the beginning of the twentieth century – experienced the general movement in the United States toward capitalist modernization and II culture. It draws on historical accounts of the Mennonites' experience and a unique archival survey data set documenting the attitudes of two generations of Mennonites living in one part of the state. More specifically, the aim of this chapter is to examine how culture is linked to particular interpretations of suffering, by demonstrating that the change in general Kansas Mennonite culture from a CV to a more individualist, secular orientation was also associated with changes in attitudes toward misfortune.

To accomplish this aim, I must preliminarily build on the framework presented in Part I by introducing a few additional concepts relevant to the relationship between modernization and attitudes toward suffering. There are many standard ways in which members of different cultures tend to interpret suffering. A distinction that will be critical for this and the following chapters is that between the normative suffering interpretations of CV cultures with a DISA threat orientation, on the one hand, and those of IV and II cultures with a DESA orientation on the other (see Chapters 4 and 5).

In the former type of culture, suffering is often interpreted in one of two ways. The first is what I have called in prior work a *repressive* interpretation of suffering (Sullivan et al., 2012b). Building on Durkheim's (1893/2014) distinction between repressive and restitutive sanctions, the concept of a repressive interpretation involves seeing suffering as caused by antisocial, deviant behavior, and as having the purpose of ultimately strengthening society through the punishment or reform of the deviant. For example, Hallowell (1967) observed that Ojibwe individuals would traditionally interpret diseases as a sign that that they had committed some offense against another person (human or nonhuman), and they believed that the best way to cure their ailment was to confess and atone for their transgression in the presence of the community. In general, the strong emphasis on injunctive norms and attachment to the group in CV culture means that when misfortune strikes, individuals are often prompted to question whether they have broken a moral law or transgressed against their fellows. Furthermore, people in such cultures often consider the suffering of individuals to be a necessary part of maintaining group cohesion and the right moral order in society.

Of course, individuals in such cultures do not always interpret suffering in a repressive fashion. Most CV cultures promote a belief system that posits two worlds or planes of existence, one "false" by virtue of being material/temporal, the other "true" by virtue of being spiritual/eternal (Jaspers, 1979; see also Chapter 4, Table 4.2, p. 101). This worldview affords a second interpretation of suffering centered on *transcendence*. While this interpretation is quite common throughout human history and takes many culturally specific guises, I will explicate here the traditional Christian variant because it is of immediate relevance in understanding the Mennonites' attitudes toward suffering. Nietzsche's late work contains an extended discussion of transcendent approaches to suffering in Christian CV culture (Valadier, 1977). Suffering is devalued in this approach because it occurs on the earthly, inferior plane. At the same time, because Christ redeemed humanity through the Crucifixion, suffering may be "transcended" by seeking spiritual comfort in the metaphysical plane. If the physical realm is viewed merely as "a bridge to that other mode of existence" (Nietzsche, 1888/1967, p. 117), then all misfortune encountered here is merely a test of one's strength and faith; as long as suffering does not cause despair and deviation from the righteous path, the true world will still be obtained. The transcendence view is important in maintaining a DISA threat orientation, because it prevents devalued suffering from calling into question the validity of cultural values.

Nietzsche contrasted this transcendence view with attitudes in modern IV and II cultures, in which the "higher" dimension has collapsed into the pure immanence of the physical world (see Chapter 4). When people no longer believe in a Heavenly sphere, there is no prospect of "vertical" transcendence; there is no higher plane to transcend *to*. Nevertheless, possibilities for new forms of transcendence emerge in secular culture (Taylor, 2007), specifically for what could be called "horizontal transcendence" (Schrag, 1997; Schwartz, 2004). Nietzsche proposed that modern culture emphasizes *self-transcendence* – not overcoming the trials of the material world, but continually overcoming the limits of the self (Kaufmann, 1968).

In the worldviews of IV and II cultures, suffering is not devalued, but rather morally elevated insofar as it is seen as the only route to transcendence. Through suffering, the individual may purge stagnant aspects of the self and encounter opportunities for growth (Reginster, 2009). From this vantage, there is an intrinsic connection between suffering and creativity or regeneration (Geniusas, 2013). The notion of suffering as trial in the classic transcendence model becomes the notion of suffering as transformation. This attitude toward suffering is discussed by psychologists as a secularized *redemptive* interpretation (e.g., McAdams, 2006) and it has become almost dominant in contemporary US discourse about suffering. The popular narrative sees suffering as a highly personal experience, and as containing opportunities for creative self-transcendence. This is one reason for the connection between DESA threat orientation and the proclivity toward anxiety (Chapter 5) – II culture especially encourages the individual to approach stressful and uncertain situations, since these are seen as a vital part of growing and bettering the self.

Thus, the modern redemptive interpretation celebrates suffering as essential to self-overcoming and self-transfiguration. This contrasts with the transcendence interpretation, which holds that suffering is a fact of life but not necessary to achieve life's aim (the salvation of one's soul). The redemptive view also differs from a repressive interpretation, which sees suffering as an indicator of deviance and hence to be avoided if possible. Quite differently, a redemptive interpretation involves the ready acceptance and even active willing of suffering in a self-focused quest for power, renewal, and creativity.

Some preliminary evidence from my laboratory supports the proposed association between different cultural orientations and these different forms of suffering interpretation. For example, in one study, undergraduate participants completed measures of immersion in the worldviews of humanism (representative of a DESA orientation) and normativism (representative of a DISA orientation; see Chapter 5). Participants then were asked to rate their level of agreement with several statements presenting possible interpretations of the suffering that comes from depression. Some of the items represented more repressive interpretations, such as "Having depression is a sign that a person needs to return to their social group, community, or family," while others captured a redemptive interpretation (e.g., "Having depression can be an opportunity for personal growth and development"). As anticipated, normativism (DISA) was positively associated with endorsement of repressive interpretations of depression, but not with redemptive interpretations; the opposite was true for humanism (DESA).

Do these theoretical relationships hold when examining the cultural situations and suffering-relevant attitudes of specific cultural groups? This will be the major theme of the present and subsequent chapters. Here, I will consider the historical question of whether modernization in the United States and a general movement toward II culture was linked with a rise in redemptive suffering interpretations. As a case study to investigate this global possibility, I will consider Kansas Mennonites, who experienced considerable modernization in the twentieth century at a more gradual pace relative to other US subgroups. To begin with, I will provide general background on Mennonite culture.

An overview of Mennonite culture

Traditionalist Mennonite culture. Before proceeding with any analysis of "Mennonite culture," it is important to acknowledge that there is and has been great variety among Mennonite groups in patterns of social organization as well as beliefs and traditions. Cultural variety among Mennonites is due not only to a historical proclivity toward ideological and social schism, but also to inevitable infringement by processes of modernization and globalization which affect different communities in different ways (Driedger, 2000; Redekop, 1989). In this section, I will be discussing Mennonite culture as an "ideal type" within the somewhat broader context of Anabaptism, averaging across the behavioral and ideological patterns of multiple subgroups that would fall on the more traditionalist end of a hypothetical spectrum. This discussion therefore applies most straightforwardly to more conservative groups such as Old Colony or Old Order Mennonites, or to other larger denominations as they existed prior to the 1950s and cultural assimilation. Detailed consideration of the particular groups of interest for the present research will follow this more general discussion.

Mennonites are part of the broader Christian family of Anabaptists, a post-Reformation branch which also includes the Amish and the Hutterites. The majority of the Mennonites in the United States emigrated from Europe or Russia at various intervals during the past 300 years. Within North America, many Mennonite groups have engaged in further patterns of internal migration. Redekop (1989) and others have argued that the strong degree of cultural cohesion displayed at one time by many Mennonites was due in large part to their historical status as a migrant people, moving both between and within nations to avoid persecution or seek better farmland. The Mennonite pattern has been to move to a new territory and establish an independent community wherein members can look inward for support rather than outward to the larger, foreign society (Redekop, 1989). Although this trend has broken down for many groups in the past half-century, for many decades Mennonite migration preempted influence by the traditions and politics of any particular nation, resulting in strong retention of Mennonite culture and a lack of assimilation to nationalist norms.

This unusual level of cultural cohesion meant that, until the mid-twentieth century (and continuing today for certain denominations), many Mennonite communities could be considered instantiations of CV culture. Relevant to the social orientation variable, Mennonite culture has traditionally been highly sociocentric (Carlson, Taylor, & Levin, 1998). In most Mennonite communities, it is implicitly accepted that the self is largely constituted by social relationships, and that the ultimate goal of behavior is to uphold the community rather than to benefit the individual (Redekop, 1989). Smucker (1986) proposes that Mennonites commonly harbor a perception of "abstract reciprocity" vis-à-vis their local community: individuals believe that they could rely heavily on aid from other families were they to somehow fall upon hard times. The Church symbolizes the cohesion of the community, and the family unit operates as a kind of symbolic mediating level between the individual and the wider community (Redekop, 1989; Smucker, 1986).

Relevant to the social control variable, many Mennonite groups possess a system of visible control that largely dictates individual behavior. Indeed, in a study of Canadian citizens, Altemeyer and Hunsberger (1992) found that Mennonite participants scored higher on Right-Wing

Authoritarianism (and lower on a religious quest scale) than participants belonging to any other religious denomination. These attitudes begin with early socialization: parenting styles in traditionalist Anabaptist communities tend to be quite authoritarian (Rubin, 2000; Schludermann & Schludermann, 1971). In Old Order Mennonite groups, children are brought up to accept an idealized code of social living that Cronk (1981) referred to as *Ordnung*: "Rules and regulations define how members live together. Although the *Ordnung* deals with ethics, it encompasses much more than the word ethics usually implies. The *Ordnung* orders all facets of life, from the furnishings of the house to the manner of earning a living" (p. 6). *Ordnung* (or visible social control) for more conservative Anabaptist groups stems from two primary sources. The first is a strict literalist interpretation of the Bible as containing all true knowledge about the world and how one should behave in it, because it provides access to the will of God (e.g., Gillin, 1948). The second, more implicit source of social control is an internalized sense of humility and deference to authority. Although ostensibly Anabaptist churches eschew centralized authority, power dynamics are nevertheless quite relevant to life in traditionalist Mennonite communities. For instance, major life decisions are almost never made without consulting one's elders and church authorities (Gillin, 1948; Hartman, 2001).

Within a world encompassed by *Ordnung*, the individual is perpetually aware of the potential penalties for breaking away from the established grid of acceptable behavior (Enns, 2010). Perceived excess egoism is punished; individualistic action that is not condoned by the community or that deviates too far from custom can result in severe excommunication and shunning behavior or boycotts (Driedger, 1982). The anthropologist Bernard Siegel (1955; 1970) described the Hutterites in particular as an example of a "defensive group": an enclave society with constant concerns about threats to their identity from a broader mainstream culture. Siegel argued that such groups develop certain visible control mechanisms to maintain their identity, including comprehensive values through which all activities and events are viewed; centralization of authority (in patriarchs and ministers); clear symbols of identity (e.g., distinct modes of dress); and the maintenance of concerns with possible guilt over deviant behavior.

Traditionally, Anabaptists instilled the sense of *Ordnung* through "comprehensive socialization" of their children into the community (Hostetler, 1974). Children in the DESA culture of the middle-class, mainstream United States are seen as uniquely attached to their parents, but they are expected to develop their own personalized worldview through a critical, liberal education. By contrast, children in traditionalist

Mennonite communities are seen as "belonging" to the community as a whole, rather than to their parents: all adults in the community display affection and secure attachment to the child, but also participate in their disciplining and socialization (Boynton, 1986; Hostetler, 1974). Children are socialized early to play clearly established roles within the community system of normative behavior. Supporting this, Carlson et al. (1998) found that children in Old Order Mennonite communities engaged in schoolyard play more focused on actual future roles (e.g., mother, father) compared to the fantasy play engaged in by more progressive Mennonite and non-Mennonite children. Earlier research (Kuhn, 1954) indicated that Amish and Mennonite children in grades 4–8, when asked to list the activities they most enjoyed and most wished to avoid, were more likely to list activities associated with adult rather than child roles (e.g., farming or housewife roles) compared to non-Anabaptist children.

All this suggests that traditionalist Mennonites best approximate the CV variant of culture. As the United States accelerated into a paradigmatic II culture over the course of the twentieth century, these "plain people" became in many ways fish out of water – a DISA enclave defining itself against a surrounding DESA society. While no culture or subculture in history has been a "pure" example of the ideal types presented in Chapter 4, traditionalist Mennonite culture can certainly not be considered "pure" CV culture insofar as it has always had to accommodate other cultural variants in order to persist (Driedger, 2000). Some Anabaptist subgroups have been relatively more successful at preserving elements of a CV and DISA cultural orientation; I will discuss in detail the case of one particular group in Chapters 7 and 8. For present purposes, we must now consider how the majority of Mennonite groups in the United States gradually shifted in the mid-twentieth century away from their traditional CV and toward mainstream II culture.

Mennonites and modernization. Redekop (1989) and Driedger (1973) propose that many Mennonites have undergone a historical process of integration into modern US culture. These scholars identify various stages in this evolution of Mennonite religiosity and social organization toward greater modernization and assimilation.

When Mennonites first established themselves in persecuted enclaves in Reformation Europe, they lived according to what Redekop calls a *theocratic* model – Mennonites lived together in a confined and geographically isolated space, and all social and economic institutions were coterminous with the religious community. Today, Redekop proposes, only the Hutterites retain the theocratic model of social life. Many non-Hutterite Anabaptist groups have historically passed through variations of what Redekop (1989) calls the *commonwealth* and *community* models, or what Driedger (1973) called the *European village* and *isolated community* models. In the former, Mennonite groups have been temporarily granted asylum within a particular nation, and largely allowed to maintain their own institutions (e.g., schools). Mennonites in this model are, however, occasionally forced to interact with political and economic representatives of the country they inhabit, and thus come to see themselves as having a certain national identity outside of their religious identity. As an example, this commonwealth model characterized life for Mennonites in mid-nineteenth-century Russia prior to their immigration to North America, including the Kansas Alexanderwohl group that will be the focus of this chapter.

Upon immigration to the United States, Mennonite groups initially endeavored to set up village structures that were self-contained and mirrored those of Europe or Russia (Driedger, 1973). However, most Mennonites were gradually forced (by US political and economic policies; Juhnke, 1975; Parker, 2005; Stevenson & Everson, 1990) to transition to the community model. In this model, congregation members still live in geographic proximity to one another and in relative rural isolation from nearby non-Mennonites, permitting the preservation of a sense of separate identity. Into the beginning of the twentieth century for most groups, and well into the century for more conservative branches, the retention of an agricultural lifestyle and traditional German dialects for services and education shielded this sense of identity (Driedger, 1973). Nevertheless, in the community model, integration with the surrounding non-Mennonite society becomes more necessary and advanced. A division arose between dealings that pertain to the group's religious identity (e.g., family prayers and celebrations; church services; Mennonite conferences) and more worldly activities (e.g., business interactions with non-Mennonites).

During the second half of the twentieth century, most Mennonites in the United States completed the transition to an *individualistic* or *ethnic urban* mode of life that is not easily distinguishable from the lifestyle of most middle-class, Caucasian Americans (Driedger, 1973; Meyer, 2003; Redekop, 1989). Global modernization processes were primarily responsible for the final shift from a relatively sheltered agricultural lifestyle dominated by religious belief to an urbanized existence guided by the same individualistic concerns found among most US citizens today. In terms of everyday experience, these broader transitions manifested for Mennonites in the formation or growth of more liberal Anabaptist denominations, increasingly greater economic and social (including intermarriage) contact with non-Mennonites, diversification of careers beyond the traditional agricultural orientation, and relocation to cities in pursuit of work (Driedger, 1973; Loewen, 2006; Stevenson & Everson, 1990).

The consequences of these changes have been empirically documented: in two large-scale survey studies of North American members of major Mennonite denominations in 1972 and 1989, Driedger (2000) and his collaborators found that those who still lived rural, farm-based lives had a stronger orientation toward moral norms and religious orthodoxy, while those who had migrated to cities were increasingly civically involved outside of their Mennonite identity. Beyond urbanism, general changes in technology that have almost universally accelerated processes of modernization also had their effect on the US Mennonites. For instance, Driedger (2000) and colleagues found substantial negative correlations in their survey between use of mainstream media (e.g., television ownership) and a host of traditional Mennonite beliefs, including moralistic behaviors and perceived conflict between Mennonite faith and the surrounding world.

It should be pointed out that, in some important ways, Mennonites have actually become *less* self-sufficient and individualistic as a result of their assimilation to US culture. Farmers always possess a certain amount of economic independence (Fromm & Maccoby, 1970), and this is especially the case in Anabaptist groups who have resisted dependence on economic systems connected to the larger society (Eaton & Weil, 1955). Naturally, as Mennonites have assimilated, they have become increasingly dependent on the products and financial institutions of commercial society. It is important, however, to recognize that this decline in *action* autonomy (i.e., in the ability to live self-sufficiently and exert control over one's economic fate) has been contemporaneous with a rise in *psychological* autonomy (Keller, 2012), as many Mennonites have broken away from the visible social control enforced in their traditional communities.

In recent decades, Mennonite theologians have grappled with the questions of what remains unique about their faith and practice as compared to other Christian traditions, and the exact manner in which traditional articles of faith should be reconciled with widespread contemporary reflexivity (A. P. Weaver, 1996; J. D. Weaver, 1997). Placing aside issues of theological detail, for many Mennonites, the end of the twentieth century brought about the completion of the evolution of Mennonitism from a religious worldview to a primarily ethnic or ancestral grouping, a process set in motion at the century's beginning (Francis, 1948). I will now consider this general process in the specific context of the Kansas General Conference Mennonites, from whom the data presented in this chapter were obtained.

A historical case study: Kansas General Conference Mennonites

Modernization and assimilation of the Kansas Mennonites. The case study presented in this chapter is based on data obtained in 1980 from members of the General Conference Mennonite denomination living in the central Kansas towns of Newton and Goessel (Engbrecht, 1985). The participants were primarily descendants of the "Alexanderwohl" group of Mennonites who immigrated to Kansas to escape persecution in Russia in the 1870s (although this group was of Prussian origin and spoke German; Kaufman, 1973). At the time of data collection, these participants ranged in age from having been born around 1900 to having been born around 1940. They came from families with an agricultural background and strong, separatist religious identity. However, following the general trends of modernization identified in the preceding section, members of these churches underwent a significant degree of incorporation over the course of their lifetimes into the wider individualist, capitalist, and urban pathways of US society (Engbrecht, 1985; Janzen, 1914).

As discussed, the period of 1900–1980 was one of substantial change and adaption to mainstream US cultural and economic values for many Mennonites (Driedger, 2000; Meyer, 2003), and the Mennonites in these particular churches were no exception. As Loewen (2006) writes of a similar Mennonite community in a nearby area of Kansas:

> Between 1930 and 1980 the majority of [Kansas] Mennonites reformulated the foundation of their culture. The social basis of a communitarian and nonconformist ethnoreligious identity had weakened. Technology, government programs, and farm markets demanded increased farm sizes, more concerted interaction with a wider world, and migration into town. (p. 100)

Alexanderwohl Mennonites born at the beginning of this transitional era experienced middle age in the 1950s, during a final period of reactionary Mennonite religious revival (Meyer, 2003). However, those born closer to 1940 were experiencing middle age at the end of this era, when Mennonite identity (for nonconservative groups such as the General Conference Mennonites) had become just one more form of denominational identity in the United States.

Two primary historical factors affected the Mennonites of Kansas in the first part of the twentieth century. The first was the advent of the World Wars, which virtually forced Mennonites to abandon the longstanding sense of cultural differentiation they derived from the German language, and also demanded a revisionary stance toward their religious ideals of pacifism and political noninvolvement (Juhnke, 1975). The second was the "Great Disjuncture": the well-documented transition of most rural family farmers in the United States to an entirely different lifestyle as a result of the onslaught of commercialized agriculture (Loewen, 2006).

Waves of nationalism coincided with spikes in urbanism, technology, and commercialization throughout the Midwest in the wake of each World War. Two institutions in General Conference Mennonite life changed dramatically during this same period, and became gateways from religious separation to assimilated urbanism. I refer to education and the practice of Mennonite religiosity itself. Whereas those Alexanderwohl Mennonites born before 1920 would likely have attended German-language, Mennonite schools, those born after World War I were educated in public schools in English, largely as a result of changes to Kansas law induced by postwar patriotism (Engbrecht, 1985; Janzen, 1914; Stevenson & Everson, 1990). Beyond linguistic assimilation, education generally played an increasingly important role in the lives of these Mennonites throughout the first half of the century. Stevenson and Everson (1990) reported that the percentage of Alexanderwohl Mennonites who attained 12 or more years of formal education increased dramatically over the period of 1900–1950, from 20% at the beginning of the period to 90% at its conclusion. Local Mennonite institutions of higher learning – the most prominent being Bethel College in North Newton – also became increasingly progressive during this time and served as a path to worldliness for many young Mennonites (Engbrecht, 1985).

A major historical event that facilitated the transition for many Mennonites in Kansas and elsewhere into mainstream US society was the spread of evangelicalism in the Midwest during the post-World War II decades. As the double threats of loosened social strictures and atheistic communism were trumpeted by the media and conservative politicians, many Americans living in more rural areas experienced a revival of religious activity. For Kansas Mennonite groups increasingly interested in expanding their economic activities into the wider social world, evangelicalism provided a theological bridge that legitimated reform of and breakout from the older, communalistic model imported from Russia. Evangelicalism's emphasis on proselytization and ideological conflict between Christians and non-Christians helped Mennonites rationalize increased contact with the wider world, travel, and even urban relocation as they began to identify more broadly with Protestantism (Loewen, 2006). Juhnke (1975) suggests that Christian fundamentalism – which often had a patriotic bent – was a stepping stone for some Mennonites away from traditional doctrines of noninvolvement and into the US political community. Furthermore, evangelicalism imported a large dose of individualism into the Mennonite religious orientation, given the stress it placed on personal conversion and individual relationship with God (Redekop, 1989).

In addition to these transformations of extant Mennonite institutions, the World Wars led to the initiation and expansion of new institutions that played a pivotal role in modernization. In particular, Driedger (2000) highlights the founding of the Mennonite Central Committee (MCC) in 1920. Initially designed as a mechanism through which flourishing US Mennonite communities could assist suffering Mennonites in other countries, the MCC transitioned during World War II to become an outlet for alternative service for pacifist Mennonite youth. Rather than travel overseas to fight, Mennonites stayed at home and worked in forestry service and mental hospitals. After the war, the MCC continued to expand, exposing Mennonite youth of the 1950s and 1960s to the wider world through agencies such as Mennonite Disaster Relief that became increasingly international (Driedger, 2000). A prototypical example is the case of Delbert Wiens, who was born in 1931 and attended Tabor College in Kansas before traveling to Vietnam in 1954 on behalf of the MCC (Homan, 2000). After a three-year stay in the country, working in the midst of a radically different culture under conditions of growing violence and poverty, Wiens had transitioned from immersion in insular Anabaptist culture to become an "ecumenical Mennonite." "[Wiens'] stay in Vietnam had been a growing experience. The same can be said of many MCC workers ... In spite of his parents' concern he had not been 'corrupted' by 'modernism,' wearing shorts, and some occasional wine drinking" (Homan, 2000, p. 23). As a largely unintended result of the global politics of the 1940s, Mennonites in Kansas and elsewhere began in the following decades to orient their traditional altruistic ideals beyond their ingroup and toward humanity as a whole, which in turn had the unintended result of facilitating assimilation.

While changes in broad US culture generated by the World Wars elicited parallel changes in Kansas Mennonite culture, the economic trials of the 1930s forced their own set of transformations to Mennonite occupational and social structure. In Kansas as elsewhere, the "Great Disjuncture" between agricultural and urbanized life was largely catalyzed by the Great Depression. Farmers who had always relied on wheat crops for their livelihood suddenly found them gone. For the Mennonites, this meant a heretofore-unprecedented reliance on government aid and insurance programs in direct contradiction to their traditional separatist convictions. When the Depression ended, Mennonites eager to recuperate from hardship were more willing than previously to adopt novel technology and approaches to land management imported from the US government and the wider world (Loewen, 2006).

In Russia, largely to accommodate national property laws, the Alexanderwohl Mennonites developed a communalized system of land allocation and centralized oversight of inheritance (Longhofer, 1986; 1993). Immediately upon immigration to the Midwest in the 1870s, conditions changed so that a more competitive and household-managed approach to ownership and inheritance took root (Longhofer, 1993). Nevertheless, throughout the nineteenth century, families continued Mennonite traditions of equality in the distribution of resources. For instance, these families practiced partible inheritance, whereby property was split equally between all offspring throughout the parents' lifetimes and upon their death, and they maintained a considerable degree of financial independence by essentially acting as their own banks, with parents managing complex loans to their offspring (Quadagno & Janzen, 1987).

However, the accelerated commercialization of agriculture in the United States in the twentieth century led the Alexanderwohl Mennonites ever further away from the communal village model they had practiced in Russia (Longhofer, 1986). The agricultural occupational structure and network of family farms that had undergirded the communal lifestyle declined. In the wake of the Depression, many Kansas Mennonites shifted toward alternative means of work, leaving their farms behind and migrating to growing cities to seek employment as wage laborers or small business owners (Loewen, 2006). For example, among the Alexanderwohl Mennonites, agricultural occupations began to decline sharply around 1920, while the percentage practicing mixed agriculture or performing nonagricultural jobs began to increase from this time and into the 1950s (Stevenson & Everson, 1990).

Empirical evidence concerning modernization of the Alexanderwohl Mennonites. As mentioned, I obtained data that had been collected from members of three Alexanderwohl Mennonite churches in central Kansas in 1980 by researchers then working at the University of Kansas. The data represent an unusually rich set of structural, behavioral, and psychological records. They were originally collected as part of a large study on lifestyle and aging that yielded several publications relating to heritability and physiological markers (e.g., Crawford, 2000).

The data came from the Goessel, Tabor, and Alexanderwohl congregations in the towns of Newton and Goessel. All these congregations were offshoots of the original "Alexanderwohl" immigrant group. The participants ranged in age at the time of data collection from 42 to 82, with the average age being 61. The participants completed a wide variety of measures (Bowerman & Penner, 1981; Stull et al., 1981). Primarily, the data I will draw upon came from a large packet of psychological questionnaires that volunteers from the congregations completed at their local churches. In addition, some of the participants were asked to complete a more extensive, ecological "diary" reporting their activities, movements, and interactions in the course of an average week. Finally, physiological and genetic measures were also obtained, which have been analyzed elsewhere (Crawford, 2000).

These data came from distinct, identifiable "generations" within the Alexanderwohl group, which makes them especially valuable for studying processes of historical transition (the first method identified in Chapter 2, Figure 2.2, p. 42). In short order, I will present analyses of these data that examine intergenerational variability in interpretations of suffering. However, prior to examining the data at an intergenerational level, it should be noted that across the entire data set, observed patterns support the general hypothesis (discussed in the preceding section) that members of these churches underwent considerable modernization in their lifetimes. More specifically, prior analyses of the data reported in Sullivan, Stewart, and Diefendorf (2015) demonstrated that there was considerable variability among these Mennonites in the extent to which they had assimilated to a more modern lifestyle and an individualist culture.

To conduct these analyses, we first classified some variables as representative of a modern habitus or lifestyle. Recall from Chapter 4 that individualist cultures are characterized by a phenomenological situation of *abstracted independence*, which includes greater geographic mobility and interaction with a wider range of individuals (strangers, as well as acquaintances who are geographically separated and communicated with indirectly via technology; Palitsky et al., in press). Drawing on this analysis, we constructed our measure of a modernized lifestyle by combining reports (for a representative week) of (1) the number of distinct settings participants visited (geographic mobility); (2) the number of strangers and non-acquaintances (e.g., commercial transaction partners) with whom they interacted; and (3) the number of indirect communications (e.g., telephone calls, letters) made. We then classified other variables as representative of more modernized attitudes and goals. The orientational framework presented in Chapter 4 (see Table 4.2, p. 101) suggests that people in II culture are oriented to see time as a valuable resource, and they are motivated for personal achievement, which implies a long-term goal structure. Accordingly, we constructed our measure of modernized attitudes and goals by combining self-reported levels of (1) valuing time as a resource and (2) possessing long-term goals. Finally, the egocentric worldview and independent self-construal characteristic of modern individualism (see Chapters 4 and 5) imply that individuals who have assimilated to modernism will be more invested in economic and leisure-related values. Thus, we constructed a measure of individualist values by combining self-reported levels of (1) investment in economic/consumer values and (2) investment in leisure-related values (e.g., expressing the self through hobbies).

Consistent with a general modernization hypothesis, we found that there was considerable variability among the Alexanderwohl Mennonites on each of these variables, but they were nevertheless related in an expected pattern. Those who scored higher on our measure of a modernized lifestyle scored higher on our measure of modernized attitudes and goals, and the latter measure was in turn positively associated with individualist values. The variability and observed patterns confirm that these were people who experienced considerable change in their group lifestyle and values over the course of their life spans. Despite the telling variability, birth year across the data set was positively associated with more modernized attitudes and goals, as well as individualist values, supporting the notion that over time the Alexanderwohl Mennonites assimilated to mainstream II culture. This contention is further borne out by intergenerational analyses of differences in suffering interpretation, to which I now turn.

Modernization and changing attitudes toward suffering among the Alexanderwohl Mennonites

I propose that as the Alexanderwohl Mennonites experienced modernization and the transition from a more CV to a more II culture characteristic of the mainstream United States, their interpretations of the causes and consequences of suffering likely underwent parallel changes driven by this broader cultural transformation. More specifically, following the general hypothesis suggested at the outset of this chapter, I would expect that as the younger Mennonites in the sample assimilated to individualism, they became more likely to interpret suffering in a redemptive light. Before discussing the results of the study, I will provide a final piece of background regarding Mennonite conceptions of suffering.

Traditional Mennonite conceptions of suffering. Because Anabaptists trace their origins to a persecuted branch of the Reformation, and see themselves as descendants of immigrants forced to move from one society to another, there is a special emphasis in traditional Mennonite theology on the role of suffering in Christian life. Indeed, the *Martyrs' Mirror* (van Braght, 1660/1938) – an edited volume compiling stories of Anabaptist martyrs – is considered a foundational text of Anabaptism and is to this day one of the few books conventionally permitted in more traditionalist Mennonite or Amish homes. In keeping with the foregoing analysis of traditional Mennonite culture as having CV characteristics, probably the most common interpretation of suffering in the tradition is that of suffering as transcendence (Dyck, 1985; Rubin, 2000). Much more will be said about this approach to suffering among a particular traditionalist Mennonite branch in Chapter 8. For now, it is sufficient to point out that in the past many Mennonites thought of suffering as an earthly trial that could be borne through God's love.

At the same time, Mennonites have also exemplified CV culture in their traditional tendency to conceive of suffering repressively, as a potential indicator of personal deviance or a "straying away" from the tenets of the faith (Redekop, 1989). This attention to deviance is exemplified by the principle of "the Ban," shunning, and excommunication, which – although currently not practiced by the majority of Mennonite groups – was formerly the most prominent mode of Mennonite social control (Redekop, 2001). The social enforcement of this principle was justified intellectually by a theodicy common among traditionalist Mennonites, which sees earthly suffering as the fate to which humans are condemned by Original Sin and their proclivity toward willful disobedience from God (J. D. Weaver, 1997). Members of some traditionalist Anabaptist communities have interpreted their own suffering repressively and been plagued by guilt when they experience dissatisfaction with group life (Rubin, 2000). This proclivity toward moralistic interpretations of suffering often coexists with a desire to heal the sick and reform the wayward in CV cultures (Braithwaite, 1989; Douglas, 1978), and the Mennonites are no exception. As will be discussed in Chapter 7, shunning is typically practiced by more traditionalist groups with the aim of eventually reaccepting reformed members, which actually occurs with high frequency.

Thus, as would be expected from a traditionally CV culture, Mennonites have historically interpreted suffering either in transcendent or in repressive terms. However, if the Kansas Alexanderwohl Mennonites shifted culturally toward individualism as a function of modernization processes over the twentieth century, then one should observe a corresponding shift toward more redemptive interpretations.

The empirical study. I tested this possibility in the aforementioned archival data, using a cross-sectional, generational approach (Elder, 1995). Approximately half the participants ($n = 29$, 18 female) belonged to the generation born between 1900 and 1920, which I refer to henceforth as the "older generation." The other half ($n = 27$, 13 female) belonged to the generation born between 1920 and 1940, which I will refer to as the "younger generation."

Generational status. Defining a "generation" in historical or longitudinal research is no easy matter. Cohler and Hostetler (2003) discuss many of the complex issues involved. Researchers agree that those born in a 15–30-year cohort experience a generally similar sociohistorical world and pattern of historical events during their lifetimes. In the present data set, the dividing line of 20 years (before and after 1920) was chosen partly for matters of practical convenience and statistical power – grouping the participants in a 20-year cohort was the best way to evenly divide the data between two generational groups, while still maintaining enough power to reasonably test basic hypotheses.

But of course the age range of a particular group of people is not the only relevant factor. At some moments in history, many more critical events (e.g., wars, major famines, technological developments) may occur in the span of a decade than may have occurred in the preceding three decades. When considering the relative weight to place on such issues, a life course approach – which emphasizes the "timing" of lives by linking structural processes of universal development to historical, generation-specific events – is useful (e.g., Cohler & Hostetler, 2003; Elder, 1995; Hareven, 1991). Within this general approach, some perspectives would suggest that infancy and childhood are a period during which the quality of social relationships and exposure to culturally significant historical events could have a lasting impact (Keller & Kärtner, 2013; Nelson, 2007; Simpson, Collins, & Salvatore, 2011). On the other hand, a great deal of research suggests that historical and person-specific events experienced in late adolescence and young adulthood are potentially of primary importance in determining not only an autobiographical self-concept but also a sense of generational belonging (Cohler & Hostetler, 2003; Habermas & Bluck, 2000).

Considering the Alexanderwohl Mennonites in the present sample, all of the members of the older generation had achieved the stage of preadolescence by 1930, and many of them were by this time well into young adulthood, while the members of the younger generation did not all achieve preadolescence until closer to 1950. Viewing the generations in this way, the 1930s appear as a pivotal decade; arguably the most important years of development were completed for most members of the older generation before or during the 1930s. Significantly, the 1930s were a critical decade for Mennonites in the United States. As Loewen (2006) argues, Kansas Mennonites

> shared a common mindset in the 1930s and even as late as 1937, when the Great Depression began lifting. Their mindset represented a "culture," a concept defined by Clifford Geertz as a "frame … of meaning within which people live and form their convictions, their selves and their solidarities." They were mostly agrarian people, committed to age-old ideas of communitarian cohesion, a stubborn anticonsumerism, a sectarian cosmology, and an implicit antimodernism … They were especially skeptical of modernity with its promises of consumer culture, government programs, and agricultural science … In this account, the 1930s marked a last decade of conservative cohesion. The cultural crescendo of this decade occurred in 1937 … [which] marked a wider recovery from the Great Depression and [the start of] four decades of profound change (pp. 229–231)

Building on Loewen's analysis, I suggest that the division of the Alexanderwohl data into an older and younger generation, however blunt and artificial, nevertheless approximates a reasonable division between those Mennonites who were primarily socialized into the "old way of life" and those who were socialized during decades of rapid assimilation.

Relevant measures. In order to examine generational differences among the Alexanderwohl Mennonites in the relation between culture and interpretations of suffering, I used the 1980 psychological data to construct measures of collectivism and individualism, as well as both redemptive and repressive interpretations of suffering (for correlations and descriptive statistics for all measures, see Appendix B).

For the cultural measures, I used items that were originally constructed and administered to test hypotheses from Bowerman's (1978) subjective competence theory (see Bowerman & Penner, 1981). Participants were asked to evaluate several different categories of activity, and rate the extent to which "My activities in this area are satisfying and meaningful for me" as well as "I find that my activities in this area are *less* satisfying and meaningful than they used to be." One additional, similar item for each activity type was included, and responses were re-coded so that higher scores indicated greater perceived meaning attached to the activity. An exploratory factor analysis suggested that ratings of the meaningfulness of seven different activities broke down into two factors, which corresponded to collectivism and individualism. Specifically, I constructed the collectivism measure based on ratings of the meaningfulness of activities related to *family, church*, and *community*, while I constructed the individualism measure based on ratings of *health, household, leisure*, and *income* activities.

To construct a measure of redemptive suffering interpretations, I averaged participants' level of agreement with the items "Many of the mistakes I make teach me lessons that are helpful later on," "When

I make a mistake I like to find out why I made it, and then try to learn from the mistake," and "I think that in the long run I just about always profit from mistakes." Higher scores indicated greater level of agreement with these items on a 1–5 scale. While these items do not necessarily address suffering directly, they were the only available items that related to redemptive interpretations, and it can be assumed that individuals who would interpret minor and major mistakes redemptively would be predisposed to interpret instances of suffering in a similar way.

To construct a measure of repressive suffering interpretations, I summed participants' responses to a series of five dichotomous questions. For three of the items, participants indicated "Yes" or "No" in response to the prompts: "I sometimes think when people have a misfortune they only got what they deserved," "I have never felt that I was punished without cause," and "I would never think of letting someone else be punished for my wrongdoings." A "Yes" response to each item was considered an indicator of repressive suffering interpretations. Additionally, for the two remaining items, participants were asked to choose between two statements. First, participants were asked whether they agreed more with the statement "Children get into trouble because their parents punish them too much," versus the statement "The trouble with most children nowadays is that their parents are too easy with them." Second, participants chose between the statements "Many of the unhappy things in people's lives are partly due to bad luck" and "People's misfortunes result from the mistakes they make." For both response pairs, choosing the second option was counted as a preference for repressive interpretations. I coded and summed the data such that higher composite scores indicate a greater proclivity toward repressive suffering interpretations.

Results. Here I will summarize the results of the study; details of the statistical analysis are provided in Appendix B. Across the entire sample, individualism was positively associated with redemptive interpretations, and negatively associated with repressive interpretations, supporting the theorized links between culture and suffering interpretation.

Findings pertinent to the differences between generations also generally supported the foregoing modernization account. For instance, one of the only observed gender differences in the data was that women in the younger generation were more individualistic compared to women in the older generation, while the latter were relatively less individualistic compared to the men of their generation. This reinforces prior analyses both of Kansas General Conference Mennonites (Loewen, 2006) and of Mennonites in general (Anderson & Driedger, 1980), suggesting that a major aspect of modernization was the increasing freedom of women to play important roles outside of housekeeping and childrearing.

Additionally, the relationship between the orientations of individualism and collectivism varied between generations. Among the older generation, these two orientations were strongly associated, while they were less so among the younger generation. One interpretation of this finding, consistent with the foregoing account, is that individualism began to emerge more clearly as a separate cultural orientation in the younger generation, reflecting its greater assimilation to the surrounding II culture. Whereas the older generation did not distinguish psychologically between, say, their economic and community-related activities, the younger generation began to recognize an increasing distinction and possible tension between individual and communal concerns.

Most importantly for a cultural-existential analysis, the *relationship* between culture and interpretations of suffering differed between the two generations. It was not the case that the younger generation showed an overall greater tendency toward redemptive interpretations. However, as indicated by Figures 6.1A and 6.1B, collectivism and individualism were differentially predictive of redemptive interpretations in a manner consistent with the modernization account. Among the older generation, collectivism was negatively associated with redemptive interpretations, suggesting that only those who were less incorporated into the dominant cultural ethos were likely to interpret suffering in a redemptive manner. However, among the younger generation, while both collectivism and individualism positively predicted redemptive interpretations, the effect

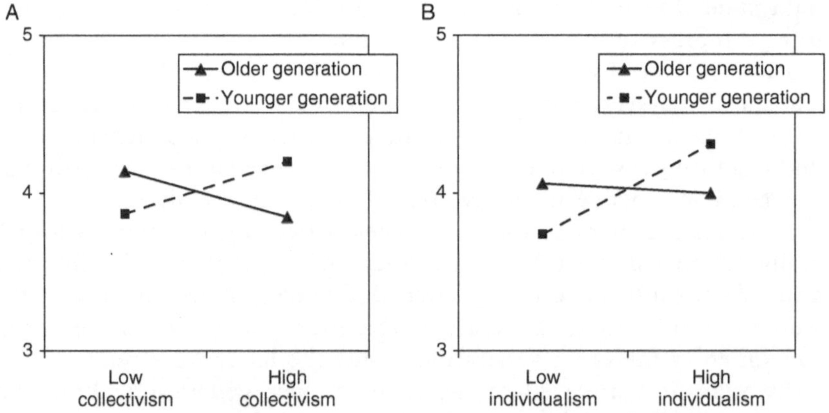

Figure 6.1. Redemptive suffering interpretation among KS Mennonites as a function of collectivism, individualism, and generation.
Note: Higher scores indicate greater redemptive interpretations.

of individualism was much larger. This demonstrates that as the Alexanderwohl Mennonites modernized across generations, a connection between cultural individualism and redemptive interpretations was forged, reflecting patterns in the larger cultural context.

Intergenerational transformations in culture and suffering interpretations

This study exemplified the theoretical principles presented in Part I by documenting how the connection between culture and suffering interpretation changes over time. Through an examination of changes in the subculture of US Mennonites – paralleling broader cultural processes of modernization – the study makes a modest advance by contributing to a wider literature on the emergence and spread of redemptive suffering interpretations. I will further consider the link between such interpretations and individualist culture in Chapter 8. At present, the primary importance of this study is its demonstration of one key facet of the cultural-existential method, namely the use of historical, cross-generational analysis to track the intertwining development of cultural forces and existentially motivated threat orientations.

The threat-culture cycle discussed in Chapter 1 has an important historical component. Rising individualism among US Mennonites, as well as increasing exposure to value systems outside of Anabaptism, pressured groups such as the Alexanderwohl Mennonites away from traditional conceptualizations of suffering as caused by deviance and to be borne through transcendence. Adaptation to II cultural values requires the individual to engage in risky economic and social behaviors that might be construed as deviant within the confines of a traditionalist community. At the same time, individualism motivates increased reliance on self-esteem as a psychological resource, generating a heightened need to protect the self against external information implying its inadequacy. One consequence of this, supported in the present study, is that transitioning to individualism encourages group members to increasingly construe their suffering as beneficial rather than punitive, as teaching them redemptive life lessons and the value of flexibility rather than the error of their waywardness.

At the same time, redemptive suffering interpretations likely facilitated the transition of the Alexanderwohl Mennonites to greater individualism. If experiences of hardship such as the Great Depression were interpreted solely as punishment for sin or a trial set by God, the Mennonites would have had fewer cultural resources to bolster the pursuit of new ways of farming, living, and worshipping. Trends in the data suggest that members of the younger generation of Alexanderwohl Mennonites likely did not see the hardships of their youth in this way. Rather, framing such instances of suffering as opportunities to learn new life strategies and discover the self's hardiness surely fortified the Mennonites in their gradual adaptation to a less traditional lifestyle.

Diachronic studies of changes within a culture can tell us much about how particular attitudes toward suffering and threat arise and play a role in cultural evolution. However, the methodological approach outlined in Chapter 2 suggests that to fully understand a group's threat orientation, it must be systematically compared to that of other groups. I turn to such a comparative analysis in the following chapter.

7 Cultural threat orientations among traditionalist Mennonites, Unitarian Universalists, and college students

Chapter 6 offered an intergenerational case study of cultural transformation among a group of (now) fairly mainstream US Mennonites. In this and the following chapter, I turn my focus to a more unique subgroup in the Anabaptist tradition, namely the Church of God in Christ, Mennonite. This group warrants study because, in comparison to the majority of Anabaptists, they have not undergone a complete historical transition from CV to more individualist culture. Rather, these Mennonites have modernized in certain aspects of their technology and lifestyle while nevertheless retaining an orthodoxly religious, communally oriented culture. They thus are an exception to the rule of II culture in the United States, and present an opportunity for examining the link between CV culture and DISA threat orientation.

In keeping with the multi-methodological approach of cultural-existential psychology, in the present and following chapters I go beyond the archival data analysis of Chapter 6 to the employ of quasi-experimental and qualitative methods. The present chapter specifically reports a cultural-comparative study. To throw into relief the DISA orientation of the members of the Church of God in Christ, Mennonite, it is necessary to compare their modal attitudes and beliefs to those of alternate subgroups in the United States. Accordingly, I conducted a survey of cultural and existential threat variables not only in a Church of God in Christ, Mennonite, congregation, but also in the standard social psychological comparison group of undergraduates, as well as in a congregation of Unitarian Universalists. The latter group was chosen as a representation of IV culture and secular tendencies, in contrast to the rigid orthodoxy and CV culture of the Church of God in Christ, Mennonite. To understand the results of the study, and the reasons why these different groups possess DISA versus DESA threat orientations, it is first essential to be acquainted with the cultural background of these groups. I will consider them each in turn, with an emphasis on the Mennonite subgroup (which will also be the focus of Chapter 8).

Church of God in Christ or "Holdeman" Mennonites

The Church of God in Christ, Mennonite, had its beginnings in the spiritual breakthrough experienced by John Holdeman in Wayne County, Ohio, in 1859 (Dyck, 1993). Holdeman had a spiritual conversion that led him to perceive extant Mennonite congregations as displaying too much conformity to the ways of the world outside the faith. Holdeman broke away from the Mennonite Church over what he perceived to be a relaxing of traditions and a compromise with worldliness (J. D. Weaver, 1997). He organized a separate following, which quickly engaged in efforts to convert Mennonites from other groups and locations outside of Ohio. Members of the Church of God in Christ, Mennonite, are typically referred to as Holdeman Mennonites after their founder.

Those who joined the Church of God in Christ, Mennonite, are now generally considered to be descended from a mixture of Pennsylvania Dutch and German Mennonites, as well as Russian Kleine Gemeinde Mennonites and others who migrated from Russia to McPherson County, Kansas, in the 1870s (Dyck, 1993; Melton, Mosher, Rubicz, Zlojutro, & Crawford, 2010). Pointing to the origins of the group in schisms and dissent from existing congregations, Redekop (1989) describes them as "a fusion of dissidents from both the Swiss and Dutch-Russian branches" (p. 42). The Holdeman congregations in Kansas with whom I conducted research represent a mixture of historical and genetic backgrounds typical for this denomination. For example, Crawford (2000) describes a typical Kansas congregation as "a composite of Molotschna Mennonites, Pennsylvania Germans, and local converts" (p. 38).

In the twentieth century, recruitment efforts for the Church of God in Christ, Mennonite, began to extend overseas in earnest (Dyck, 1993). The Holdeman Mennonites now number over 21,000, with several congregations in the Midwestern part of the United States, as well as congregations and missions all over North and South America, Africa, and Asia (Church of God in Christ, Mennonite, 2012).

Redekop (1989) argues that Holdeman Mennonites are among the Anabaptist groups that have most strongly demonstrated fundamentalist tendencies, which he defines as reactions "against the increasing threat of the modern scientific ethos and worldview" (p. 288). Indeed, the Holdemans would be considered culturally and religiously conservative or fundamentalist by the standards of most social scientists (e.g., Altemeyer & Hunsberger, 1992; Stevenson & Everson, 1990). It should also be noted that most other Mennonites consider the Holdemans to be quite conservative (Dyck, 1993). Barclay (1967) devised a scale for ranking different Anabaptist groups on their degree of "plainness," with higher ratings being associated with a stronger negative reaction to various individualist or materialist behaviors (e.g., watching television, marrying a non-Church member, wearing decorative attire), as well as stricter enforcement of church discipline (i.e., shunning of apostates). Out of seven relevant denominations ranked by Barclay, only the Old Order Amish ranked higher than the Holdemans on the scale. One year later, a survey of attitudes toward various elements of modern culture (e.g., going to the movies, smoking, attending public dance establishments) carried out among ministers from all the major Anabaptist groups found that Holdeman ministers exhibited the most conservative and rejecting attitudes (even more so than the Amish; Hiebert, 1973).

Based on these observations, as well as more recent ethnographies of the cultural patterns of this particular denomination (e.g., Arthur, 1998; Boynton, 1986), it is clear that Holdeman Mennonites belong to a CV culture. Indeed, Arthur (1998) has analyzed a community of Holdeman Mennonites in Northern California using Mary Douglas' grid/group framework (see Chapter 4), and concluded that the Holdemans are strong on both the social orientation/group variable ("Identity in Holdeman society refers to group identity, which subsumes personal identity," p. 86) and the social control/grid variable ("The Holdeman social body controls the expression of identity through intense scrutiny of rigid norms," p. 86).

The Holdeman Mennonites' CV culture revolves around their strong sense of Christian faith, which guides all their beliefs and daily behaviors. An important aspect of the Holdeman faith is the principle of "nonconformity to the world" (Church of God in Christ, Mennonite, 1998). The Holdeman Mennonites perceive that the world (i.e., mainstream commercialized society, especially modern culture in the United States) is characterized by widespread materialism and numerous opportunities for pursuing individualistic or selfish goals and desires. It is stressed that individuals must remain true to the Church and the principles of Christian faith in order to maintain separation from the temptations and sins of the world. This viewpoint does not imply complete isolation from the world or its technological and financial developments, but it does advocate a strong commitment to the Holdeman community, and avoidance of worldly activities such as political or military involvement. Congregations negotiate local normative practices, which typically involve unspoken rules for plain attire (especially for women) and the avoidance of any objects, entertainments, or activities that might be construed as unrewarding, gluttonous, materialistic, or promoting of carnality or selfishness (Arthur, 1998). The Holdemans are not opposed, however, to the use of technologies or the purchase of commodities that facilitate personal comfort, social communication with family or other "brethren," or enhanced productivity and labor.

I will illustrate the Holdemans' CV culture, and the processes through which it is sustained, through consideration of a few specific areas.

Discipline and repressive sanctions. Holdeman Mennonites emphasize the importance of excommunication and avoidance ("shunning") behavior to sanction individuals who deviate from communally prescribed norms (Boynton, 1986; Dyck, 1993; Hiebert, 1973). Redekop (1989) notes the important interrelatedness of the threat of such behavior and maintenance of the traditional Mennonite concept of community: "Shunning serve[s] as a prime expression of disapproval and, as such, strongly reinforce[s] the group's religious norms. But the existence of a strong sense of community [is] fundamental for this sanction to have any power against the sinning individual" (p. 133). Although shunning was an important element of Anabaptist social organization for centuries, it has now been largely abandoned by most Mennonite groups. The continued emphasis on this practice is one of the distinguishing features of the Holdemans.

Within a Holdeman community, when an individual deviates from local norms for behavior, a lengthy process of reintegrative reprimanding is set in motion, which may ultimately result in excommunication and shunning from the faith community and family members (Barclay, 1967; Hiebert, 1973). Excommunicated Holdemans are often reaccepted back into the Church after a short ritual of repentance. However, those who are not reaccepted typically have difficulty adjusting to mainstream society (Hiebert, 1973; McAvoy, 2012).

Generally speaking, excommunication and shunning are "last resorts" within Holdeman culture. As the process of church discipline is described in the foundational volume *The Confession of Faith and Minister's Manual* (1952):

> When any member of the church walks disorderly, and does not observe the Gospel of Jesus Christ, and the rules and ordinances of the church, he shall be visited by the ministry, as well as individuals, who shall faithfully endeavor to bring him to a sense of his duty, to show him the error of his ways, and thus bring him to confess the transgression, to repent of his sins, and ask forgiveness and forbearance of the church. But if by repeated efforts this cannot be done, the matter must also be brought before the church, council held, and the transgressor dealt with ... (pp. 82–83)

Based on her ethnographic work with a Holdeman community in Glenn, California, Boynton (1986) observed that the group's approach to visible social control in practice remarkably paralleled the abstract description in *The Confession.*

Each person in the society has the responsibility of monitoring not only his or her own behavior but also that of others. For example, if one girl sees that another is frequently wearing dresses that somehow call attention to herself, then the first girl would discuss this behavior with the second girl. This type of behavior is seen as symptomatic of the weakening of spiritual strength. If this discussion did not result in a change in her behavior, the girl would be visited by the Minister. If he were unsuccessful, she would be "reproved" at a meeting of the church members. If she continued to show prideful behavior, she would be expelled. Generally, problems are resolved at the first stage of the process. The peer pressure to conform is extremely strong in Holdeman society. (p. 62)

The family and other congregation members are expected not to eat at the same table or fraternize with an excommunicated Holdeman, and if the wayward member attends church, he or she must sit in a separate section and avoid contact with others. This process is painful for loved ones as well as for the shunned member, and the fear of excommunication drives Holdeman parents to sternly discipline their children in the hope that they will never undergo this process (Hiebert, 1973). In this manner, visible control patterns operate to insure the transmission of and adherence to cultural values.

Socialization practices. Within a Holdeman community, the highly visible net of social control operating to restrain potential deviants also influences the socialization of children (Boynton, 1986). Holdeman culture is transmitted through narrow socialization practices, which involve communal participation in child-rearing, exclusive attendance at local church schools, and avoidance of higher education except in special circumstances.

The kin group, and by extension the entire community, has the right and responsibility to direct the behavior of any child ... Members of the community feel no hesitation when it comes to correcting a child who is misbehaving. This is consistent with the entire sphere of Holdeman life in that each member of the community is charged with the responsibility of advising his or her fellow Christians concerning their behavior. Additionally, each person is expected to accept advice without rancor. This type of behavior is believed to exhibit the concern and love that one Christian feels for another. (Boynton, 1986, pp. 102–103)

This emphasis on communally reinforced, tight socialization practices extends very much to the Holdeman view and method of child education. Traditionally, it was believed that Holdeman children required only 8 years of formal schooling, unless they were being trained for a more advanced profession (Ediger, 1984). Holdeman Mennonites tend to shelter their children in parochial schools from what are perceived to be the potential pernicious influences of public institutions. The limitation of education to parochial schools has produced some minor controversy but has been legally upheld (Bergen, 1981). Boynton's (1986) ethnography details how, in a multitude of ways, the Holdeman parochial schools exemplify what Bernstein (1990) calls the "visible pedagogy" common in CV cultures:

> Speaking out-of-turn, and walking about the classroom are permitted only with the permission of the teacher ... Teachers and students are expected to use self-discipline at all times. Corporal punishment, used at the teacher's discretion, is considered an acceptable form of punishment ... The Code of Ethics [for the school] sets clear-cut expectations and standards ... Curricula in Holdeman schools must deal with reality, not fantasy. The curriculum in Holdeman schools is traditional in nature ... Rotating schedules, unstructured time, and flexible schedules are not used ... (pp. 190–202)

Interestingly, historical and survey research (Parker, 2005) lends some credence to the Holdeman view that attendance at public schools and institutions of higher learning would reduce the effectiveness of their socialization practices. This research demonstrates that public school attendance among non-Holdeman Mennonites (e.g., the Alexanderwohl community considered in Chapter 6) historically led to a considerable degree of cultural assimilation into broader national values and opinions. The Holdeman schools attempt to circumvent this potentiality, and do so through the employ of a rather different pedagogic approach compared to the mainstream US education system:

> Public schools emphasize the uniqueness of the individual, and adapt materials and methods to meet the needs of the individual student. The student is frequently tested, and his progress is charted on a continuum of skills previously established by his teachers. This method of tracking is entirely absent in the Holdeman school ... Teaching methods rely on drill, memorization, recitation ... repetitious learning techniques are preferred by Holdeman teachers. Whereas some techniques, such as behavior modification and competition between individuals and groups, are widely used in public schools, they are avoided in the Holdeman school. According to the Holdemans, since these techniques focus attention on the individual, they could encourage prideful behavior. (Boynton, 1986, pp. 203–204)

Economic practices. In the past, the Holdemans have upheld their visibly controlled culture and strong sense of shared faith by isolating themselves to a considerable degree from mainstream society, a goal that has been greatly facilitated by their traditionally agricultural lifestyle. Historically, the members of the Kansas congregations with whom I worked cultivated wheat in order to earn their living (Crawford,

Demarchi, Ellerd, & Puppala, 2000). However, the processes of capitalism, globalization, and technological and media infiltration which modernized the Alexanderwohl Mennonites (see Chapter 6) have also had their impact on the Holdemans. These processes have made it difficult for them both to isolate themselves from the ideas and influences of commercialized society and to maintain agricultural careers (Hiebert, 1973). In lieu of the farmsteading of their forefathers, many contemporary Holdemans have adopted alternate ways of earning a living that remain rooted in either agriculture or craftsmanship, such as operating farm supply stores, restaurants, or floral shops; raising poultry; carpentry; oil extraction; and so on.

Critical for contemporary Holdemans is the struggle to maintain economic insulation and self-sufficiency in a world driven by market capitalism. They have devised a variety of practices for avoiding too much integration into the mainstream economy (Barclay, 1969), which broadly fit Polanyi's pre-market model of the "householding" economic organization (Halperin, 1994). These practices have included – in addition to unspoken bans on the purchase of certain kinds of materialist commodities – resistances to purchasing commercial insurance, accruing debt, overuse of credit cards, becoming too involved in business ventures with non-Holdemans, and investing in the stock market (e.g., Boynton, 1986). The prohibition by the ministry of private insurance, along with the provision of internal means of insurance, is a particularly important mechanism. In mainstream US II culture, insurance operates widely on a principle of *quantitative* individualization that views all persons as potential risks (liabilities) to the broader collective (Ewald, 1991). For the individual in such a setting, insurance is often viewed as a means of using the calculus of risk and uncertainty to buffer the self against danger and provide a foundation for individualist enterprise. The Holdemans, however, prefer to build a communal safety net of mutual aid (and control) around their members.

In a related fashion, the Holdemans avoid accruing personal debt: "Although credit cards are used, the principal of the debt is paid off monthly in order to avoid the payment of interest" (Boynton, 1986, p. 113). Whereas household debt is a common form of invisible social control in modern capitalist society (Lazzarato, 2011; McNally, 2011), as well as a means of sustaining the capitalist growth imperative and modern consumer culture, the communal interdependence and "householding" self-sufficiency of the Holdemans obviate the need for individual debt to perform these functions.

In the present study, survey data obtained from a congregation of Holdeman Mennonites were compared to those obtained from a congregation of Unitarian Universalists, as well as a standard social psychological sample of university undergraduates. The goal in comparing data from these three groups was to evaluate the different threat orientations of a CV (Holdeman) culture as compared to an IV (Unitarian Universalist) and an II (undergraduate) culture. I will now summarily discuss how the two comparison groups represent IV and II culture, respectively.

Unitarian Universalists

Unitarian Universalism has historical roots in various strands of Reformation-era Unitarian Christianity – which rejected the doctrine of the Holy Trinity and advocated religious tolerance – as well as Universalism – an open form of Christianity that developed in parallel with eighteenth-century Enlightenment Deism and American Transcendentalism (Greenwood & Harris, 2011; McKanan, 2013). In general, the three cornerstones of Enlightenment idealism – the sanctity of the individual, the shift from "revelation" to "reason" in religiosity, and the Utopian call for massive social reform – remain an adequate summation of Unitarian Universalist beliefs (Leitgeb, 2009; Tapp, 1973). In the United States, the Unitarian and Universalist churches consolidated in 1961 with the formation of the Unitarian Universalist Association. There are currently 161,000 members of the Unitarian Universalist Association (McKanan, 2013).

Unitarian Universalism is considered by many (but not all) of its adherents to be a religion, yet it represents the near extreme of possibilities for religiosity in the contemporary age. As a leading liberal church, this "faith" eschews many traditional religious concepts. For example, Unitarian Universalists tend not to believe in immortality (Tapp, 1973), and many also find the idea of a personified God to be not only false or misleading but harmful (Greenwood & Harris, 2011). Furthermore, it is technically possible to be a Unitarian Universalist but also belong to any other denomination or belief system; for example, one can be a Unitarian Buddhist, a Unitarian Muslim, a Unitarian atheist, and so on. In short, Unitarian Universalism is an *ethical* rather than a *creedal* religion (Greenwood & Harris, 2011): its practitioners are united by a set of moral convictions, rather than an explicit belief system.

One of the few "creedal" elements of Unitarian Universalism is the set of seven principles which its members follow (Buehrens & Church, 1998). These principles may be summarized thus: respect for individual dignity is to be maintained through justice and equality; tolerance of others and their viewpoints is essential; truth and meaning should always be sought; we are part of a world community and connected to our natural environment. Their principles indicate that Unitarian Universalists have a fairly abstract belief system. Supporting this, members of this denomination demonstrate "postconventional morality" (defined according to Kohlberg's stages of moral development) compared to members of fundamentalist religions (Ernsberger & Manaster, 1981). Their beliefs are abstract enough to accommodate a variety of individual personalities and perspectives.

Indeed, the denomination may be characterized as individualism attached to and instantiated in a worldview, the essence of IV culture. Unitarian Universalism represents an attempt to ground individualism in a local and global community. Accordingly, liberal theologians affiliated with the denomination stress the idea of the "social self" (Rasor, 2008). A 1960s questionnaire study of eighty different Unitarian Universalist churches and fellowships found that one of the more prominent impacts of conversion to a Unitarian Universalist community is an increased integration between personal values and social-ethical values (Tapp, 1973). This consonance between personal conviction and a social orientation is reflected in Unitarian Universalists' deep concern with *generativity* – connecting to subsequent generations and making a lasting contribution to their lives (McAdams, 2006).

The religiosity of Unitarian Universalists is expressed not only through their common moral code, but also through the enactment of community in periodic rituals. Unitarian Universalists practice a model of congregational polity (Greenwood & Harris, 2011), and the organization, atmosphere, and emphases of congregations vary considerably; for example, some congregations have ministers, while others do not. Typically, most congregations hold Sunday services that are not structurally dissimilar from those of many US mainline Christian denominations (Elliott & Hayward, 2007). However, Sunday gatherings and sermons tend to emphasize intellectual issues and social justice activism, rather than theological content. Congregants are encouraged to play an active role in shaping the structure and content of church activities and worship (Leitgeb, 2009).

The IV culture of Unitarian Universalists can be clearly seen in the responses given by many congregation members to a series of open-ended questions I asked them as part of the present study (see Appendix C). When asked to describe what "faith" means to them, Unitarian Universalists expressed their belief in the general benevolence of human nature and the importance of connection to others. For example: "I believe that all beings have at least a spark of basic goodness in their hearts," and "I have faith in the goodness of humans and the dignity and worth of every person." Not uncommonly, this faith in human benevolence was linked either to dedication to social justice ("People must band together to confront injustice but we are all capable of choosing selfishly or acting kindly") or to a sense of generativity ("I believe that I have a sense of duty to work hard in the path that I have chosen ... and to protect my children ... [they] will always cherish my contributions to them"). The Unitarian Universalists responded similarly to questions about the importance and meaning of their community; indeed, some insisted that for them, their only sense of "faith" came from community belongingness. For example, one participant wrote: "My faith means community to me, this means diversity but also shared values"; another wrote, "My faith ... reminds me that I'm part of a community of people that care about me." Several participants stressed the need to be politically and locally involved: "I ... have become more aware of social injustice ... My involvement in fellowship activities gives me purpose – I know I make a difference," and "Being with others who have similar political views is very comforting. I enjoy volunteering in the context of the Fellowship ..."

In clear contrast to the Holdeman Mennonites, Unitarian Universalists come from a variety of backgrounds, and do not share a particular type of career or lifestyle. The denomination is sometimes characterized as a "religion of converts," because the majority of Unitarian Universalists are not "born" or socialized into the religion, but rather adopt it in young or middle adulthood, often after youthful experiences with a different religion (Leitgeb, 2009; Tapp, 1973). However, common characteristics are found in urban living and higher education. Compared to many other denominations, Unitarian Universalists not only overwhelmingly tend to have college educations, but they quite often have academic careers (Tapp, 1973). Some evidence tentatively suggests that better-educated Unitarian Universalists are the most adept at deriving a sense of personal well-being from their seemingly incoherent or open-ended belief system (Elliott & Hayward, 2007).

Unitarian Universalists are clearly on the individualist side of the social orientation dimension. However, their belief system and emphasis on community participation distinguish them from other individualists in contemporary US culture, because they represent IV culture: an attempt to embed individualism in a collectively shared worldview. The third group in the present study – university undergraduates – comes closer to encapsulating the dominant cultural model on the US landscape, namely II culture.

Undergraduates

Admittedly, the identity of "undergraduate" is different from that of Holdeman Mennonite or Unitarian Universalist. The latter two groups are organized on the basis of a religious identity; for the quasi-isolationist Holdemans, this serves as an individual's most important identification, whereas for the more cosmopolitan Unitarian Universalists this may be only one source of identity among others. Undergraduates are grouped together on the basis of a common social role, one that is also recognized as inherently temporary. However, this does not connote that undergraduates do not constitute a unique subculture with particular characteristics. Because of social psychologists' tendency to rely on undergraduate samples in their research and generalize from findings with these samples, as well as their own nearness to undergraduate culture, they are perhaps disinclined to think of undergraduates as representing a "culture." Nevertheless, it is clear that they do; what is more, as has recently been argued, undergraduates constitute a cultural group that has many unique and extreme tendencies with comparison to much of the rest of the world population (Henrich, Heine, & Norenzayan, 2010b).

Naturally, undergraduates differ from members of many other cultural groups – including the others in the present study – in terms of their restricted age range and common life stage. But age differences can be accounted for in statistical analyses, and undergraduate culture differs from that of the other two groups in a variety of ways. In particular, the fact that undergraduates are grouped together only by a common role identity – and one that places them in a context of performative competition with all other members of their group – makes them an ideal instantiation of an II culture. Although undergraduates can certainly embrace their local college identity, the typical college environment affords a highly individualistic self-concept (Stephens, Fryberg, Markus, Johnson, & Covarrubias, 2012). In college, students often experimentally join and leave multiple groups, acquiring the sense of a "protean self" (Lifton, 1987) with fragmentary allegiances that ultimately reinforces their sense of personal uniqueness (Simmel, 1955). College students most often conceive of themselves as unique individuals subject to continual evaluation and intragroup comparison – the epitome of II culture. The competitive, isolationist atmosphere of the college milieu is well summarized by an ethnographer of undergraduates:

> undergraduates did not ignore the [social] world in conceptualizing the self . . . They simply saw it as a different place, requiring a different, more artificial social self. The true self had to disguise itself in the wider world, they believed. It had to wear masks. It had to play roles. It had to manipulate other people. Personal

development of the sort that most students expected to accomplish in college was thus a complicated business . . . you had to come to know, or to construct, your "real" personal identity as you came of age. At the same time, you had to polish the practical skills of masking this same true self in the public world. You had to refine your ability to influence others if you wanted to get ahead in life. (Moffatt, 1989, p. 41)

Scholars have presented evidence that the conversion of the undergraduate university environment to an II setting has been, in many ways, a deliberate part of the neoliberal agenda of politicians and the capitalist and managerial classes of the world economy over the past 35 years (Duménil & Lévy, 2011; Harvey, 2005; Lazzarato, 2015; Ratner, 2013). Following several economists (see, in overview, Smith et al., 2011) and the theorizing of Harvey (2005), I define neoliberalism as a political compromise between the capitalist and managerial classes beginning prominently in the late 1970s, intended to resolve economic crises and promoting the following agenda: (1) maintaining and/or reestablishing US (and, to a lesser extent, European) political and economic hegemony; (2) the deregulation of markets; (3) the financialization of capital; (4) the globalization of capital. Although there is insufficient space here to discuss the neoliberal movement in any detail, it should be acknowledged that this movement has accelerated the processes of US modernization described in the Alexanderwohl Mennonite case study (Chapter 6), with the end result being an ongoing transition of mainstream US culture toward a "pure" II pattern.

Even prior to the rise of neoliberalism as a dominant cultural force, college students perceived individualism and competitive assertiveness to be important aspects of their social role (Reitzes, 1980). These elements have been exacerbated by the trend, in recent decades, for universities in the United States either to be directly privatized or commercialized, or to adopt models of privatization and commercialization. This results in undergraduates increasingly viewing their college experience in commoditized terms: the university and its instructors are providing a product (a degree) that will facilitate their future career goals (Tomlinson & Lipsitz, 2013). However, undergraduates also view the quality of the product they obtain through their education as contingent on their own performance, meaning they have been socialized to understand that universities submit them to an "order of rank," an abstract bell curve along which they are hoping to achieve the highest possible score (Foucault, 1977). Indeed, undergraduates know that they themselves are the product being produced: "every piece of knowledge one acquires can be interpreted and assessed as a *skill*, an aspect of oneself that can be considered productive by prospective employers. *Skills* thus become a form of self-marketing, and students readily come to imagine themselves as bundles of skills" (Urciuoli, 2010).

In these senses, the university environment not only is reflective of broader movements in the United States toward increased II culture, but can even be seen as a kind of laboratory in which II ideals are being created, tested, and transmitted (Lazzarato, 2015). For this reason, scholars have argued that undergraduates represent "the future" of II culture in the United States, meaning that the majority of US citizens (and even citizens of other nations) will eventually become more like contemporary undergraduates as a result of capitalist modernization and globalization (Rozin, 2010). This conclusion has been partly supported already by recent studies showing high levels of similarity between undergraduate research participants and non-college US participants recruited using other means (Goodman, Cryder, & Cheema, 2013. Indeed, Ratner (2013) has argued that the increased emphasis on college education in the United States, and the increasing number of college-educated citizens, is the direct result of attempts by corporations and politicians to socialize a greater number of citizens into II culture.

DISA and DESA orientations among the three groups

The primary predictions for the present study were that Holdeman Mennonites – a CV subculture – would demonstrate tendencies indicative of a DISA threat orientation, while Unitarian Universalists and undergraduates – representative of IV and II culture, respectively – would show, in somewhat different ways, DESA threat orientations. In other words, drawing on the analysis in Chapter 5, Holdemans should have a relative tendency to interpret suffering and misfortune in terms of personal culpability or waywardness, and therefore be relatively predisposed toward feelings of guilt, but they should be very unlikely to experience meaninglessness angst. By contrast, Unitarian Universalists and undergraduates should have a relative tendency to interpret suffering as caused by external factors such as randomness or social injustice, and therefore be relatively predisposed toward feelings of anxiety, but they should be comparatively unlikely to experience guilt and condemnation angst.

Ample evidence could be marshaled to suggest that the Holdemans have a DISA orientation. Like many other fundamentalist Christian writers, their founder John Holdeman (1890) assumed that the starting point for all human suffering was the Original Sin of Adam and Eve. In this view, human and individual deviance – *sin* – is the ultimate source of all suffering. For the Holdemans, sin is always the result of individual greed, weakness, and selfishness. As an important piece of their interpretive religious literature reads:

> Selfishness is at the heart of every sin. Indeed, selfishness and sin are synonyms because self-interests are the motivation of disobedience. *Selfish* is defined as being concerned excessively or exclusively with oneself; seeking or concentrating on one's own advantage, pleasure, or well-being without regard for others ... In contrast, love, by its unselfish nature, produces holy living by preferring God and others above oneself. (Church of God in Christ, Mennonite, 1998, pp. 99–100; italics in original)

In data from the current study that I have presented elsewhere (Sullivan et al., in press b), we found that Holdemans are more predisposed than Unitarian Universalists and undergraduates toward repressive interpretations of suffering (see Chapter 6). Specifically, Holdemans are relatively more likely than members of the other groups to agree with statements such as "By and large, the people who suffer most severely in life are immoral people" and "In many cases, it is necessary for people to suffer to protect the well-being of the community as a whole." Further evidence of the Holdeman tendency toward repressive suffering and DISA interpretations can be seen in their attitudes toward child-rearing. In prior research, my colleagues and I (Sullivan et al., 2012b) found that in a sample of US parents, those who were more likely to interpret suffering as caused by individual deviance were also more likely to support corporal punishment of children. Similarly, Holdemans believe that children must sometimes suffer punishment to curb their selfish and individualistic desires: "Because sin is prevalent and human nature accords with sin, teaching alone will not meet all the goals of child nurture ... Discipline reinforces teaching and helps establish order and routine. It establishes the fact that there are consequences for disobeying any code of conduct" (Church of God in Christ, Mennonite, 1998, p. 360). In keeping with a DISA threat orientation, the purpose of strict discipline is seen as instilling a sense of guilt consciousness that will allow the individual to avoid misfortune and anxiety in the future: "punishment ... brings home the truth that transgression of the commandment will result in disaster and that one can avoid this by making proper choices" (Church of God in Christ, Mennonite, 1998, pp. 360–361). Accordingly, being able to interpret suffering through the frame of discipline and preparedness for life allows the Holdemans to equate the experience of punishment with psychological well-being: "A properly disciplined child is a secure child. Discipline brings or provides a strong sense of security" (Church of God in Christ, Mennonite, 1998, p. 360).

The fact that Holdemans interpret negative events largely in terms of personal culpability and responsibility suggests that they will be relatively susceptible to guilt feelings. But, importantly, such feelings should be understood within the overall context of a DISA cultural threat orientation, where the capacity to interpret misfortune as caused by individual deviance neutralizes the threat of nihilism. In keeping with most fundamentalist Christian doctrines, John Holdeman (1890) saw a solution to the problem of human suffering in the New Testament's "redeemer theodicy" (Berger, 1967; Weber, 1946). God assumed human form through His Son, and sacrificed Himself for our sins. In other words, John Holdeman and his followers fully subscribed to what is often called a "penal substitutionary" or "satisfaction" theology of atonement (J. D. Weaver, 1997): Christ's death was the price paid for humanity's sinful nature, so that all faithful souls would ultimately be redeemed and guaranteed entrance to the higher world upon death. For Holdemans, the belief that all suffering stems from humanity's deviant nature provides a clear explanation for misfortune and is accompanied by the reassuring belief that suffering may be overcome through obedient submission to God.

Holdeman literature is often very explicit about the fact that this belief system protects the individual from anxiety and meaninglessness angst, and that the price for this psychological protection is a perennial view of the self as potentially guilt-worthy. Consider the following passage which appeared on the Church's website (churchofgodinchristmennonite.net):

> Many search among outward and tangible things, but neglect to look within ... They would like to blame a troubled world for their troubled minds, but the cure must begin within their own hearts ... when you are out of tune with God, fears and anxieties crowd into your life. When you focus your attention on the uncertainties of life, on a changing, decaying world, your security and confidence are shaken. Your peace is disturbed ... When you become self-centered in your wants and ambitions, you become anxious and fretful. The longer you travel the path of self-centeredness, the more troubled you become ... Instead of seeing yourself as the center of existence, you need to turn to God and make Him your central purpose in life. Without God as your center, you fall easy prey to petty worries, self-pity, fears, and anxiety. With God in the center, every area of your life will reach out from the "hub" like spokes in a wheel and make your life complete and worth living ... Faith and trust are the antidotes for fear and anxiety. How restful it is to trust in the only God who is from everlasting to everlasting, to have a Friend who never changes, whose love never dies ... Maybe you feel the heavy load of past sins weighing you down, and you feel you have more than you can bear. The Lord offers the remedy in Acts 3:19. "Repent ye therefore, and be converted, that your sins may be blotted out, when the times of refreshing shall come from the presence of the Lord." 1 John 1:9 also says, "If we confess our sins, he is faithful and just to forgive us our sins, and to cleanse us from all unrighteousness." As a result, you will have peace with God through our Lord Jesus Christ. (Romans 5:1)

In stark contrast to the DISA orientation evident in Holdeman beliefs and practices, Unitarian Universalists seem to have a pronounced DESA orientation. Although the beliefs of this denomination are difficult to codify summarily, since they can vary between congregations and individuals, it is nevertheless clear that the Unitarian Universalist value system prioritizes the well-being and value of the individual over and above any concerns about the collective or a set of norms. Unitarian Universalists believe that people are fundamentally good, rather than sinful, and that suffering in life often results from low self-esteem and needless self-blame. As one participant in the present study described their Unitarian Universalist "faith": "[it is] a life force, maybe collective life force, love force. It is that which keeps me putting one foot in front of the other . . . all in imperfect but perfectly human growth toward light." In interviews with converts to Unitarian Universalism from other religions, Jindra (2008) found that many individuals described being attracted to the belief system as a way out of guilt-focused models, as in this example: "I grew up very this is right, this is wrong, you don't drink, ah, you don't have sex before your marriage, you don't, you don't, you don't, and it never said what you do. And a lot of guilt and shame, and it was just completely external" (p. 212). Unitarian Universalist "hymns" define the denomination's belief system in opposition to others that create the potential for nihilistic despair: "Some beliefs weaken a person's selfhood. They blight the growth of resourcefulness . . ." (Leitgeb, 2009, p. 251). Given the Unitarian Universalist belief that undue feelings of guilt are a major source of suffering, it is not surprising that my comparative survey revealed that members of this group were the least likely to endorse repressive interpretations of suffering (Sullivan et al., in press b).

Unitarian Universalism orients the individual away from experiences of guilt and condemnation angst because its DESA worldview stresses the incontestable value of each individual. In a large-scale study employing the Rokeach Values Survey, Miller (1976) found that, compared to members of major US religious groups, Unitarian Universalists endorsed a unique constellation of values emphasizing respect and love for individuals and the maintenance of a beautiful world, while de-emphasizing moralistic values and obedience. At the same time that this value system discourages guilt, it affords potential anxiety and meaninglessness angst because it is not "closed" but rather open-ended. Unitarian Universalists see their lives as an ongoing search for meaning; this connotes that meaninglessness can be a problem for them in a way it is not for the Holdemans. Their beliefs also make Unitarian Universalists susceptible to various anxieties about the course of world events; like most contemporary liberals, they see themselves as battling forces of social injustice and environmental destruction that are rampant in the world.

Just as the Holdemans' DISA orientation affords both the threat of guilt and the defense of redemptive confession, the DESA orientation of the Unitarian Universalists makes anxiety more palatable by presenting it as a necessary component of growth and accomplishment. As one minister wrote in an introductory textbook for converts to the denomination:

> The sense of self-control, of self-containment, and of self-realization is a necessary aspect of meeting crises and tension ... Religious liberals take [such crises and tension] on their own shoulders. Their problem is not how to live without tension, but how to live with it. They can accept the tensions of the moment, because they see that they offer a challenge to creative living. (Marshall, 1966, pp. 39–40)

Unitarian Universalists' DESA orientation, which affords anxiety and concern about meaning but also protects against these threats by stressing the sacred self as a coping resource, is well summarized in the following passage written by another minister:

> Only as I have the courage to accept my supreme aloneness and vulnerability can I turn to full participation. Only as I am brave enough to know that, even in my own warm home I am but on a visit, only as I can face the fact that everything I build will someday crumble am I free to give that which endures on this earth, the spirit in which I live my life and do my part... The comfort of my religion rests not on any of the conventional but questionable "proofs" of God's personal concern and care, but on the encouragement I find in my aloneness, and in an appreciation of the aloneness of others, to accept and trust life without such proofs. If the world of nature is impersonal, so be it. If the universe plays no favorites ... isn't that after all a necessary condition of whatever dependability we can find? My liberal religion offers me the comfort of spiritual solitude in a world where I can rise in hope to meet, or compensate for, most of my problems, where, in fact, I can intelligently anticipate many of the stresses I must solve or bear. In brief, mine is a religion that cares more about me as a person – my potential resources and strengths – than it does about theological explanations or atonements of the dilemmas and failures that beset me ... My human limitations I cannot abolish, but within the limitations are the meanings I am free to create. (Mendelsohn, 2006, p. 168)

Undergraduates in the United States are part of the same mainstream individualist culture as Unitarian Universalists, and should be expected to share many aspects of a DESA threat orientation. It is certainly clear from prior work that undergraduates are susceptible to relatively high levels of anxiety. Throughout the duration of their college careers, undergraduates are consistently evaluating themselves against both an abstract internal standard and the performances of their peers, all in the pursuit of ultimate personal success. Their daily lives are marked by a high degree of "status anxiety" (de Botton, 2004). Studies suggest that undergraduates often react with greater defensiveness to threat inductions than members of non-undergraduate samples (Burke et al., 2010). Supporting the notion that the DESA threat orientation of undergraduates has arisen in response to a historical transition toward II culture, Twenge (2000) reported a large meta-analysis showing that college students' average levels of anxiety steadily and dramatically increased over the period of 1950–1990.

How do undergraduates defend against the anxiety that they face? In this regard, we might expect the DESA pattern of undergraduates to differ somewhat from that of Unitarian Universalists. Because undergraduates are immersed in an II culture, they often lack a stable, comprehensive worldview and community on which they can rely to cope with experienced stressors. Indeed, the undergraduate role is a *liminal* identity (Nathan, 2006), a prototypic transitional period during which students are encouraged to adopt and discard various identities in a quest for self-knowledge. While Unitarian Universalists maintain a minimal level of visible control by attaching their individualism to a pro-social worldview and denominational community, undergraduates generally lack these resources. Thus, undergraduates must primarily rely on themselves – specifically their own feelings of personal control and self-value – to protect themselves against threats. Accordingly, in addition to periodic bouts of hedonistic or materialist excess, undergraduates cope with their anxiety by employing a variety of self-serving biases acquired through socialization in II culture (Griffin, 2004; Vaillancourt, 2013). The DESA emphasis on maintaining high perceived self-value means that high-functioning undergraduates will be relatively inoculated against experiences of guilt and condemnation angst. They will tend to externalize blame for negative events.

Thus, although undergraduates and Unitarian Universalists would be expected to demonstrate more of a DESA orientation pattern compared to Holdemans – that is, comparatively low levels of guilt and higher levels of anxiety – they would likely differ in the particular defensive patterns they would show. Specifically, Unitarian Universalists should primarily defend against threats by relying on their individualistic *worldview*, while undergraduates will primarily defend by relying on the individualistic resource of *self-esteem*.

A study of cultural threat orientations

Participants in the study were 28 Holdeman Mennonites (9 female), 29 undergraduate students at the University of Kansas in Lawrence, Kansas (17 female), and 24 Unitarian Universalists (15 female, 1 unidentified).

All Holdeman participants belonged to the same central Kansas congregation. I obtained participation from this congregation by initially contacting its ministers and deacon via phone and post. At an initial meeting with these congregation leaders, the general purpose of the study was discussed and a preliminary copy of the questionnaire was presented for inspection. The ministers approved the project and made only two small requests to modify the questionnaire (an item referring to potential guilt feelings over interpersonal aggression was removed, since this is a very sensitive topic among the Holdemans; an item referring to anxiety about the possibility of divorce was also removed, since they do not practice divorce). The ministers arranged a date and time for data collection and announced the project at a preceding church service, inviting any interested congregation members to attend and participate. Data were collected from the participants in a single sitting at their church building. After the surveys were completed, the congregation collectively prayed that they had answered the questions correctly and to the best of their ability. They also shared a meal that they provided with myself and my research assistant. A few months after the data were preliminarily analyzed, I sent a report of the results (written in non-specialized language) to the ministers, and they generally approved of the findings.

All Unitarian Universalists also belonged to the same congregation, which was located in a major Kansas city. I solicited participation from this congregation by making contact with their minister (note that not all Unitarian Universalist congregations have acting ministers). The governing congregational board was given an opportunity to review and approve the study questionnaire and general project. A date was arranged by the minister for data collection to occur after a Sunday service. The week prior to this date, I attended the service and gave some summary remarks about the purpose of the project, inviting any interested congregation members to participate. About one-third of the participants completed the questionnaire at the fellowship building after the following service, while the remaining participants took questionnaires home and mailed them to me upon completion. A few months after the data were preliminarily analyzed, I gave a presentation of the results to the congregation. They generally approved of the findings and expressed considerable interest in the project.

Data from the University of Kansas undergraduates were collected in a single sitting in a large university classroom. The participants completed the study in exchange for course credit, and were individually recruited through the university's psychology participant pool recruiting system. After all three data collection sessions, the purpose of the study was explained in detail to each group of participants, and they were given an opportunity to ask any questions. For more details regarding instructions given, see Appendix C.

At the beginning of the survey, undergraduates and Unitarian Universalists indicated their religious affiliation. The majority of undergraduates identified as "Christian" or "Catholic" (a few identified as "nonreligious"), while the majority of Unitarian Universalists identified as "Unitarian Universalist" (a few identified as "atheist").

Broadly, the survey given to each group included minimal demographic items and two primary sets of variables relevant to the hypotheses. These were (1) religious, cultural, and worldview orientation variables, which were included primarily to validate my assumptions regarding the relative positions of the groups in the conceptual space generated by the two-variable cultural model; and (2) threat and defense variables, which were used to test the hypotheses regarding DISA/DESA orientations among the groups. For all specific items included in the study, and details regarding the composition of measurement scales, see Appendix C. For details of the statistical analyses underlying the summary discussions that follow, see Appendix D.

Influence of demographic variables. Average ages within groups were 50 years for the Holdemans, 18.5 years for the Undergraduates, and 65 years for the Unitarian Universalists. Effects of age both across the entire sample and within groups were surprisingly few. Nevertheless, age certainly had an influence on some of the variables measured; for instance, across the full sample, age was negatively correlated with death angst. While I do not deny the influential role of development in many existential issues (consider, for example, the discussions of generational status in the prior chapter), there are several reasons why I believe that this factor alone cannot account exclusively for any of the findings that I will presently discuss. First, age was controlled for in all between-group statistical analyses. Second, while undergraduates and Unitarian Universalists were the youngest and oldest groups, respectively, they were more similar to each other in their general cultural pattern (despite important differences) than to the Holdemans, a finding understandable from a cultural but not a pure developmental perspective. Third, mediational analyses controlling for age (described below) suggest that cultural differences between groups play a significant role in many of the threat-related differences, whereas age does not. Fourth, age was only correlated with six of the other variables across the entire sample.

Gender also did not appear to play a substantial role, although some effects were observed that are consistent with common findings (e.g., across the entire sample, men perceived the world to be more controlled than women, whereas women expressed greater anxiety than men). The sample was somewhat underpowered to detect interactions between gender and culture, although a few interesting (but unsystematic) interactions emerged (described in Appendix D). Nevertheless, controlling for gender in all analyses did not alter any of the effects that will be described here.

It could be argued that education differences may have played a role in some of the effects I will present. As mentioned, the Holdemans generally do not pursue higher education, whereas many Unitarian Universalists are well educated and undergraduates are, by virtue of their group membership, immersed in higher education. However, no formal measures of education level were taken in this study. I did not take this step because, in this context, education level and type is really inseparable from culture. For instance, Holdeman Mennonites, while not college-educated in many instances, nevertheless often possess considerable training in their profession, whether agricultural or related to some form of commerce or craftsmanship; many are also well traveled. In short, they are educated people, but in a nonconventional sense. Thus, education and/or social class do not, to my mind, qualify in this context as "alternative" or "control" variables. Rather, they are basic elements of the cultural differences between these groups, which I now will consider in detail.

Religious, cultural, and worldview orientations among the three groups. Table 7.1 provides a conceptual summary of the results concerning religious and cultural differences. Mean differences on the key religious and cultural variables are graphically displayed in Figure 7.1. As can be seen, the groups generally evinced the expected patterns. Holdemans had elements of a CV culture: in terms of social orientation, they were higher than the other groups in collectivism, and in terms of social control, they had comparatively high levels of orthodox and intrinsic religiosity, suggesting that their religious beliefs are rigid and guide all

Table 7.1. *Summary of religious, cultural, and worldview orientations among the three comparison groups.*

	Holdeman Mennonites	Undergraduates	Unitarian Universalists
Religiosity	*High orthodox and intrinsic religiosity*	*Moderate religiosity*	*High secularism*
Cultural type	*High collectivism*	*High vertical and horizontal individualism*	*High horizontal individualism*
Assumptions about world	*Controlled world*	*Random world*	*Benevolent world and people*

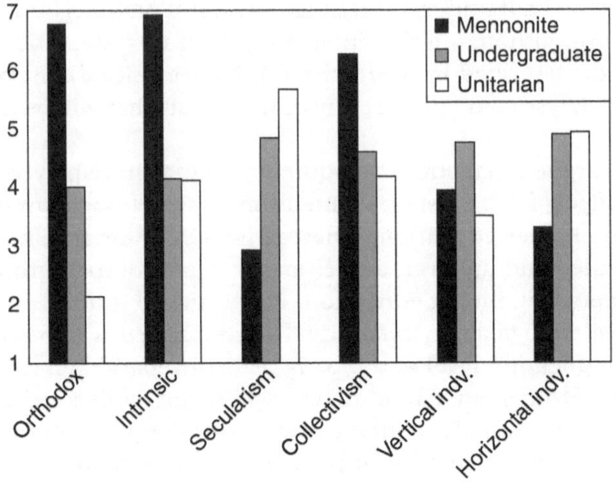

Figure 7.1. Mean differences on religiosity and cultural variables among the three comparison groups.

their daily behaviors. As a result, they tended to see the world as a controlled and orderly place.

By contrast, undergraduates and Unitarian Universalists displayed patterns fitting II and IV cultures, respectively. The undergraduates were comparatively high in the vertical, competitive individualism that is characteristic of II culture (for discussion of vertical vs. horizontal forms of individualism, see Chapter 4). Attesting to the invisible social control pattern dominating their experience, they tended to see the world as a fairly random and unordered place. They did not score particularly high in religiosity or secularism, indicating that there is no common worldview which grounds their competitive individualism. Demonstrating more of an IV configuration, the Unitarian Universalists were oriented not only toward a horizontal, expressive form of individualism but also toward a generally individualistic worldview. They scored comparatively high on secular attitudes, as well as beliefs in the general benevolence of the world and of humanity. The Unitarian Universalists share a common understanding of reality as a meaningful place where people can achieve knowledge and understanding through cooperation. Their individualism is grounded in a worldview.

Threat and defense patterns among the three groups. As expected, the groups also differed substantially in proclivity toward certain threat experiences. Table 7.2 provides a conceptual summary of

Table 7.2. *Summary of threat and defense patterns among the three comparison groups.*

	Holdeman Mennonites		Undergraduates		Unitarian Universalists	
First-level threat orientation	Toward ***Guilt***		Toward ***Anxiety***		Toward ***Anxiety***	
	Cause: *Orthodox religiosity*	**Defense:** *Reparative behavior*	**Cause:** –	**Defense:** *Self-esteem*	**Cause:** –	**Defense:** *Horizontal individualism*
Second-level threat orientation	Away from ***Meaninglessness Angst***		Toward ***Death Angst***		Away from ***Condemnation Angst***	
	Cause: *Less randomness and secularism*	**Defense:** –	**Cause:** *Vertical individualism*	**Defense:** *Self-esteem*	**Cause:** *Less vertical individualism*	**Defense:** *Benevolence of people*

Note. En dashes indicate that the data were not conclusive on this issue.

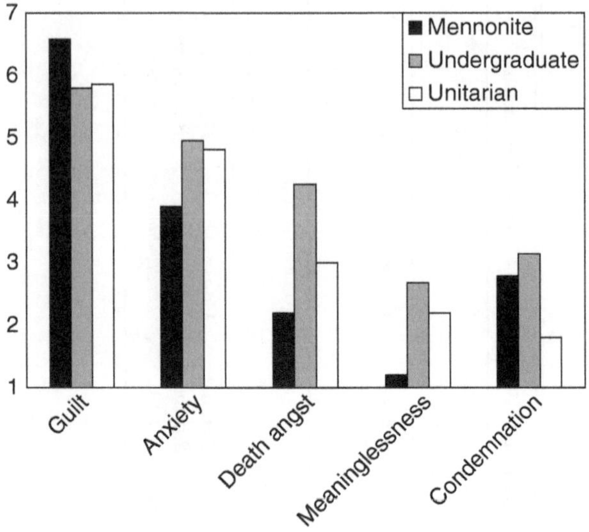

Figure 7.2. Mean differences on threat variables among the three comparison groups.

these results, while Figure 7.2 presents the relevant mean differences. Generally, the Holdemans displayed a DISA threat orientation: they scored comparatively high in proclivity toward the first-level threat of guilt, but low with regard to the second-level threat of meaninglessness angst. The Unitarian Universalists, by contrast, displayed a clear DESA pattern: higher scores on first-level anxiety, but low scores on second-level condemnation angst. Undergraduates also evinced a DESA pattern, in that (compared to Holdemans) they were oriented away from guilt and toward anxiety. However, they were distinguishable from Unitarian Universalists in that they did not score any lower than the Holdemans on condemnation angst, and they scored higher than both other groups on death angst.

What is the source of undergraduates' comparatively high level of death angst? Interestingly, analysis of the data suggests that this effect was not primarily due to the general age difference between undergraduates and the other groups, but rather to their relatively high degree of competitive individualism. Indeed, across the entire sample, those participants who tended to have a more vertical, competitive form of individualist social orientation also tended to express more death angst.

In general, analyses revealed compelling relationships between the cultural and threat variables within each group, testifying to the second principle of cultural-existential psychology that culture is both a source of and a solution to the problems of threat and suffering. Among Holdemans, proclivity toward guilt seems to have been driven by their high levels of orthodox religiosity; at the same time, however, the reverse relationship was also in evidence, meaning that those Holdemans who experience more guilt turn to their beliefs partly as a source of solace. Additionally, a tendency to engage in reparative behavior toward others seemed to be a culturally conditioned defense against guilt for the Holdemans. Keeping with a DISA orientation, the Holdemans' cultural values seemed to be their primary defense against threat – for them (but not the other groups), belief in God was negatively correlated with death angst, and their relatively low levels of meaninglessness angst are related to their lack of investment in secular ideas or perceptions that the world is random.

The Unitarian Universalists, on the other hand, displayed further elements of a DESA pattern insofar as their individualistic worldview seemed to be their primary defense against threat. Among members of this group, anxiety was negatively correlated with horizontal individualism. Furthermore, their relatively low levels of condemnation angst seem to result from their tendency to endorse the fundamental benevolence and dignity of each person over and above a more competitive form of individualism. Again, undergraduates displayed a DESA pattern that was somewhat different from that of the Unitarian Universalists. Although the latter scored highest on self-esteem overall, the undergraduates were more likely to rely on their self-esteem (rather than any worldview) to protect themselves from threat. Among undergraduates, self-esteem was negatively correlated with death angst, anxiety, and meaninglessness angst. This suggests the possibility that self-esteem is more fragile and defensive among undergraduates (and in II culture generally) compared to among Unitarian Universalists (and in IV culture generally).

Implications of an in-depth cultural-comparative study

This study offers support for the model of cultural threat orientations presented in Part I. Holdeman Mennonites displayed a DISA orientation – comparatively high in guilt proneness, and low in concerns with anxiety and meaninglessness – which follows from their high levels of collectivism and orthodox religiosity. By contrast, the more individualistic and secularized Unitarian Universalists and undergraduates displayed variations of a DESA orientation – comparatively high in anxiety proneness, and low in concerns with guilt and condemnation. Furthermore, cultural variables were linked to threat variables in mediational chains that follow from my theoretical analysis. In some instances, a cultural variable seems to heighten group members' sensitivity to threat, but the reverse was also observed – heightened threat sensitivity seems to bind the group to their cultural values. For example, greater orthodoxy among the Holdemans generates more guilt proneness, which in turn also contributes to orthodoxy, a testament to the threat-culture cycle discussed in Chapter 1.

The observation of these bidirectional links between culture and threat might call into question some of the causal assertions assumed in this chapter. For instance, how can we be certain that participants' cultural background causes them to spontaneously interpret information in such a way that they are more prone to experience one or the other type of threat (e.g., guilt or anxiety)? Is it not equally plausible that participants have certain inborn ways of interpreting information and experiencing threat that have caused them to gravitate toward particular religious identities?

This concern is largely misguided because the cultural-existential perspective holds both possibilities to be valid and likely. Indeed, I can summarily report the results of two experiments from my laboratory that provide direct causal evidence for both an influence of culture on threat interpretation and an influence of threat interpretation on culture. Considering first the more intuitive direction – cultural background affording particular threat interpretations – I exposed Kansas undergraduates to a hypothetical existential threat and assessed culturally based variation in their reactions. I first measured participants' dispositional levels of religiosity and secularism using scales similar to those in Appendix C. I then randomly assigned them to watch either an intense, immersive video of a tornado destroying a small Midwestern town, or a nonthreatening video with routine imagery of Midwestern countryside and small-town life. Participants in the tornado video condition wrote about their imagined experience of the hypothetical threat, and their responses were coded for salient themes. Finally, participants completed measures of their current emotional state, perceived control, and belief in a just world. I assessed the written descriptions of the threatening situation, as well as responses to the subsequent measures, to determine if more religious versus more secular undergraduates would differentially interpret the threat.

Highly religious participants in the tornado video condition reported heightened negative affect, including elevated guilt, and imagined turning toward sources of external support – such as family, community members, or God – for assistance in the hypothetical disaster situation. By contrast, more secular undergraduates reacted in characteristically DESA ways, demonstrating meaninglessness angst in their reflections on the hypothetical tornado. They defended against this angst by reporting greater perceived personal control in the tornado (as opposed to the neutral) condition, an effect that was mediated by elevated belief in a just world. In short, the more secular participants relied on individualistic, rather than external or community-based, defenses. Thus, results from an experiment in which exposure to threat was controlled and manipulated reinforce the general assumption that cultural background influences the cognitions, emotions, and standard responses that are activated in the presence of threat.

Another experiment found evidence supporting the opposite causal direction, namely threat encounters influencing attachment to culture. Participants initially completed a measure of their dispositional tendency to interpret suffering repressively (i.e., as an indication of personal deviance and need to reintegrate with the collective). They then were randomly assigned to imagine either an instance of major personal suffering – being in a car accident and becoming paralyzed – or minor personal suffering – being in a car accident but sustaining no injury. After engaging with one of these hypothetical scenarios, participants were asked to report their level of individualism and collectivism. Imagining an experience of major personal suffering led individuals with a high (as opposed to low) dispositional tendency to interpret suffering repressively to report more vertical collectivism (CV tendencies). I also found that, among those low in a dispositional tendency to interpret suffering repressively, imagining personal suffering *decreased* vertical collectivism, and increased horizontal individualism (IV tendencies). This suggests that those people who do not typically interpret misfortune in repressive terms respond to personal suffering by becoming more focused on unique aspects of the self, and psychologically distancing from the collective. In short, individuals learn certain ways of interpreting suffering from their culture, and when these interpretations become active during suffering, they reorient the individual toward their particular cultural worldview.

Of course, both these experiments and the culture-comparative study leave open the question of how participants might respond in the presence of an actual threat. It is important to note in this regard that the measures of guilt and anxiety were assessments of proneness to these emotions in the context of imagined hypothetical scenarios (see Appendix C). Thus, the results of the present study do not necessarily imply that Holdemans *actually experience* more guilt than Unitarian Universalists or undergraduates, for example. Indeed, some prior research (Fayard, Roberts, Robins, & Watson, 2012) suggests that individuals high in guilt proneness actually tend to experience *less* guilt than others, because their concern about guilt inhibits them from engaging in blameworthy activities (although, importantly, this work focused on personality, rather than cultural differences). What can be concluded on the basis of my findings is that in the event a Holdeman commits an act they consider blameworthy, they will almost certainly feel a greater emotional "depth" of guilt than members of the other groups (see Ratcliffe, 2015). Furthermore, the range of events which Holdemans construe as possibly blameworthy is almost certainly wider than that of the other two groups. A key implication of these findings is that different cultural groups have different thresholds and environmental affordances for different forms of negative affect – in short, differing threat orientations.

The question of how the groups studied would react to the actual experience of a threat is partly addressed in the following chapter, which reports a qualitative study of Holdeman responses to a natural disaster. Before considering the Holdeman DISA orientation in greater detail, however, let me dwell for a moment on the comparison groups in the present study. Although Unitarian Universalists and undergraduates both evinced a DESA orientation, the differences observed testify to the distinction between IV and II cultures.

The IV background of Unitarian Universalists grounds their individualism in a worldview, which shelters them from threat experiences. Thus, IV DESA orientation involves a denial of condemnation angst that is scaffolded by a metaphysical prioritization of the value of individual persons and the broader human community. Although secular rationalists such as the Unitarian Universalists experience considerable anxiety about the future – indeed, their commitment to social justice and environmental protection is fueled by this anxiety – they take a firm stance against the possibility of nihilistic despair, succored by their conviction that each human life is inherently valuable.

In their attempt to straddle the line between individual and community, IV cultures such as the Unitarian Universalists define themselves not only in opposition to the fundamentalism and group-centrism of CV culture, but against the egocentric utilitarianism of II culture as well. The pattern of results suggests that undergraduates – immersed in an II environment – are actually oriented *toward* both anxiety and death angst. Rather than relying on a community identity or worldview to defend against threat, the undergraduates' primary resource is their self-esteem. Importantly, it was not only the case that vertical individualism explained undergraduates' greater tendency toward death angst; death angst was also shown to contribute to vertical individualism. I will reconsider related aspects of II threat orientation in the concluding chapter.

While tracing the history of US Mennonites in Chapter 6, I presented evidence that the majority of these people assimilated to modern individualist culture, bringing their interpretations of misfortune in line with a standard II approach. The evidence presented in the current chapter, however, suggests that – at least compared to other groups more representative of contemporary US culture – some Mennonites have retained many elements of CV culture and a DISA orientation. In particular, the Church of God in Christ, Mennonite, appears to have preserved deeply held religious convictions and feelings of attachment to ingroup members, even at the expense of greater proclivity toward guilt. But do the comparative results of a survey truly map the ways in which Holdemans respond to experiences of profound threat? I address this question in the following chapter.

8 Transcendence versus redemption in the experience of a natural disaster

Following the methodological principle of cultural-existential psychology presented in Chapter 2, it is insufficient to consider the threat experience of a particular cultural group only through eco-historical or comparative quantitative data. Such studies – like those presented in the prior two chapters – are vital to understanding how one group's experience of suffering and threat is shaped by their cultural milieu, and how it differs from that afforded by other milieus. Nevertheless, historical and socio-ecological studies are limited by the available data, which are often somewhat sparse, and comparative surveys or experiments have difficulty examining people's *actual experience* of threatening situations.

This chapter presents my attempt – through the use of qualitative methods – to overcome these limitations and flesh out our understanding of how the CV culture of Holdeman Mennonites affords particular experiences of suffering and threat. I conducted an interview-based ethnographic study to determine how one congregation of Holdeman Mennonites experienced a particular threatening event, namely the major tornado that destroyed their home town of Greensburg, Kansas, in 2007. Another goal was to determine points of contrast between the method of coping and recovery employed by this CV cultural group with that of the other residents of Greensburg, who are more integrated into mainstream US culture.

I will focus on two primary narratives that emerged from the Greensburg disaster. One of those narratives was a redemptive suffering interpretation, as this construct was described in Chapter 6. Presently I will elaborate on redemptive narratives as they appear in the contemporary psychological literature on suffering. I will then begin my discussion of the Greensburg tornado by outlining the mainstream redemptive narrative that emerged almost immediately after the storm. This narrative will be contrasted with that given by the Holdemans. I will argue that the Mennonites recovered more completely from the tornado than the townspeople of Greensburg as a whole, and that they did so not by constructing an individualistic redemption story, but by relying on the assistance of their faith-based community and meaning-conferring narratives of religious transcendence.

Redemptive suffering

Redemptive suffering narratives can take many forms in academic, therapeutic, media, and popular discourses. At base, however, they share an overarching structure: the individual moves from an initial state of negative suffering to an improved (or at least positive) state of "posttraumatic growth" (Tedeschi & Calhoun, 1996), through a process of "benefit-finding" (Davis, Nolen-Hoeksema, & Larson, 1998) that prototypically involves both a revaluation *of* the suffering and a revaluation of one's life *based on* the suffering. In short, an experience of suffering is positively incorporated into the self's autobiography (McAdams, 2006).

Increasingly in the past few decades, redemptive narratives have been touted as both a common and a beneficial way of construing suffering in North American psychology. In many expositions of this construct, it is common for the researcher or practitioner to claim that while in the past suffering was viewed as inherently negative, we now know that suffering can have "surprising" positive benefits for the self. There is insufficient space to examine in detail the large amount of research and writing that has described variations on the redemptive narrative and demonstrated its relation to positive outcomes, such as recovery from trauma or possession of a well-adjusted self-concept. In overview, however, it will suffice to observe that redemptive narratives have been examined in qualitative work from sociological and psychological perspectives (e.g., Frank, 1993; McAdams, 2006; Sandstrom, 1990); in the "posttraumatic growth" empirical literature in clinical psychology (e.g., Tedeschi & Calhoun, 1996; Triplett et al., 2012); in experimental studies demonstrating that people spontaneously rely on redemptive ideas to make sense of others' suffering (e.g., Hafer & Gosse, 2011); in comprehensive mixed-methods approaches examining outcomes for victims of traumatic suffering (e.g., Janoff-Bulman, 1992); in books on medical ethics intended for practitioners (e.g., May, 1994); and, finally, in psychology trade books intended for a popular audience (e.g., Joseph, 2011).

It should be observed that of all the scholars listed here, only two (Frank, 1993; McAdams, 2006) even broach the question of whether redemptive narratives are healthy and normative (the rest – and many others not cited – either assume they are, or present evidence supporting this). Furthermore, all of this research was conducted with moderate- to high-income participants in the contemporary United States. McAdams (2006) has identified the redemptive narrative as a uniquely American view of adversity. Calhoun, Cann, and Tedeschi (2010) similarly suggest that the posttraumatic growth concept is strongly ingrained in contemporary US culture, and therefore may be a prototype for coping with suffering in this context.

A few identifiable elements are common to most redemptive narratives as they are employed by research participants and as they are operationally defined by researchers. One aspect of these narratives is the *individualization of suffering*: suffering is primarily conceptualized as something that happens to an individual (even if it occurred in the context of a far-reaching event, such as a natural disaster), and it is also seen as an isolating, private experience (Frank, 1993; Kleinman, 1988). At the same time that suffering is individualized, it is also in many instances *intensified* – meaning that in a redemptive narrative, the experience of suffering itself is typically viewed as especially harsh and negative. Construing an initial experience of suffering as intense supports the arc of a redemptive narrative; it creates an initial "low point" from which the sufferer can rise to a "higher place" through processes of redemption.

Redemption occurs through the process of reevaluating one's suffering (initially viewed as extremely negative) and incorporating it into the self's narrative by discovering *opportunities for growth* latent in the suffering. An assumption of redemptive narratives is that extreme suffering requires a change in one's understanding of the world and the self, because people typically view the world as a just place and themselves as good (meaning that a bad experience for the self produces dissonance; Janoff-Bulman, 1992). Growth occurs when one allows either one's worldview or one's self-concept to change positively as the autobiographical meaning of the suffering is formulated (e.g., Triplett et al., 2012). Crucial for such positive growth is the sense that either *new knowledge*, *enhanced creativity*, or both are being gained as a result of the suffering. New knowledge usually involves becoming aware of resources of which one was previously unaware (e.g., learning through the survival of suffering that one is stronger than one thought), and enhanced creativity often involves taking advantage of new knowledge to transform one's life after the suffering.

At the conclusion of a prototypic redemptive narrative, positive growth has brought one to a state where one's life is actually *improved* compared to the pre-suffering state. The sufferer may not believe that the suffering was a necessary event in their life story, but ideally they will be convinced that they are better off in some ultimate sense because they suffered.

Theory and research both suggest that the idea of improvement through suffering is often conveyed in redemptive narratives by translating classic religious notions of death and rebirth into secular ideas about the active construction of personality across the life span (Becker, 1997;

Deardorff, 2009; Rank, 1958). It is clear that the elements of *individualization* and *intensification of suffering*, followed by *opportunities for growth* through *new knowledge* and/or *enhanced creativity*, culminating in overall *personal improvement* connect the redemptive narrative to the ideal of self-transcendence in IV and II cultures (see Chapter 6). Rather than an ultimate threat to the self, in light of this narrative, suffering becomes the platform for a new self-enhancement project. Religious ideas and even broadly endorsed worldviews of any kind are not strictly necessary for redemption to occur.

Writing in a philosophic frame, Phillips (2000) summarizes how, with the advent of the modern secular worldview and the collapse into pure immanence, narratives of religious transcendence became narratives of individual redemption, requiring suffering to be recast as something inherently positive:

> When transience is not merely an occasion for mourning, we will have inherited the earth ... making sense of our lives as bound by mortality not seduced by transcendence ... Modern lives, unconsoled by religious belief, could be consumed by the experience of loss. So what else could a life be now but a grief-stricken project, a desperate attempt to make grief itself somehow redemptive, a source of secular wisdom? (pp. 12–14)

Nevertheless, it is important to note that redemptive suffering narratives need not be couched in exclusively secular terms. Of course, the notion of redemption itself, and the overall pattern of this form of narrative, is steeped in historically Christian ideas (Janoff-Bulman, 1992; McAdams, 2006). Furthermore, the new knowledge that is gained through redemptive suffering can sometimes be spiritual in nature, as when people report a renewed, deepened, or acquired sense of faith after a traumatic experience (e.g., Tedeschi & Calhoun, 1996). And of course Christian and other religious perspectives can – especially in contemporary guises – be drawn upon as lenses through which to view suffering as an opportunity for personal growth (Hall & Johnson, 2001). Nonetheless, the pattern of redemptive narratives allows an individual to make sense of suffering without necessarily relying on religion or other collective structures, and interpreting suffering this way typically reinforces processes of individualization and worldview-questioning that are associated with the decline of religious conviction.

I will argue that the dominant discourse surrounding the Greensburg tornado – that is, the discourse adopted by the media, outside institutions, and city officials – has been one that is highly resonant with the redemption narrative popular among contemporary psychologists. One would expect such a narrative to emerge from social forces and agents representing mainstream contemporary II culture in the United States. However, this narrative is quite different from that offered by the Holdemans who lived through the tornado, as I will show later in this chapter.

Greensburg's redemption story

Greensburg is a small town, the seat of Kiowa County in south central Kansas near the Oklahoma border. Its population in 2000 was 1,574; two years after the tornado, this figure had been cut in half to 777 (Smith & Cartlidge, 2011). On the night of Friday, May 4, 2007, an extremely powerful tornado (which received the highest potential rating on the Enhanced Fujita scale used to rank tornadoes), 1.7 miles wide with estimated wind speeds of over 200 mph, tore through the town and the surrounding countryside in about half an hour (Monfredo, 2008). When the storm had passed and the damage was reckoned, 95 percent of the town had been laid waste, with 1,000 homes in the area either destroyed or severely damaged. In addition, ten people had been instantly killed (because they lacked adequate shelter), and ninety injuries were reported in the first 24 hours after the storm (a few more people were to die soon afterward from complications related to their injuries; Ablah, Tinius, Konda, Synovitz, & Subbarao, 2007). Kiowa County was declared the site of a national disaster, and state and national government representatives, Federal Emergency Management Agency (FEMA) workers, volunteers, and concerned relatives swarmed into the area. Over the weekend following the storm, access to the town was heavily restricted, and it continued to be restricted more loosely for some time afterward during the recovery process. In time, "FEMAville" – a trailer park – was constructed for those who were displaced by the storm, where utilities were charged for the first 18 months and rent and utilities were charged after this time (Paul & Che, 2011).

Almost immediately after the initial shock of the storm, ideas of redemptive suffering started to percolate into the discourse surrounding Greensburg. Firsthand accounts of the tornado (Haney, 2008; 2009; Unruh & Unruh, 2007) all triangulate on the existence in the immediate aftermath of what Wolfenstein (1957) referred to as the "post-disaster utopia": people from inside and outside the community coming together in an outpouring of sympathy and positive affect, with intentions of helping each other to achieve normalcy in the chaos left by the storm. Such outbreaks of altruism and perceived positive emotional exchanges between individuals are especially common in the wake of large-scale tornadoes (Taylor, Zurcher, & Key, 1970). In the midst of the post-disaster utopia, within a week of the storm, the idea was voiced by local officials and Kansas Governor Kathleen Sebelius that the town should be rebuilt "green," with an eye toward sustainability and energy efficiency (White, 2010).

The idea of reconstructing the town in a completely different way took hold and began to guide much of the official discourse surrounding the event. For example, a Long-Term Community Recovery Plan for Greensburg – drafted by FEMA officials (2007) working in collaboration with local politicians, the Kansas government, a Kansas nonprofit organization, and the displaced citizens of Kiowa County (White, 2010) – centered almost exclusively on the idea of transforming the town into a model of green energy for the nation. The document is filled with language fitting the redemptive suffering narrative:

> With great destruction comes opportunity; you are seizing this opportunity to create a Greensburg that will shine in the future . . . Extraordinary circumstances have demanded extraordinary resolve. Faced with the daunting tasks of rebuilding home and hearth, many of you have devoted energy, thought, and creativity to envisioning the "new Greensburg." (FEMA, 2007, p. 6)

Language that reframes the near-total destruction of the community in terms of opportunity for transformation and improvement is also used to specifically describe the "green" initiative:

> Greensburg and Kiowa County have the unique opportunity to rebuild in a way that will not only replace the parts of the community that were destroyed but will look at the real impact of that rebuilding on the community and the environment. Sustainable or "green" development creates livable, inspirational, and enduring places where the quality of life and the long-term quality of the community will be enhanced rather than depleted . . . Greensburg and Kiowa County have a unique opportunity to become the national leader in the design and construction of highly efficient and environmentally sound facilities. (FEMA, 2007, pp. 15–17)

Naturally, part of the appeal of this particular redemptive narrative stems from the fact that a worldwide reputation for green energy is not something that would typically be associated with a small Midwestern town. Indeed, accounts of the town's trajectory put forward by local officials – for example, in the three-season reality TV series *Greensburg* dedicated to the topic – bring the redemptive arc into sharp relief by emphasizing that the town was in decline (in terms of population and productivity) prior to the tornado (see White, 2010). This narrative suggests that without the tornado's utter devastation, the unprecedented chance for Greensburg's total rebirth would never have occurred (see Jones, 2011). From at least one perspective, in the years since the tornado, Greensburg has largely succeeded in its mission of becoming "stronger, better, greener!" (a slogan now prominently displayed on several new billboards around town). Most of the city's power is now supplied by a series of wind turbines, and it is the first city in the nation where all official city buildings have been built to the platinum standards of Leadership in Energy and Environmental Design (LEED). However, the population has not recovered to pre-tornado levels, and many townspeople moved away from Greensburg because of the slowness of the recovery and obstacles to building new homes, which resulted in part from the collective decision to rebuild green (Paul & Che, 2011).

The redemptive vision for Greensburg was "in the air" almost immediately after the catastrophe. This is partly a testament to the fact that Greensburg's redemption story was crafted and promoted by representatives of outside institutions and the local and national media as much as local community leaders. For example, content analysis reveals that the words "opportunity" and "resilience" appeared with unusually high frequency in local newspapers for the first two years after the tornado (White, 2010). Consider one typical example from a local paper:

> That rumble [of post-disaster cleaning and construction] has yet to cease. The sounds of construction are as persistent as the wind. But now, it sounds like progress, like lives being rebuilt with nails, boards, and iron will. It sounds like hope and excitement, something for residents to rally around besides their loss. Greensburg is rebuilding "green," a town-wide effort to use as many environmentally friendly materials as it can to bring the town back to life ... The people of Greensburg are facing the daunting challenge before them. Watch. Nail by nail, strangers and friends are linking the past to the future, and slowly rebuilding the spirit within the city limits. (Nickelson, 2008)

Evidence that the townspeople of Greensburg themselves endorsed the redemptive narrative is less conclusive. Some accounts compiled and published by local residents in the two years after the tornado suggest an adoption of the narrative to make sense of their suffering. For example, one resident wrote: "It is now November 9th and Greensburg is building a new history. We're building a green, sustainable community. I feel proud to be a pioneer of this new city. I may have lost all of my possessions, my home, and my job, but it seems there is possibly much more to gain" (qtd. in Haney, 2008, p. 45). Another claimed, "We're a lot stronger and better than we used to be. While I would never wish this type of experience on anyone, I am very thankful for the life lessons I've learned" (qtd. in Haney, 2008, p. 29). Some of the townspeople explicitly couched the redemption narrative in religious terms: "God has blessed us all ... He hasn't stripped us of anything. He has presented us with glorious and unprecedented opportunities of growth that exceed even our wildest expectations ..." (qtd. in Haney, 2008, p. 19). Others discussed how learning about energy efficiency was part of a larger growth in knowledge and a shifting life philosophy necessitated by the disaster:

> Our lives have been changed forever. The things that were important before have no meaning to us now. We have decided to make our lives simpler ... We are introducing the green initiative into our lives. It's amazing how we've always done these things but never thought it to be eco-friendly. We always thought it was a way of living on the prairie ... It's the little things that make life worth living. Enjoy the great environment that God has so preciously molded on this earth. Don't take life for granted! As we all know, life can be changed and taken away from us in an instant. (Qtd. in Haney, 2009, p. 78)

Yet, despite these instances, a comprehensive examination of the first-hand accounts produced by Greensburg survivors, coupled with information from research reports, calls into question the idea that Greensburg's redemption story was universally accepted. Indeed, reactions of some of the townspeople to the greening process have been mixed to negative, as evidenced by some of the documented meetings and interviews in the *Greensburg* TV series (see also Smith & Cartlidge, 2011). Even those who have adopted the redemptive narrative themselves recognize that it might not apply to all locals; as one resident put it in a newspaper interview: "I've heard it said the tornado was a blessing ... I like to stay away from saying that because there are ... people who are (not) in a better situation ... But as far as myself and my wife, we are in a better place today than we were before the storm" (Tanner, 2010). Many survivors feel that rebuilding green was not in their best financial interest; others evince a lack of understanding of the initiative and its importance, and a concern that they have been marginalized in the reconstruction project. Economic issues seemed to play a significant role in the difficulty some survivors had in adopting the redemptive narrative or rebuilding in Greensburg. In 2009, Greensburg had a lower median household and average per capita income compared to the national figures (Hernandez, 2011), and local incomes tended to be beneath the national average even prior to the storm (Paul & Che, 2011). Furthermore, the amount of insurance compensation the average household received after the storm was less than 40% of the amount required to build a new home in the town, a situation partly resulting from the difficulties involved in relying on contractors in a remote, rural area (Paul & Che, 2011). After the "post-disaster utopia" faded and the practical obstacles to Greensburg's redemption story became apparent in the following years, many residents expressed frustration at the slow pace of the town's recovery (Smith & Cartlidge, 2011).

For those who were unable to wholeheartedly embrace the redemption narrative, a profound sense of loss and disorientation regarding the tornado sometimes emerged. Many of the elderly residents of Greensburg, who lived there most of their lives, were disoriented by the loss of all familiar landmarks for a long period afterward, and express a sadness that the green transformation of the town has fundamentally altered its appearance (Smith & Cartlidge, 2011). One account is representative of many of the narratives offered by this group of disenchanted survivors:

> No matter how nice Greensburg is built back, no matter how much we grow and prosper . . . we will never have our home back. The Greensburg I grew up in will never be the same. So many familiar places are gone forever . . . there's always an underlying sadness for those of us whose roots are deep in Greensburg. One friend commented, "I wonder when I can drive down Main Street and not cry?" (Haney, 2009, p. 28)

In sum, the "mainstream" narrative that emerged in the immediate aftermath of the devastating Greensburg tornado bore many of the characteristics of a prototypic redemptive suffering interpretation. A terrible calamity was recast as a once-in-a-lifetime opportunity for the complete transformation of the community, to be achieved through ingenuity and perseverance. The town was to be changed – and *improved* – because of its collective trauma. This narrative, although adopted by some local residents, was primarily supplied and reinforced by city officials, members of the state and national government, outside businesses, and the media. Many Greensburg citizens found themselves unable to adopt this narrative, and have continually expressed a sense that their lives were fundamentally changed, in negative ways, by the storm. Some of these citizens have left the town forever.

An overlooked perspective: Bethel Mennonite Church

Despite the considerable amount of scrutiny the town of Greensburg has received since the tornado, both from the media and academic researchers, very little attention has been paid to the perspective of a Holdeman congregation living just outside the town limits. I assumed that the members of this congregation probably experienced the post-disaster recovery in a different way from the townspeople of Greensburg, and, given their CV culture, that their interpretation of the event's significance would not conform to the mainstream redemptive narrative. To determine how this congregation experienced the disaster and recovered from it, and whether their culture influenced this process in unique ways, I conducted a series of interviews with tornado survivors from the Bethel Mennonite congregation.

Bethel Mennonite Church – located to the southwest of Greensburg proper – is a mid-sized Holdeman congregation of 116 current members.

The congregation was founded in 1908 by members of the Lone Tree congregation in Moundridge, Kansas (one of the earliest Holdeman congregations, and the site of John Holdeman's final years and burial in 1900; Hiebert, 1973). The members of this congregation have largely succeeded in maintaining a fairly agricultural lifestyle. Even prior to the 2007 tornado, the Holdemans at Bethel were more integrated with the local townspeople than might be typical for a Holdeman congregation. This is due partly to the small size of the Greensburg community and the fact that many Bethel members perform various kinds of contract work or provide services for non-Mennonite residents (e.g., house remodeling and construction). It is my impression that the tornado experience brought the Bethel congregation even closer to the surrounding community.

Significantly, because it was outside the town, Bethel Mennonite Church was not destroyed by the tornado (all seven other local churches, located within town limits, were demolished; Smith & Cartlidge, 2011). Furthermore – and most significantly, as the Holdemans stress in their accounts of the event – no members of the congregation perished during the storm. Despite these good fortunes, the congregation certainly suffered as a whole; out of fifty-four total households in the congregation, seventeen were destroyed and thirteen severely damaged (Unruh & Unruh, 2007).

I first approached one of the ministers of the Bethel congregation with a letter in which I asked to arrange a meeting. In February 2013, I met with the minister and one deacon at the church and explained to them that I was interested in interviewing tornado survivors from their congregation. The church leaders assented to the project and agreed to assist me in soliciting participation from members of the congregation. We arranged a date for three weeks in the future when I would return to Greensburg and interview any willing participants. In the meanwhile, the minister announced the study to the congregation during a service.

I prepared an interview guide with six major, open-ended questions and several potential follow-up questions, following the specific method and recommendations of Carspecken (1996). In line with existential anthropology (Jackson, 2005; see Chapter 1), the study was thoroughly event focused, concentrating on participants' experience and meaning-making with regard to the May 4, 2007, tornado. Questions focused on participants' experiences and emotions on the night of the tornado and in the weeks and months afterward; how the Bethel congregation coped with the aftermath of the storm and recovered from it; and their interpretations of the significance and impact of the tornado in their lives, including comparisons of life "before and after" the storm. In

March 2013, I interviewed four separate couples at the Bethel church. In total, then, I interviewed eight Holdeman tornado survivors, 7 percent of the total population at a conservative estimate. Interviews were conducted with each couple (i.e., husband and wife responded to questions simultaneously) and lasted about an hour each. With permission from the participants, I audio-recorded the interviews. Although I prepared with a detailed interview guide, the interviews were basically unstructured and interactive in style (e.g., Corbin & Morse, 2003).

After the interviews were complete, I fully transcribed them. In the tradition of grounded theory (Charmaz, 2006), I engaged in two major waves of coding the interview data in an attempt to discern important analytic codes that distilled the subjective impressions and lived events of the participants. In the first wave of descriptive coding, I developed 104 lower-level codes using line-by-line coding (Miles & Huberman, 1994). In the second wave of pattern coding, I developed seven higher-order analytic categories, summarizing participants' experiences and interpretations, through a process of conceptually grouping the descriptive codes. Two of these analytic categories will be the primary focus of the present discussion.

To facilitate the development of the analytic categories, and to check their validity, I also compared the interview data to data obtained from three other relevant sources. First, I examined six written accounts of the storm by Bethel Holdemans included in locally published anthologies (Haney, 2008; 2009; one of these accounts was written by one of the couples whom I interviewed). Second, I examined a collective written account of the storm and its aftermath prepared by the Bethel congregation itself (Unruh & Unruh, 2007). And third, I searched through all issues of the Church of God in Christ, Mennonite, newsletter "Messenger of Truth" between the years 2007 and 2009 for material relevant to the storm and the Bethel congregation. As additional checks on the validity of my findings, I submitted my codes to critical scrutiny from two groups of academic peers during the process of code development, one group in sociology and the other in psychology (Carspecken, 1996). Finally, as recommended by Carspecken (1996), I sent a copy of my report of the results (revised with less technical language) to the Bethel church leaders for distribution among the interviewed participants. I received feedback from a deacon, and – apart from a few details which I corrected – the presented information was approved as accurate by the congregation.

To maintain anonymity, when quoting the transcripts, I refer to my participants using numbers (i.e., P1–P8).

It is my distinct impression, based on analysis of the interview data and other materials, that the Bethel congregation has recovered rather well from the 2007 tornado, and, although it was a major upset in the course of their lives, its effects were ultimately temporary for them. When asked whether their lives or beliefs were changed significantly because of the storm, two of the four couples answered in the negative. The other two couples mentioned changes that were not very profound and were localized to the experience of storms (P5 primarily discussed a fear of bad weather that he and his wife did not have prior to the tornado, and P7, who works with the Holdeman organization Christian Disaster Relief, mentioned that his experience has made him more empathetic toward survivors of other disasters). As far as I can ascertain, nearly all members of the congregation who lost their homes felt that their lives had returned to normalcy and were living in new or rebuilt houses within 1 or 2 years of the tornado. When I first met with the Bethel minister to discuss the project, he informed me that he could only think of two families in the congregation that had moved away because of the tornado. Comparing these observations to the fact that the total population of Greenburg was almost cut in half, and that as of January 2010 many houses in the town were still only under construction (Paul & Che, 2011), it is reasonable to conclude that the recovery of the Bethel community was swifter and more complete than the recovery of the town community at large.

The question then becomes: What about the Holdeman community facilitated their recovery? What resources did the survivors draw on, which may have been less available or unavailable to other Greensburg residents outside their congregational community? Based primarily on the themes that emerged from the interviews, I propose that the Holdemans in Greensburg had access to two primary resources that facilitated their recovery. The first of these is more material, while the second is psychological. The first resource I refer to using the analytic category *Community*; it is, quite simply, the material ways in which the traditional practices and solidarity of the Bethel church and the broader Holdeman faith community facilitated recovery by providing labor, financial support, food, building materials, and replacement of lost property. Of course, this largely material-behavioral category is not without its psychological component – the Holdeman survivors certainly experienced an assuring sense of solidarity as they were physically and financially aided by their "brothers and sisters," and opportunities to help fellow sufferers were doubtless therapeutic. But when grappling with the psychological issues raised by the tornado – possibilities of meaninglessness, despair, or a loss of self-confidence – the Bethel congregation members primarily relied on the second resource, to which I refer with the analytic category *Transcendence*. The two analytic categories of *Community* and *Transcendence* encompass the descriptive codes that appeared most often across the interview transcripts. I will outline these two major resources in detail, drawing on representative examples from the transcripts.

The material resource of *Community*

The *Community* analytic category encapsulates the many references made throughout the interviews and Holdeman written accounts to the wealth of material and emotional support the survivors received from the Holdeman faith community. Tornado survivors not only received; they also gave support to others who were either in the same situation as themselves or even less fortunate, and this generosity toward others was also psychologically beneficial for the survivors. Some of the most commonly referenced events in the interviews were occasions when the Holdeman community was able to show solidarity and fortitude even in the days immediately following the disaster. Accordingly, the *Community* category consists of three primary subcomponents – *Receiving from the Community, Giving to the Community,* and the *Communal Practices* in which the emotional solidarity of the community was made materially manifest. An overview of the *Community* category and its components is provided in Table 8.1.

It is important to make clear from the outset that in developing this analytic category, I focused on the Church of God in Christ, Mennonite, community in particular. By this I mean the Bethel Mennonite congregation – both those who were personally affected by the storm, and those who were relatively unaffected by virtue of being outside the storm's path – as well as the many other Holdeman congregations that provided

Table 8.1. *The analytic category of* Community, *its major components, and constituent descriptive codes.*

Community		
Receiving from the Community	Giving to the Community	Communal Practices
Assistance from Family	Concern for Others	Power to Rebuild
Assistance from the Bethel Congregation	Protection of Others	Church Meals
Assistance from Other Congregations	Helping Others	Survival of the Church
Mennonite Disaster Relief	Providing Shelter	Shared Experience
Mennonite Insurance (Aid Plans)	Children	Narration

support, primarily coming from (but by no means limited to) the rest of Kansas and nearby Oklahoma.

The Bethel survivors readily acknowledge that they received ample and important assistance from many "outsiders," that is, non-Holdeman individuals and institutions. Occasionally, participants fondly recalled non-Holdeman friends who showed up right after the disaster with "a will to help" (P5). One couple mentioned receiving helpful funds to rebuild their homes in the form of government loans. Many Holdemans spent some amount of time in FEMA trailers (often stationed in the yards of relatives whose houses had withstood) before they were able to reconstruct their homes. And one participant told a heartwarming anecdote about how he learned from the tornado that the Holdeman people are somewhat reluctant to offer each other open displays of affection. When he went into the disaster-stricken town in the days following, this man received numerous embraces from non-Holdemans, and found this to be an important emotional resource that was a little lacking in his more reserved community.

It is not only the case that the Bethel members received support from non-Holdeman sources; the relationship was reciprocal. The astonishing labor power and work ethic, coupled with knowledge of construction processes, displayed by the Holdeman Christian Disaster Relief organization made it a valuable asset to the town community in the days, weeks, and months after the storm. By June 24, 2007, the Christian Disaster Relief workers (from Greensburg and other Holdeman congregations) had cleared and cleaned up over one hundred damaged homes and foundations (Unruh & Unruh, 2007). And because the Bethel church was the only church building in the Greensburg area unscathed by the storm, the Holdemans were able to organize massive meals there in the days afterward, which they shared with hundreds of non-Holdemans.

Although these experiences and many others were certainly important to the Bethel survivors, and although they probably forged a stronger bond between the congregation and the other townspeople than might exist for many Holdeman communities, the participants placed primary emphasis on the overwhelming support they received from family members and other Holdemans. As mentioned, the Bethel congregation seems to have been on a different recovery trajectory from the other townspeople of Greensburg, doubtless due to the congregation's faith-based community network.

Receiving from the Community. All accounts from Bethel survivors contain numerous references to the tremendous material and emotional support they received from other Holdemans. This support came in three primary forms: *Assistance from Family* and *Assistance from the Bethel*

Congregation, which was most important immediately after the storm and in the years afterward, and *Assistance from Other Congregations*, which was primarily important in the days after the storm and for about a year or two later, while the survivors were rebuilding their homes. These forms of assistance were often recounted in the interviews in ways consonant with the Holdeman emphasis on humility and dependence. As one participant put it: "that was a real morale booster to see that, you know, we had friends from away that were coming in and doing for us what we couldn't do ourselves" (P3). A passage from the congregation's written account echoes this sentiment: "If you have never been there yourself, you cannot imagine the immense comfort to see brethren driving in to help when you are walking about in shock, not knowing what to do first" (Unruh & Unruh, 2007, p. 98). Another couple described the assistance they received this way:

P1: I feel like we have probably the greatest support group in the world, as far as a support group, and that is our church, here.
P2: They were there immediately.
P1: Yeah.
P2: The next day . . . was that on a Friday?
P1: It was on a Friday, when the tornado was, yeah.
P2: But they started coming *immediately*. Meals were being served already the next day here at the church. There was no electricity but they set up, you know, with generators, they brought generators and were serving meals to everybody. Anybody in town that needed a place.

Family members and non-relatives from other congregations flooded into Greensburg to help with the disaster relief effort. Assistance came in a variety of forms. First, damaged foundations were cleared and destroyed. Women often helped by preparing food or by cleaning and repairing salvaged belongings. Massive amounts of food, clothing, and other goods were donated. Collections were taken up at neighboring churches for money to be donated to the survivors. One participant – a carpenter by trade – had lost his shop and all of his tools (including several very costly pieces of equipment). He described how, miraculously, he received a call from a Holdeman deacon (an acquaintance) in Michigan about ten days after the tornado. A carpenter in the deacon's congregation had gone bankrupt, and they not only offered to sell the participant his tools at a very generous price, but to deliver them all by truck to him in Greensburg.

Much of the assistance the Bethel survivors received was facilitated by institutions within the church community that have a long history. Because Anabaptists of all varieties subscribe to ideals of pacifism and nonresistance, members of these groups have been historically required to find alternative means of service during periods of national military involvement (Chapter 6). Among the Holdemans and other denominations, this has led to the development of *Mennonite Disaster Relief* organizations. Much of the labor involved in cleaning up the post-disaster homesteads, rebuilding fences, and other tasks was accomplished by volunteers for Christian Disaster Relief. Most Holdeman congregations possess a "Sewing Circle" organized by the female members, and these groups donated many supplies (blankets, etc.) to the Bethel congregation (Unruh & Unruh, 2007). Because of their historical stance against insurance, the Holdemans also have developed a set of alternative institutions internal to their faith community, including Mennonite Union Aid and Brotherhood Auto Aid (Unruh & Unruh, 2007, p. 144). These *Aid Plans* operate similarly to insurance on a small scale. As one participant explained, "we had 56 policy-holders in our congregation ... And I think there was like, around forty of 'em had claims from the tornado ... I was just impressed with how, how liberally they settled those claims. How, how compassionate they were. It taught me a lesson" (P5).

Giving to the Community. In addition to the assistance the Bethel survivors received from relatives and other Holdemans around the country, as well as from their Church's extant institutions, their post-disaster experience was characterized by *Helping Others* in an equally impressive variety of ways. This was especially true for those who had not suffered massive loss of property: "some of those that just *completely* lost their homes, and their buildings, and so forth, which we, we didn't ... for the ones that were left that had resources, and we, we were able to help them. That was more our part, to help where we could, and we were, we were happy to do that" (P6).

Regardless of what they had lost in the storm, all the Bethel survivors began their experience of giving to the community on May 4. All four interviews made it clear that the primary thought running through the survivors' minds in the immediate passing of the tornado was a deep *Concern for Others.* Concern for frightened *Children* who might be injured or traumatized in the experience was especially prevalent. Six years later, one participant still experienced emotional difficulty recounting the "overwhelming fear" he felt upon realizing that his son, daughter-in-law, and infant grandson were potentially in danger. Already when the storm hit, some of the participants were helping others by *Providing Shelter* to those who did not have secure basements or who happened to be with them at the time. After the immediate danger was over, all the participants (particularly the men) went by foot or in salvaged vehicles through the wreckage of Greensburg and the surrounding countryside, checking on relatives, neighbors, and other Holdeman households, looking to see where damage had been done and to offer help to those who were in trouble. *Protection of Others* was an important theme in the interviews, with the male participants often assuming the traditional masculine role characteristic for this community, protecting their wives and family during the storm (including sheltering others' bodies with their own against flying debris). Women also protected the children.

In the weeks and months after the storm, mutual assistance among the Bethel congregation was normative, as work parties were routinely organized to help those who had lost their homes or sustained damage salvage whatever they could. Those with intact properties provided temporary shelter to displaced relatives, allowing them to stay for a time either in the house or in a FEMA trailer set up on the lawn. The feeling that they were helping their friends and neighbors provided psychological solace to the participants. One interviewee in particular felt blessed that she had a newborn baby at the time the tornado struck, because her need to care for the infant helped her forget about her own troubles. Another summarized his experience of the storm as giving him a desire to help others founded on the generosity that he had witnessed:

> P5: And I think that's the one thing that's impressed me the most with this tornado experience, the way our surrounding congregations . . . and others, other volunteers, not only our own people – the way they came into Greensburg with a will to help. And give of themselves. It made me vow at one point if there's ever a disaster anywhere that I can somehow help out someway, I want to do it.

Communal Practices. The experiences of giving and receiving that the Bethel survivors underwent in the aftermath of the storm were materialized in several *Communal Practices* – collective actions that made manifest the solidarity felt by the Holdemans in the face of disaster. On several occasions, the interviewees spoke with an air of near disbelief about how efficiently they and the outside congregations were able to effect repairs and restore what had been damaged. One participant found his courage renewed after the disaster by seeing how quickly the roof of the damaged Holdeman school building was repaired:

> P3: By Monday morning, though, the volunteer crews, when we went by Monday morning the roof was back on and they had it sheeted and tar-papered and that was such a morale booster to me. I can still remember that. I just couldn't believe it, that they had actually got rafters built, and got 'em on, and got new sheeting, and had it weather-tight. By Monday morning.

The carpenter participant – who received the discounted tools from the Michigan congregation – similarly expressed amazement at the fact that he and his brothers were able to reconstruct his shop in two weeks (it should have taken double that time, he said). The *Power to Rebuild* manifested by the Holdeman community and the Bethel congregation in particular clearly played a pivotal role in the congregation's relatively swift recovery.

While physical acts of rebuilding catalyzed the recovery and boosted morale, the *Church Meals* organized by the Holdemans were another material practice that had important consequences for solidarity. All participants mentioned these meals with fondness, gratitude, and awe. They were massive affairs held routinely at Bethel Church for the first few weeks after the tornado. Although they primarily served to provide displaced congregation members and Holdeman volunteers with breakfast, lunch, and dinner, on several occasions any individuals in town who desired to attend were given free food and temporary reprieve from the weather and surrounding devastation. Massive amounts of food were donated from other congregations, sometimes appearing with no explanation or obvious source (Unruh & Unruh, 2007). The Bethel survivors were very grateful for this particular form of outside assistance, and were also glad that the *Survival of the Church* allowed them to help other townspeople:

> P7: We, we felt very blessed ... all these different congregations coming in and bringing the food, you know ... Noon and supper, we were always in good hands ... But I think it was very nice, very appropriate that this building stood. To help the people in town, that was very nice, it was a very good gesture that we could show the community, I feel.

One participant summarized the extent and significance of the undertaking in this way: "Ours was the only church left standing, and many, many townspeople came and ate out here. I think they fed around, anywhere from 5, 6, 7 or 800 people every day. And uh, people were very grateful to have a place to come and eat and share with other people" (P6). This remark points to some of the psychological significance of these events, underscored by other comments and accounts. When coming together for the church meals, survivors were able to gain an important sense of *Shared Experience* with others, and to begin the process of *Narration* – making sense of the traumatic event and incorporating it into a meaningful account of their life experience.

The importance that these communal practices were accorded in the interviews and written accounts can hardly be overstated. They were concrete processes of recovery, as well as material displays of solidarity and perseverance. It should not go unremarked that these practices had their basis in cultural and behavioral patterns present among the Holdeman people prior to the disaster. The Holdemans are typically skilled in manual labor and construction, and possess equipment relevant to such tasks; they possess a spirit of collective belonging and mutual charity among their fellows; and they have institutions internal to their community designed to help others in times of need. The fact that the Bethel survivors were able to draw on these community-specific resources – as well as other forms of assistance available to all the townspeople of Greensburg, such as FEMA's operations and the work of miscellaneous volunteers – clearly aided their comparatively complete recovery. If the Holdeman people did not possess these cultural elements, the Bethel congregation – and indeed the town of Greensburg as a whole – would have suffered to a considerably greater extent.

The psychological resource of *Transcendence*

Obviously, a major natural disaster bringing significant loss of property raises the problem of theodicy for a devout people. The *Transcendence* category captures the primary interpretive framework relied on by the Bethel survivors in making sense of the tornado.

As described in Chapter 6, suffering interpretations involving transcendence are grounded in a dualistic worldview that contrasts a true, eternal world with a false, temporal one. Proceeding from this distinction, what I refer to as the resource of transcendence involves three primary components. First, the Bethel survivors *Preserve the "True World" (the Sacred)* through a variety of means. By seeing the tornado as fitting into God's ultimate plan, and by refusing to question God's motives (which they believe to be unknowable), the Holdemans inoculate the true world against the threat of doubt. Second, the suffering caused by the tornado is rendered less problematic by *Degrading the "False World" (the Profane)*. Through the conviction that we currently exist in a temporal order that is inferior to the eternal plane, the Bethel survivors trivialize the threat implied by loss of property and disrupted routines. Third, in relating the experience of the tornado, the Bethel survivors point to several apparent *Mediations*, wherein the true world was made temporarily manifest in the false, or the inhabitants of the false world reached out to the true. Especially significant were instances in which the Holdemans saw God's hand protecting them during the storm. An overview of the *Transcendence* category and its components is provided in Table 8.2.

Preservation of the "True World" (the Sacred). It is through the prospect of eventual vertical transcendence into Heaven that Holdemans maintain a sense of the meaningfulness of their often materially difficult

Table 8.2. *The analytic category of* Transcendence, *its major components, and constituent descriptive codes.*

Transcendence		
Preservation of the "True World" (the Sacred)	Degradation of the "False World" (the Profane)	Mediations
God's Security God's Purpose/Truth Trust/Faith Unknowable Reasons Avoidance/Resisting Analysis Common Faith	Suffering as Trial (Acceptance) Nonattachment Temporal Order Property Unimportant Future Focus	God's Assistance God's Power Fortunate Circumstances (Blessings) Prayer/Devotions

lives and labors. It is therefore important that when seemingly random or threatening events occur, they are not allowed to call the true world, or God's benevolence and control, into question. When I asked the Bethel survivors why they thought the storm had happened, or whether it had any meaning for them, they often responded in ways that drew on the true world as a source of meaningful interpretation, while also circumventing the problem of theodicy.

This was generally accomplished by insisting that the individual must maintain *Trust* and *Faith* in *God's Purpose* and *Truth.* From the perspective of the Holdemans I interviewed, God has a reason for everything that happens, including negative events such as the tornado, and we should simply trust in His wisdom. One excerpt is particularly representative:

> P3: I believe that God can ... um, overrule the natural course of events at any time, and I believe He does. So when something like this happens I believe He knew in advance this was going to happen, He allowed it to happen. But He ... He sees from an eternal perspective, whereas our thinking is human, it's, it's restricted by time and circumstance, and we don't have the true perspective that He has ... one message that came through loud and clear to me was set your affection on things above, not on things on the earth ... through it, we learned to trust, we learned to trust more than we had, probably.

This quote demonstrates an aspect of preserving the true world that is closely related to the insistence on *God's Purpose/Truth.* This is the tactic of positing that *God's Purpose/Truth* consists of *Unknowable Reasons.* Although there was unquestionably a meaning and intention behind the tornado, we cannot understand it, and should not attempt to. An exchange between one couple is representative here:

P5: Well I think everything happens for a reason. And it's our choice, oftentimes, how it, how we can use it, for the good.
P6: We just don't know the reason.
P5: We don't know the reason, necessarily. I don't think that's for us to know.

In an effort to preserve the true world by insisting on God's *Unknowable Reasons*, some participants went so far as to engage in deliberate strategies of *Avoidance/Resisting Analysis*. In other words, when questions arose about why the tornado occurred, what meaning it had, or why some people were severely affected and not others, participants would occasionally state that they refuse to think too deeply about such issues. This refusal would be coupled with appeals to *God's Truth/Purpose* and *Unknowable Reasons*. An example of this was the fact that two of the four men interviewed qualified their statements on the psychological significance of the tornado with phrases such as "I'm not sure that I'm enough of an analyst to be able to tell you . . ." (P5) and "I'm not the kind of person to do so much analyzing" (P7).

I asked one couple to reflect on the differences between life in their old home and in their new home, and the emotions they experience thinking about those differences. This seemed to be a mildly upsetting question for the couple, who remarked on some of the property they had lost, and then responded with a motto: "*you don't go there*" (P7). I refer to this phrase as a motto because the couple used it four times during the interview, and it also appears in one of their published accounts of the experience. As the wife put it, "if I start analyzing, then I tell myself: You don't go there. Because, I'm the kind that . . . it would just get too depressing" (P8). In the first instance in which the couple invoked the motto, the husband immediately linked this tactic of *Avoidance/Resisting Analysis* to the idea of *Unknowable Reasons*:

P7: OK, it's in Deuteronomy, the 29th Chapter, the 29th Verse, if I remember right. It says, "The secret things belong to the Lord." There's some things about this tornado – for instance, *why*. [*brief pause*] That's, that's, that's really not our business, as far as I'm concerned. [*slight chuckle*] That belongs to the Lord. And why He, why it didn't go 500 feet over, and why it had to hit us, why, I don't know, that . . . There are no answers for that kind of thing, I don't think, that belongs to the Lord.

In Deuteronomy 29, Moses outlines the natural disasters and calamities that befall those who break the Covenant with the Lord, and concludes with the phrase "The secret things belong to the Lord our God." This scriptural line is invoked in official Holdeman texts regarding other situations of moral ambiguity (Church of God in Christ, Mennonite, 1998, pp. 413–414).

Of course, the ultimate significance of the true world concept for the Bethel survivors lies not in their various tactics for inoculating it against the theodicy problem, but in its role as a psychological resource. Here the notion of *God's Security* is most important. It is clear from the interviews that the Holdemans look to the true world for a reservoir of security and comfort that cannot be infringed on by earthly suffering, whether it be caused by natural disaster or by some other tragedy.

P3: These temporal things that we see and touch – in a sense they don't matter, so much. I mean, in a way they do to us, because we need 'em. But . . . I, I feel like God wants us to have a sense of security that's not just based on those things. We need to have a sense of security in Him, based on our faith, that He loves us, He's taking care of us, He's gonna be there no matter what happens. And that way we have a sense of security that's not shaken or taken away when we do have an event like the tornado.

The reliance on *God's Security* is a very common theme throughout nearly all Holdeman writings, especially those that are concerned with the realities of misfortune. As the excerpt from P3 demonstrates, this security is usually presented as the victory of love over fear. Love – especially God's perfect love – is an affective bridge to the true world, while fear is an emotion binding us to the false world. This is well captured in a testimonial given by one Bethel survivor, with which the congregation closes its written account of the tornado:

> He holds us with sustaining arms. Think of the love God has for us, and the undergirding strength. This gives us the ability to trust and look to God in a right way. Fear of the future, fear of failure, wondering how all this will work out troubles us. God showed me the future is there; there can be a reaching out in faith and trust . . . That little world I was holding on to too tightly, too comfortably . . . it doesn't bring the security we once thought it did. As we look to God, there is hope, there is direction. Fear brings darkness . . . God is light. (Unruh & Unruh, 2007, p. 155)

Degradation of the "False World" (the Profane). At the same time that participants gestured toward and protected the true world into which they will transcend, they also devalued or degraded the false world of the *Temporal Order*, with the result that any suffering because of the storm seemed less significant. An important aspect of degrading the false world is to adopt the viewpoint of *Suffering as Trial*, or to achieve an *Acceptance* of suffering. In this view, suffering "just is"; it is not necessarily meaningful or desired, but it is the fate of humankind and something to be borne. This view is well summarized in the first article written in the newsletter "Messenger of Truth" by a Bethel member after the storm, almost exactly two years later:

Matthew 24:13 reads, "But he that shall endure unto the end, the same shall be saved" ... If we endure something, we bear it to attain. Are we willing to suffer? In 1 Peter 4:12,13, we read that we should not think it strange concerning the fiery trial that comes, but we can rejoice that we are partakers of Christ's suffering ... There will always be some suffering in the Christian walk. (Unruh, 2009, p. 3)

Almost everywhere the word *Leid* ("suffering") appears in John Holdeman's writing (particularly in *Ein Spiegel der Wahrheit/Mirror of Truth*, 1880), it is accompanied by the word *Geduld* ("patience"). "Patient suffering" was an ideal for John Holdeman, reinforcing the idea that, among his followers, misfortunes are loads to be borne along a straight path, rather than signposts of a path toward change.

Significantly, suffering can be seen as a trial or a test of one's faith in the prospect of transcendence. As one participant described the tornado and its aftermath: "it was a test, I guess you'd say. You know we had to turn those feelings over to the Lord, and pray many times, to just help us to trust, because that fear, fear is such a tormenting, crippling emotion. It takes away your ability to cope, you know, when you're feeling very fearful" (P3). One "passes" the test or trial of suffering by preserving the true world and learning to accept the hardships undergone in the false world.

In addition to conceiving of earthly suffering as a kind of insignificant trial, another tactic for degrading the false world was stressing *Nonattachment* to the *Temporal Order*, which meant viewing *Property as Unimportant*. Participants insisted that only property or material things were lost in the storm, and that these were replaceable or ultimately unimportant, as in the following examples:

P1: It's very real that the things of this life are very temporal.
P2: You can just not hold on to anything ...
P1: That's one thing that's become very real to us, that nothing that we have ...
P2: In just a minute, it can go.
P1: ... is something that you can take with you ... we would come back in the morning wondering if our house would actually be there the next morning, our new house.
P7: My attachment to these earthly things is way less than it used to be. Cause you know, this table's worth so terrible much to you [*indicating the table at which we were sitting*]. Well, tomorrow it may not be here! Well, it may not be here, so why even get so attached to it? [*brief pause*] Some people think that's a fatalistic view, I don't know. You know, maybe it's realistic.

At one point during an interview, one participant (P8) handed me a slip of paper on which she had written a piece of scripture: "But this one thing I do, forgetting those things which are behind and reaching forth unto those things which are before" (Philippians 3:13). This line conveyed the theme of *Future Focus*: not dwelling on the past and simply moving on with one's life after a tragedy or setback. P7 and P8 in fact expressed at one point that many people in their community were tired of talking about the tornado and have a desire to "keep going" or move past the event. The tactic of maintaining a *Future Focus* serves as a final means of degrading the false world: whatever happens in the *Temporal Order* of the past and present is insignificant when one fixates on the horizon of the future.

Mediations. The third component of the *Transcendence* category refers to the concrete practices and events mentioned by the Bethel survivors in which they experienced a consoling, temporary bridging of the two worlds. In one direction, the Holdemans all mentioned reaching out from the false world of earthly existence toward the true world, in acts of *Prayer* or family and congregational *Devotions*. Virtually every Holdeman account of the tornado mentions praying (usually audibly, in a group of relatives sheltered in a basement) up to and during the time when the storm hit. Often, prayers were said for the safety of others in the family or community not immediately present. Most accounts also mention giving thanks to God immediately after the storm had passed. *Prayer/Devotion* continued to be important as a source of succor and meaning-making in the weeks and months after the storm. P6 mentioned being comforted by a church service, held shortly after the event, where members of the congregation were permitted to stand and share their experiences of the tornado. And P1 indicated that an especially important turning point came during family devotions held in a trailer 1 or 2 weeks after the tornado, when reading a piece of scripture brought the whole family to tears with the realization that they could let go of any anger and embrace *God's Security*.

Mediations not only occurred in this direction. Most Holdeman accounts of the tornado also mention feeling God's very real presence during the storm, manifest in his *Power* and *Assistance*, which kept them from any loss of life. As a result of God's interventions to shelter them during the storm, the participants reported either feeling calm and secure as their homes were battered or destroyed around them, or feeling an ambivalent mixture of fear and security: "Even when we were afraid, at the same time, and that's why, it's a little bit hard to explain that, I mean even though . . . I mean, it's an experience that we had never been through before, and we never want to again, and yet, overall we felt like God was watching over us" (P2). One participant in fact asserted that angels were with them as the tornado passed overhead.

Beyond sensing God's protective presence, the participants also saw evidence for His intervention in a number of *Fortunate Circumstances*, which they would refer to as *Blessings*. These were unlikely circumstances in the absence of which (the participants believe) damage from the storm would have been worse and probably resulted in serious injury or loss of life. For one couple, these *Blessings* were largely framed in terms of the unlikelihood of their survival in light of the severe damage done mere inches away from their bodies. For another couple, the *Blessings* had more to do with fortuitous timing: the family should have realized earlier that the tornado was approaching, but if they had, they would have taken shelter sooner, and missed an opportunity to help some relatives who came to their house for shelter right before the storm hit. As Janoff-Bulman (1992) indicated, it is not unusual for survivors of natural disasters to engage in advantageous comparisons, reflecting on how "it could have been worse" or it may in fact have been worse for others. What might be less typical, however, is to see in such *Fortunate Circumstances* unambiguous evidence for God's mediation between the true and false worlds.

The connection between *Community* and *Transcendence*

I will now expand upon the significance of the ideas and processes distilled in the analytic categories for the Bethel congregation's recovery from the tornado, and their place in Holdeman CV culture.

Communal practices undergirded transcendence interpretations. Although the Holdemans themselves might not see the matter in the same light, it is fairly clear that the presence of community in the aftermath was a necessary material foundation for the psychological method of coping through transcendence. In contrast to the typical redemption narrative valorized by contemporary psychology, the Bethel survivors do not feel that their worldview and life patterns were challenged or altered in any significant way by the experience of the tornado. This was in large part due to the fact that the survivors were able to interpret the event in light of their preexisting views, using the narrative of transcendence. It seems reasonable to assert, however, that without the outpouring of communal support that the Bethel congregation experienced in the weeks after the tornado, their material experience would have been much more difficult, and therefore posed more of a challenge to their worldview. Without the institutions and behavioral routines that were already in place among the Holdeman people, the survivors may have found it less easy to assimilate the event and its consequences into their preexisting cognitive structures.

This contention is supported by comparing the Greensburg Holdeman experience to other instances of natural disaster. In post-disaster situations where communities have been severely disrupted, and unable to perform their prior functions of providing solidarity and support (e.g., through the forced resettlement of survivors in new neighborhoods), the likelihood of experiencing posttraumatic stress and difficulty in assimilating the event to previous views has been much greater (e.g., Erikson, 1978; 1994; Zaumseil et al., 2013). Even in situations where the community structure is not completely altered by a disaster, in the absence of preexisting high levels of solidarity, the ephemeral "post-disaster utopia" of fellow-feeling and cooperation fades fairly quickly, leaving the process of long-term recovery largely to the individual and bureaucratic institutions (Taylor et al., 1970). When individuals are forced to rebuild their lives in isolation, adjustments in worldview are more likely to be necessary (Herman, 1997; Janoff-Bulman, 1992).

An interesting possibility suggested by the threat-culture cycle (Chapter 1) is that disasters or other calamities are occasionally necessary to maintain high levels of solidarity in a CV subculture such as the Holdeman Mennonites. At the very least, the occurrence of such events reinforces their solidarity through a process that might be termed "collective resilience" (to be contrasted with the individual resilience typical of redemptive suffering narratives). Along these lines, a few of the Bethel participants mentioned their regret that some of the anxiety they felt after the storm was dissipating 6 years later. The implication was that felt security makes it easier to become attached to worldly concerns and possessions, and from thence to engage in more individualistic behavior. Concern about suffering, by contrast, forces one to recognize one's dependence on others. Rather than prompting Holdemans to recognize their self-sufficiency and grow in unique ways – as per the classic redemption story – suffering interpreted in this way tightens the web of group solidarity in which they are enmeshed.

Transcendence as a solution to the theodicy problem. When seemingly unjust or random suffering occurs, the problem of theodicy arises. The construct of transcendence captures the way in which the Bethel survivors solved this problem and avoided nihilistic disorientation. Specifically, by preserving the true world, the Holdeman Mennonites definitively resolved the search for a causal account of their suffering. Belief in the true world and God's purpose convinces the Holdemans that their suffering happened for a meaningful reason. However, because of their conviction that the reason is unknowable, they need search no further for causes, and there is no threat that meaninglessness angst might arise due to a failure to provide a causal account. Similarly, the degradation of the false world obviates the search for a teleological account of the tornado. If the events that happen to us in this world are ultimately insignificant compared to our final existence in the true world, then the suffering we encounter does not need to possess profound significance for our lives.

In these ways, Holdeman Mennonites transcend the problem of theodicy. Indeed, in many instances both during the interviews and in their publications, Holdemans express an active reticence to delve into theodicy questions. Consider the following passage from the Bethel congregation's written account of the storm, which appears in a chapter entitled "Awe at God's Great Power": "Why were some neighbors' homes and lives left unscathed when others lost everything? It seems that, in disaster, all men are equal and common, born of the same human family. The rich, the poor, the old, the young, the sick, the healthy, the proud, the influential, all become equal when calamities strike" (Unruh & Unruh, 2007, p. 83). This passage is interesting in a few ways. First, the idea that suffering brings equality, presented in response to the objectively uneven distribution of destruction, can buttress ideals of solidarity in a situation that might quickly undermine them (for a contrasting case, see Zaumseil et al., 2013). Second, in a subtle way, this passage represents a classic Christian approach to the theodicy problem: what starts as a potential questioning of God for uneven outcomes shifts to a focus on the uneven outcomes that humans apparently create for themselves. Rather than wondering why the storm affected some instead of others, the passage points toward the question of why some people enjoy more wealth or have more pride than others, and reframes the storm as a "great equalizer."

This type of interpretation is related to repressive interpretations of suffering. As mentioned in the previous chapter, Holdemans are more likely to interpret suffering repressively compared to undergraduates and Unitarian Universalists. In the specific case of the Greensburg tornado, I found very little evidence that the storm was interpreted in this way by the Bethel congregation. However, another Holdeman wrote an article in "Messenger of Truth" raising the issue of whether the Greensburg tornado may have been a punishment for the sins of local people (Schmidt, 2007). Ultimately, he concludes that this was not the case, and once again insists that God possessed an unknowable reason for allowing the event. It is quite possible that calamities affecting multiple Holdeman people at once are less likely to be interpreted repressively, and more likely to be coped with via the transcendence method (Wolfenstein, 1957). One of the participants (P7) expressed this in their interview when contemplating the possibility that only he and his wife might have been hit: "if it had only been us, I would've almost taken it personally . . . I'd of had to go through quite a bit more than I did now. I'd of probably asked the Lord, you know, why, why just us? What did we do wrong, you know? Or what do we need to learn out of this thing?" Although the participants and other Holdemans did not seem to interpret the Greensburg tornado as a specific instance of repressive suffering, it is important to remember their general DISA orientation and redeemer theodicy (discussed in the previous chapter), which ultimately traces all earthly suffering to human inferiority and original sin.

Transcendence versus redemption. An important difference between the narratives of redemption and transcendence lies in the significance accorded to the focal event. In redemptive narratives, suffering is treated as a relatively personal and isolating affair, and its magnitude is typically seen as quite large. Transcendence narratives tend to pay less attention to the terrible nature of suffering and more to the forces of security and benevolence that deliver one from suffering. The importance accorded to suffering in redemptive narratives is probably part of a causal loop. Redemptive narratives are more likely in IV and II cultures, whose members are in fact more likely to experience their suffering in an isolated way. Thus, it is quite possible that in many situations people in individualist cultures experience "objectively" worse hardship than those in collectivist environments (although this is significantly impacted by economic factors; Zaumseil et al., 2013). However, regardless of the actual magnitude of the suffering in a given instance (which is difficult to gauge), redemptive narratives encourage an interpretive ratcheting-up of that magnitude.

In the case of natural disasters, this is most obvious in the differential significance placed on the loss of property by people from IV or II as opposed to CV or CI backgrounds. As is clear from the words of the Bethel survivors, the primary role of property in the transcendence narrative is that of devaluation – emphasis is placed on the ideal of nonattachment and the transitoriness of worldly goods. By contrast, in many disaster narratives from individuals more integrated into mainstream US culture, loss of property plays a very important role in descriptions of the extent of the suffering. This loss is often described less in terms of financial hardship and more in terms of the disorientation produced by losing defining material instantiations of the self, such as sentimental keepsakes or old photographs (e.g., Taylor et al., 1970). One non-Holdeman wrote rather poetically about how the loss of family possessions in the Greensburg tornado implied a loss of self:

> The first thing I thought about salvaging was not family photographs, or china or furniture. Thoughts of valuable, precious items would come later, poking their

heads out of the fog of disbelief. First, though, were two glass jars full of marbles my grandfather collected on the porch ... I had no idea, in all those years of growing up, how valuable they were to become ... They are small things, still caked with mud. But underneath it, they have spent a lifetime wrapping up quiet secrets of a house that no longer exists, in a town where I can no longer find my history. Maybe once I clean them up, they will let me in on those secrets about the places and the people from which I have come. (Qtd. in Haney, 2008, p. 90)

Closely related to the differential emphases on the significance and extent of the relevant suffering are differences in the level of past focus involved in transcendence and redemption narratives. The avoidance of the past and the focus on the future present in the Bethel accounts contrast sharply with the prototypic redemptive suffering interpretation. Redemptive narratives require a focus on past hardship in order to demonstrate through contrast how much the individual has grown, and to redeem the suffering by integrating it into a positive trajectory (Furedi, 2004; Herman, 1997; McAdams, 2006).

Some Holdeman leaders have explicitly recognized the distinction between secular psychology – which is heavily invested in redemptive narratives – and their own religious approach to coping with life's travails. In an article entitled "The Beguiling Influence of Psychology and Psychiatry," one Holdeman minister argued that psychology's obsession with positive self-esteem and overcoming past traumas is a thin veil covering a self-centered and irresponsible way of life:

A forward movement in consecration and sanctification is paramount. Paul writes about forgetting those things that are behind (Phil. 3:13). Forgiveness allows us to forget the things of the past ... Psychology and psychiatry want us to believe that there is a subconscious where hurts and memories may be suppressed with denial that they exist. Therefore psychologists and psychiatrists stir, question, and suggest, digging this out so it can be remembered. When we have faith and confidence in God, He will bring to our remembrance those things that need to be addressed. The rest isn't there as far as He is concerned ... If we approach our problems from the humanistic standpoint, we will get its kind of results. Its teaching does not bring deliverance but negotiates a settlement with the past that gives no permanent rest. (Klassen, 2010, p. 3)

Beyond these fairly general differences in the perspectives on suffering of the Holdemans compared to mainstream US society, we can point to more specific contrasts between the Bethel survivors and the townspeople of Greensburg. As mentioned, the Holdemans in Greensburg do not generally feel that their lives have been significantly changed by the tornado, whereas massive change is a common theme in many of the narratives of the townspeople (Haney, 2008; 2009). Based on the interview data, it also does not seem to be the case that the Bethel congregation has placed much stock in the mainstream redemption story of Greensburg. Their religious beliefs and practical, simplistic approach to living and building mean that they are generally skeptical of the "green" movement, although they have adopted certain energy-efficient building practices that they see as making "common sense."

To summarize, it is perhaps most instructive to compare the redemptive and transcendence suffering narratives in terms of their different implied life trajectories. According to the redemptive narrative, the individual is proceeding along a straight line, and then the disruption of suffering causes a major dip, after which – through the posttraumatic growth process – the line soars to a level higher than it was prior to the suffering. The redemptive teleology is one of change. The alternate teleology implied by the transcendence narrative is stable rather than transformative. The Holdemans were proceeding in a straight line toward their goal of Heaven – then the tornado struck, but they were carried over this hurdle by their faith and solidarity. Now, after the tornado, they have returned to the same place they were before and continue to move forward. These alternate individual-psychological trajectories parallel two different trajectories undergone by broader social and eco-systems in the wake of disasters, namely adaptation and transformation (Tidball & Krasny, 2013). When a community or environment is radically changed by a disaster in a way that produces a new state of resilience, this is called transformation – the ecological parallel of the redemption narrative. The transcendence narrative instead mirrors the experience of communities that have the capacity for adaptation, or returning to a prior desired state after a disaster.

If the tornado experience did anything for the Bethel congregation, it simply reinforced the beliefs they always had: beliefs in their dependence on others, in the necessity of charity, and in the importance of feelings of gratitude and love. As one participant said,

> P5: Well, I believe there's many people without a sense of direction in life, and a disaster dis-, derails them worse than it has us ... We have an anchor, I feel like, that we can always go back to, and redirect as we need to ... And yeah, you know, when you think about, why did it have to happen, maybe, maybe all that ... needed to happen, for people to learn to, help others, and for those in this community who were affected, for them to learn to be gracious and receive.

It should be noted that when one reads or hears the accounts of the night of and morning after the storm, very few differences emerge between Holdeman and non-Holdeman narratives. The same elements recur in account after account: looking for shelter; fear for the survival of one's family; prayers; feelings of gratitude and shock after emerging from the shelter alive and witnessing the destruction; the "post-disaster utopia" of warmth and altruism. Although religious themes are probably more prominent in the Holdeman narratives overall, they occur to some extent in almost every account of the Greensburg tornado.

The real differences in the narratives seem to emerge over the long term, from accounts taken 1 or 2 years after the event. This is a familiar theme from prior research on natural disasters, which generally documents a "disaster management cycle" involving several distinct stages, including initial response and long-term recovery (Zaumseil et al., 2013). Differences between subgroups within a disaster-stricken community become much more pronounced in the recovery phase, with some groups achieving a return to relative normalcy much more rapidly than others (Berke, Kartez, & Wenger, 1993). Beyond extending prior research, the present study underscores the important role that cultural differences and material practices play in processes of retrospective meaning-making.

Different stories of the Greensburg tornado

Three predominant narratives emerged out of the Greensburg tornado experience. The Holdeman narrative, stemming from a CV cultural enclave, is one of transcendence and community. By contrast, what might be called the mainstream narrative has been a redemption story typical for IV or II culture – after the utter destruction of the town, Greensburg is rising Phoenix-like and embracing a radically new vision of green energy. This narrative comes primarily from city leaders, outside institutions, and the media.

A third, less coherent story that nevertheless seems apparent is an unfortunate one of fatalism and frustration. Many of the residents of Greensburg were profoundly disoriented by the storm, and of those several have found themselves unable to return (Haney, 2009; Paul & Che, 2011; Smith & Cartlidge, 2011). By and large, these individuals do not endorse the decision to rebuild the town green, and feel that their old home has been lost forever. To some extent, they have experienced the disaster as a form of "collective trauma" (Erikson, 1994), of permanent disruption of their community's prior way of life. Social class and age seem to have been prominent factors in determining who was forced toward this more fatalistic narrative, with the older and less well-off residents of Greensburg denied access to stories of collective or individualistic resilience (Hernandez, 2011; Paul & Che, 2011). Although I do not personally have data that can speak to these issues definitively, the data available suggest – in line with a great deal of research on other disasters (Zaumseil et al., 2013) – that differences in cultural patterns and social practices profoundly impact how different segments of a community are impacted by disaster, psychologically and otherwise.

Discussions of the experience and interpretation of suffering in the psychological literature often invoke metaphors. More often than not, these are metaphors of transformation and the change brought about by an incorporation of suffering into the self. For example, in their discussion of the narratives of Hurricane Katrina survivors, Marks, Cherry, and Silva (2009) quote Viktor Frankl, one of the early pioneers of redemptive psychology: "If architects want to strengthen a decrepit arch, they increase the load which is laid upon it, for thereby the parts are joined more firmly together" (p. 197). In his book on the psychology of trauma survivors, Joseph (2011) advocates his "theory of the shattered vase" as the key to successfully overcoming suffering. According to this conceit, the self is a vase, which is shattered after an instance of trauma. Rather than awkwardly attempt to glue the pieces back together in a fragile reconstruction of the original, Joseph argues, it is better to rearrange them into a completely different design, such as a new mosaic.

> When adversity strikes, people often feel that at least some part of them – their views of the world, their sense of themselves, their relationships – have been smashed. Those who try to put their lives back together exactly as they were remain fractured and vulnerable. But those who accept the breakage and build themselves anew become more resilient and open to new ways of living. (Joseph, 2011, p. xiv)

After his interview, when I was explaining the purpose of my study to one of the participants, one Holdeman Mennonite offered his own metaphoric understanding of the matter. He asked me if I had ever noticed that when a storm is coming, all the birds seem to go away somewhere, and after the storm has passed, they all return. He told me that the birds always have a place to go, and they know where it is. Other Holdemans have also found solace in the seeming capacity of the natural world to restore itself to a pre-disaster state. As Wedel (September 26, 2007) wrote:

> God has made this earth with that ability to recreate what was destroyed or damaged by a storm . . . For those homes and individuals who have felt the storms of life and experienced loss, may our hope be renewed with the words of Job. He said that in the natural world, even the scent of water could stimulate new growth. (pp. 2–3)

In the estimation of one Holdeman Greensburg survivor, the sense of God's security is like the shelter which in some deeply significant way the birds know and rely upon. This metaphor is not one of transformation through suffering; indeed, the birds escape the trauma of the storm altogether. It is instead a metaphor of transcendence, intended to express the stability that comes from knowing an alternate plane of existence that is immune to the sufferings of the flesh and the chaos of the natural world. For the Holdeman Mennonites, it is perhaps accurate to say that the only significant transformation comes when one leaves the earthly plane altogether, on the day when the birds do not come back. One of the interviewed couples concluded a personal narrative of the storm, written about a month afterward, with this reflection: "[Because of the storm] our lives will never be the same again and it reminds me of a much bigger change that is coming that will make this one seem so insignificant. We could well be going about our everyday life, thinking it's a normal day when the great Judgment Day comes. Where will our FINAL home be?"

Part III

Implications

9 Cultural-existential psychology and contemporary society

The aim of this book was to provide an outline for a cultural-existential psychology. Part I presented the theoretical grounding of this new approach by reviewing relevant prior movements in the social sciences, offering three fundamental principles, and combining separate models of existential threat and cultural variation into a comprehensive account of variation in cultural threat orientations. The core idea of this book is not a complex one; indeed, it is another of those dichotomies which perennially haunt the social sciences. Quite simply, some cultures are *disorientation-avoidant* (DISA), meaning individuals are encouraged to avoid nihilistic disorientation by interpreting threatening events less in terms of their implication for one's meaning system or surrounding environment, and more in terms of their implication for the self's possible inadequacy or need for reconciliation. Other cultures are *despair-avoidant* (DESA), meaning individuals are encouraged to avoid nihilistic despair by interpreting threatening events less in terms of their implication for the self, and more in terms of their implication for the potential invalidity of meaning systems and insecurity of the environment.

Part II presented a program of research demonstrating how different methods can be used to apply cultural-existential ideas to the understanding of how specific cultural groups experience existential threat. I focused on a unique subgroup in US culture, namely traditionalist Kansas Mennonites. I set the general context for the research with a historical study showing that over the course of the twentieth century, most Kansas Mennonites assimilated to US II culture, and as they did so, redemptive suffering notions became fused with individualist attitudes. I subsequently turned to more focused, contemporary investigations of a particular denomination – the Church of God in Christ or "Holdeman" Mennonites – which has largely retained its CV cultural orientation despite making progressive adjustments toward economic integration with the broader society. A cultural-comparative survey demonstrated that, relative to IV Unitarian Universalists and a standard II undergraduate sample, the Holdemans have a DISA threat orientation: they show higher levels of guilt and lower levels of meaninglessness angst and anxiety. Among the three groups, cultural variables predicted threat experiences, but the opposite patterns were also observed, providing evidence for the threat-culture cycle (Chapter 1). Finally, an in-depth interview study examined how one Holdeman congregation experienced the threat of a destructive tornado. I found that the Holdemans recovered from the storm fairly well compared to other non-Holdeman citizens, a divergent experience driven by the material resources they obtain from their collectivist community and the psychological resources offered by their religious narrative of transcendence.

It is my hope that the two parts of this book provide a preliminary "proof of concept" for how cultural and existential psychological ideas may be profitably combined, at the level of both theory and research. Of course, a great deal more research needs to be done to establish the overall usefulness of this framework, and far more to uphold the validity of the particular categories I have proposed, for example, guilt and anxiety, or DISA versus DESA orientations. But a blueprint is now available to researchers interested in the intersection between cultural background and the individual's experience of suffering and threat. Those who pursue research in this area will be adding to a great body of important but often-neglected work in philosophical and psychological anthropology, as well as existential anthropology and sociology (Chapter 1).

In this final chapter, I would like to draw out more clearly some of the practical scientific and social implications of the foregoing analysis and data. I will begin with the potential implications of the cultural-existential approach for contemporary social psychology. I will then turn to broader considerations of the DISA/DESA dualism, particularly as it pertains to pressing social problems in modern society.

Methodological implications of cultural-existential psychology

In the 1970s, social psychology (along with most other branches of psychology and social science) went through a well-known epistemic crisis. Many have recently proposed that the field is currently in the midst of another crisis (e.g., Funder et al., 2014). The difference between these two crises, and the proposed resolutions to them, is telling. The earlier crisis basically centered around whether or not the common methods of social psychologists – laboratory experiments, surveys built on the assumption of stable traits and reliable attitudes – tell us *anything meaningful* about the social world. The current crisis is instead one of "dependability," which has arisen from a concern with empirical "false positives" and a widespread absence of replication in science. In short, the earlier crisis was one of *external*, whereas the current one is of *internal* validity (Campbell, 1957). Whereas earlier social psychologists questioned the general usefulness of their methods, they are now obsessed with how well their methods work.

One of my aims in proposing cultural-existential psychology is to encourage social psychologists to move away from an obsessive concern with the functionality of their methods and back toward the broader concern that was raised in the 1970s: What do these methods actually tell us about human functioning? What kinds of questions do they answer? In 1977, the influential social psychologist Muzafer Sherif proposed that the way forward for social psychology was to borrow from other disciplines to answer two fundamentally important questions: (1) What is the nature of social systems? (2) What is the nature of human psychology? In proposing the second question, he emphasized the importance of determining whether human nature is cross-culturally invariant or variable. It is clear that a quest to develop more advanced statistical methods and more honest means of reporting results – however laudable these goals may be – does relatively little to answer these fundamental questions.

Indeed, the emphasis on particular methods and statistical approaches in social psychology (e.g., random assignment to condition, statistics requiring independence of observations), which became more resolute as a result of the 1970s crisis, is one of the primary reasons why the "social" has been largely eliminated from social psychology (Greenwood, 2004). For decades, social factors – meaning any commitments participants might have to particular belief systems or cultural and habitual modes of life – have been treated as "noise" and "confounds" to be "controlled" in psychological experiments. The "new statistics" (Cumming, 2014) that are being advocated in contemporary social psychology, which involve a move away from traditional hypothesis testing, could certainly be a step in the right direction toward reincorporating the "noise" of actual life into the discipline. However, many of the calls for these new approaches are accompanied by calls for greater statistical power and larger sample sizes (Funder et al., 2014; Simmons, Nelson, & Simonsohn, 2011), which in the highly competitive academic environment discourages researchers from working with understudied populations and encourages instead the use of convenience (e.g., online) samples.

Cultural psychology should be applauded for making space for the reincorporation of social factors into the discipline. But recently cultural psychology has also become burdened with the weight of methodological concerns. Researchers have become preoccupied with assessing the "equivalence" of constructs measured in different cultural settings, in order to separate "true" cultural differences from bias. They have also attempted to separate cultural-level from individual-level differences, as if culture and the individual could actually be dichotomized in reality. There is nothing wrong with these methodological concerns per se; indeed, they can do much to illuminate certain problems. But if they become the focus of the discipline, they will preclude the investigation of the very complex differences and interconnections between radically diverse cultures and between cultures and individuals. "Bias" and "true" differences between cultures are not easily separated; indeed, at some level, they are always meaningfully interrelated (Poortinga, 1989; van de Vijver, 2011). For instance, I have no doubt whatsoever that the Holdeman Mennonites experienced the completion of a survey in a very different way from my undergraduate participants (Chapter 7). But this "noise" in the data is one small part of the very meaningful differences between these cultural groups. It is not a separate factor to be controlled or eliminated; it is part of the story told by these data.

When we look past such methodological concerns – again, significant as they are – to the true potential impact of cultural psychology, it lies in the aims of anthropology and sociology: to understand, as Sherif (1977) put it, the nature of human social systems. But following Sherif's propositions, this is only half of what we need to accomplish. Psychology also needs to reveal the essence of human nature. As Cantril (1988) wrote:

> Psychology will meet the challenge it has imposed on itself and which men everywhere expect it to meet only when it becomes fully emancipated from a point of view which permits or encourages the study of isolated individuals, isolated experiences, isolated relationships ... If the nature of man's everyday life experience is to be fathomed, it is necessary first of all to try to describe man's experience in appropriate terms. Those processes that play significant roles in man's living and their cross-relationships must be sought and understood ... the *why* of man's striving [cannot] be explained by recognizing that men want to belong to some group and to have some status within that group. The questions remain as to *why* all men want to belong to a group, *why* all men want to be loved and appreciated, *why* nearly all men strive for some kind of status. (pp. 18–20, emphasis added)

These *why* questions are rarely posed by social psychology, which typically contents itself with the smaller task of describing processes. Experimental existential psychology holds out the promise of understanding why people do the things they do – why they invest in culture, why they are concerned with self-esteem, why they sacralize their relationships.

But just as in cultural psychology and the rest of the discipline, XXP is losing sight of the important concerns that prompted its initiation as it becomes mired in method fetishism. Researchers are preoccupied with the question of which threats are most motivating in human experience, and they have used the mortality salience experimental paradigm developed through terror management theory in an attempt to resolve this question (Hart, 2014; Jonas et al., 2014; see also Chapters 1 and 3). This has led to frequent debates about whether, say, meaninglessness or death is more aversive. Because researchers have convinced themselves that laboratory experiments are the only valid arbiter of such a question, they have moved toward a reductionist stance that holds that all symbolic threats are more or less equivalent, and indeed no different from threat experiences in nonhuman animals. This position not only is the exact opposite of what the existentialists themselves believed, but it does nothing to answer Cantril's and Sherif's call for understanding human experience in relevant human terms.

Thus, while cultural and existential psychology offer the necessary tools for accomplishing what social psychology was intended to accomplish – namely, providing a thorough understanding of the interplay between social systems and human nature – they cannot fulfill their potential unless they are allowed to go beyond current disciplinary obsessions with methodological fine-tuning. It is my hope that this book makes some modest contribution by showing how these subdisciplines might achieve more by learning from each other, and hearkening back to common threads in the other social sciences (Chapter 1). The use of mixed qualitative and quantitative methods seems an increasingly promising way out for a field in crisis.

These methodological considerations prompt me to probe and even problematize some of the concepts I have relied on throughout this book. Cultural-existential psychology is in its infancy, so there is no guarantee that the hypotheses and distinctions I have made will withstand empirical scrutiny and cross-cultural comparison. I believe that the prior literatures reviewed in Chapters 3–5 as well as the studies in Part II offer initial testimony to the validity of these ideas, enough to warrant further research. However, certain questions and issues have arisen throughout the prior chapters that I was unable to fully address before.

While DISA orientation is associated with collectivism and DESA with individualism, how do these threat orientations manifest differently as a function of visible versus invisible control? How can secular individualists be more likely to interpret suffering redemptively when ideas of redemption have been prominent throughout religious and especially Christian traditions? Even if culture influences experiences of lower-level threat, such as guilt and anxiety, does it truly have an influence on the experience of second-level angst? And is it indeed the case that meaninglessness angst is less common in DISA, and condemnation angst less common in DESA cultures? Depression rates are on the rise in II cultures such as the United States, which seems to belie the notion that a DESA orientation prevents condemnation angst.

There are doubtless many other questions which could be raised about the foregoing analyses, but these are a few important ones that I would like to address. Doing so will complicate the concept of DISA and DESA orientations, serving as a reminder that the theoretical edifice presented in Part I is an ideal-typical analysis. Psychological categories and generalizations are never watertight and consistent; rather, they can at best illuminate connections between diverse but related findings, and provide the impetus for future discoveries. As the methodological third principle of cultural-existential psychology holds, we should use multiple methods to avoid being shackled by the vantage of our generalizations, while not stretching them so far that they lose their usefulness.

Culturally specific forms of DISA and DESA orientation

In Chapter 5, the DISA/DESA threat orientations were presented as if they are more or less consistent patterns across contexts. However, even the somewhat limited empirical data in Part II suggest that these orientations manifest differently in different groups, including among subgroups coexisting in the same society. For instance, Chapter 7's comparative survey found that Unitarian Universalists and undergraduates both evince more of a DESA orientation compared to Holdemans – both groups are comparatively lower in guilt and higher in anxiety. But while they share this general tendency, they also differed from each other in important ways. The undergraduates showed higher levels of vertical individualism, which drove their higher reported death anxiety. And while the undergraduates defended against threat primarily through self-esteem, Unitarian Universalists relied more on their individualistic worldview and belief in the fundamental benevolence of humanity.

Chapter 4's model suggests that there are four primary cultural types arising as a combination of different modes of social orientation and control, and this indicates that there should be at least two ways in which DISA and DESA orientations each manifest across these four types. Considering Chapter 7's data, let us first turn to the distinction between different manifestations of a DESA orientation in IV versus II culture. Both cultural types orient their members away from condemnation angst, but in different ways. In IV culture – exemplified by the Unitarian Universalists – the abstract value of each individual is paramount, and leaders within the culture are driven by the desire to grant equal self-esteem, public representation, and access to resources for all individuals. Nihilistic despair is avoided in such cultures by never questioning the primacy of human value. This is the ideal of expressive individualism and the Enlightenment (Bellah, Madsen, Sullivan, Swidler, & Tipton, 1985; Taylor, 2007). II culture also orients its members away from condemnation angst, but in a rather different way. The utilitarian individualism (Bellah et al., 1985) of II culture is built on the assumption that some individuals are inferior in terms of aptitude and character, and hence worthy of condemnation. But for this cultural system to be psychologically tenable, it encourages each (adjusted) member to believe that *they* personally are worthy and deserving, that they should never be condemned. One can see clearly how this cultural type has its origin in the doctrine of predestination in Calvinism, as identified by Weber (1904/2009). In II culture, competition for self-esteem becomes the psychological motive for nearly all activity. So the individual develops a variety of psychological strategies (i.e., self-serving biases) for preserving their self-esteem. But, unlike in the case of IV culture, the protection of self-esteem is an individual, rather than a humanistic, enterprise. A person in II culture believes self-esteem to be a zero-sum game, and indeed it is in a competitive market for access to psychological and material resources. This is why, in Chapter 7, we saw that Unitarian Universalists (IV) defend against threat through an individualistic *worldview*, while undergraduates (II) defend against threat through individualized *self-esteem*.

How might a DISA orientation manifest differently in CV versus CI culture? Before considering this question, we should explicate an important distinction between visibly and invisibly controlled cultures, one which clarifies the two manifestations of DESA culture just discussed. This is the difference between cultures of transcendence and immanence, as discussed in Chapters 6 and 8. Similar dualisms appear in anthropological treatments of forms of religiosity: for instance, we have *doctrinal* and *imagistic* religions (Whitehouse & Laidlaw, 2004); *ritual theory* and *ritual practice* (Bell, 1992); and *orthodoxy* and *orthopraxy* (Asad, 1993). In visibly controlled cultures, a fully symbolized and injunctively normative meaning system insures some horizon of transcendence toward which the individual is oriented (Diken, 2009). In the case of a CV culture, this connotes the prospect of *vertical* transcendence, of orientation toward a sacred dimension that is superior to the material plane (Chapter 8). In an IV culture, it is a question of *horizontal* transcendence, of overcoming narrow self-focus and identity through constant dialogue with others and the world. But regardless of the important differences, in both these cultures, the individual has a coherent worldview supplying them with a goal through which they can achieve transcendence of current existence.

By contrast, invisibly controlled cultures are cultures of immanence – the individual is primarily oriented toward the here and now, not toward some distal horizon (Diken, 2009; Schroeder, 1987). Again, the exact manifestation of immanence differs as a form of social orientation – II cultures instruct their members that the material world of the present is all that exists, while CI cultures breed the sense that the present is in continuous contact with the deep past, an originary moment fused with the present through contact with departed ancestors (Gauchet, 1997). But setting these distinctions aside, members of both cultures are not oriented toward some ideal alternate conception of the world or the self.

The implication of this for defenses against existential threat is that in visibly controlled cultures, *beliefs take primacy*, whereas in invisibly controlled cultures, *actions take primacy*. This fact facilitates understanding of the possible manifestations of DISA orientation. In Part II, I was unable to present data relevant to this distinction, because CI cultures – epitomized by small-scale societies and hunter-gatherer groups – are difficult to find in contemporary society and even more difficult to systematically compare with other cultures. Nevertheless, the ethnographic literature allows us to speculate on how the beliefs/actions distinction might yield varying DISA forms. In CV cultures such as the Holdemans', nihilistic disorientation is avoided through the maintenance of an abstract meaning system replete with theodicies and apologetics (Berger & Luckmann, 1966). By contrast, in often-smaller-scale CI groups, nihilistic disorientation is avoided almost through the very *absence* of the articulation of values, a disavowal of human potential for transformation of the social or natural world (Boehm, 1999; Clastres, 1974/1987; Gauchet, 1997). Relative equality is maintained in such settings because individuals share a common fear that anyone who advances too far beyond the rest, who claims too much power, wealth, or knowledge, will suffer retribution from invisible forces (ancestors, spirits, witches). Thus, in CI cultures, disorientation is avoided not through the hyper-articulation of values – as in a complex scriptural religious system – but rather through the ongoing performance of ritualized actions in a local web of social interdependence.

In sum, the transcendence/immanence, beliefs/actions distinction is crucial for understanding how DISA and DESA orientations might manifest differently as a function of mode of social control. Visibly controlled cultures emphasize the prospect of transcendence, be it vertical in a collectivist context or horizontal in an individualist context. Thus, meaning-making is a primary form of existential defense in both configurations, the key difference being whether the locus of meaning is the divine world (in CV DISA orientation) or the sacred individual (in IV DESA orientation). By contrast, individuals in invisibly controlled cultures negotiate reality in what they perceive to be relatively immanent frames. Here the regulation of individual actions occurs largely as a result of invisible social configurations. In CI culture, there is an emphasis on avoiding nihilistic disorientation through the preservation of social harmony, whereas II cultures emphasize avoiding despair at the expense of social harmony.

In the absence of systematic data, these comparisons have been necessarily abstract and speculative, although they should shed some light on the differences between Unitarian Universalists and undergraduates found in Chapter 7. Let us revisit the distinction between DISA and DESA cultures now in a slightly different way, working with a more concrete set of empirical observations. In Part II, the data primarily focused on how culture shapes individuals' encounters with events that fall in a relatively normal range of human experiences (pangs of guilt, experiences of loss, and so on). Here I turn to a brief consideration of how more extreme instances of threat – namely manifestations of angst – may also be shaped by cultural forces.

Possession and depersonalization: angst experiences in DISA and DESA culture

In Chapter 3, I presented the categories of meaninglessness and condemnation angst to distinguish between more severe, second-level threat experiences that occur across cultures when the individual's routine defenses against anxiety and guilt prove inadequate. Here I would like to show preliminary evidence for the usefulness of the DISA/DESA distinction when it comes to understanding not only everyday experiences of threat, but more extreme and potentially clinical cases. In particular, I will consider how meaninglessness angst might manifest differently in DISA versus DESA cultures.

One extreme way in which meaninglessness angst can manifest is through forms of *dissociation* – an experience of being cut off from the world, or of the world suddenly seeming unreal and untrustworthy. Clinical psychologists in individualist, postindustrial settings have become increasingly interested in dissociation as a reaction to traumatic experiences such as child abuse (e.g., Herman, 1997). But anthropologists have also investigated what are summarily referred to as "altered states of consciousness" (Klass, 2004), and the possible connections between dissociative phenomena in postindustrial societies and the many forms of religiously couched spirit possession observed elsewhere (Bourguignon, 1978).

In this connection, it is important to distinguish between normative and pathological understandings of possession (Douglas, 1970). Culturally normative *ritual possession* is practiced in many cultures as a key part of religious life, as in the Haitian *voudoun* worldview, wherein individuals are traditionally "mounted" by distinct spirits during ceremonies (Bourguignon, 1978). This is quite different from harmful *peripheral possession*, where the taking over of the body by a spirit is seen as pathological within the culture, and seems to be the result of stress or threat (Ward, 1980). An example of this pathological form can be seen in the following report of a patient in Uganda:

> A 33-year-old woman came to our mental health clinic accompanied by her sister. For many years she had regularly suffered from attacks in which, according to her sister, she displayed aggressive and strange behavior, after which she started talking in different voices, which were not recognized as her own.
>
> These attacks occurred when the family prepared to go to Christian church or to say prayers. During our session, the client shifted into a trancelike state, and started to move her hands like claws and made animal-like noises, after which she began to speak in a strange language and voice. Her sister explained that this was the voice of an uncle who had died many years ago. This uncle still valued traditional cultural beliefs, while their father had turned to Christianity. There had been an unsolved conflict between their father and this uncle as their father refused to perform rituals for the ancestors. (van Duijl, Nijenhuis, Komproe, Gernaat, & de Jong, 2010, p. 385)

The authors who collected this case study have proposed that possession trance disorders in Uganda are perhaps reactions to trauma similar to dissociation in the United States (van Duijl, Kleijn, & de Jong, 2012). In this vein, Castillo (1994) argues that pathological spirit possession in South Asian countries and dissociative identity (formerly "multiple personality") disorders in North America are similar but culturally patterned responses to traumatic events. In an important demonstration of such claims, a quasi-experimental study in Uganda revealed that those who had experienced harmful spirit possession (compared to control participants) reported not only more dissociation experiences, but more prior experiences of trauma (van Duijl et al., 2010). Related survey and interview evidence (Igreja et al., 2010) suggests that harmful experiences of possession by *gamba* spirits in rural Mozambique are caused in part by traumatic experiences during the local civil war (1976–1992). In turn, these experiences of possession seem to be related to subsequent health problems, such as reproductive difficulties.

Experiences of possession in more rural or religious CV and CI cultures may then be comparable to what in postindustrial settings is called dissociation. But how does this typically appear in the IV/II cultures of

Western Europe and the United States? Here, dissociation is also associated with the experience of earlier trauma (Simeon, Guralnik, Schmeidler, Sirof, & Knutelska, 2001). However, it often manifests as *depersonalization*, which is possibly the third most common psychiatric symptom in the United States after anxiety and depression (Simeon et al., 1997). Rather than a sense that the self has been overtaken by a spirit or ancestor, depersonalization involves a felt loss of control of the self and distancing from reality, as in the following patient accounts: "It is as if the real me is taken out and put on a shelf or stored somewhere inside of me. Whatever makes me me is not there. It is like an opaque curtain ... like going through the motions and having to exert discipline to keep the unit together" (Simeon et al., 1997, p. 1109); or "a feeling of unreality and distance, like I am a spectator of my own movements and of what is going on" (Simeon et al., 1997, p. 1110). Diagnostic criteria for depersonalization disorder include "Persistent or recurrent experiences of feeling detached from, and as if one is an outside observer of, one's mental processes or body (e.g., feeling like one is in a dream)" and "Derealization symptoms, i.e. objects, people, and/or surroundings seem unreal, distant, artificial, colourless, lifeless, etc." (Spiegel et al., 2011, p. E23).

Why is it that when people reach clinically severe levels of meaninglessness angst, they experience these states differently across cultures, in some settings as spirit possession and in others as depersonalization? I propose that these different experiences of angst can be understood as patterned – at least at the level of the sufferer's phenomenological experience – by normative cultural expectations. In other words, when culture seems to break down and the threat of meaninglessness overwhelms the self, that impending meaninglessness *must nevertheless be filtered through meaningful categories* set by one's culture. Meaninglessness angst is experienced by the individual as a hypertrophied version of cultural beliefs that, in less severe doses, might actually be quite meaningful.

Consider, for instance, what is at the core of depersonalization. The person has a sense that they are cut off from reality, isolated, a spectator of their own actions. But is this not a slightly exacerbated version of the independent self-construal promoted by an individualist social orientation (Chapter 4)? Consider Landrine's (1995) description of the independent self in Western culture:

> The self is represented as existing free of any and all contexts: The self is here; the context is there. Given that the self is seen as an emotional and cognitive universe above, beyond, and without a context, the self is believed to possess attributes of its own, in isolation from other selves, over time, and across situations. (pp. 747–748)

Given the heightened level of cultural and individual reflexivity experienced in IV and II cultures (Chapter 5), such independently construed selves are accustomed to "standing outside" of themselves, to experiencing objective self-awareness. So in many ways, depersonalization may be an amplification of processes that are typically considered normative and even healthy in individualist cultures. Many philosophers in the Western canon wrote about the virtues of distancing from the self in order to obtain a more rational ethical perspective (Smith, 1759/2009). And social psychological research shows that people in individualist cultures will often distance themselves from the reality of a situation, and see that situation as less valid or compelling, if the situation in any way threatens their self-esteem (Sullivan et al., 2014). Conceptually, the sense of unreality and self-distance present in depersonalization is only a haywire manifestation of cognitive experiences that individualism trains the person to be capable of. Hence, it is not surprising that in a review of published studies (Sierra-Siegert & David, 2007), frequency of reported depersonalization was positively associated with the level of individualism in a country.

By contrast, spirit possession could be seen as an intensification of religious and social attitudes that are pervasive and often psychologically beneficial in CV or CI cultures. Such settings are characterized by psychological and material interdependence between group members, and local beliefs typically reflect this sense of a "porous self" by stressing an embodied connection to ancestors, spirits, and other religiously filtered entities (Hsu, 1967; Sow, 1980). Individualism prioritizes the self's sense of value and control, and hence meaninglessness in individualist settings manifests as a loss of the self's taken-for-granted relationship with the world. Collectivism, on the other hand, emphasizes the self's embeddedness in several layers of social relationship, and so meaninglessness is experienced as a perversion of such relationship, a domination of the self by a spirit or ancestor who is unsatisfied and wishes harmony to be restored. In another way of framing the distinction, the self theodicy of DESA culture insures that even in the experience of meaninglessness angst, the self remains prominent – it is the self from which one is estranged, and with which one must reconnect to restore meaning. Very differently, the world theodicy of DISA culture causes culturally sanctioned beliefs to be prominent even in the self's experience of mental breakdown. As Klass (2004) points out, even negative, demonic experiences of possession are always *patterned* in CV and CI culture: the identities possessing the self are recognizable, if feared.

One might suggest that the adequate comparison to pathological possession in postindustrial contexts is not really depersonalization, but rather a more extreme form of dissociation such as dissociative identity disorder wherein the self is also "possessed" by alternate identities. But even when such cases are considered, there is marked evidence for cultural variation in this manifestation of meaninglessness angst. Consider the following discussion in Spiegel et al. (2011) of differences between dissociative identity disorder (DID), observable in IV and II contexts, and pathological possession trance (PPT), more characteristic of CV and CI contexts:

> Both DID and PPT manifest incompatible identities that are separated by an amnestic barrier; these identities occur during an altered state of consciousness and display distinct cognitions, affects, and behaviors. Perhaps the primary distinction between DID and PPT involves the attributed origin and features of the alternate identities. DID is hypothesized to evolve during a traumatic, neglectful, and/or abusive early childhood. These developmental disturbances prevent the dissociative child from developing a unified sense of self; instead, the child develops multiple senses of self that continue to evolve over developmental time ... Alternate identities in PPT tend to represent supernatural agents, typically the spirit of a dead person, or a culturally accepted spirit, demon, god, animal, or mythical figure. Unlike DID alters, possessing entities display a collective existence. For example, the same spirit may possess different family members down the generations (or different villagers in the same generation) ... It is of interest that in the more sociocentric Eastern cultures, dissociative identities take the form of a member of the community, while in the more individually focused Western cultures, the dissociation involves a variety of internal individual identities. (pp. E37–E38)

In sum, while this book primarily focused on how culture influences people's interpretations and reactions to threats that fall within a normative psychological range, there is interesting evidence that culture plays a fairly prominent role even in the shaping of more severe and pathological threat experiences. There are a few implications of this, which I will briefly mention here. First, clinicians and relief workers operating in unfamiliar settings should be very mindful of the ways in which psychological disturbances might manifest in novel, culturally patterned forms. Phenomenologically oriented treatments may need to take very different courses. In a DESA setting, where meaninglessness tends to involve a felt loss of control and ability to connect the self to the world, it may be appropriate to focus on restoring felt personal agency and responsibility through therapy. In DISA cultures, however, meaninglessness may more often manifest as a sense of social chaos or disrupted relationships, and interpreting disturbances in a way that is respectful of these relationships and how they might be repaired could be vital.

Second, there is a great deal more research that could be conducted from a cultural-existential perspective, investigating a number of problems that go beyond the primary interests of social psychology and which may fall more in the purview of clinical or health psychology. For example, beyond considering psychopathology, researchers might also investigate the extent to which culture shapes the experience of *physical* pain. Again, the material in this book was largely limited to experiences of symbolic threats, but such experiences are often intimately connected to physical pain and health difficulties, suggesting that these may also permit cultural influence. One possible direction for such research might be the very different experiences of veteran amputees in different cultures (French, 1994; Messinger, 2010).

Considering a cultural-existential perspective on pathological experiences points to the relevance of this view for contemporary social dilemmas. In the globalized world, experiences of meaninglessness and condemnation angst are perhaps increasingly common. A corollary of this observation is that the DISA and DESA threat orientations are possibly less effective than they were at sheltering individuals from nihilism prior to the dominance of capitalism and globalization. To understand why this might be the case, we must explore one final distinction between DISA and DESA cultures, namely how they orient the individual toward different understandings of redemption.

Redemption of the self and redemption of the world

Chapters 6 and 8 presented evidence that people from IV and II backgrounds are more likely to interpret suffering redemptively, that is, to see suffering as a necessary and desirable part of personal improvement. This may have surprised some readers. The idea of redemption is often associated with religious ideology, particularly the Christian tradition. Why, therefore, would it be the case that the relatively more secularized members of IV and II cultures would be oriented toward "redemptive" suffering interpretations?

This question indicates an important ambiguity in the meaning of "redemption," which in turn points to another way of framing the distinction between DISA and DESA cultures. Psychologists have secularized the word, and I have followed them in referring to an individualistic interpretation of suffering as "redemptive." But ultimately the word can have multiple meanings: what is significant is what the individual seeks *to redeem* or *be redeemed from*. As Hostetler (1996) wrote in his analysis of the Amish, an important meaning of redemption is *the desire to make whole again*. What do people in DISA and DESA cultures want to make whole again? Framed another way, where do they see emptiness (nonbeing)?

At the end of Part I, I distinguished between DISA and DESA cultures by proposing that they offer theodicies of world and self, respectively. These correspond to two opposing ideas of redemption, identified by Jung (1940) as the redemption of Christianity versus that of alchemy, and also described as the religious versus secular mode of redemption by Nietzsche (see Shulman's, 2006, analysis). If DISA culture has a world theodicy – it attempts to inoculate the world, as interpreted through a coherent meaning system, against suffering and threat – it correspondingly identifies the self as the entity requiring redemption. In DISA belief systems, the self is invariably portrayed as incomplete and inferior, requiring union with the collective or a deity to be made whole again. The experience of guilt is the embodiment of this emptiness within the self. By contrast, the self theodicy of DESA culture – which immunizes the self against suffering and threat – corresponds with a world-focused redemption system. From this perspective, manifest in Rousseau and other foundational individualist thinkers, the self should be an auto-sustaining entity, and it is rather the world (or culture) that is found damaged and lacking, and which requires active, positive transformation. This is why the humanistic worldview associated with a DESA orientation is so often the foundation for radical political projects and social justice movements, as in the case of the Unitarian Universalists.

In these conflicting concepts of redemption, we find the seeds of the different social psychological problems inherent in exclusive reliance on a DISA or DESA orientation. The problems associated with DISA culture are very well recognized in contemporary social science, and so do not need special attention here. Many politicians, educators, and scientists have argued against the crippling effects that follow from a focus on the self's inadequacy and a rigid meaning system. Such a focus can lead to the development of psychopathology or a general inflexibility when DISA-oriented individuals are confronted by change or members of outside groups.

However, the dangers of DESA culture are equally troubling. As Nietzsche (1874/1997) and Charles Taylor (1991) have argued, the self requires a "horizon of significance" against which to define its ability and prospects. In the language of terror management theory, the individual requires a cultural worldview to set meaningful standards for the pursuit of self-esteem. The world-focused redemption ideal of DESA culture encourages the individual to constantly push back, redefine, or collapse the cultural horizons of significance around them. The individual converts from one belief system to another, pursues one major project after another, and comes to embrace change and suffering as necessary elements in the interminable pursuit of growth. If Buddhism traditionally advocated the dissolution of the self into the world, secular individualism fosters instead the impossible goal of consuming the entire world in the ongoing expansion of the self's capabilities and experience (Durkheim, 1897). This is why Simmel (1918/2010) argued that existing in an epistemological plane of immanence – that is, the secularism of contemporary IV and II cultures – actually makes the self *more* rather than less dependent on the idea of transcendence and the beyond. If the individual believes they exist in a "horizonless" material world, they are perennially engaged in the struggle to redeem that world by finding some elusive horizon within the self.

The endless quest to reinvent the self and tear down existing horizons in DESA culture can lead to nihilistic disorientation, as has been argued in numerous philosophical discussions of modernity (e.g., Taylor, 2007). However, in an ironic twist, the "horizonless" world of contemporary II culture can ultimately generate high levels of condemnation angst as well. Although DESA culture was born in the attempt to uphold the self's value through the project of redeeming a problematic world, the psychological destruction of one's world – the decline of clear meaning systems, the movement away from a sociocentric worldview – ultimately leaves the self fragile and susceptible to condemnation. If the self has no horizons, it cannot be judged – and this means the absence not only of negative, but also of positive judgments. Individualist culture seeks to immunize the self against condemnation (Esposito, 2013), but in so doing incorporates the threat of condemnation within the self. If the ego is never convinced that it has attained its ideal because that ideal is constantly shifting, then the ego can become a harsher judge of itself than the superego ever was.

Problems of modern society, and possible solutions

DISA culture developed to protect individuals from meaninglessness angst, and DESA culture to protect them from condemnation angst. However, in modern, globalized society, people are increasingly exposed to the threats that their culture developed to protect them against. These more and more frequent cases are examples of what Habermas (1987) referred to as the modern "uncoupling of system and lifeworld." To unpack these terms, the cultural lifeworld is the phenomenological arena of symbolic meaning provided to individuals by their cultural *Existenzielle*, the five orientations discussed in Chapters 2 and 4. Under situations of existential security, these orientations filter threats for individuals, allowing them to make sense of dangers in light of meaningful cultural categories. The uncoupling of lifeworld and system refers to a process whereby the globalized institutions of modern capitalism grow beyond the boundaries of what is interpretable by the lifeworld, infiltrating all aspects of life. For example, whereas processes of economic exchange in CI cultures used to be normatively understood as sacred exchanges binding together individuals in the *Mitwelt* (Mauss, 1950/1990), the financial economy has now grown to global proportions that are beyond the cognitive capacity of any single individual to remotely comprehend (Allen & Pryke, 1999). The processes of modern politics, even in representative democracies, are similarly beyond the understanding and cultural interpretations available to most citizens (Hibbing & Theiss-Morse, 2002). It is certainly the case that culture has never represented to individuals' conscious awareness the full complexity of the economic and political institutions that influence their lives; indeed, a primary function of meaning systems has always been, through religious or other means, to simplify a complex world and provide the individual with the illusion that they understand and have some influence over their fate. However, contemporary globalization and capitalism have widened the gap between the simplicity of cultural meanings and the complexity of social institutions and intersocietal exchange to a profound extent. In short, meaning systems have not been able to keep pace with the acceleration of technological and economic development, leaving people vulnerable to psychopathologies that were previously kept at bay.

For instance, individuals in DISA cultures are increasingly exposed to possibilities of meaninglessness angst that have emerged as direct or indirect consequences of globalization (Wieviorka, 2012). As only one of many possible examples, Kai Erikson (1994) reports how a group of Ojibwe American Indians living on the Grassy Narrows reservation in Canada suffered a series of blows to their traditional belief system over the course of the twentieth century resulting from encroaching globalizing forces. For centuries, Ojibwe had lived in the region in an insulated and intact variant of CI culture. However, a flu epidemic imported by European Americans in the 1910s destroyed the Ojibwe's faith in the power of their healers to cope with suffering, the first of a series of externally originating events that would gradually erode their culture. By the 1970s, government takeover of Ojibwe land and the marketization of the region, combined with the group's exposure to debilitating toxins infiltrating their water from a nearby factory, had created a situation that one local leader referred to as living in a "broken culture" (Erikson, 1994). With their traditional faith marginalized, humiliated, and forgotten, and yet unable to psychologically embrace the Christianity forced on them by missionaries, the Grassy Narrows Ojibwe reportedly live a life characterized by high rates of depression, suicide, and violent alcoholism.

While isolated DISA cultures have been able to shelter their members from nihilistic disorientation for centuries, the insidious manner in which modern capitalism infiltrates and connects diverse cultural groups can corrode traditional beliefs in less than a generation, suddenly exposing previously buffered individuals to threats for which they are psychologically unequipped. An impressive aspect of Holdeman Mennonites – as summarized in Chapters 7 and 8 – is the disciplined work that members and especially leaders of this community do to maintain boundaries around their CV culture in the midst of modernity. But the Holdemans too will have increasing difficulty upholding their way of life as farming and other agricultural practices become increasingly commercialized throughout the world.

At the opposite end of the spectrum, as neoliberal capitalism facilitates a worldwide transition toward increased income inequality and II culture, individuals socialized with a DESA threat orientation are increasingly exposed to condemnation angst. The hyper-individualism of II culture breeds a consumerist, aestheticist approach to identity (Featherstone & Hepworth, 1991), including an ongoing search for personal authenticity (Giddens, 1990; Potter, 2010) combined with a preoccupation with self-esteem and career advancement (de Botton, 2004). Summarily, these conditions make up the experience of what has been called "hypermodernity" (e.g., Dubouloy, 2011) – the self, its close relationships, and worldly successes constitute the individual's supreme and only value system, and there are constant demands on this system for improvement and reinvention, as well as rampant processes of evaluative comparison. Horizons against which the self might be judged are perennially torn down and rebuilt. Under such straining circumstances, theodicies of the self often break down, yielding to condemnation angst. Although the DESA orientation of immunizing individualist ideologies was originally intended to buffer the self against perceived limitations, the growing weight of a competitive individualism that stresses the divide between an ever-smaller number of "winners" and an ever-growing number of "losers" generates historically unprecedented depression rates (Ehrenberg, 2010).

Worse still, the outpacing of meaning systems by capitalism does not only result in greater psychological suffering for individuals within cultures. This suffering often feeds back into the system and spreads through acts of violence, oppression, or indifference toward members of other groups. We are all too familiar with acts of political extremism, ranging from terrorist bombings to institutionalized racism, that are gradually gaining in their appeal to segments of the world population whose DISA orientations no longer provide them with a bedrock of unassailable meaning (Wieviorka, 2012). And the condemnation angst percolating through DESA culture only generates greater defensive narcissism, which distracts those with resources from interfering with the injustices of neoliberal expansion. If the wealthiest people in the world desperately need new products to convince themselves that they have value, they will not bother asking questions about who had to suffer in their production.

How can we, as a global society, confront the problems we face and restore culture's potential to provide the individual with acceptable interpretations of suffering and threat, to allow the individual to die, as Weber (1946) wrote, "old and satiated with life" (p. 140)? One of the central claims of cultural-existential psychology is that this is no easy task; indeed, it might well be an impossible dream. The existential condition is one of suffering and mortality, and, due to our dialectical nature, culture can only channel us toward the minimization of some threats while exacerbating the potency of others. The outpacing of meaning systems by capitalism seems to be usurping culture's potential to do even this. And unprecedented threats of environmental destruction, mass poverty, and technological warfare cry out for culture to do more than it has ever done to elevate our existential situation, at the very moment when culture has been weakened to an unprecedented degree.

The cultural and threat orientations identified in Chapters 4 and 5 offer a framework for at least conceptualizing ways in which new cultural patterns might emerge that could be better suited for coping with the modern situation. Given that humans are torn between dialectical poles of self and world, disorientation and despair (as seen in Chapter 3), the most viable way of life would be one that can balance and integrate these potentialities and threats. Thus, the most resilient cultural pattern would be one that could combine elements of a DISA and DESA orientation. There are clear advantages to living under the religious canopy and interwoven community of a DISA culture – consider how the Holdeman Mennonites were able to weather the Greensburg storm with a strength that was not readily available to mainstream residents (Chapter 8). And yet the reflexivity of DESA culture has equipped humanity with the critical reason that is alone capable of recognizing and anticipating mass-scale disasters – from tornadoes to poverty to global warming – and potentially mitigating or avoiding them.

How can a common ground be reached between DISA and DESA orientations? Again, this might seem an impossible task. The psychological force and efficacy of these radically different visions of the world stems precisely from their magnification of certain values and threats over and above others. Can humans truly be motivated toward the good without simultaneously being oriented *away from the evil*? It would seem, perhaps, that any attempt to reconcile DISA and DESA orientations would dilute them, and thus further impair their capacity to offer psychological shelter.

Nevertheless, examples have been identified of ways in which DISA and DESA cultures might grow closer to and learn from one another, and hence more flexibly meet the challenges of the globalized world and strengthen the individual. These examples primarily consist of social control in individualist cultures becoming more visible, or becoming more invisible in collectivist cultures. For instance, the reflexivity and self-questioning of II culture can be grounded if the individual pursues paths of self-cultivation through critical engagement with ritual practices (Rosati, 2009). Traditional Judaism, for instance, offers a set of rituals that can structure a person's life, set limits to their aspirations, and reduce uncertainty, while not necessitating a commitment to dogma or ethnocentrism. Such paradoxical commitment to subordination may offer surprising relief from anxiety for the individual. On the other hand, the rigidity of CV culture can be loosened through the careful introduction of more reflexive elements and skeptical engagement with modern institutions. Madsen (2012) points to the example of the Buddhist Compassion Relief Society and similar organizations in contemporary Taiwan. These groups are engaged in ongoing efforts to retain the essential elements of classic Buddhist and Confucian teaching, modifying them to incorporate and improve upon modern transformations in lifestyle.

The combining of beneficial elements from DISA and DESA perspectives – of finding some middle ground between visible and invisible modes of social control, between an emphasis on belief and on practice – is a painstaking process. There are no simple and efficient paths toward this goal. If the secular individualist self-consciously attempts to construct a patchwork of religious rituals – sampling from various traditions at will like stations in a buffet – or to use meditation techniques to alleviate stress with the aim of working longer hours, they will never leave the hold of DESA egocentrism. And there is great danger in the opening up of DISA traditions to modern reflexivity, however small the initial steps might be. Religions are the product of centuries of effort to inoculate humanity's fragile symbol systems against threat, and in the dialogue with secular ideas, they may lose the compelling force that alone fostered this inoculation. Even setting aside these problems of discursive meaning, there is a deeper issue involved, namely the anonymous hostility of capitalist social structures to any culturally grounded attempt to limit them. As suggested by the responses of undergraduate students in Chapter 7's survey, competitive individualism is indifferent to the psychological suffering of persons – indeed, it flourishes as a consequence of such suffering.

Ultimately, then, we are left with the rather unsurprising conclusion that while small moderations of the more extreme tendencies of DISA and DESA culture may improve the lot of certain groups and individuals, confronting the collective dilemmas of humanity will be far more difficult. That this is the case should be clear when we reflect upon the work of the social scientists and philosophers that has appeared throughout these pages. The tremendous challenge lies in the tragic collision of the existential and cultural elements of human being. Across time, those who have sought a way out of the chaos of worldly suffering in the redemption of the self have failed to admit an indisputable fact, namely that humans are mortal and base creatures. And those who have looked to the redemption of the world have been comparably blind to the reality that our consciousness binds us to symbol systems and institutions that transcend us and are immortal in a very meaningful, even oppressive sense. Any cultural system that might hold forth the promise of our flourishing must pay equal homage to our animal bodies and our proliferating tools. No worldview has yet struck such a balance between our flesh and the Word.

Appendix A Guide to key abbreviations and terms

Anxiety – A first-level threat experience involving unpleasant, abstract uncertainty about one or more of the following: the significance of one's actions and cultural beliefs; how to achieve a particular higher-order aim; whether one will be able to act efficaciously. Anxiety tends to be directed toward the future. If unresolved, anxiety can elevate to second-level meaninglessness angst.

CI – Collectivist, invisibly controlled culture; a (sub)culture that has a collectivist social orientation and invisible social control, as described in Chapter 4. A paradigmatic example would be a seminomadic hunter-gatherer group.

Collectivism vs. individualism – A continuum of cultural differences in social orientation; collectivist cultures orient their members toward social relationships and embeddedness in a group, whereas individualist cultures orient their members away from social relationships and toward a sense of their own independence.

Condemnation angst – A second-level threat experience involving prolonged negative existential feelings (as discussed in Chapter 3) centering around a sense of the self's unworthiness. Condemnation angst arises from first-level guilt if the latter is not defused. In extreme instances, condemnation angst can give rise to nihilistic despair.

CV – Collectivist, visibly controlled culture; a (sub)culture that has a collectivist social orientation and visible social control, as described in Chapter 4. A paradigmatic example would be a fundamentalist religious group.

DESA – Despair-avoidant cultural threat orientation; being oriented away from nihilistic despair, through a defensive commitment to preserving either the self's unique value, the value of all human life, or both. People socialized in DESA cultures tend to prioritize the preservation of their self-esteem and the avoidance of guilt. They have less rigid meaning systems and are therefore comparatively vulnerable to anxiety.

DISA – Disorientation-avoidant cultural threat orientation; being oriented away from nihilistic disorientation, through a defensive commitment to preserving sacred cultural values, beliefs, and practices. People socialized in DISA cultures tend to prioritize the preservation of meaning and order and the avoidance of anxiety. They have less buffered self-concepts and are therefore comparatively vulnerable to guilt.

Eigenwelt – One of the three "worlds of experience" in which people simultaneously live, the *Eigenwelt* is the "personal world," consisting of aspects of experience that are uniquely connected to self and identity.

Existenzial – Pertaining to universal, structural aspects of human existence arising from the unique biological situation of humanity, as discussed in Chapter 2. *Existenzial* exigencies must be dealt with by people in all cultures. Paradigmatic examples include existence in the *Umwelt, Mitwelt,* and *Eigenwelt* (discussed in Chapter 2), or experiencing the dialectic of anxiety and guilt (Chapter 3).

Existenziell – Pertaining to concrete instantiations of universal *Existenzial* exigencies in specific cultural contexts. Structural features of human biology are made manifest in different ways according to *existenziell,* culture-specific features of environment and social custom. Paradigmatic examples are the different orientations presented in Table 4.2 (Chapter 4).

First-level, dialectical threats – Relatively minor threats that the individual may encounter on an everyday basis and against which they possess defenses acquired through socialization. Such threats typically evoke a "dialectical" response: the abstract threat of anxiety is responded to with investment in concrete goals and meanings, while the concrete threat of guilt is responded to with investment in abstract identities and possibilities.

Guilt – A first-level threat experience involving unpleasant, concrete certainty that the self has transgressed against or deviated from an internalized behavioral standard, moral code, or ego-relevant goal. Guilt tends to be directed toward a past event. If unresolved, guilt can elevate to second-level condemnation angst.

II – Individualist, invisibly controlled culture; a (sub)culture that has a collectivist social orientation and visible social control, as described in Chapter 4. A paradigmatic example would be the elite members of a capitalist company.

Immanence – The attitudes, beliefs, and experience associated with living in "one world," to be contrasted with transcendence. Immanent existence posits one material plane, without any higher or alternate reality. Secularism promotes belief in immanence.

IV – Individualist, visibly controlled culture; a (sub)culture that has an individualist social orientation and visible social control, as described in Chapter 4. A paradigmatic example would be members of a democratic commune.

Meaninglessness angst – A second-level threat experience involving prolonged negative existential feelings (as discussed in Chapter 3) centering around a perceived breakdown of culturally normative meaning categories. Meaninglessness angst arises from first-level anxiety if the latter is not defused. In extreme instances, meaninglessness angst can give rise to nihilistic disorientation.

Mitwelt – One of the three "worlds of experience" in which people simultaneously live, the *Mitwelt* is the "social world," consisting of aspects of experience that are uniquely connected to living in cultural groups and social relationships.

Nihilistic despair – The conviction that one is not capable of achieving one's highest values. If an individual or culture suffers from nihilistic despair, one feels that one cannot do anything that is worth doing. It is an extreme outcome of guilt and condemnation angst.

Nihilistic disorientation – The conviction that there are no values worth achieving. If an individual or culture suffers from nihilistic despair, one feels that no action is worth doing, that no goal is of greater importance than any other. It is an extreme outcome of anxiety and meaninglessness angst.

Redemptive suffering interpretation – In a secular sense, interpreting suffering as ultimately positive for the individual because it contributes to the individual's growth. Such interpretations are afforded by individualist culture.

Reflexivity – Generally, the human ability to reflect upon and question culturally given beliefs and practices. Individual reflexivity involves an actor's recognition of the socially constructed nature of her values and activities. Cultural reflexivity involves a society's construction of a knowledge base about the origin of its practices that can be used to critique those practices.

Repressive suffering interpretation – Interpreting suffering as caused by an individual's deviance or anti-sociality, and as having the ultimate purpose of strengthening society through the punishment or reform of the deviant. Such interpretations are afforded by collectivist culture.

Second-level, non-dialectical threats – Relatively extreme threats experienced during unusual negative events or after prolonged exposure to a first-level threat. Unlike in the case of first-level threats, the individual does not typically have reliable defenses against second-level threats, and so cannot shift "dialectically" away from them. These threats manifest as negative existential feelings of meaninglessness angst or condemnation angst.

Threat dialectic – In existentialist theory, the assumption that individuals cycle routinely between experiences of anxiety that prompt investment in concrete goals and identities, and experiences of guilt that prompt abstract flights from past goals and identities.

Transcendence – The attitudes, beliefs, and experience associated with living in "two worlds," to be contrasted with immanence. Transcendent existence posits an inferior, temporal plane to be contrasted with a superior, eternal plane. Religiosity typically promotes belief in transcendence.

Transcendence suffering interpretation – Within a transcendent (typically religious) worldview, interpreting suffering as a trial to be borne on the inferior, earthly plane, with the consequence of downplaying the significance of suffering and highlighting the superiority of the supramaterial plane. Such interpretations are afforded by CV culture.

***Umwelt* –** One of the three "worlds of experience" in which people simultaneously live, the *Umwelt* is the "natural world," consisting of aspects of experience that are uniquely connected to biological existence in a culturally filtered material environment.

Visible vs. invisible social control – A continuum of cultural differences in social control; visibly controlled cultures regulate their members through moralized norms, clear punishments, and concentrated sources of surveillance, whereas invisibly controlled cultures regulate their members through environmentally structured or behavioral norms and more diffuse forms of surveillance.

Appendix B Data analyses, Chapter 6

Descriptive statistics: correlations, reliabilities (Cronbach's alpha), range of observed scores, means, and standard deviations for all variables.

	1	2	3	4	5
1. Birth Year	–				
2. Individualism	0.20	–			
3. Collectivism	0.35**	0.63**	–		
4. Repressive Suffering	0.09	−0.28*	−0.15	–	
5. Redemptive Suffering	−0.04	0.36**	0.03	0.09	–
SCALE α	N/A	0.87	0.84	N/A	0.58
RANGE	1898–1938	2.7–4.7	2.3–4.7	2–5	3–5
VARIABLE MEAN	1919	3.53	3.54	3.50	4.05
STANDARD DEVIATION	11.66	0.49	0.50	0.95	0.41

$N = 57$; $^{*}p < 0.10$; $^{**}p < 0.05$.

Correlational analyses. Considering the data set as a whole, individualism was negatively correlated with repressive suffering construals, $r = -0.28$, $p = 0.08$, and positively correlated with redemptive suffering construals, $r = 0.36$, $p = 0.01$.

Examining correlations within generations, in the older generation, individualism and collectivism were strongly positively correlated, $r = 0.78$, $p < 0.001$. By contrast, in the younger generation, these two variables were only moderately correlated, $r = 0.48$, $p = 0.02$. The difference between these associations is significant, $z = 1.69$, $p = 0.05$.

Regression analyses. Redemptive suffering scores were regressed onto generation (categorical), collectivism (continuous), and their interaction (see Figure 6.1A). The interaction term was significant, $\beta = 2.67$, SE = 0.26, $t(44) = 2.37$, $p = 0.02$. Simple slopes analysis revealed that among the older generation, collectivism was negatively associated with redemptive suffering interpretations, $\beta = -0.33$, SE = 0.18,

$t(44) = -1.57$, $p = 0.11$. However, among the younger generation, collectivism was positively associated with redemptive suffering interpretations, $\beta = 0.38$, SE = 0.18, $t(44) = 1.77$, $p = 0.08$. Considering the data another way, at high levels of collectivism (i.e., one standard deviation above the mean), those in the older generation were less endorsing of redemptive suffering than those in the younger generation, $\beta = 0.40$, SE = 0.18, $t(44) = 1.91$, $p = 0.06$.

The same analysis was performed substituting individualism for collectivism as a continuous predictor, and again the interaction term was significant, $\beta = 2.79$, SE = 0.24, $t(44) = 2.66$, $p = 0.01$ (see Figure 6.1B. In this analysis, among the older generation, there was no relationship between individualism and redemptive suffering interpretations, $p = 0.74$. However, among the younger generation, there was a substantial positive association between individualism and redemptive suffering interpretations, $\beta = 0.65$, SE = 0.15, $t(44) = 3.79$, $p < 0.001$.

Importantly, considering the zero-order correlations for the younger generation, the relationship between individualism and redemptive suffering ($r = 0.67$, $p < 0.001$) was stronger than the relationship between collectivism and redemptive suffering ($r = 0.34$, $p = 0.11$), $z = 1.44$, $p = 0.08$.

The same analyses performed on repressive suffering scores did not approach significance.

Gender effects. The sample included 32 female and 24 male participants. Examining gender in the analyses presented above did not yield any significant effects, with two exceptions. First, there was a marginally significant interaction between gender and generation on individualism, $F(1, 43) = 3.60$, $p = 0.06$. Pairwise comparisons (Fisher's LSD) revealed that this effect was primarily driven by the higher scores of women in the younger generation, $M = 3.74$, SD = 0.64, compared to women in the older generation, $M = 3.33$, SD = 0.46, $t(43) = 2.23$, $p = 0.03$. Additionally, within the older generation, women tended to score lower compared to men, $M = 3.60$, SD = 0.30.

Second, on the measure of repressive interpretations, there was an overall tendency for women to score higher, $M = 3.70$, SD = 1.00, than men, $M = 3.23$, SD = 0.87, $t(44) = 1.74$, $p = 0.09$. This finding is notable because prior research has suggested that men are more likely to interpret suffering repressively than women (Sullivan et al., 2012b).

Appendix C Methodology and questionnaire items, Chapter 7

Study instructions. At the beginning of all sessions (or in instruction sheets in the case of Unitarian Universalists who completed the survey at home), it was stressed that whenever they encountered the word *community* in the survey, participants were to think specifically about the local community on the basis of which they had been recruited. In other words, Holdemans thought about their congregation as a whole, Unitarian Universalists similarly thought about their local fellowship, and undergraduates thought about the undergraduate community at their university. It was made clear to all participants that other potentially ambiguous terms encountered throughout the survey (e.g., "God," "faith," "people") should be interpreted in whatever way seemed most natural to them.

After answering a few demographic questions, participants responded to several items pertaining to the cultural factors of primary interest: *Religiosity* and *Collectivism-individualism.* Participants responded to all items in this section of the survey on 1 = *Strongly disagree*, 7 = *Strongly agree* scales (exceptions noted below).

Religiosity. Religiosity measures included previously validated measures of intrinsic religiosity (Hoge, 1972) and existential quest (van Pachterbeke, Keller, & Saroglou, 2012), as well as an additional item assessing perceived control of one's life by God. To determine how the measures of religiosity related to one another in this religiously diverse sample, I submitted scores on all religiosity measures to an exploratory factor analysis, using maximum-likelihood estimation and Promax rotation. The analysis and corresponding scree plot suggested that the variables loaded onto three distinguishable factors. The eight existential quest items loaded at 0.45 or higher on only one factor. Conceptually, these items represent open-minded and skeptical approaches to religiosity, or more accurately secularism in Taylor's (2007) sense (see also Hall, Koenig, & Meador, 2008). I created a composite measure of these items, which I refer to as a *secularism* index ($\alpha = 0.87$). Four items mentioning God or religious strictness loaded at 0.80 or higher on only one factor, which I averaged to create an *orthodox religiosity* index ($\alpha = 0.95$). The four remaining items assessed the pervasiveness and importance of religiosity in one's life, and loaded at 0.80 or higher on only one factor. I averaged responses to these items to create an *intrinsic religiosity* index ($\alpha = 0.94$). Across the entire sample, secularism correlated negatively with orthodox and intrinsic religiosity, $rs > -0.60$, $ps < 0.001$, and the latter two factors correlated at $r = 0.77$, $p < 0.001$. The specific items for each religiosity variable were as follows:

Secularism

- Today, I still wonder about the meaning and goal of my life.
- My attitude toward religion/spirituality is likely to change according to my life experiences.
- Being able to doubt about one's convictions and to reappraise them is a good quality.
- In my opinion, doubt is important in major questions about life.
- My way of seeing the world is certainly going to change again.
- My opinion varies on a lot of subjects.
- I know perfectly well what the goal of my life is. (reverse-scored)
- Years go by but my way of seeing the world doesn't change. (reverse-scored)

Orthodox religiosity

- One should seek God's guidance when making every important decision.
- Nothing is as important to me as serving God as best I know how.
- My faith sometimes restricts my actions.
- Do you believe that you yourself, or that God controls your life and the events in it? (1 = *I entirely control my life*, 4 = *God has some control over my life*, 7 = *God entirely controls my life*).

Intrinsic religiosity

- My faith involves all my life.
- In my life I experience the presence of the divine.
- I try hard to carry my religion over into all my other dealings in life.
- My religious beliefs are really what lie behind my whole approach to life.

Individualism-collectivism. Social orientation measures were adapted from the dimensional individualism-collectivism scale (Singelis et al., 1995), with three items each intended to assess vertical collectivism, horizontal collectivism, vertical individualism, and horizontal individualism. I performed an exploratory factor analysis (using maximum-likelihood estimation and promax rotation) on these items; the analysis and corresponding scree plot suggested that they loaded onto only three (rather than the hypothesized four) distinguishable factors. Specifically, all six collectivism items loaded at 0.50 or higher on only one factor, so rather than creating separate vertical and horizontal collectivism indices, I created a single collectivism composite ($\alpha = 0.80$). The EFA suggested meaningful differentiation between the two dimensions of individualism, however, so I created separate vertical ($\alpha = 0.55$) and horizontal individualism indices ($\alpha = 0.50$). The specific items included in each index were as follows:

Collectivism

- I would do what would please my family, even if I detested that activity.
- I would sacrifice an activity that I enjoy very much if my community did not approve of it.
- Children should be taught to place duty before pleasure.
- It is important to maintain harmony within my community.
- My happiness depends very much on the happiness of those around me.
- I feel good when I cooperate with others.

Vertical individualism

- Competition is the law of nature.
- I enjoy working in situations involving competition with others.
- When another person does something better than I do, I get tense and upset.

Horizontal individualism

- I enjoy being unique and different from others in many ways.
- One should live one's life independently of others.
- What happens to me is my own doing.

After completing the cultural variables, participants then completed measures designed to assess more specific components of their worldview, which, in addition to the more general belief systems of religiosity-secularism and collectivism-individualism, were hypothesized to act as culturally derived defensive structures against existential threat. Participants responded to all items in this section of the survey on 1 = *Strongly disagree*, 7 = *Strongly agree* scales.

Worldview components. Worldview components were assessed using a modified version of the World Assumptions Scale (Janoff-Bulman, 1989), with three items each assessing the components of *controllability* ($\alpha = 0.63$), *self-controllability* ($\alpha = 0.52$), *justice* ($\alpha = 0.52$), *randomness* ($\alpha = 0.45$), *benevolence of the world* ($\alpha = 0.70$), *benevolence of* *people* (α = 0.33), and *luck* (α = 0.71), and with four items assessing the component of *self-esteem* (α = 0.79). The low reliabilities observed for some of the subscales were probably due to the fact that the original four items were reduced to three. Because of the theoretical specificity of the World Assumptions subscales and their prior validation (Janoff-Bulman, 1992), the separate scales were nevertheless maintained. The specific items measuring each component were as follows:

Justice

- Misfortune is least likely to strike worthy, decent people.
- Generally, people deserve what they get in this world.
- People will experience good fortune if they themselves are good.

Self-controllability

- I usually behave in ways that are likely to maximize good results for me.
- I almost always make an effort to prevent bad things from happening to me.
- I take the actions necessary to protect myself against misfortune.

Controllability

- People's misfortunes result from mistakes they have made.
- Through our actions we can prevent bad things from happening to us.
- If people took preventive actions, most misfortune could be avoided.

Self-esteem

- I often think I am no good at all. (reverse-scored)
- I have a low opinion of myself. (reverse-scored)
- I am very satisfied with the kind of person I am.
- I have reason to be ashamed of my personal character. (reverse-scored)

Randomness

- Bad events are distributed to people at random.
- The course of our lives is largely determined by chance.
- Life is too full of uncertainties that are determined by chance.

Luck

- I am basically a lucky person.
- Looking at my life, I realize that chance events have worked out well for me.
- I am luckier than most people.

Benevolence of people

- Human nature is basically good.
- People don't really care what happens to the next person. (reverse-scored)
- People are basically kind and helpful.

Benevolence of the world

- The good things that happen in this world far outnumber the bad.
- There is more good than evil in the world.
- If you look closely enough, you will see that the world is full of goodness.

Reparative behaviors. Besides the World Assumptions Scale components, I assessed one additional culturally derived defensive structure, namely the tendency to engage in reparative behavior after a guilt-inducing situation. Specifically, participants were asked to recall a time when they had said or done something to offend or harm someone whom they cared about. They then responded to the item, "I made very strong efforts to apologize and reconcile with this person."

Having completed measures of cultural variables, worldview components, and reparative behaviors, in the final questionnaires participants completed several measures of threat experience.

First-level threats. I assessed the first-level existential threat experiences of *guilt* and *anxiety* using previously validated measures. Specifically, guilt was assessed using five items from the Guilt and Shame Proneness Scale (Cohen, Wolf, Panter, & Insko, 2011). Participants rated the negative affect they would feel in hypothetical situations in which they might experience guilt or shame. All responses were given on 1 = *Very unlikely*, 7 = *Very likely* scales. I used five guilt and shame feelings items from the measure, selecting scenarios that would be equally applicable to each group, and created a composite guilt measure ($\alpha = 0.70$).

Anxiety was assessed using two kinds of items. Four items were adopted from a previous measure (Sullivan, Landau, & Rothschild, 2010) that assesses anxious concern over potential future risks, and to which participants responded on the scale 1 = *Not anxious at all*, 4 = *Neutral*, 7 = *Very anxious*. Two additional items came from the *emptiness* subscale of the Existential Anxiety Questionnaire (Weems, Costa, Dehon, & Berman, 2004). Participants responded to these items on the scale 1 = *Strongly disagree*, 7 = *Strongly agree*. The six items were averaged to create a composite measure of proclivity toward anxiety ($\alpha = 0.63$). The specific items used to measure guilt and anxiety were as follows:

Guilt

- After realizing you have received too much change at a store, you decide to keep it because the clerk doesn't notice. What is the likelihood you would feel uncomfortable about this?
- You make a big mistake at work. Afterward your boss criticizes you in front of the other people you work with. What is the likelihood you would feel like you behaved foolishly?
- You secretly commit a felony crime. What is the likelihood that you would feel remorse about breaking the law?
- You accidentally damage your neighbor's car, but another neighbor is blamed for the damage. Later, this person confronts you about what you have done. What is the likelihood that you would feel like a coward?
- You lie to people but they never find out about it. What is the likelihood that you would feel terrible about the lies you told?

Anxiety

- You might have a major health problem. How anxious or worried do you feel thinking about this possibility?
- Due to changes in circumstances, you might be separated for a while from some people who are close to you. How anxious or worried do you feel thinking about this possibility?
- Due to rising costs of living, at some point in your life your income might not be enough to support your lifestyle. How anxious or worried do you feel thinking about this possibility?
- You might develop dental problems. How anxious or worried do you feel thinking about this possibility?
- I often think that the things that were once important in life are empty.
- I never think about emptiness. (reverse-scored)

Second-level threats. I administered the two-item *death* ($r = 0.41$, $p < 0.001$), *meaninglessness* ($r = 0.38$, $p < 0.001$), and *condemnation* ($r = 0.45$, $p < 0.001$) subscales of the Existential Anxiety Questionnaire (Weems et al., 2004). Responses to all angst measures were given on 1 = *Strongly disagree*, 7 = *Strongly agree* scales. The specific items used to measure each form of angst were as follows:

Death angst

- I often think about death and this causes me anxiety.
- I am not anxious about death because I am prepared for whatever it may bring. (reverse-scored)

Meaninglessness angst

- I often feel anxious because I am worried that life might have no meaning.
- I know that life has meaning. (reverse-scored)

Condemnation angst

- I often feel anxious because I feel condemned.
- I never feel anxious about being condemned. (reverse-scored)

Open-ended questions. After completing the rest of the questionnaires, participants in all three groups responded to open-ended questions. The Holdeman Mennonites responded to three questions about their religiosity: "What does your Christian faith mean to you? How does it influence your daily life?"; "How does your Christian faith give your life meaning and purpose?"; and "How does your Christian faith help you cope with times of trouble, suffering, or misfortune?" Undergraduates and Unitarian Universalists responded to the same three prompts, but with the adjective "Christian" removed (i.e., they answered the questions with reference to "faith," however they understood that concept). Additionally, because of their focus on community belonging as opposed to traditional religiosity, Unitarian Universalists responded to three questions about community: "What does the idea of community mean to you?"; "How does belonging to the Unitarian Universalist community influence your life? Does this community help give your life meaning and purpose?"; and "How does your participation in this community help you cope with times of trouble, suffering, or misfortune?" Holdemans and undergraduates did not complete the questions about community.

Appendix D Data analyses, Chapter 7

Influence of demographic variables. Age was controlled for in all reported analyses, with the exception of within-group correlations. Across the entire sample, age was significantly negatively correlated with vertical and horizontal individualism, and with death and condemnation angst, $rs > -0.33$, $ps < 0.01$, and significantly positively correlated with guilt and perceived benevolence of the world, $rs > 0.29$, $ps < 0.01$. Within groups, the only significant associations found were that older undergraduates professed less orthodox religiosity, $r = -0.53$, $p < 0.01$, and they tended to be more horizontally individualist, $r = 0.35$, $p = 0.06$.

When gender was included along with group as a between-subjects variable in all analyses, the following effects emerged: a main effect of gender on perceived justice, $F(1, 72) = 5.72$, $p = 0.02$, such that men scored higher ($M = 3.53$, SD = 1.23) than women ($M = 2.84$, SD = 1.06); a main effect of gender on perceived controllability, $F(1, 72) = 7.38$, $p < 0.01$, such that men again scored higher ($M = 4.72$, SD = 1.02) than women ($M = 3.86$, SD = 1.21); a main effect of gender on anxiety, $F(1, 73) = 4.07$, $p = 0.05$, such that women scored higher ($M = 4.87$, SD = 0.89) than men ($M = 4.21$, SD = 1.03); an interaction effect on guilt, $F(2, 72) = 3.09$, $p = 0.05$, driven by the tendency for undergraduate men to score lower ($M = 5.04$, SD = 1.57) than all other groups; an interaction effect on intrinsic religiosity, $F(2, 73) = 5.81$, $p < 0.01$, driven by the tendency for Unitarian Universalist women to score higher ($M = 4.86$, SD = 1.50) than Unitarian Universalist men ($M = 2.66$, SD = 1.90); and an interaction effect on collectivism, $F(1, 73) = 3.59$, $p = 0.03$, driven by the tendency for Unitarian Universalist men to score higher ($M = 4.88$, SD = 0.65) than Unitarian Universalist women ($M = 3.84$, SD = 0.91). When gender was added as a second covariate to each of the analyses described below, all between-group effects remained significant, with the exception of the effect on perceived benevolence of the world, which became marginal, $p = 0.08$.

Religious and cultural orientations. I submitted each of the relevant variables to a between-subjects (Holdeman Mennonites vs. undergraduates vs. Unitarian Universalists) ANCOVA, with age entered as the covariate. For all means, see Figure 7.1.

Orthodox religiosity. The omnibus effect was significant, $F(2, 76) = 107.81$, $p < 0.001$, partial-$\eta^2 = 0.74$. Pairwise comparisons (Fisher's LSD) revealed that Holdemans had higher orthodox religiosity scores compared to undergraduates, $p < 0.001$, and Unitarian Universalists, $p < 0.001$. Undergraduates also displayed greater orthodox religiosity relative to Unitarian Universalists, $p < 0.01$.

Intrinsic religiosity. The omnibus effect was significant, $F(2, 76) = 34.02$, $p < 0.001$, partial-$\eta^2 = 0.47$. Pairwise comparisons suggested that Holdemans had higher intrinsic religiosity scores compared to undergraduates, $p < 0.001$, and Unitarian Universalists, $p < 0.001$. The latter two groups did not differ in intrinsic religiosity, $p = 0.97$.

Secularism. The omnibus effect was significant, $F(2, 76) = 67.21$, $p < 0.001$, partial-$\eta^2 = 0.64$. Unitarian Universalists had higher secularism scores than undergraduates, $p = 0.04$, and Holdemans, $p < 0.001$. Undergraduates also had higher secularism scores compared to Holdemans, $p < 0.001$.

Collectivism. The omnibus effect was significant, $F(2, 76) = 48.54$, $p < 0.001$, partial-$\eta^2 = 0.56$. Holdemans were more collectivist than undergraduates, $p < 0.001$, and Unitarian Universalists, $p < 0.001$. The latter two groups did not differ in collectivism, $p = 0.28$.

Vertical individualism. The omnibus effect was significant, $F(2, 76) = 3.21$, $p = 0.05$, partial-$\eta^2 = 0.08$. Undergraduates were more vertically individualist than Holdemans, $p = 0.04$, and Unitarian Universalists, $p = 0.01$. The latter two groups did not differ in vertical individualism, $p = 0.17$.

Horizontal individualism. The omnibus effect was significant, $F(2, 76) = 17.73$, $p < 0.001$, partial-$\eta^2 = 0.32$. Holdemans were less horizontally individualist than undergraduates, $p < 0.001$, and Unitarian Universalists, $p < 0.001$. The latter two groups did not differ in horizontal individualism, $p = 0.95$.

Worldview components. In order to reduce the number of analyses and simplify presentation, planned contrasts were conducted rather than omnibus one-way ANOVAs. The contrasts were planned based on my analysis and preliminary inspection of the data from the cultural variables. Specifically, the following predictions were tested:

(1) Relative to the other groups, Holdeman Mennonites were expected to score higher on *controllability* and *reparative behavior.* A planned contrast found that Holdemans perceived the world to be more

controlled ($M = 4.98$, SD = .97) compared to the other two groups ($M = 3.91$, SD = 1.19), $F(1, 76) = 16.90$, $p < 0.001$. Holdemans also scored higher ($M = 6.77$, SD = 0.68) on the measure of reparative behavior compared to the other two groups ($M = 5.13$, SD = 2.00), $F(1, 70) = 14.04$, $p < 0.001$.

(2) Relative to the other groups, undergraduates were expected to score higher on *randomness*. A planned contrast found that undergraduates perceived the world to be more random ($M = 5.71$, SD = 1.02) compared to the other two groups ($M = 4.23$, SD = 1.14), $F(1, 76) = 14.23$, $p < 0.001$.

(3) Relative to the other groups, Unitarian Universalists were expected to score higher on *self-esteem, benevolence of the world*, and *benevolence of people*. A planned contrast found that Unitarian Universalists had higher self-esteem ($M = 6.16$, SD = 1.00) compared to the other two groups ($M = 5.01$, SD = 1.35), $F(1, 76) = 8.30$, $p < 0.01$. Unitarian Universalists perceived the world to be more benevolent ($M = 5.46$, SD = 1.42) compared to the other two groups ($M = 4.61$, SD = 1.18), $F(1, 76) = 4.61$, $p = 0.04$. They also perceived human nature in general to be more benevolent ($M = 5.48$, SD = 0.78) compared to the other two groups ($M = 4.43$, SD = 1.08), $F(1, 76) = 10.92$, $p < 0.01$.

Threat experiences. For means of the groups on all threat variables, see Figure 7.2. Planned contrasts were carried out to test group differences on these variables.

Guilt. A planned contrast found that Holdemans had a greater proclivity toward feelings of guilt ($M = 6.58$, SD = 0.59) compared to the other two groups ($M = 5.84$, SD = 1.06), $F(1, 76) = 11.42$, $p < 0.01$. Only among the Holdemans was there a significant positive correlation between guilt and reparative behavior, $r = 0.53$, $p < 0.01$.

Anxiety. A planned contrast found that Holdemans showed less proclivity toward feelings of anxiety ($M = 3.94$, SD = 0.93) compared to the other two groups ($M = 4.86$, SD = 0.92), $F(1, 77) = 17.90$, $p < 0.001$. Undergraduates and Unitarian Universalists did not differ in anxiety scores, $p = 0.74$. Only among undergraduates was anxiety significantly negatively correlated with self-esteem, $r = -0.46$, $p = 0.01$, while only among Unitarian Universalists was anxiety significantly negatively correlated with horizontal individualism, $r = -0.52$, $p = 0.01$.

Death angst. A planned contrast found that undergraduates showed a greater level of death angst ($M = 4.44$, SD = 1.62) compared to the other two groups ($M = 2.43$, SD = 1.29), $F(1, 77) = 14.70$, $p < 0.001$. Only among undergraduates was self-esteem negatively correlated with death angst, $r = -0.48$, $p < 0.01$. By contrast, only among Holdemans was orthodox religiosity negatively correlated with death angst, $r = -0.59$, $p < 0.01$. All three within-group correlations between vertical individualism and death angst were significant and positive (Holdemans: $r = 0.39$, $p = 0.04$, undergraduates: $r = 0.55$, $p < 0.01$, Unitarian Universalists: $r = 0.45$, $p = 0.03$).

Meaninglessness angst. A planned contrast found that Holdemans showed a lower level of meaninglessness angst ($M = 1.25$, SD = 0.42) compared to the other two groups ($M = 2.43$, SD = 1.34), $F(1, 77) = 19.51$, $p < 0.001$. Only among undergraduates was meaninglessness angst significantly negatively correlated with self-esteem, $r = -0.78$, $p < 0.001$, while among Unitarian Universalists, meaninglessness angst was significantly negatively correlated with perceived world benevolence, $r = -0.44$, $p = 0.03$ (somewhat surprisingly, this was also the case with undergraduates, $r = -0.45$, $p = 0.01$, although this association was significantly less than that between meaninglessness angst and self-esteem, $z = -2.02$, $p = 0.04$).

Condemnation angst. A planned contrast found that Unitarian Universalists showed a lower level of condemnation angst ($M = 1.98$, SD = 1.01) compared to the other two groups ($M = 2.91$, SD = 1.43), $F(1, 77) = 5.70$, $p = 0.02$. Only among Unitarian Universalists was condemnation angst significantly negatively correlated with the perceived benevolence of people, $r = -0.49$, $p = 0.02$, while among undergraduates, condemnation angst was significantly negatively correlated with self-esteem, $r = -0.38$, $p = 0.04$ (this was also the case with Unitarian Universalists, $r = -0.41$, $p = 0.04$).

Mediation analyses. To determine whether particular differences in religious, cultural, or worldview orientation might be driving differences in threat experience between the groups, I performed analyses testing whether the effect of group (contrast-coded) on each of the threat variables occurred indirectly through one or more of the cultural variables. Specifically, I used Preacher and Hayes' (2008) bootstrapping approach. This approach tests the significance of the multiplicative parameter $a \times b$ (where a represents the predictor's effect on the mediator, and b represents the mediator's effect on the outcome controlling for the predictor). My bootstrapping tests sampled 5,000 times from the data (with replacement) to create an approximate distribution for this parameter. Confidence intervals of 95% were generated to test the null hypothesis that $a \times b = 0$. If a 95% CI does not contain 0, this indicates evidence at $\alpha = 0.05$ of a significant indirect effect. Reverse-mediational analyses were also conducted to determine if it was the case not only that particular cultural tendencies influenced participants' proclivity toward threat, but also that particular threat experiences influenced participants' attachment to cultural beliefs.

Guilt. Because Holdemans scored higher than the other two groups on orthodox religiosity, intrinsic religiosity, and collectivism, and because these three variables were positively correlated with guilt, an analysis was performed with the three variables entered as potential mediators. No results were significant at $\alpha = 0.05$. However, the indirect effect of group via the mediator of orthodox religiosity was significant at $\alpha = 0.10$, 90% CI (0.06, 0.96). A reverse-mediational analysis with guilt entered as the mediator and orthodox religiosity as the outcome yielded a significant effect, 95% CI (0.05, 0.37).

Death angst. Because undergraduates scored higher than the other two groups on vertical individualism and the randomness WAS subscale, and because these two variables were positively correlated with death angst, an analysis was performed with the two variables entered as potential mediators. Only the mediational path through vertical individualism was significant, 95% CI (0.02, 0.72). A reverse-mediational analysis with death angst entered as the mediator and vertical individualism as the outcome also yielded significance, 95% CI (0.20, 0.83).

Meaninglessness angst. Because Holdemans scored lower than the other two groups on secularism, horizontal and vertical individualism, and perceived randomness, and because these four variables were positively correlated with meaninglessness angst, an analysis was performed with the four variables entered as potential mediators. The 95% CIs for secularism (−0.94, −0.06) and randomness (−0.37, −0.002) yielded significant effects. Reverse-mediational analyses were also significant, with meaninglessness angst entered as the mediator, and secularism, 95% CI (−0.30, −0.03), and randomness, 95% CI (−0.36, −0.03), as the outcomes.

Condemnation angst. Because Unitarian Universalists scored lower than the other two groups on orthodox religiosity and vertical individualism, and because these two variables were positively correlated with condemnation angst, an analysis was performed with the two variables entered as potential mediators. No results were significant at $\alpha = 0.05$. However, the indirect effect of group via the mediator of vertical individualism was significant at $\alpha = 0.10$, 90% (−0.25, −0.001). The reverse-mediational model was nonsignificant.

No other significant mediational results were found.

References

Abdel-Khalek, A. M. (2002). Age and sex differences for anxiety in relation to family size, birth order, and religiosity among Kuwaiti adolescents. *Psychological Reports*, *90*, 1031–1036.

Abelson, R. P. (1995). *Statistics as Principled Argument*. Hillsdale, NJ: Psychology Press.

Ablah, E., Tinius, A. M., Konda, K., Synovitz, C., & Subbarao, I. (2007). Regional health system response to the 2007 Greensburg, Kansas, EF5 tornado. *Disaster Medicine and Public Health Preparedness*, *1*(2), 90–95.

Adams, G., & Dzokoto, V. A. (2007). Genital-shrinking panic in Ghana: A cultural psychological analysis. *Culture and Psychology*, *13*(1), 83–104.

Adams, G., & Markus, H. R. (2004). Toward a conception of culture suitable for a social psychology of culture. In M. Schaller, & C. S. Crandall (Eds.), *The Psychological Foundations of Culture* (pp. 335–360). Mahwah, NJ: Lawrence Erlbaum.

Adams, G., & Plaut, V. C. (2003). The cultural grounding of personal relationship: Friendship in North American and West African worlds. *Personal Relationships*, *10*(3), 333–347.

Adams, G., & Stocks, E. L. (2008). A cultural analysis of the experiment and an experimental analysis of culture. *Social and Personality Psychology Compass*, *2*(5), 1895–1912.

Adorno, T. W. (2010). *Guilt and Defense: On the Legacies of National Socialism in Postwar Germany*. Cambridge, MA: Harvard University Press.

Albertsen, E. J., O'Connor, L. E., & Berry, J. W. (2006). Religion and interpersonal guilt: Variations across ethnicity and spirituality. *Mental Health, Religion, and Culture*, *9*, 67–84.

Alford, C. F. (2014). *Trauma and Forgiveness*. New York: Cambridge University Press.

Allen, J., & Pryke, M. (1999). Money cultures after Georg Simmel: Mobility, movement, and identity. *Environment and Planning D: Society and Space*, *17*(1), 51–68.

Altemeyer, B., & Hunsberger, B. (1992). Authoritarianism, religious fundamentalism, quest, and prejudice. *International Journal for the Psychology of Religion*, *2*(2), 113–133.

Anderson, A., & Driedger, L. (1980). The Mennonite family: Culture and kin in rural Saskatchewan. In K. Ishwaren (Ed.), *Canadian Families: Ethnic Variations*. Toronto: McGraw-Hill Ryerson.

Anderson, S. L., Adams, G., & Plaut, V. C. (2008). The cultural grounding of personal relationship: The importance of attractiveness in everyday life. *Journal of Personality and Social Psychology, 95*(2), 352–368.

Angyal, A. (1941). *Foundations for a Science of Personality*. New York: Commonwealth Fund.

Arndt, J., Greenberg, J., Solomon, S., Pyszczynski, T., & Schimel, J. (1999). Creativity and terror management: Evidence that creative activity increases guilt and social projection following mortality salience. *Journal of Personality and Social Psychology, 77*(1), 19–32.

Arthur, L. B. (1998). Deviance, agency, and the social control of women's bodies in a Mennonite community. *NWSA Journal, 10*, 75–99.

Asad, T. (1993). *Genealogies of Religion: Discipline and Reasons of Power in Christianity and Islam*. Baltimore: The Johns Hopkins University Press.

Barash, D. P. (2000). Evolutionary existentialism, sociobiology, and the meaning of life. *BioScience, 50*(11), 1012–1017.

Barclay, H. B. (1967). The plain people of Oregon. *Review of Religious Research, 8*, 140–165.

(1969). The Protestant ethic versus the spirit of capitalism? *Review of Religious Research, 10*, 151–158.

Bargh, J. A. (1997). The automaticity of everyday life. In R. S. Wyer, Jr. (Ed.), *The Automaticity of Everyday Life: Advances in Social Cognition* (Vol. 10, pp. 1–61). Mahwah, NJ: Erlbaum.

Barrett, W. (1962). *Irrational Man: A Study in Existential Philosophy*. Garden City, NY: Doubleday.

Bauman, Z. (1992). *Mortality, Immortality, and Other Life Strategies*. Stanford, CA: Stanford University Press.

Baumeister, R. F. (Ed.). (1986). *Public Self and Private Self*. New York: Springer.

(1987). How the self became a problem: A psychological review of historical research. *Journal of Personality and Social Psychology, 52*(1), 163–176.

(Ed.). (1999). *Self in Social Psychology: Essential Readings*. Philadelphia, PA: Psychology Press.

Baumeister, R. F., Stillwell, A. M., & Heatherton, T. F. (1994). Guilt: An interpersonal approach. *Psychological Bulletin, 115*(2), 243–267.

Bear, G. G., Uribe-Zarain, X., Manning, M. A., & Shiomi, K. (2009). Shame, guilt, blaming and anger: Differences between children in Japan and the U.S. *Motivation and Emotion, 33*, 229–238.

Beardsworth, S. (2004). *Julia Kristeva: Psychoanalysis and Modernity*. Albany, NY: State University of New York.

Beck, U. (1992). *Risk Society: Towards a New Modernity*. Thousand Oaks, CA: SAGE Publications, Inc.

Becker, E. (1969). *Angel in Armor*. New York: The Free Press.

(1973). *The Denial of Death*. New York: The Free Press.

(1975). *Escape from Evil*. New York: The Free Press.

Becker, G. (1997). *Disrupted Lives: How People Create Meaning in a Chaotic World*. Berkeley: University of California Press.

Becker, H. S. (1963). *Outsiders: Studies in the Sociology of Deviance*. New York: Free Press of Glencoe.

Bedford, O. A. (2004). The individual experience of guilt and shame in Chinese culture. *Culture and Psychology*, *10*, 29–52.

Bell, C. (1992). *Ritual Theory, Ritual Practice.* New York: Oxford University Press.

Bellah, R. N. (1964). Religious evolution. *American Sociological Review*, *29*(3), 358–374.

Bellah, R. N., & Joas, H. (Eds.). (2012). *The Axial Age and Its Consequences.* Cambridge, MA: Belknap Press.

Bellah, R. N., Madsen, R., Sullivan, W. M., Swidler, A., & Tipton, S. M. (1985). *Habits of the Heart: Individualism and Commitment in American Life*. Berkeley: University of California Press.

Bensman, J., & Lilienfeld, R. (1991). *Craft and Consciousness: Occupational Technique and the Development of World Images*. New York: Walter de Gruyter & Co.

Bergen, J. J. (1981). Freedom of education in a religious context: The Alberta Holdeman private school case. *Mennonite Quarterly Review*, *55*, 75–85.

Berger, P. L. (1967). *The Sacred Canopy: Elements of a Sociological Theory of Religion*. Garden City, NY: Doubleday.

Berger, P. L., & Luckmann, T. (1966). *The Social Construction of Reality: A Treatise in the Sociology of Knowledge*. New York: Anchor.

Berke, P. R., Kartez, J., & Wenger, D. (1993). Recovery after disaster: Achieving sustainable development, mitigation and equity. *Disasters*, *17*(2), 93–109.

Bernstein, B. (1990). *Class, Codes and Control: The Structuring of Pedagogic Discourse v. 4*. London; New York: Routledge.

Bernstein, B., & Henderson, D. (1973). Social class differences in the relevance of language to socialization. In B. Bernstein (Ed.), *Class, Codes and Control. Vol. 2: Applied Studies towards a Sociology of Language* (pp. 24–47). Boston, MA: Routledge & Kegan Paul.

Bettelheim, B. (1976). *The Uses of Enchantment – The Meaning and Importance of Fairy Tales*. London: Thames and Hudson.

Bierbrauer, G. (1992). Reactions to violation of normative standards: A cross-cultural analysis of shame and guilt. *International Journal of Psychology*, *27*, 181–193.

Billig, M. (2006). Is my home my castle? Place attachment, risk perception, and religious faith. *Environment and Behavior*, *38*, 248–265.

Binswanger, L. (1958). The existential analysis school of thought. In R. May, E. Angel, & H. Ellenberger (Eds.), *Existence: A New Dimension in Psychology and Psychiatry* (pp. 191–213). New York: Basic Books.

Bjorklund, D. F. (1997). The role of immaturity in human development. *Psychological Bulletin*, *122*(2), 153–169.

Bloch, M., & Parry, J. (Eds.). (1982). *Death and the Regeneration of Life.* Cambridge; New York: Cambridge University Press.

Block, J. (2002). *Personality as an Affect-Processing System: Toward an Integrative Theory*. New York: Taylor & Francis.

Blumer, H. (1969). *Symbolic Interactionism: Perspective and Method.* Englewood Cliffs, NJ: Prentice Hall.

Boehm, C. (1999). *Hierarchy in the Forest: The Evolution of Egalitarian Behavior.* Cambridge, MA: Harvard University Press.

Boesch, E. E. (1991). *Symbolic Action Theory and Cultural Psychology*. Berlin: Springer-Verlag.

Boiger, M., Mesquita, B., Uchida, Y., & Feldman Barrett, L. (2013). Condoned or condemned: The situational affordance of anger and shame in the United States and Japan. *Personality and Social Psychology Bulletin, 39*, 540–553.

Bonanno, G. A., Goorin, L., & Coifman, K. G. (2008). Sadness and grief. In M. Lewis, J. Haviland-Jones, & L. Feldman Barrett (Eds.), *The Handbook of Emotion*. New York: Guilford.

Bornemark, J. (2006). Limit-situation. Antinomies and transcendence in Karl Jaspers' philosophy. *SATS: Northern European Journal of Philosophy, 7*(2), 63–85.

Botton, A. de. (2004). *Status Anxiety*. New York: Pantheon.

Bourdieu, P. (1977). *Outline of a Theory of Practice*. Cambridge: Cambridge University Press.

Bourguignon, E. (1978). Spirit possession and altered states of consciousness: The evolution of an inquiry. In G. D. Spindler (Ed.), *The Making of Psychological Anthropology* (pp. 478–515). Berkeley: University of California Press.

Bowerman, W. R. (1978). Subjective competence: The structure, process and function of self-referent causal attributions. *Journal for the Theory of Social Behaviour, 8*(1), 45–75.

Bowerman, W. R., & Penner, D. A. (1981). "*Dimensions of subjective competence and life-satisfaction by age*." Unpublished manuscript. Lawrence, KS: University of Kansas.

Boynton, L. L. (1986). *The Plain People: An Ethnography of the Holdeman Mennonites*. Salem, WI: Sheffield Press.

Braithwaite, J. (1989). *Crime, Shame and Reintegration*. New York: Cambridge University Press.

Brown, K. W., Ryan, R. M., & Creswell, J. D. (2007). Mindfulness: Theoretical foundations and evidence for its salutary effects. *Psychological Inquiry, 18*(4), 211–237.

Brown, N. O. (1959). *Life against Death*. New York: Vintage.

Buehrens, J. A., & Church, F. (1998). *A Chosen Faith: An Introduction to Unitarian Universalism*. Boston, MA: Beacon Press.

Burke, B. L., Martens, A., & Faucher, E. H. (2010). Two decades of terror management theory: A meta-analysis of mortality salience research. *Personality and Social Psychology Review, 14*(2), 155–195.

Cacioppo, J. T., & Patrick, W. (2008). *Loneliness: Human Nature and the Need for Social Connection*. New York: W. W. Norton & Company.

Calhoun, L. G., Cann, A., & Tedeschi, R. G. (2010). The posttraumatic growth model: Socio-cultural considerations. In T. Weiss, & R. Berger (Eds.), *Posttraumatic Growth and Culturally Competent Practice: Lessons Learned from Around the Globe* (pp. 1–14). Hoboken, NJ: Wiley.

Campbell, D. T. (1957). Factors relevant to the validity of experiments in social settings. *Psychological Bulletin, 54*, 297–312.

(1961). The mutual methodological relevance of anthropology and psychology. In F. L. K. Hsu (Ed.), *Psychological Anthropology: Approaches to Culture and Personality* (pp. 333–352). Homewood, IL: The Dorsey Press.

Campbell, D. T., & Fiske, D. W. (1959). Convergent and discriminant validation by the multitrait-multimethod matrix. *Psychological Bulletin, 56*(2), 81–105.

Camus, A. (1991). *The Myth of Sisyphus: And Other Essays*. New York: Vintage.

Cantril, H. (1988). *Psychology, Humanism, and Scientific Inquiry*. New Brunswick, NJ: Transaction.

Carlsmith, J. M., Ellsworth, P. C., & Aronson, E. (1976). *Methods of Research in Social Psychology*. Reading, MA: Addison Wesley.

Carlson, S. M., Taylor, M., & Levin, G. R. (1998). The influence of culture on pretend play: The case of Mennonite children. *Merrill-Palmer Quarterly, 44*(4), 538–565.

Carspecken, F. P. (1996). *Critical Ethnography in Educational Research: A Theoretical and Practical Guide*. New York: Routledge.

Carver, C. S., & Scheier, M. F. (1981). *Attention and Self-Regulation: A Control-Theory Approach to Human Behavior*. New York: Springer.

Casanova, J. (2012). Religion, the Axial Age, and secular modernity in Bellah's theory of religious evolution. In R. N. Bellah, & H. Joas (Eds.), *The Axial Age and Its Consequences* (pp. 191–221). Cambridge, MA: Harvard University Press.

Castillo, R. J. (1994). Spirit possession in South Asia: Dissociation or hysteria? Part 2: Case histories. *Culture, Medicine, and Psychiatry, 18*, 141–162.

Charmaz, K. (2006). *Constructing Grounded Theory: A Practical Guide through Qualitative Analysis*. London; Thousand Oaks, CA: SAGE Publications, Inc.

Cheng, C., Cheung, S., Chio, J. H., & Chan, M. S. (2013). Cultural meaning of perceived control: A meta-analysis of locus of control and psychological symptoms across 18 cultural regions. *Psychological Bulletin, 139*, 152–188.

Church of God in Christ, Mennonite. (1952). *Confession of Faith and Minister's Manual*. USA: Church of God in Christ, Mennonite.

(1998). *Bible Doctrine and Practice*. Moundridge, KS: Gospel Publishers.

(2012). *2012 Yearbook*. Moundridge, KS: Gospel Publishers.

Cialdini, R. B., Reno, R. R., & Kallgren, C. A. (1990). A focus theory of normative conduct: Recycling the concept of norms to reduce littering in public places. *Journal of Personality and Social Psychology, 58*(6), 1015–1026.

Clark, A., & Chalmers, D. J. (1998). The extended mind. *Analysis, 58*(1), 7–19.

Clarke, A. E. (2005). *Situational Analysis: Grounded Theory after the Postmodern Turn*. Thousand Oaks, CA: SAGE Publications, Inc.

Clastres, P. (1987). *Society against the State: Essays in Political Anthropology* (R. Hurley, & A. Stein, Trans.). New York; Cambridge, MA: Zone Books.

Cohen, D., Kim, E., & Hudson, N. W. (2014). Religion, the forbidden, and sublimation. *Current Directions in Psychological Science, 23*(3), 208–214.

Cohen, S. (1985). *Visions of Social Control: Crime, Punishment and Classification*. Cambridge: Polity Press.

Cohen, S., & Taylor, L. (1978). *Escape Attempts: The Theory and Practice of Resistance to Everyday Life*. New York: Penguin.

Cohen, T. R., Wolf, S. T., Panter, A. T., & Insko, C. A. (2011). Introducing the GASP scale: A new measure of guilt and shame proneness. *Journal of Personality and Social Psychology, 100*, 947–966.

Cohler, B. J., & Hostetler, A. J. (2003). Linking life course and life story: Social change and the narrative study of lives over time. In J. T. Mortimer, & M. J.

Shanahan (Eds.), *Handbook of the Life Course* (pp. 555–576). New York: Springer.

Cole, M. (1998). Can cultural psychology help us think about diversity? *Mind, Culture, and Activity*, *5*(4), 291–304.

Cooper, D. E. (1990). *Existentialism: A Reconstruction*. Oxford; Cambridge, MA: Blackwell Publishers.

Corbin, J., & Morse, J. M. (2003). The unstructured interactive interview: Issues of reciprocity and risks when dealing with sensitive topics. *Qualitative Inquiry*, *9*(3), 335–354.

Cox, C. R., Goldenberg, J. L., Pyszczynski, T., & Weise, D. (2007). Disgust, creatureliness and the accessibility of death-related thoughts. *European Journal of Social Psychology*, *37*(3), 494–507.

Crawford, M. H. (Ed.). (2000). *Different seasons: Biological aging among the Mennonites of the Midwestern United States*. Lawrence, KS: University of Kansas Press.

Crawford, M. H., Demarchi, D., Ellerd, M., & Puppala, S. (2000). Body morphology and aging among the Mennonites of Kansas and Nebraska. In M. H. Crawford (Ed.), *Different seasons: Biological aging among the Mennonites of the Midwestern United States* (pp. 55–68). Lawrence, KS: University of Kansas Press.

Cronk, S. (1981). *Gelassenheit*: The rites of the redemptive process in Old Order Amish and Old Order Mennonite Communities. *Mennonite Quarterly Review*, *55*, 5–40.

Cross, S. E., Hardin, E. E., & Gercek-Swing, B. (2011). The what, how, why, and where of self-construal. *Personality and Social Psychology Review*, *15*(2), 142–179.

Csikszentmihalyi, M. (1991). *Flow – The Psychology Optimal Experience – Steps toward Enhancing the Quality of Life*. New York: Harper Perennial.

Cumming, G. (2014). The new statistics: Why and how. *Psychological Science*, *25*, 7–29.

Cumming, R. D. (1980). *Starting Point: An Introduction to the Dialectic of Existence*. Chicago, IL: University of Chicago Press.

Dalferth, I. U. (2012). The idea of an Axial Age. A phenomenological reconsideration. *Neue Zeitschrift Für Systematicsche Theologie Und Religionsphilosophie*, *54*(2), 127–146.

Daniel, E. V. (1994). The individual in terror. In T. J. Csordas (Ed.), *Embodiment and Experience: The Existential Ground of Culture and Self* (pp. 229–247). Cambridge: Cambridge University Press.

Davis, C. G., Nolen-Hoeksema, S., & Larson, J. (1998). Making sense of loss and benefiting from the experience: Two construals of meaning. *Journal of Personality and Social Psychology*, *75*(2), 561–574.

Deacon, T. W. (1998). *The Symbolic Species: The Co-evolution of Language and the Brain*. New York: W. W. Norton & Company.

Deardorff, D. (2009). *The Other Within*. Berkeley: North Atlantic Books.

Dennett, D. C. (1984). *Elbow Room: The Varieties of Free Will Worth Wanting*. Cambridge, MA: A Bradford Book.

Denzin, N. K., & Lincoln, Y. S. (Eds.). (2008). *Strategies of Qualitative Inquiry*. Los Angeles, CA: SAGE Publications, Inc.

De Sousa, R. (2010). Existentialism as biology. *Emotion Review*, *2*, 76–83.

De St. Aubin, E. (1996). Personal ideology polarity: Its emotional foundation and its manifestation in individual value systems, religiosity, political orientation, and assumptions concerning human nature. *Journal of Personality and Social Psychology*, *71*(1), 152–165.
Dick, B. W. (1983). Psychology and Mennonite studies. *Journal of Mennonite Studies*, *1*, 149–160.
Diken, B. (2009). *Nihilism*. Abingdon; New York, NY: Routledge.
Dilthey, W. (1961). *Meaning in History*. London: Allen and Unwin.
Donald, M. (2012). An evolutionary approach to culture: Implications for the study of the Axial Age. In R. N. Bellah, & H. Joas (Eds.), *The Axial Age and Its Consequences* (pp. 47–66). Cambridge, MA: Belknap Press.
Douglas, J. D., & Johnson, J. M. (Eds.). (1977). *Existential Sociology*. Cambridge; New York: Cambridge University Press.
Douglas, M. (1966). *Purity and Danger*. London; New York: Routledge.
(1970). *Natural Symbols Explorations in Cosmology*. New York: Pantheon.
(1978). *Cultural Bias*. London: Humanities Press.
(1994). *Risk and blame: Essays in cultural theory*. New York: Routledge.
Douglas, M., & Wildavsky, A. (1982). *Risk and Culture*. Berkeley: University of California Press.
Draguns, J. G. (1980). Psychological disorders of clinical severity. In H. C. Triandis, & J. G. Draguns (Eds.), *Handbook of Cross-Cultural Psychology* (Vol. 6). Boston, MA: Allyn & Bacon.
Dreyfus, H. L. (1991). *Being-in-the-World: A Commentary on Heidegger's Being and Time, Division I*. Cambridge, MA: MIT Press.
Dreyfus, H. L., & Rabinow, P. (1983). *Michel Foucault: Beyond Structuralism and Hermeneutics*. Chicago, IL: University of Chicago Press.
Driedger, L. (1973). Impelled group migration: Minority struggle to maintain institutional completeness. *International Migration Review*, *7*, 257–269.
(1982). Individual freedom vs. community control: An adaptation of Erikson's ontogeny of ritualization. *Journal for the Scientific Study of Religion*, *21*(3), 226–241.
(2000). *Mennonites in the Global Village*. Toronto: University of Toronto Press.
Dubouloy, M. (2011). Is recognition a prerequisite for citizenship for managers? In L. J. Gould, A. Lucey, & L. Stapley (Eds.), *The Reflective Citizen: Organizational and Social Dynamics* (pp. 131–148). London: Karnac Books.
Duménil, G., & Lévy, D. (2011). *The Crisis of Neoliberalism*. Cambridge, MA: Harvard University Press.
Duncan, H. D. (1968). *Symbols in Society*. New York: Oxford University Press.
Durkheim, E. (1893/2014). *The Division of Labor in Society*. New York: Simon and Schuster.
(1897/2007). *On Suicide*. (A. Riley, Ed., R. Buss, Trans.). London; New York: Penguin Classics.
(1972). *Emile Durkheim: Selected Writings*. (A. Giddens, Ed.). Cambridge: Cambridge University Press.
(1978). ... *On Institutional Analysis* (M. Traugott, Trans.). Chicago, IL: University of Chicago Press.

Durkheim, É., & Mauss, M. (2009). *Primitive Classification*. New York: Routledge.
Duval, S., & Wicklund, R. A. (1972). *A Theory of Objective Self Awareness*. New York: Academic Press.
Dyck, C. J. (1985). The suffering church in Anabaptism. *Mennonite Quarterly Review, 59*, 5–23.
(1993). *An Introduction to Mennonite History*. Scottdale, PA: Herald Press.
Eaton, J. W., & Weil, R. J. (1955). *Culture and Mental Disorders: A Comparative Study of the Hutterites and Other Populations*. Glencoe, IL: Free Press.
Ediger, M. (1984). *Mennonites in American Society*. Retrieved from http://eric.ed.gov/?id=ED248178
Edwards, R. (1979). *Contested Terrain*. New York: Basic Books.
Ehrenberg, A. (2010). *The Weariness of the Self: Diagnosing the History of Depression in the Contemporary Age*. Montreal: Mcgill Queens University Press.
Eid, M., & Diener, E. (2001). Norms for experiencing emotions in different cultures: Inter- and intranational differences. *Journal of Personality and Social Psychology, 81*, 869–895.
Elder Jr., G. H. (1995). The life course paradigm: Social change and individual development. In P. Moen, G. H. Elder, Jr., & K. Lüscher (Eds.), *Examining Lives in Context: Perspectives on the Ecology of Human Development* (pp. 101–139). Washington, DC: American Psychological Association.
Elias, N. (1969). *Die Hofische Gesellschaft*. Neuwied: Hermann Luchterhand.
Elkholy, S. N. (2011). *Heidegger and a Metaphysics of Feeling: Angst and the Finitude of Being*. London: Continnuum-3PL.
Ellenberger, H. F. (1958). A clinical introduction to psychiatric phenomenology and existential analysis. In R. May, E. Angel, & H. F. Ellenberger (Eds.), *Existence: A New Dimension in Psychiatry and Psychology* (pp. 92–124). New York: Basic Books.
Elliott, M., & Hayward, D. (2007). Religion and well-being in a church without a creed. *Mental Health, Religion, and Culture, 10*, 109–126.
Engbrecht, D. D. (1985). *The Americanization of a Rural Immigrant Church: The General Conference Mennonites in Central Kansas, 1874–1939*. Doctoral Dissertation. Lincoln, NE: University of Nebraska.
English, T., Chen, S., & Swann, W. B. (2008). A cross-cultural analysis of self-verification motives. In R. M. Sorrentino, & S. Yamaguchi (Eds.), *Handbook of Motivation and Cognition across Cultures* (pp. 119–142). San Diego, CA: Academic Press.
Enns, D. (2010). For the love of paradox: Mennonite morality and philosophy. In *Religious Upbringing and the Costs of Freedom: Personal and Philosophical Essays* (pp. 176–191). University Park, PA: Pennsylvania State University Press.
Erikson, K. (1994). *A New Species of Trouble: Explorations in Disaster, Trauma, and Community*. New York: W W Norton & Co Inc.
Erikson, K. T. (1978). *Everything in Its Path: Destruction of Community in the Buffalo Creek Flood*. New York: Simon & Schuster.
Ernsberger, D. J., & Manaster, G. J. (1981). Moral development, intrinsic/extrinsic religious orientation, and denominational teachings. *Genetic Psychology Monographs, 104*, 23–41.

Esposito, R. (2011). *Immunitas: The Protection and Negation of Life*. Cambridge; Malden, MA: Polity.

(2013). *Terms of the Political: Community, Immunity, Biopolitics* (R. N. Welch, Trans.). New York: Fordham University Press.

Estrada-Hollenbeck, M., & Heatherton, T. F. (1997). Avoiding and repairing guilt through prosocial behavior. In J. Bybee (Ed.), *Guilt and Shame in Children* (pp. 215–231). San Diego, CA: Academic.

Evans-Pritchard, E. E. (1939). Nuer time-reckoning. *Africa: Journal of the International African Institute, 12*(2), 189–216.

Ewald, F. (1991). Insurance and risk. In G. Burchell, C. Gordon, & P. Miller (Eds.), *The Foucault Effect: Studies in Governmentality* (pp. 197–210). London: Harvester/Wheatsheaf.

Fayard, J. V., Roberts, B. W., Robins, R. W., & Watson, D. (2012). Uncovering the affective core of conscientiousness: The role of self-conscious emotions. *Journal of Personality, 80*(1), 1–32.

Featherstone, M., & Hepworth, M. (1991). The mask of ageing and the post-modern life course. In M. Featherstone, M. Hepworth, & B. S. Turner (Eds.), *The Body: Social Processes and Cultural Theory*. London: SAGE Publications, Inc.

FEMA (August 2007). *Long-Term Community Recovery Plan: Greensburg + Kiowa County, Kansas*. Retrieved from www.greensburgks.org/residents/recovery-planning/long-term-community-recovery-plan

Firestone, W. A. (1987). Meaning in method: The rhetoric of quantitative and qualitative research. *Educational Researcher, 16*(7), 16–21.

Fischer, R. (2009). Where is culture in cross-cultural research?: An outline of a multilevel research process for measuring culture as a shared meaning system. *International Journal of Cross-Cultural Management, 9*, 25–49.

Fiske, A. P. (1991). *Structures of Social Life: The Four Elementary Forms of Human Relations: Communal Sharing, Authority Ranking, Equality Matching, Market Pricing*. New York: Free Press.

(2004). Relational models theory 2.0. In N. Haslam (Ed.), *Relational Models Theory: A Contemporary View* (pp. 3–26). Mahwah, NJ: Lawrence Erlbaum Associates.

Florian, V., & Kravetz, S. (1983). Fear of personal death: Attribution, structure, and relation to religious belief. *Journal of Personality and Social Psychology, 44*(3), 600–607.

Florian, V., & Mikulincer, M. (1997). Fear of death and the judgment of social transgressions: A multidimensional test of terror management theory. *Journal of Personality and Social Psychology, 73*(2), 369–380.

Fontana, A. (1984). Introduction: Existential sociology and the self. In J. A. Kotarba, & A. Fontana (Eds.), *Existential Self in Society* (pp. 3–17). Chicago, IL: University of Chicago Press.

Förster, J., Liberman, N., & Friedman, R. S. (2007). Seven principles of goal activation: A systematic approach to distinguishing goal priming from priming of non-goal constructs. *Personality and Social Psychology Review, 11*(3), 211–233.

Foucault, M. (1977). *Discipline and Punish: The Birth of the Prison*. New York: Pantheon Books.

Francis, E. K. (1948). The Russian Mennonites: From religious to ethnic group. *American Journal of Sociology, 54*, 101–107.

Frank, A. W. (1993). The rhetoric of self-change: Illness experience as narrative. *Sociological Quarterly, 34*(1), 39–52.

French, L. (1994). The political economy of injury and compassion: Amputees on the Thai-Cambodia border. In T. J. Csordas (Ed.), *Embodiment and Experience: The Existential Ground of Culture and Self* (pp. 69–99). Cambridge: Cambridge University Press.

Friedman, M. (1967). *To Deny Our Nothingness: Contemporary Images of Man*. New York: Delacorte Press.

Fromm, E., & Maccoby, M. (1970). *Social Character in a Mexican Village*. Englewood Cliffs, NJ: Prentice Hall.

Frosh, S., & Saville Young, L. (2008). Psychoanalytic approaches to qualitative psychology. In W. S. Rogers, & C. Willig (Eds.), *The SAGE Handbook of Qualitative Methods in Psychology*. London: SAGE Publications, Inc.

Fuchs, T. (2011). The brain – A mediating organ. *Journal of Consciousness Studies, 18*, 196–221.

(2013). Temporality and psychopathology. *Phenomenology and the Cognitive Sciences, 12*, 75–104.

Funder, D. C., Levine, J. M., Mackie, D. M., Morf, C. C., Sansone, C., Vazire, S., et al. (2014). Improving the dependability of research in personality and social psychology: Recommendations for research and educational practice. *Personality and Social Psychology Review, 18*, 3–12.

Furedi, F. (2004). *Therapy Culture*. New York: Routledge.

Furukawa, E., Tangney, J., & Higashibara, F. (2012). Cross-cultural continuities and discontinuities in shame, guilt, and pride: A study of children residing in Japan, Korea, and the U.S.A. *Self and Identity, 11*, 90–113.

Gabriel, Y. (1983). *Freud and Society*. Boston, MA: Routledge & Kegan Paul.

Gardner, W. L., Gabriel, S., & Dean, K. K. (2004). The individual as "melting pot": The flexibility of bicultural self-construals. *Cahiers de Psychologie Cognitive, 22*, 181–201.

Gardner, W. L., Gabriel, S., & Lee, A. Y. (1999). "I" value freedom, but "we" value relationships: Self-construal priming mirrors cultural differences in judgment. *Psychological Science, 10*(4), 321–326.

Garfinkel, H. (1972). Studies of the routine grounds of everyday activities. In D. Sudnow (Ed.), *Studies in Social Interaction* (pp. 1–30). New York: The Free Press.

Gauchet, M. (1997). *The Disenchantment of the World: A Political History of Religion*. Princeton, NJ: Princeton University Press.

Gauchet, M., & Swain, G. (1999). *Madness and Democracy* (C. Porter, Trans.). Princeton, NJ: Princeton University Press.

Geertz, C. (1975). *The Interpretation of Cultures: Selected Essays*. London: Hutchinson.

Gehlen, A. (1980). *Man in the Age of Technology*. New York: Columbia University Press.

Gelfand, M. J., Lim, B.-C., & Raver, J. L. (2004). Culture and accountability in organizations: Variations in forms of social control across cultures. *Human Resource Management Review, 14*(1), 135–160.

Gelfand, M. J., Nishii, L. H., & Raver, J. L. (2006). On the nature and importance of cultural tightness-looseness. *Journal of Applied Psychology, 91*(6), 1225–1244.

Gelfand, M. J., Raver, J. L., Nishii, L., Leslie, L. M., Lun, J., Lim, B. C., . . . Yamaguchi, S. (2011). Differences between tight and loose cultures: A 33-nation study. *Science, 332*(6033), 1100–1104.

Geniusas, S. (2013). On Nietzsche's genealogy and Husserl's genetic phenomenology. In C. Daigle, & É. Boublil (Eds.), *Nietzsche and Phenomenology: Power, Life, Subjectivity* (p. 44). Bloomington: Indiana University Press.

Gergen, K. J. (1973). Social psychology as history. *Journal of Personality and Social Psychology, 26*(2), 309–320.

(2015). Culturally inclusive psychology from a constructionist standpoint. *Journal for the Theory of Social Behaviour, 45*(1), 95–107.

Gervais, W. M., & Norenzayan, A. (2012). Analytic thinking promotes religious disbelief. *Science, 336*(6080), 493–496.

Gibson, J. J. (1979). *The Ecological Approach to Visual Perception.* Boston, MA: Houghton Mifflin.

Giddens, A. (1971). *Capitalism and Modern Social Theory: An Analysis of the Writings of Marx, Durkheim and Max Weber.* London: Cambridge University Press.

(1983). *A Contemporary Critique of Historical Materialism.* Berkeley: University of California Press.

(1984). *The Constitution of Society: Outline of the Theory of Structuration.* Cambridge: Polity Press.

(1986). Action, subjectivity, and the constitution of meaning. *Social Research,* 53, 529–545.

(1990). *The Consequences of Modernity.* Cambridge: Cambridge University Press.

Gillin, J. (1948). *The Ways of Men: An Introduction to Anthropology.* New York: D. Appleton-Century.

(1954a). Methods of approach to the study of human behavior. In F. L. K. Hsu (Ed.), *Aspects of Culture and Personality.* New York: Abelard-Schuman.

(1954b). The forward view. In J. Gillin (Ed.), *For a Science of Social Man* (pp. 257–276). New York: Macmillan.

(1967). The balance of threat and security in Mesoamerica: San Carlos. In R. Hunt (Ed.), *Personalities and Cultures: Readings in Psychological Anthropology* (pp. 139–149). Garden City, NY: Natural History Press.

Gillin, J., & Nicholson, G. (1951). The security functions of cultural systems. *Social Forces, 30,* 179–184.

Glaser, B. G., & Strauss, A. L. (1967). *The Discovery of Grounded Theory: Strategies for Qualitative Research.* Aldine de Gruyter.

Goffman, E. (1959). *The Presentation of Self in Everyday Life.* New York: Anchor.

(1963). *Stigma: Notes on the Management of Spoiled Identity.* Englewood Cliffs, NJ: Prentice Hall.

(1967). *Interaction Ritual.* New York: Doubleday.

Gomm, R., Hammersley, M., & Foster, P. (Eds.). (2000). *Case Study Method: Key Issues, Key Texts.* Thousand Oaks, CA: SAGE Publications, Inc.

Goodman, J. K., Cryder, C. E., & Cheema, A. (2013). Data collection in a flat world: The strengths and weaknesses of Mechanical Turk samples. *Journal of Behavioral Decision Making, 26*(3), 213–224.

Greenberg, J., & Arndt, J. (2012). Terror management theory. In A. Kruglanski, E. Tory Higgins, & P. A. M. Van Lange (Eds.), *Handbook of Theories of Social Psychology: Vol. 1* (pp. 398–415). London: SAGE Publications, Inc.

Greenberg, J., Koole, S. L., & Pyszczynski, T. (2004). *Handbook of Experimental Existential Psychology*. New York: The Guilford Press.

Greenberg, J., Martens, A., Jonas, E., Eisenstadt, D., Pyszczynski, T., & Solomon, S. (2003). Psychological defense in anticipation of anxiety: Eliminating the potential for anxiety eliminates the effect of mortality salience on worldview defense. *Psychological Science, 14*(5), 516–519.

Greenberg, J., Pyszczynski, T., & Solomon, S. (1986). The causes and consequences of a need for self-esteem: A terror management theory. In R. F. Baumeister (Ed.), *Public Self and Private Self* (pp. 189–212). New York: Springer.

Greenberg, J., Pyszczynski, T., Solomon, S., Rosenblatt, A., Veeder, M., Kirkland, S., & Lyon, D. (1990). Evidence for terror management theory II: The effects of mortality salience on reactions to those who threaten or bolster the cultural worldview. *Journal of Personality and Social Psychology, 58*(2), 308–318.

Greenberg, J., Solomon, S., & Arndt, J. (2008). A basic but uniquely human motivation: Terror management. In J. Shah (Ed.), *Handbook of Motivation Science*. New York: Guilford Press.

Greenfield, P. M. (1997). You can't take it with you: Why ability assessments don't cross cultures. *American Psychologist, 52*(10), 1115–1124.

Greenwood, A., & Harris, M. W. (2011). *An Introduction to the Unitarian and Universalist Traditions*. Cambridge: Cambridge University Press.

Greenwood, J. D. (2004). What happened to the "social" in social psychology? *Journal for the Theory of Social Behaviour, 34*, 19–34.

Griffin, B. W. (2004). Grading leniency, grade discrepancy, and student ratings of instruction. *Contemporary Educational Psychology, 29*, 410–425.

Guignon, C., & Pereboom, D. (1995). *Existentialism: Basic Writings/Kierkegaard, Nietzsche, Heidegger, Sartre*. Indianapolis: Hackett Pub Co Inc.

Habermas, J. (1985). *The Theory of Communicative Action, Volume 1: Reason and the Rationalization of Society* (T. McCarthy, Trans.). Boston, MA: Beacon Press.

(1987). *Theory of Communicative Action: Lifeworld and System – A Critique of Functionalist Reason, Vol. 2*. Boston, MA: Beacon Press.

Habermas, T., & Bluck, S. (2000). Getting a life: The emergence of the life story in adolescence. *Psychological Bulletin, 126*, 748–769.

Hafer, C. L., & Gosse, L. (2011). Predicting alternative strategies for preserving a belief in a just world: The case of repressive coping style. *European Journal of Social Psychology, 41*, 730–739.

Haidt, J. (2013). *The Righteous Mind: Why Good People Are Divided by Politics and Religion*. New York: Vintage.

Hall, D. E., Koenig, H. G., & Meador, K. G. (2008). Hitting the target: Why existing measures of "religiousness" are really reverse-scored measures of "secularism." *Explore, 4*, 368–373.

Hall, M. E. L., & Johnson, E. L. (2001). Theodicy and therapy: Philosophical/theological contributions to the problem of suffering. *Journal of Psychology and Christianity, 20*, 5–17.

Hallowell, A. I. (1965). Hominid evolution, cultural adaptation, and mental dysfunctioning. In. A. V. S. de Reuck, & R. Porter (Eds.), *Transcultural Psychiatry* (pp. 26–53). Boston, MA: Little, Brown & Co.

(1967). *Culture and Experience*. New York: Schocken Books.

Halperin, R. H. (1994). *Cultural Economies Past and Present*. Austin: University of Texas Press.

Hammack, P. L. (2010). Identity as burden or benefit? Youth, historical narrative, and the legacy of political conflict. *Human Development, 53*(4), 173–201.

Hammersley, M. (1992). *What's Wrong with Ethnography?: Methodological Explorations*. New York: Psychology Press.

Haney, J. (Ed.). (2008). *Greensburg: The Twisted Tales*. Newton, KS: Mennonite Press Inc.

(Ed.). (2009). *Greensburg: The Twisted Tales* (Vol. 2). Newton, KS: Mennonite Press Inc.

Hankiss, E. (2001). *Fears and Symbols: An Introduction to the Study of Western Civilization*. Budapest: CEU Press.

Harding, S. (1993). Rethinking standpoint epistemology: What is "strong objectivity"? In L. Alcoff, & E. Potter (Eds.), *Feminist Epistemologies* (pp. 49–82). New York: Routledge.

Hareven, T. K. (1991). Synchronizing individual time, family time, and historical time. In J. Bender, & D. E. Wellberry (Eds.), *Chronotypes: The Construction of Time* (pp. 167–182). Stanford: Stanford University Press.

Hart, J. (2014). Toward an integrative theory of psychological defense. *Perspectives on Psychological Science, 9*(1), 19–39.

Hartman, J. (2001). Power under the cover of tradition: A case study of a "Plain Community." In B. W. Redekop, & C. W. Redekop (Eds.), *Power, Authority, and the Anabaptist Tradition* (pp. 115–137). Baltimore: Johns Hopkins University Press.

Harvey, D. (2005). *A Brief History of Neoliberalism*. Oxford; New York: Oxford University Press.

Haslam, N. (2004). Research on the relational models: An overview. In N. Haslam (Ed.), *Relational Models Theory: A Contemporary Overview* (pp. 27–60). Mahwah, NJ: Lawrence Erlbaum.

Hayes, J., Schimel, J., Arndt, J., & Faucher, E. H. (2010). A theoretical and empirical review of the death-thought accessibility concept in terror management research. *Psychological Bulletin, 136*(5), 699–739.

Hayim, G. J. (2007). *Existentialism and Sociology*. New Brunswick, NJ: Transaction.

Heft, H. (2005). *Ecological Psychology in Context: James Gibson, Roger Barker, and the Legacy of William James*. Hillsdale, NJ: Lawrence Erlbaum.

(2012). Foundations of an ecological approach to psychology. In S. D. Clayton (Ed.), *The Oxford Handbook of Environmental and Conservation Psychology* (pp. 11–40). Oxford: Oxford University Press.

Heidegger, M. (1962). *Being and Time* (J. Macquarrie & E. Robinson, Trans.). New York: Harper & Row.

Heine, S. J., & Hamamura, T. (2007). In search of East Asian self-enhancement. *Personality and Social Psychology Review, 11*(1), 4–27.

Henrich, J., Ensminger, J., McElreath, R., Barr, A., Barrett, C., Bolyanatz, A., et al. (2010a). Markets, religion, community size, and the evolution of fairness and punishment. *Science, 327*, 1480–1484.

Henrich, J., Heine, S. J., & Norenzayan, A. (2010b). The weirdest people in the world? *Behavioral and Brain Sciences, 33*, 61–135.

Herman, J. (1997). *Trauma and Recovery: The Aftermath of Violence – From Domestic Abuse to Political Terror* (14th printing). New York: Basic Books.

Hernandez, E. P. (2011). Twice uprooted: How government policies exacerbate injury to low-income Americans following natural disasters. *The Scholar: St. Mary's Law Review on Minority Issues, 14*, 220–250.

Hibbing, J. R., & Theiss-Morse, E. (2002). *Stealth Democracy: Americans' Beliefs about How Government Should Work.* Cambridge; New York: Cambridge University Press.

Hiebert, C. (1973). *The Holdeman People: Church of God in Christ, Mennonite, 1859–1969.* South Pasadena, CA: William Carey Library.

Higgins, E. T. (1987). Self-discrepancy: A theory relating self and affect. *Psychological Review, 94*(3), 319–340.

Hindmoor, A. (2010). The banking crisis: Grid, group and the state of the debate. *Australian Journal of Public Administration, 69*(4), 442–456.

Hirsh, J. B., Mar, R. A., & Peterson, J. B. (2012). Psychological entropy: A framework for understanding uncertainty-related anxiety. *Psychological Review, 119*(2), 304–320.

Hofstede, G. H., & Hofstede, G. J. (2005). *Cultures and Organizations: Software of the Mind* (2nd Ed.). New York: McGraw-Hill.

Hoge, D. R. (1972). A validated intrinsic religious motivation scale. *Journal for the Scientific Study of Religion, 11*, 369–376.

Hoge, E. A., Tamrakar, S. M., Christian, K. M., Mahara, N., Nepal, M. K., Pollack, M. H., et al. (2006). Cross-cultural differences in somatic presentation in patients with generalized anxiety disorder. *Journal of Nervous and Mental Disease, 194*, 962–966.

Hogg, M. A., Adelman, J. R., & Blagg, R. D. (2010). Religion in the face of uncertainty: An uncertainty-identity theory account of religiousness. *Personality and Social Psychology Review, 14*(1), 72–83.

Holbrook, C., Sousa, P., & Hahn-Holbrook, J. (2011). Unconscious vigilance: Worldview defense without adaptations for terror, coalition, or uncertainty management. *Journal of Personality and Social Psychology, 101*(3), 451–466.

Holdeman, J. (1880). *Ein Spiegel der Wahrheit.* Lancaster, PA: Johann Bär's Sons.
(1890). *A Treatise on Redemption, Baptism, and the Passover and the Lord's Supper.* Carthage, MO: Free Press Book and Job Printing House.

Homan, G. D. (2000). Innocents abroad?: Mennonite Central Committee's beginnings in Vietnam, 1954–1957. *Journal of Mennonite Studies, 18*, 10–28.

Homans, G. C. (1941). Anxiety and ritual: The theories of Malinowski and Radcliffe-Brown. *American Anthropologist, 43*(2), 164–172.

Horwitz, A. V. (1990). *The Logic of Social Control.* New York: Plenum Press.

Hostetler, J. A. (1974). *Hutterite Society*. Baltimore: Johns Hopkins University Press.

(1996). The Amish as a redemptive community. In L. Hege, & C. Wiebe (Eds.), *The Amish: Origin and Characteristics, 1693–1993* (pp. 346–355). Ingersheim: Association Française d'Histoire Anabaptiste-Mennonite.

Hsu, F. L. K. (1961). Psychological anthropology in the behavioral sciences. In F. L. K. Hsu (Ed.), *Psychological Anthropology*. Homewood, IL: Dorsey Press.

(1967). *Under the Ancestor's Shadow*. New York: Anchor Books.

Hull, D. L. (1988). *Science as a Process: An Evolutionary Account of the Social and Conceptual Development of Science*. Chicago, IL: University of Chicago Press.

Huppert, J. D., Siev, J., & Kushner, E. S. (2007). When religion and obsessive-compulsive disorder collide: Treating scrupulosity in ultra-orthodox Jews. *Journal of Clinical Psychology*, *63*(10), 925–941.

Husserl, E. (2000). *Logical Investigations, 2 Volume-Set*. Amherst, NY: Humanity Books.

Hwang, W.-C., Myers, H. F., Abe-Kim, J., & Ting, J. Y. (2008). A conceptual paradigm for understanding culture's impact on mental health: The cultural influences on mental health (CIMH) model. *Clinical Psychology Review*, *28*(2), 211–227.

Igreja, V., Dias-Lambranca, B., Hershey, D. A., Racin, L., Richters, A., & Reis, R. (2010). The epidemiology of spirit possession in the aftermath of mass political violence in Mozambique. *Social Science & Medicine*, *71*, 592–599.

Imada, T., & Kitayama, S. (2010). Social eyes and choice justification: Culture and dissonance revisited. *Social Cognition*, *28*(5), 589–608.

Inglehart, R. (1997). *Modernization and Postmodernization*. Princeton, NJ: Princeton University Press.

Inkeles, A., & Levinson, D. J. (1954). National character: The study of modal personality and sociocultural systems. In G. Lindzey (Ed.), *Handbook of Social Psychology:* (Vol. 2).

Innis, R. E. (2009). *Susanne Langer in Focus: The Symbolic Mind*. Bloomington: Indiana University Press.

Inozu, M., Karanci, A. N., & Clark, D. A. (2012). Why are religious individuals more obsessional? The role of mental control beliefs and guilt in Muslims and Christians. *Journal of Behavior Therapy and Experimental Psychiatry*, *43*, 959–966.

Jackson, M. (Ed.). (1996). *Things As They Are: New Directions in Phenomenological Anthropology*. Bloomington: Indiana University Press.

(2005). *Existential Anthropology: Events, Exigencies, and Effects*. New York: Berghahn Books.

(2013). *Lifeworlds: Essays in Existential Anthropology*. Chicago, IL: University of Chicago Press.

Jahoda, M., Lazarsfeld, P. F., & Zeisel, H. (1971). *Marienthal: The Sociography of an Unemployed Community*. New Brunswick, NJ: Transaction.

Jankélévitch, S. (2008). *Le suicide* and psychological suffering. In W. S. F. Pickering, & M. Rosati (Eds.), *Suffering and Evil: The Durkheimian Legacy* (pp. 31–48). New York: Berghahn Books.

Janoff-Bulman, R. (1989). Assumptive worlds and the stress of traumatic events: Applications of the schema construct. *Social Cognition*, *7*, 113–136.

(1992). *Shattered Assumptions: Towards a New Psychology of Trauma*. New York; Toronto; New York: Free Press; Maxwell Macmillan Canada; Maxwell Macmillan International.

Janoff-Bulman, R., & Carnes, N. C. (2013). Surveying the moral landscape: Moral motives and group-based moralities. *Personality and Social Psychology Review*, *17*, 219–236.

Janoff-Bulman, R., & Yopyk, D. (2004). Random outcomes and valued commitments: Existential dilemmas and the paradox of meaning. In J. Greenberg, S. L. Koole, & T. Pyszczynski (Eds.), *Handbook of Experimental Existential Psychology*. New York: Guilford.

Janzen, C. C. (1914). *Americanization of the Russian Mennonites in Central Kansas*. Doctoral Dissertation. University of Kansas.

Jaspers, K. (1970). *Philosophy* (Vol. 2). Chicago, IL; London: University of Chicago Press.

(1979). *Nietzsche: An Introduction to the Understanding of His Philosophical Activity* (C. F. Wallraff, & F. J. Schmitz, Trans.). South Bend, IN: Regnery/Gateway.

Jilek, W. G. (1971). Review of Vergleichende Untersuchungen über depressive Erkrankungen in Japan und in Deutschland by B. Kimura. *Transcultural Psychiatry*, 8, 23–28.

Jindra, I. W. (2008). Religious stage development among converts to different religious groups. *International Journal for the Psychology of Religion*, *18*(3), 195–215.

Johnson, D., & Bering, J. (2006). Hand of God, mind of man: Punishment and cognition in the evolution of cooperation. *Evolutionary Psychology*, *4*, 219–233.

Johnston, A., & Malabou, C. (2013). *Self and Emotional Life: Philosophy, Psychoanalysis, and Neuroscience*. New York: Columbia University Press.

Johnston-Robledo, I., & Chrisler, J. C. (2011). The menstrual mark: Menstruation as social stigma. *Sex Roles*, *68*(1–2), 9–18.

Jonas, E., Fritsche, I., & Greenberg, J. (2005). Currencies as cultural symbols – An existential psychological perspective on reactions of Germans toward the Euro. *Journal of Economic Psychology*, *26*(1), 129–146.

Jonas, E., McGregor, I., Klackl, J., Agroskin, D., Fritsche, I., Holbrook, C., et al. (2014). Threat and defense: From anxiety to approach. *Advances in Experimental Social Psychology*, *49*, 219–286.

Jonas, H. (1966). *The Phenomenon of Life: Toward a Philosophical Biology*. Evanston, IL: Northwestern University Press.

Jones, A. R. (2011). *Sustainable Growth and Redevelopment of Wadena: Evoking Meaningful Change*. BA Thesis. Fargo: North Dakota State University.

Joseph, S. (2011). *What Doesn't Kill Us: The New Psychology of Posttraumatic Growth*. New York: Basic Books.

Juhnke, J. C. (1975). *A People of Two Kingdoms: The Political Acculturation of the Kansas Mennonites*. Newton, KS: Faith & Life Press.

Jung, C. G. (1940). *The Integration of the Personality*. London: Routledge & Kegan Paul.

Kaufman, E. G. (1973). *General Conference Mennonite Pioneers*. Newton, KS: Bethel College.

Kaufmann, W. (1968). *Nietzsche: Philosopher, Psychologist, Antichrist*. New York: Vintage Books.

Kay, A. C., & Sullivan, D. (2013). Cultural unity and diversity in compensatory control processes. In M. J. Gelfand, C. Chiu, & Y. Hong (Eds.), *Advances in Culture and Psychology: Vol. 3* (pp. 181–226). New York: Oxford University Press.

Keller, H. (2012). Autonomy and relatedness revisited: Cultural manifestations of universal human needs. *Child Development Perspectives, 6*, 12–18.

Keller, H., & Kärtner, J. (2013). Development – The culture-specific solution of universal developmental tasks. In M. L. Gelfand, C.-Y., Chiu, & Y. Y. Hong (Eds.), *Advances in Culture and Psychology, Vol. 3* (pp. 63–116). Oxford; New York: Oxford University Press.

Kelly, G. (1955). *The Psychology of Personal Constructs*. New York: Norton.

Keltner, D., & Haidt, J. (2003). Approaching awe, a moral, spiritual, and aesthetic emotion. *Cognition and Emotion, 17*(2), 297–314.

Kesebir, P., & Kesebir, S. (2012). The cultural salience of moral character and virtue declined in twentieth century America. *Journal of Positive Psychology, 7*, 471–480.

Kierkegaard, S. (1981). *The Concept of Anxiety* (Original work published 1844). (R. Thomte, Trans.). Princeton, NJ: Princeton University Press.

(2004). From *The sickness unto death*. In G. Marino (Ed.), *Basic Writings of Existentialism* (pp. 41–110). New York: Modern Library (Original work published 1849).

Kihlstrom, J. F. (1990). The psychological unconscious. In L. Pervin (Ed.), *Handbook of Personality: Theory and Research* (pp. 445–464). New York: Guilford.

Kimura B. (1965). Vergleichende untersuchungen über depressive erkrankungen in Japan und in Deutschland. *Fortschritte der Neurologie & Psychiatrie*, 93: 202–215.

(1967). Phänomenologie des Schulderlebnisses in einer vergleichenden psychiatrischen Sicht. *Aktuelle Fragen der Psychiatrie und Neurologie, 6*, 54–65.

Kincaid, H., Dupré, J., & Wylie, A. (Eds.). (2007). *Value-Free Science?: Ideals and Illusion*. Oxford; New York: Oxford University Press.

Kitayama, S., Park, H., Sevincer, A. T., Karasawa, M., & Uskul, A. K. (2009). A cultural task analysis of implicit independence: Comparing North America, Western Europe, and East Asia. *Journal of Personality and Social Psychology, 97*(2), 236–255.

Klapp, O. (1986). *Overload and Boredom: Essays on the Quality of Life in the Information Society*. New York: Praeger.

Klass, M. (2004). *Mind over Mind: The Anthropology and Psychology of Spirit Possession*. Lanham, MD: Rowman & Littlefield.

Klassen, R. J. (May 19, 2010). The beguiling influence of psychology and psychiatry. *Messenger of Truth*, 108(10), 2–3.

Kleinman, A. (1988). *The Illness Narratives: Suffering, Healing, and the Human Condition*. New York: Basic Books.

Koltko-Rivera, M. E. (2004). The psychology of worldviews. *Review of General Psychology*, *8*(1), 3–58.

Konner, M. (2007). Evolutionary foundations of cultural psychology. In S. Kitayama, & D. Cohen (Eds.), *Handbook of Cultural Psychology* (pp. 77–105). New York: Guilford Press.

Kotarba, J. A. (1977). The chronic pain experience. In J. D. Douglas, & J. M. Johnson (Eds.), *Existential Sociology* (pp. 257–272). New York: Cambridge University Press.

(1979). Existential sociology. In S. McNall (Ed.), *Theoretical Perspectives in Sociology* (pp. 348–368). New York: St. Martin's Press.

Kotarba, J. A., & Johnson, J. M. (Eds.). (2002). *Postmodern Existential Sociology.* Walnut Creek, CA: AltaMira Press.

Kraus, M. W., Piff, P. K., & Keltner, D. (2011). Social class as culture: The convergence of resources and rank in the social realm. *Current Directions in Psychological Science*, *20*(4), 246–250.

Kristeva, J. (1982). *Powers of Horror: An Essay on Abjection* (L. S. Roudiez, Trans.) New York: Columbia University Press.

Kugler, K., & Jones, W. H. (1992). On conceptualizing and assessing guilt. *Journal of Personality and Social Psychology*, *62*(2), 318–327.

Kuhn, M. H. (1954). Factors in personality: Socio-cultural determinants as seen through the Amish. In F. L. K. Hsu (Ed.), *Aspects of Culture and Personality* (pp. 43–60). New York: Abelard-Schuman.

Kvale, S. (1995). The social construction of validity. *Qualitative Inquiry*, *1*(1), 19–40.

Laing, R. D. (1960). *The Divided Self.* New York: Pantheon Books.

Landau, M. J., Greenberg, J., & Sullivan, D. (2009). Managing terror when self-worth and worldviews collide: Evidence that mortality salience increases reluctance to self-enhance beyond authorities. *Journal of Experimental Social Psychology*, *45*(1), 68–79.

Landrine, H. (1995). Clinical implications of cultural differences: The referential versus the indexical self. In N. R. Goldberger, & J. B. Veroff (Eds.), *The Culture and Psychology Reader* (pp. 744–766). New York: New York University Press.

Langer, S. K. (1957). *Philosophy in a New Key: A Study in the Symbolism of Reason, Rite, and Art.* Cambride, MA: Harvard University Press.

(1982). *Mind: An Essay on Human Feeling, Vol. 3.* Baltimore: The Johns Hopkins University Press.

(1988). Mind: An Essay on Human Feeling *(Abridged Ed.)*. Baltimore: The Johns Hopkins University Press.

Langevoort, D. C. (2011). Chasing the greased pig down Wall Street: A gatekeeper's guide to the psychology, culture, and ethics of financial risk-taking. *Cornell Law Review*, *96*, 1209–1246.

Langford, I. H. (2002). An existential approach to risk perception. *Risk Analysis*, *22*(1), 101–120.

Lazarus, R. S. (1991). Cognition and motivation in emotion. *American Psychologist*, *46*(4), 352–367.

Lazarus, R. S., & Lazarus, B. N. (1994). *Passion and Reason: Making Sense of Our Emotions.* New York: Oxford University Press.

Lazzarato, M. (2011). *The Making of the Indebted Man: An Essay on the Neoliberal Condition* (J. D. Jordan, Trans.). Los Angeles, CA: Semiotext(e).

(2015). *Governing by Debt* (J. D. Jordan, Trans.). Los Angeles, CA: Semiotext(e).

Leichty, M. M. (1961). Family attitudes and self concept in Vietnamese and U.S. children. *American Journal of Orthopsychiatry, 33*, 38–50.

Leitgeb, L. E. (2009). *Building Theology, Reinscribing Subjectivity: Cultivating a Liberal Identity in Unitarian Universalism*. Doctoral Thesis. Buffalo: SUNY.

Lerner, M. (1980). *The Belief in a Just World: A Fundamental Delusion*. New York: Springer.

Lester, M. (1984). Self: Sociological portraits. In J. A. Kotarba, & A. Fontana (Eds.), *Existential Self in Society* (pp. 18–68). Chicago, IL: University of Chicago Press.

LeVine, R. A. (1973). *Culture, Behaviour and Personality*. London: Hutchinson.

(2001). Culture and personality studies, 1918–1960: Myth and history. *Journal of Personality, 69*(6), 803–818.

Lewis, M. (1997). The self in self-conscious emotions. *Annals of the New York Academy of Sciences, 818*(1), 119–142.

Lifton, R. J. (1968). *Death in Life: Survivors of Hiroshima*. New York: Random House.

(1987). *The Future of Immortality*. New York: Basic Books.

Ligotti, T. (2012). *The Conspiracy against the Human Race: A Contrivance of Horror*. New York: Hippocampus Press.

Loewen, R. (2006). *Diaspora in the Countryside: Two Mennonite Communities and Mid-twentieth Century Rural Disjuncture*. Toronto: University of Toronto Press.

Longhofer, J. (1986). *Land, Household, and Community: A Study of the Alexanderwohl Mennonites*. Ph.D. Dissertation. Lawrence, KS: Department of Anthropology, University of Kansas.

(1993). Toward a political economy of inheritance: Community and household among the Mennonites. *Theory and Society, 22*, 337–362.

Luckhurst, R. (2008). *The Trauma Question*. London; New York: Routledge.

Lupton, D. (2013). *Risk* (2nd Ed.). New York: Routledge.

Lyman, S. M., & Scott, M. B. (1970). *A Sociology of the Absurd*. Pacific Palisades, CA: Goodyear.

Ma, M., & Agarwal, R. (2007). Through a glass darkly: Information technology design, identity verification, and knowledge contribution in online communities. *Information Systems Research, 18*(1), 42–67.

Macho, T. H. (1987). *Todesmetaphern: Zur Logik der Grenzerfahrung*. Frankfurt am Main: Suhrkamp.

Madsen, R. (2012). The future of transcendence: A sociological agenda. In R. N. Bellah, & H. Joas (Eds.), *The Axial Age and Its Consequences* (pp. 430–446). Cambridge, MA: Belknap Press.

Marino, G. D. (1998). Anxiety in the Concept of Anxiety. In A. Hannay, & G. D. Marino (Eds.), *The Cambridge Companion to Kierkegaard* (pp. 308–328). New York: Cambridge University Press.

Marks, H. M. (2003). Rigorous uncertainty: Why RA Fisher is important. *International Journal of Epidemiology, 32*(6), 932–937.

Marks, L. D., Cherry, K. E., & Silva, J. (2009). Faith, crisis, coping, and meaning making after Katrina: A qualitative, cross-cohort examination. In K. Cherry

(Ed.), *Lifespan Perspectives on Natural Disasters: Coping with Katrina, Rita and Other Storms* (pp. 195–215). New York: Springer.

Markus, H. R., & Conner, A. (2013). *Clash!: 8 Cultural Conflicts That Make Us Who We Are*. New York: Hudson Street Press.

Markus, H. R., & Kitayama, S. (1991). Culture and the self: Implications for cognition, emotion, and motivation. *Psychological Review, 98*(2), 224–253.

(2010). Cultures and selves a cycle of mutual constitution. *Perspectives on Psychological Science, 5*(4), 420–430.

Marsella, A. J. (1980). Depressive experience and disorder across cultures. In H. Triandis, & J. Draguns (Eds.), *Handbook of Cross-Cultural Psychology: Volume 6 Mental Health* (pp. 237–289). Boston, MA: Allyn & Bacon.

Marshall, G. N. (1966). *Challenge of a Liberal Faith*. Boston, MA: Skinner House Books.

Martens, A., Burke, B. L., Schimel, J., & Faucher, E. H. (2011). Same but different: Meta-analytically examining the uniqueness of mortality salience effects. *European Journal of Social Psychology, 41*, 6–10.

Martin, T. (2002). *Oppression and the Human Condition: An Introduction to Sartrean Existentialism*. Lanham, MD: Rowman & Littlefield.

Mauss, M. (1990). *The Gift: The Form and Reason for Exchange in Archaic Societies* (W. D. Hall, Trans.). New York: W. W. Norton & Co., Inc.

May, R. (1983). *The Discovery of Being, Writings in Existential Psychology*. New York: Norton.

May, W. F. (1994). *The Patient's Ordeal*. Bloomington: Indiana University Press.

McAdams, D. P. (2006). *The Redemptive Self: Stories Americans Live by*. New York: Oxford University Press.

McAdams, D. P., Josselson, R., & Lieblich, A. (Eds.). (2006). *Identity and Story: Creating Self in Narrative*. Washington, DC: American Psychological Association.

McAvoy, P. (2012). "There are no housewives on *Star Trek*": A reexamination of exit rights for the children of insular fundamentalist parents. *Educational Theory, 62*, 535–552.

McGraw, K. M. (1987). Guilt following transgression: An attribution of responsibility approach. *Journal of Personality and Social Psychology, 53*(2), 247–256.

McGregor, I. (2006). Offensive defensiveness: Toward an integrative neuroscience of compensatory zeal after mortality salience, personal uncertainty, and other poignant self-threats. *Psychological Inquiry, 17*(4), 299–308.

McKanan, D. (2013). Unitarianism, universalism, and unitarian universalism. *Religion Compass, 7*, 15–24.

McKinnon, S. (2005). *Neo-Liberal Genetics: The Myths and Moral Tales of Evolutionary Psychology*. Chicago, IL: Prickly Paradigm Press.

McNally, D. (2011). *Global Slump: The Economics and Politics of Crisis and Resistance*. Oakland, CA: PM Press.

Mead, G. H. (1934). *Mind, Self, and Society*. Chicago, IL: University of Chicago Press.

Meier, R. F. (1982). Perspectives on the concept of social control. *Annual Review of Sociology, 8*(1), 35–55.

Melton, P. E., Mosher, M. J., Rubicz, R., Zlojutro, M., & Crawford, M. H. (2010). Mitochondrial DNA diversity in Mennonite communities from the Midwestern United States. *Human Biology*, *82*, 267–289.

Mendelsohn, J. (2006). *Being Liberal in an Illiberal Age: Why I am a Unitarian Universalist* (2nd Ed.). Boston: Skinner House Books.

Messinger, S. D. (2010). Getting past the accident: Explosive devices, limb loss, and refashioning a life in a military medical center. *Medical Anthropology Quarterly*, *24*, 281–303.

Meyer, J. W. (2003). Reflections on a half-century of Mennonite change. *Mennonite Quarterly Review*, *77*(2), 257.

Mikulincer, M., & Florian, V. (1997). Do we really know what we need? A commentary on Pyszczynski, Greenberg, & Solomon. *Psychological Inquiry*, *8*, 33–36.

Miles, M. B., & Huberman, A. M. (1994). *Qualitative Data Analysis: An Expanded Sourcebook* (2nd Ed.). Thousand Oaks, CA: SAGE Publications, Inc.

Miller, G. A. (2010). Mistreating psychology in the decades of the brain. *Perspectives on Psychological Science: A Journal of the Association for Psychological Science*, *5*(6), 716–743.

Miller, J. G. (1997). Culture and the self: Uncovering the cultural grounding of psychological theory. In J. G. Snodgrass, & R. L. Thompson (Eds.), *Annals of the New York Academy of Sciences: Vol. 818. The Self across Psychology: Self-Recognition, Self-Awareness, and the Self Concept* (pp. 217–231). New York: New York Academy of Sciences.

Miller, R. L'H. (1976). The religious value system of Unitarian Universalists. *Review of Religious Research*, *17*(3), 189–208.

Mingers, J. (2001). Combining IS research methods: Towards a pluralist methodology. *Information Systems Research*, *12*(3), 240–259.

Minkowski, E. (1970). *Lived Time: Phenomenological and Psychopathological Studies*. (N. Metzel, Trans.). Evanston, IL: Northwestern University Press.

Mischel, W., & Shoda, Y. (1995). A cognitive-affective system theory of personality: Reconceptualizing situations, dispositions, dynamics, and invariance in personality structure. *Psychological Review*, *102*(2), 246–268.

Mitscherlich, A. (1970). *Society without the Father*. New York: Schocken.

Miyamoto, Y., Nisbett, R. E., & Masuda, T. (2006). Culture and the physical environment. Holistic versus analytic perceptual affordances. *Psychological Science*, *17*(2), 113–119.

Moffatt, M. (1989). *Coming of Age in New Jersey*. New Brunswick, NJ: Rutgers University Press.

Monfredo, W. (2008). Blown away in Greensburg, USA: Prediction and analysis of an EF-5 tornado. *Weather*, *63*, 116–120.

Morelli, G. A., & Rothbaum, F. (2007). Situating the child in context: Attachment relationships and self-regulation in different cultures. In S. Kitayama, & D. Cohen (Eds.), *Handbook of Cultural Psychology* (pp. 500–527). New York: Guilford Press.

Morling, B., & Lamoreaux, M. (2008). Measuring culture outside the head: A meta-analysis of individualism-collectivism in cultural products. *Personality and Social Psychology Review*, 12, 199–221.

Morozov, E. (2013a). *To Save Everything, Click Here: The Folly of Technological Solutionism*. New York: PublicAffairs.
(2013b). The real privacy problem. *MIT Technology Review, 116*(6), 32–43.
Morton, T. (2013). *Hyperobjects: Philosophy and Ecology after the End of the World*. Minneapolis: University of Minnesota Press.
Mowrer, O. H. (1950). Pain, punishment, guilt, and anxiety. In *Anxiety: The Proceedings of the Thirty-Ninth Annual Meeting of the American Psychopathological Association* (pp. 27–48). New York: Grune & Stratton.
Nagel, T. (1993). Death. In J. M. Fischer (Ed.), *The Metaphysics of Death* (pp. 59–70). Stanford: Stanford University Press.
Namihira, E. (1987). Pollution in the folk belief system. *Current Anthropology, 28*(4), S65–S74.
Nasby, W., & Read, N. W. (1997). The life voyage of a solo circumnavigator: Integrating theoretical and methodological perspectives. *Journal of Personality, 65*(4), 785–1068.
Nash, K., McGregor, I., & Prentice, M. (2011). Threat and defense as goal regulation: From implicit goal conflict to anxious uncertainty, reactive approach motivation, and ideological extremism. *Journal of Personality and Social Psychology, 101*(6), 1291–1301.
Nathan, R. (2006). *My Freshman Year: What a Professor Learned by Becoming a Student*. New York: Penguin Books.
Neimeyer, R. A., & Hogan, N. S., (2001). Quantitative or qualitative? Measurement issues in the study of grief. In M. S. Stroebe, R. O. Hansson, W. Stroebe, & H. Schut (Eds.), *Handbook of Bereavement Research: Consequences, Coping, and Care* (pp. 89–118). Washington, DC: American Psychological Association.
Nelson, K. (2007). *Young Minds in Social Worlds*. Cambridge, MA: Harvard University Press.
Nickelson, A. (May 13, 2008). Resounding spirit fills quiet little town. *Greeley Colorado Tribune*. Retrieved from www.greeleytribune.com/article/20080514/NEWS/563034513
Nicolaisen, I. (1995). Persons and nonpersons: Disability and personhood among the Punan Bah of central Borneo. In B. Ingstad, & S. R. Whyte (Eds.), *Disability and Culture*. Berkeley: University of California Press.
Nietzsche, F. (1964). *The Joyful Wisdom* (T. Common, Trans.). New York: Russell & Russell (Original work published 1887).
(1967). *On the Genealogy of Morals/Ecce Homo*. New York: Vintage.
(1997). *Twilight of the Idols* (R. Polt, Trans.). Indianapolis: Hackett Publishing Co. (Original work published 1889).
(1997). *Untimely Meditations* (D. Breazeale, Ed., R. J. Hollingdale, Trans.). New York: Cambridge University Press (Original work published 1874).
Nilsson, A. (2014). Humanistic and normativistic worldviews: Distinct and hierarchically structured. *Personality and Individual Differences, 64*, 135–140.
Nisbett, R. E., Peng, K., Choi, I., & Norenzayan, A. (2001). Culture and systems of thought: Holistic versus analytic cognition. *Psychological Review, 108*(2), 291–310.
Nisbett, R. E., & Wilson, T. D. (1977). Telling more than we can know: Verbal reports on mental processes. *Psychological Review, 84*(3), 231–259.

Norenzayan, A. (2013). *Big Gods: How Religion Transformed Cooperation and Conflict*. Princeton, NJ: Princeton University Press.

Norenzayan, A., & Lee, A. (2010). It was meant to happen: Explaining cultural variations in fate attributions. *Journal of Personality and Social Psychology*, *98*(5), 702–720.

Norris, P., & Inglehart, R. (2012). *Sacred and Secular: Religion and Politics Worldwide*. Cambridge: Cambridge University Press.

O'Dea, T. F. (1966). *The Sociology of Religion*. Englewood Cliffs, NJ: Prentice Hall.

Ohnuki-Tierney, E. (1984). *Illness and Culture in Contemporary Japan: An Anthropological View*. Cambridge; New York: Cambridge University Press.

Oishi, S. (2014). Socioecological psychology. *Annual Reviews of Psychology*, *65*, 581–609.

Oishi, S., & Kisling, J. (2009). The mutual constitution of residential mobility and individualism. In R. S. Wyer, C. Chiu, & Y. Hong (Eds.), *Understanding culture: Theory, research, and application* (pp. 223–238). New York: Psychology Press.

Ong, W. J. (1982). *Orality and Literacy*. London; New York: Routledge.

Ostrander, D. (1982). One and two dimensional models of the distribution of beliefs. In M. Douglas (Ed.), *Essays in the Sociology of Perception* (pp. 14–30). London: Routledge & Kegan Paul.

Otto, R. (1958). *The Idea of the Holy* (J. W. Harvey, Trans.). New York: Oxford University Press.

Oyserman, D., Coon, H. M., & Kemmelmeier, M. (2002). Rethinking individualism and collectivism: Evaluation of theoretical assumptions and meta-analyses. *Psychological Bulletin*, *128*(1), 3–72.

Oyserman, D., & Lee, S. W. S. (2008). Does culture influence what and how we think? Effects of priming individualism and collectivism. *Psychological Bulletin*, *134*(2), 311–342.

Palitsky, R., Sullivan, D., Keefer, L. A., & Stewart, S. A. (in press). The cultural backdrop to modern prospection: Exploring the relevance of time-space distanciation. *Review of General Psychology*.

Parker, T. (2005). Education and ethnicity: The relationship between Russian Mennonites and school district formation in Buhler and Goessel, Kansas. *Journal of American Ethnic History*, *24*, 34–69.

Parsons, T. (1971). *System of Modern Societies*. Englewood Cliffs, NJ: Prentice Hall.

Paul, B. K., & Che, D. (2011). Opportunities and challenges in rebuilding tornado-impacted Greensburg, Kansas as "stronger, better, and greener." *GeoJournal*, *76*, 93–108.

Pelto, P. J. (1968). The differences between "tight" and "loose" societies. *Trans-Action*, *5*(5), 37–40.

Pepper, S. C. (1942). *World Hypotheses: A Study in Evidence*. Los Angeles, CA: University of California Press.

Peregrine, P. (1996). The birth of the gods revisited: A partial replication of Guy Swanson's (1960) cross-cultural study of religion. *Cross-Cultural Research*, *30*(1), 84–112.

Perloff, L. S. (1987). Social comparison and illusions of invulnerability to negative life events. In C. R. Snyder, & C. E. Ford (Eds.), *Coping with Negative*

Life Events: Clinical and Social Psychological Perspectives (pp. 217–242). New York: Plenum.

Phillips, A. (2000). *Darwin's Worms: On Life Stories and Death Stories*. New York: Basic Books.

Pinel, E. C., & Long, A. E. (2012). When I's meet: Sharing subjective experience with someone from the outgroup. *Personality & Social Psychology Bulletin, 38*(3), 296–307.

Pitts, J. R. (1961). Introduction to part three. In T. Parsons, E. Shils, K. D. Naegele, & J. Pitts (Eds.), *Theories of Society: Foundations of Modern Sociological Theory* (pp. 685–716). New York: Free Press.

Poortinga, Y. H. (1989). Equivalence of cross-cultural data: An overview of basic issues. *International Journal of Psychology, 24*, 737–756.

Potter, A. (2010). *The Authenticity Hoax: How We Get Lost Finding Ourselves*. New York: Harper.

Preacher, K. J., & Hayes, A. F. (2008). Asymptotic and bootstrapping strategies for assessing and comparing indirect effects in multiple mediator models. *Behavior Research Methods, 40*, 879–891.

Proulx, T. (2012). Threat-compensation in social psychology: Is there a core motivation? *Social Cognition, 30*, 643–651.

Proulx, T., & Heine, S. J. (2008). The case of the transmogrifying experimenter: Affirmation of a moral schema following implicit change detection. *Psychological Science, 19*(12), 1294–1300.

(2010). The frog in Kierkegaard's beer: Finding meaning in the threat-compensation literature. *Social and Personality Psychology Compass, 4*(10), 889–905.

Proulx, T., & Inzlicht, M. (2012). The five "A"s of meaning maintenance: Finding meaning in the theories of sense-making. *Psychological Inquiry, 23*(4), 317–335.

Pyszczynski, T., & Greenberg, J. (1992). *Hanging On and Letting Go: Understanding the Onset, Progression and Remission of Depression*. New York: Springer-Verlag Berlin and Heidelberg GmbH & Co. K.

Pyszczynski, T., Greenberg, J., & Goldenberg, J. (2003). Freedom vs. fear: On the defense, growth, and expansion of the self. In M. Leary, & J. Tangney (Eds.), *Handbook of Self and Identity*. New York: Guilford Press.

Pyszczynski, T., Greenberg, J., Solomon, S., & Hamilton, J. (1990). A terror management analysis of self-awareness and anxiety: The hierarchy of terror. *Anxiety Research, 2*(3), 177–195.

Pyszczynski, T., Sullivan, D., & Greenberg, J. (2015). Experimental existential psychology: Living in the shadow of the facts of life. In E. Borgida, & J. Bargh (Eds.), *American Psychological Association Handbook of Personality and Social Psychology* (pp. 279–308). Washington, DC: American Psychological Association.

Quadagno, J. B., & Janzen, J. M. (1987). Old age security and the family life course: A case study of 19th century Mennonite immigrants to Kansas. *Journal of Aging Studies*, 1(1), 36–54.

Radin, P. (1927). *Primitive Man as Philosopher*. New York: D. Appleton & Company.

Rai, T. S., & Fiske, A. P. (2011). Moral psychology is relationship regulation: Moral motives for unity, hierarchy, equality, and proportionality. *Psychological Review*, *118*(1), 57–75.

Rank, O. (1947). *Will Therapy and Truth and Reality*. New York: A.A. Knopf.

(1958). *Beyond Psychology*. New York: Dover Publications.

(1996). *A Psychology of Difference: The American Lectures*. Princeton, NJ: Princeton University Press.

(1998). *Psychology and the Soul: A Study of the Origin, Conceptual Evolution, and Nature of the Soul*. Baltimore: The Johns Hopkins University Press.

Rasor, P. (2008). Theological and political liberalisms. *Journal of Law and Religion*, *24*, 433–462.

Ratcliffe, M. (2008). *Feelings of Being: Phenomenology, Psychiatry and the Sense of Reality*. Oxford; New York: Oxford University Press.

(2012). The phenomenology of existential feeling. In J. Fingerhut, & S. Marienberg (Eds.), *Feelings of Being Alive* (pp. 23–54). Berlin: Walter de Gruyter.

(2015). *Experiences of Depression: A Study in Phenomenology*. New York: Oxford University Press.

Ratcliffe, M., & Broome, M. (2012). Existential phenomenology, psychiatric illness and the death of possibilities. In S. Crowell (Ed.), *Cambridge Companion to Existentialism* (pp. 361–382). Cambridge: Cambridge University Press.

Ratner, C. (2013). Macro-cultural psychology: Its development, concerns, politics, and future direction. In M. J. Gelfand, C. Chiu, & Y. Hong (Eds.), *Advances in Culture and Psychology: Vol. 3* (pp. 283–326).

Redekop, C. W. (1989). *Mennonite society*. Baltimore: The Johns Hopkins University Press.

(2001). Power in the Anabaptist community. In B. W. Redekop, & C. W. Redekop (Eds.), *Power, Authority, and the Anabaptist Tradition* (pp. 174–192). Baltimore: The Johns Hopkins University Press.

Reginster, B. (2009). *The Affirmation of Life: Nietzsche on Overcoming Nihilism*. Cambridge, MA: Harvard University Press.

Reis, H. T. (2012). Why researchers should think "real-world": A conceptual rationale. In M. R. Mehl, & T. S. Conner (Eds.), *Handbook of Research Methods for Studying Daily Life* (pp. 3–21). New York: Guilford Press.

Reitzes, D. C. (1980). College student identities and behaviors. *Sociological Focus*, *13*, 113–124.

Richards, P. S. (1991). Religious devoutness in college students: Relations with emotional adjustment and psychological separation from parents. *Journal of Counseling Psychology*, *38*(2), 189–196.

Ricœur, P. (1967). *The Symbolism of Evil*. Boston, MA: Beacon Press.

(1970). *Freud and Philosophy: An Essay on Interpretation* (D. Savage, Trans.). New Haven, CT: Yale University Press.

Robinson, S., & Mendelson, A. L. (2012). A qualitative experiment: Research on mediated meaning construction using a hybrid approach. *Journal of Mixed Methods Research*, doi: 10.1177/1558689812444789.

Roes, F. L., & Raymond, M. (2003). Belief in moralizing gods. *Evolution and Human Behavior, 24*(2), 126–135.

Rorty, R. (1999). *Philosophy and Social Hope*. Penguin Books.

Rosati, M. (2009). *Ritual and the Sacred*. Burlington, VT: Ashgate.

Rosenberg, A. (2000). *Darwinism in Philosophy, Social Science, and Policy*. New York: Cambridge University Press.

Rosenblatt, A., Greenberg, J., Solomon, S., Pyszczynski, T., & Lyon, D. (1989). Evidence for terror management theory: I. The effects of mortality salience on reactions to those who violate or uphold cultural values. *Journal of Personality and Social Psychology, 57*(4), 681–690.

Ross, L. & Nisbett, R. (2011). *The Person and the Situation: Perspectives of Social Psychology*. London: Pinter & Martin Ltd.

Rothschild, Z. K., Landau, M. J., Keefer, L. A., & Sullivan, D. (2015). Another's punishment cleanses the self: Evidence for a moral cleansing function of punishing transgressors. *Motivation and Emotion, 39*, 722–741.

Rothschild, Z. K., Landau, M. J., Sullivan, D., & Keefer, L. A. (2012). A dual-motive model of scapegoating: Displacing blame to reduce guilt or increase control. *Journal of Personality and Social Psychology, 102*(6), 1148–1163.

Rozin, P. (2010). The weirdest people in the world are a harbinger of the future of the world. *Behavioral and Brain Sciences*, 33, 108–109.

Rubin, J. (2000). *The Other Side of Joy: Religious Melancholy among the Bruderhof*. New York: Oxford University Press.

Ryan, R. M., & Deci, E. L. (2000). Self-determination theory and the facilitation of intrinsic motivation, social development, and well-being. *American Psychologist, 55*, 68–78.

Sahlins, M. (2008). *The Western Illusion of Human Nature*. Chicago, IL: Prickly Paradigm Press.

Saldaña, J. (2009). *The Coding Manual for Qualitative Researchers*. Los Angeles, CA: SAGE Publications, Inc.

Sales, S. M. (1972). Economic threat as a determinant of conversion rates in authoritarian and nonauthoritarian churches. *Journal of Personality and Social Psychology, 23*(3), 420–428.

Sampson, E. E. (1988). The debate on individualism: Indigenous psychologies of the individual and their role in personal and societal functioning. *American Psychologist, 43*(1), 15–22.

Sampson, R. J., Raudenbush, S. W., & Earls, F. (1997). Neighborhoods and violent crime: A multilevel study of collective efficacy. *Science, 277*(5328), 918–924.

Sandstrom, K. L. (1990). Confronting deadly disease: The drama of identity construction among gay men with AIDS. *Journal of Contemporary Ethnography, 19*(3), 271–294.

Sandywell, B. (1996). *Reflexivity and the crisis of Western reason: Logological investigations Vol. 1*. New York: Routledge.

Sartre, J. P. (1948). *Existentialism and Humanism*. New York: Methuen.

(1965). *Essays in Existentialism*. New York: Citadel.

(2001). *Being and Nothingness: An Essay in Phenomenological Ontology* (H. Barnes, Trans.). New York: Citadel.
Savani, K., Markus, H. R., Naidu, N. V. R., Kumar, S., & Berlia, N. (2010). What counts as a choice? U.S. Americans are more likely than Indians to construe actions as choices. *Psychological Science, 21*(3), 391–398.
Savani, K., Morris, M. W., & Naidu, N. V. R. (2012). Deference in Indians' decision making: Introjected goals or injunctive norms? *Journal of Personality and Social Psychology, 102*, 685–699.
Scheff, T. (2015). Toward defining basic emotions. *Qualitative Inquiry, 21*, 111–121.
Schieffelin, E. (1983). Anger and shame in the tropical forest: On affect as a cultural system in Papua New Guinea. *Ethos, 11*(3), 181–191.
Schluchter, W. (1981). *The Rise of Western Rationalism*. Berkeley: University of California Press.
Schludermann, S., & Schludermann, E. (1971). Adolescents' perception of themselves and adults in Hutterite communal society. *Journal of Psychology, 78*(1st Half), 39–48.
Schmidt, E. (November 21, 2007). Wind, storms, hail, and rain. *Messenger of Truth, 105*(24), 12–13.
Schnall, S., Haidt, J., Clore, G. L., & Jordan, A. H. (2008). Disgust as embodied moral judgment. *Personality and Social Psychology Bulletin, 34*(8), 1096–1109.
Schneider, K. J. (1999). *The Paradoxical Self: Toward an Understanding of Our Contradictory Nature*. Amherst, NY: Humanity Books.
(2013). *The Polarized Mind: Why It's Killing Us and What We Can Do about It.* Colorado Springs, CO: University Professors Press.
Schooler, C. (1996). Cultural and social-structural explanations of cross-national psychological differences. *Annual Review of Sociology, 22*(1), 323–349.
Schrag, C. (1961). *Existence and Freedom: Towards an Ontology of Human Finitude*. Evanston, IL.: Northwestern University Press.
Schrag, C. O. (1969). *Experience and Being: Prolegomena to a Future Ontology*. Evanston, IL: Northwestern University Press.
(1997). *The Self after Postmodernity*. New Haven, CT: Yale University Press.
Schroeder, R. (1987). Nietzsche and Weber: Two prophets of the modern age. In S. Lash, & S. Whimster (Eds.), *Max Weber, Rationality, and Modernity* (pp. 207–221). London: Allen & Unwin.
Schutz, A. (1970). *On Phenomenology and Social Relations*. Chicago, IL: University of Chicago Press.
Schwartz, B. (2005). *The Paradox of Choice: Why More Is Less*. New York: Harper Perennial.
Schwartz, R. M. (2004). *Transcendence: Philosophy, Literature, and Theology Approach the Beyond*. New York: Routledge.
Scott, A. (2000). Risk society or angst society? Two views of risk, consciousness, and community. In B. Adam, U. Beck, & J. van Loon (Eds.), *The Risk Society and Beyond: Critical Issues for Social Theory* (pp. 33–46). Thousand Oaks, CA: SAGE Publications, Inc.
Sharpless, B. A. (2013). Kierkegaard's conception of psychology. *Journal of Theoretical and Philosophical Psychology, 33*(2), 90–106.

Shavitt, S., Torelli, C. J., & Riemer, H. (2011). Horizontal and vertical individualism and collectivism: Implications for understanding psychological processes. *Advances in Culture and Psychology, 1*, 309–350.

Sherif, M. (1977). Crisis in social psychology: Some remarks towards breaking through the crisis. *Personality and Social Psychology Bulletin, 3*(3), 368–382.

Sherif, M., & Harvey, O. J. (1952). A study in ego functioning: Elimination of stable anchorages in individual and group situations. *Sociometry, 15*(3/4), 272–305.

Shreve-Neiger, A. K., & Edelstein, B. A. (2004). Religion and anxiety: A critical review of the literature. *Clinical Psychology Review, 24*, 379–397.

Shulman, G. (2006). Redemption, secularization, and politics. In D. Scott, & C. Hirschkind (Eds.), *Powers of the Secular Modern: Talal Asad and His Interlocutors* (pp. 154–179). Stanford: Stanford University Press.

Shweder, R. A. (1984). Anthropology's romantic rebellion against the enlightenment, or there's more to thinking than reason and evidence. In R. A. Shweder, & R. A. Levine (Eds.), *Culture Theory* (pp. 27–66). New York: Cambridge University Press.

(1995). Cultural psychology: What is it? In N. R. Goldberger, & J. B. Veroff (Eds.), *The Culture and Psychology Reader* (pp. 744–766). New York: New York University Press.

Shweder, R. A., & Bourne, E. (1984). Does the concept of the person vary cross-culturally? In R. A. Shweder, & R. LeVine (Eds.), *Culture Theory: Essays on Mind, Self, and Emotion* (pp. 158–199). New York: Cambridge University Press.

Shweder, R. A., Much, N. C., Mahapatra, M., & Park, L. (1997). The "big three" of morality (autonomy, community, divinity) and the "big three" explanations of suffering. In A. Brandt, & P. Rozin (Eds.), *Morality and Health* (pp. 119–169). New York: Routledge.

Sidanius, J., & Pratto, F. (2001). *Social Dominance: An Intergroup Theory of Social Hierarchy and Oppression*. New York: Cambridge University Press.

Siegel, B. J. (1955). High anxiety levels and cultural integration: Notes on a psycho-cultural hypothesis. *Social Forces, 34*, 42–48.

(1970). Defensive structuring and environmental stress. *American Journal of Sociology, 76*, 11–32.

Sierra-Siegert, M., & David, A. S. (2007). Depersonalization and individualism: The effect of culture on symptom profiles in panic disorder. *Journal of Nervous and Mental Disease, 195*, 989–995.

Silvia, P. J. (2001). Nothing or the opposite: Intersecting terror management and objective self-awareness. *European Journal of Personality, 15*(1), 73–82.

Simeon, D., Gross, S., Guralnik, O., Stein, D. J., Schmeidler, J., & Hollander, E. (1997). Feeling unreal: 30 Cases of DSM-III-R depersonalization disorder. *American Journal of Psychiatry, 154*, 1107–1113.

Simeon, D., Guralnik, O., Schmeidler, J., Sirof, B., & Knutelska, M. (2001). The role of childhood interpersonal trauma in depersonalization disorder. *American Journal of Psychiatry, 158*, 1027–1033.

Simmel, G. (1955). *Conflict and the Web of Group-Affiliations*. New York: MacMillan Publishing Company.

(1971). *On Individuality and Social Forms* (D. N. Levine, Ed.). Chicago, IL: University of Chicago Press.

(1982). *Philosophy of Money* (T. Bottomore & D. Frisby, Trans.). New York: Routledge.

(2010). Life as transcendence. In G. Simmel (Ed.), *The View of Life: Four Metaphysical Essays* (J. A. Y. Andrews & D. N. Levine, Trans.) (pp. 1–18). Chicago, IL: University of Chicago Press.

Simmons, J. P., Nelson, L. D., & Simonsohn, U. (2011). False-positive psychology: Undisclosed flexibility in data collection and analysis allows presenting anything as significant. *Psychological Science, 22*, 1359–1366.

Simpson, J. A., Collins, W. A., & Salvatore, J. E. (2011). The impact of early interpersonal experience on adult romantic relationship functioning: Recent findings from the Minnesota Longitudinal Study of Risk and Adaptation. *Current Directions in Psychological Science, 20*(6), 355–359.

Singelis, T. M., Bond, M. H., Sharkey, W. F., & Lai, C. S. Y. (1999). Unpackaging culture's influence on self-esteem and embarrassability: The role of self-construals. *Journal of Cross-Cultural Psychology, 30*, 315–341.

Singelis, T. M., Triandis, H. C., Bhawuk, D. P. S., & Gelfand, M. J. (1995). Horizontal and vertical dimensions of individualism and collectivism: A theoretical and measurement refinement. *Cross-Cultural Research, 29*(3), 240–275.

Smith, A. (2009). *The Theory of Moral Sentiments.* New York: Penguin Books (Original work published 1759).

Smith, D. N., Ternes, B., Ordner, J. P., Schloemer, R., Moran, G., Goode, C., et al. (2011). Mapping the Great Recession: A reader's guide to the first crisis of 21st century capitalism. *New Political Science, 33*(4), 577–601.

Smith, J. S., & Cartlidge, M. R. (2011). Place attachment among retirees in Greensburg, Kansas. *Geographical Review, 101*, 536–555.

Smucker, J. (1986). Religious community and individualism: Conceptual adaptations by one group of Mennonites. *Journal for the Scientific Study of Religion, 25*(3), 273–291.

Sorrentino, R. M., Szeto, A., Nezlek, J. B., Yasunaga, S., Kouhara, S., & Ohtsubo, Y. (2008). Uncertainty regulation: The master motive? In R. M. Sorrentino, & S. Yamaguchi (Eds.), *Handbook of Motivation and Cognition across Cultures* (pp. 49–70). San Diego, CA: Academic Press.

Sow, A. I. (1980). *Anthropological Structures of Madness in Black Africa.* New York: International Universities Press.

Spencer-Rodgers, J., Peng, K., Wang, L., & Hou, Y. (2004). Dialectical self-esteem and East-West differences in psychological well-being. *Personality and Social Psychology Bulletin, 30*(11), 1416–1432.

Spiegel, D., Loewenstein, R. J., Lewis-Fernández, R., Sar, V., Simeon, D., Vermetten, E., et al. (2011). Dissociative disorders in DSM-5. *Depression and Anxiety, 28*, E17–E45.

Spierenburg, P. (2004). Social control and history: An introduction. In H. Roodenburg, & P. Spierenburg (Eds.), *Social Control in Europe Volume 1: 1500–1800* (pp. 1–22). Columbus, OH: Ohio State University Press.

Spiro, M. (1961). An overview and a suggested reorientation. In F. L. K. Hsu (Ed.), *Psychological Anthropology*. Homewood, IL: Dorsey Press.

Spiro, M. E. (1965). Religious systems as culturally constituted defense mechanisms. In M. E. Spiro (Ed.), *Context and Meaning in Cultural Anthropology* (pp. 100–113). New York: Free Press.

(1967). *Burmese Supernaturalism: A Study in the Explanation and Reduction of Suffering*. Englewood Cliffs, NJ: Prentice Hall.

Staples, W. G. (2003). Surveillance and social control in postmodern life. In T. G. Blomberg, & S. Cohen (Eds.), *Punishment and Social Control* (pp. 191–214). New York: Walter de Gruyter.

Steele, C. M. (1988). The psychology of self-affirmation: Sustaining the integrity of the self. In L. Berkowitz (Ed.), *Advances in Experimental Social Psychology* (Vol. 21, pp. 261–302). San Diego, CA: Academic Press.

Stephan, A. (2012). Emotions, existential feelings, and their regulation. *Emotion Review*, *4*(2), 157–162.

Stephens, N. M., Fryberg, S. A., Markus, H. R., Johnson, C. S., & Covarrubias, R. (2012). Unseen disadvantage: How American universities' focus on independence undermines the academic performance of first-generation college students. *Journal of Personality and Social Psychology*, *102*, 1178–1197.

Stephens, N. M., Hamedani, M. G., Markus, H. R., Bergsieker, H. B., & Eloul, L. (2009). Why did they "choose" to stay? Perspectives of Hurricane Katrina observers and survivors. *Psychological Science*, *20*, 878–886.

Stevenson, J. C., & Everson, P. M. (1990). The cultural context of fertility transition in immigrant Mennonites. In J. Landers, & V. Reynolds (Eds.), *Fertility and Resources: Society for the Study of Human Biology Symposium 31*. Cambridge; New York: Cambridge University Press

Stiker, H.-J. (1999). *A History of Disability* (T. Common, Trans.). Ann Arbor, MI: University of Michigan Press.

Stull, D. D., Bowerman, W. R., Crawford, M. H., Haas, J. D., Hiebert, D. L., Janzen, J. M., et al. (1981). "Aging among the Mennonites of Kansas and Mexico." Proposal for renewal of KU Aging Grant (Principal Investigator D. D. Stull). Lawrence, KS.

Suddendorf, T., & Corballis, M. C. (1997). Mental time travel and the evolution of the human mind. *Genetic, Social, and General Psychology Monographs*, *123*(2), 133–167.

Suh, E. M. (2000). Self, the hyphen between culture and subjective well-being. In E. Diener, & E. M. Suh (Eds.), *Culture and Subjective Well-Being* (pp. 63–86). Cambridge, MA: MIT Press.

(2002). Culture, identity consistency, and subjective well-being. *Journal of Personality and Social Psychology*, *83*(6), 1378–1391.

Suhail, K., & Cochrane, R. (2002). Effect of culture and environment on the phenomenology of delusions and hallucinations. *International Journal of Social Psychiatry*, *48*(2), 126–138.

Sullivan, D. (2013). From guilt-oriented to uncertainty-oriented culture: Nietzsche and Weber on the history of theodicy. *Journal of Theoretical and Philosophical Psychology*, *33*(2), 107–124.

Sullivan, D., Keefer, L. A., Stewart, S. A., & Palitsky, R. (in press a). Time-space distanciation: An interdisciplinary account of how culture shapes the implicit and explicit psychology of time and space. *Journal for the Theory of Social Behaviour*.

Sullivan, D., Landau, M. J., & Kay, A. C. (2012a). Toward a comprehensive understanding of existential threat: Insights from Paul Tillich. *Social Cognition*, *30*(6), 734–757.

Sullivan, D., Landau, M. J., Kay, A. C., & Rothschild, Z. K. (2012b). Collectivism and the meaning of suffering. *Journal of Personality and Social Psychology*, *103*(6), 1023–1039.

Sullivan, D., Landau, M. J., & Rothschild, Z. K. (2010). An existential function of enemyship: Evidence that people attribute influence to personal and political enemies to compensate for threats to control. *Journal of Personality and Social Psychology*, *98*, 434–449.

Sullivan, D., Landau, M. J., Young, I. F., & Stewart, S. A. (2014). The dramaturgical perspective in relation to self and culture. *Journal of Personality and Social Psychology*, *107*(5), 767–790.

Sullivan, D., & Stewart, S. A. (in press). Perceived uncontrollability as a coping resource: The control-serving function of enemies and uncertainty. In M. Bukowski, I. Fristche, A. Guinote, & M. Kofta (Eds.), *Coping with Lack of Control in a Social World*. New York: Psychology Press.

Sullivan, D., Stewart, S. A., & Diefendorf, J. (2015). Simmel's time-space theory: Implications for experience of modernization and place. *Journal of Environmental Psychology*, *41*, 45–57.

Sullivan, D., Stewart, S. A., Landau, M. J., Liu, S., Yang, Q., & Diefendorf, J. (in press b). Exploring repressive suffering construal as a function of collectivism and social morality. *Journal of Cross-Cultural Psychology*.

Swanson, G. E. (1964). *The Birth of the Gods: The Origin of Primitive Beliefs*. Ann Arbor, MI: University of Michigan Press.

Talle, A. (1995). A child is a child: Disability and equality among the Kenya Maasai. In B. Ingstad & S. Whyte (Eds.), *Disability and Culture* (pp. 56–72). Berkeley: University of California Press.

Tambiah, S. J. (1973). Classification of animals in Thailand. In M. Douglas (Ed.), *Rules and Meanings: The Anthropology of Everyday Knowledge* (pp. 127–166). Baltimore: Penguin.

Tangney, J. P., & Dearing, R. L. (2002). *Shame and Guilt*. New York: The Guilford Press.

Tanner, B. (April 20, 2010). On tornado anniversary, Greensburg reflects. *The Wichita Eagle*. Retrieved from www.kansas.com/2010/04/20/1277208/on-tornado-anniversary-town-reflects.html

Tapp, R. B. (1973). *Religion among the Unitarian Universalists*. New York: Seminar Press.

Taylor, C. (1991). *The Ethics of Authenticity*. Cambridge, MA: Harvard University Press.

(2007). *A Secular Age*. Cambridge, MA: The Belknap Press of Harvard University Press.

Taylor, J. B., Zurcher, L. A., & Key, W. H. (1970). *Tornado: A Community Responds to Disaster*. Seattle: University of Washington Press.

Taylor, S. J., & Bogdan, R. (1998). *Introduction to Qualitative Research Methods*. New York: Wiley.

Teddlie, C., & Tashakkori, A. (2006). A general typology of research designs featuring mixed methods. *Research in the Schools*, 13, 12–28.

Tedeschi, R. G., & Calhoun, L. G. (1996). The posttraumatic growth inventory: Measuring the positive legacy of trauma. *Journal of Traumatic Stress*, *9*(3), 455–471.

TenHouten, W. D. (2005). *Time and Society*. Albany, NY: SUNY Press.

Tesser, A. (1988). Toward a self-evaluation maintenance model of social behavior. *Advances in Experimental Social Psychology*, *21*, 181–228.

Thapar, R. (2002). Cyclical and linear time in early India. In K. Ridderbos (Ed.), *Time* (pp. 27–45). Cambridge: Cambridge University Press.

Thompson, B. (1989). Statistical significance, result importance, and result generalizability: Three noteworthy but somewhat different issues. *Measurement and Evaluation in Counseling and Development*, *22*(1), 2–6.

Thompson, E., & Varela, F. J. (2001). Radical embodiment: Neural dynamics and consciousness. *Trends in Cognitive Sciences*, *5*(10), 418–425.

Thorlindsson, T., & Bjarnason, T. (1998). Modeling Durkheim on the micro level: A study of youth suicidality. *American Sociological Review*, *63*(1), 94–110.

Tidball, K. G., & Krasny, M. E. (Eds.). (2013). *Greening in the Red Zone: Disaster, Resilience and Community Greening*. Berlin: Springer.

Tillich, P. (1952). *The Courage to Be*. New Haven, CT: Yale University Press.

(1959). *The Theology of Culture*. Oxford: Oxford University Press.

Tipton, S. M. (2002). Social differentiation and moral pluralism. In R. Madsen, W. M. Sullivan, A. Swidler, & S. M. Tipton (Eds.), *Meaning and Modernity: Religion, Polity, and Self* (pp. 15–40). Berkeley: University of California Press.

Tiryakian, E. A. (1962). *Sociologism and Existentialism*. Englewood Cliffs, NJ: Prentice Hall.

Tomasello, M. (1999). *The Cultural Origins of Human Cognition*. Cambridge, MA: Harvard University Press.

Tomlinson, B., & Lipsitz, G. (2013). Insubordinate spaces for intemperate times: Countering the pedagogies of neoliberalism. *Review of Education, Pedagogy, and Cultural Studies*, *35*, 3–26.

Tonnies, F. (1971). *Ferdinand Toennies on Sociology Pure, Applied and Empirical Sociology*. Chicago, IL: University of Chicago Press.

Tracy, J. L., & Robins, R. W. (2007). The self in self-conscious emotions: A cognitive appraisal approach. In J. L. Tracy, R. W. Robins, & J. P. Tangney (Eds.), *The Self-Conscious Emotions: Theory and Research* (pp. 3–20). New York: Guilford Press.

Triandis, H. C. (1989). The self and social behavior in differing cultural contexts. *Psychological Review*, *96*(3), 506–520.

(1995). *Individualism and Collectivism*. Boulder: Westview Press.

Triandis, H. C., & Gelfand, M. J. (1998). Converging measurement of horizontal and vertical individualism and collectivism. *Journal of Personality and Social Psychology, 74*(1), 118–128.

Triplett, K. N., Tedeschi, R. G., Cann, A., Calhoun, L. G., & Reeve, C. L. (2012). Posttraumatic growth, meaning in life, and life satisfaction in response to trauma. *Psychological Trauma, 4*, 400–410.

Trompf, G. W. (1994). *Payback: The Logic of Retribution in Melanesian Religions*. Cambridge; New York: Cambridge University Press.

Tuan, Y. (1977). *Space and Place: The Perspective of Experience*. Minneapolis: Hodder & Stoughton Educational.

Twenge, J. M. (2000). The age of anxiety? The birth cohort change in anxiety and neuroticism, 1952–1993. *Journal of Personality and Social Psychology, 79*(6), 1007–1021.

Unruh, E. (May 20, 2009). Vision. *Messenger of Truth, 107*(10), 2–3.

Unruh, E., & Unruh, F. (2007). *Tornado! Up from the Debris to Thank God*. Newton, KS: Mennonite Press Inc.

Urciuoli, B. (2010). Neoliberal education: Preparing the student for the new workplace. In C. J. Greenhouse (Ed.), *Ethnographies of Neoliberalism* (pp. 162–176). Philadelphia: University of Pennsylvania Press.

Vaillancourt, T. (2013). Students aggress against professors in reaction to receiving poor grades: An effect moderated by student narcissism and self-esteem. *Aggressive Behavior, 39*, 71–84.

Valadier, P. (1977). Dionysus versus the crucified. In D. B. Allison (Ed.), *The New Nietzsche: Contemporary Styles of Interpretation* (pp. 247–264). New York: Delta Books.

Vallacher, R. R., & Wegner, D. M. (1987). What do people think they're doing? Action identification and human behavior. *Psychological Review, 94*(1), 3–15.

van Braght, T. J. (1660/1938). *Martyrs Mirror: The Story of Seventeen Centuries of Christian Martyrdom from the Time of Christ to A.D. 1660*. (J. F. Sohm, Trans.). Scottdale, PA: Herald Press.

van de Vijver, F. J. R. (2011). Bias and real differences in cross-cultural differences: Neither friends nor foes. In F. J. R. van de Vijver, A. Chasiotis, & S. M. Breugelmans (Eds.), *Fundamental Questions in Cross-Cultural Psychology* (pp. 235–258). New York: Cambridge University Press.

van Duijl, M., Kleijn, W., & de Jong, J. (2012). Are symptoms of spirit possessed patients covered by the DSM-IV or DSM-V criteria for possession trance disorder? A mixed-method explorative study in Uganda. *Social Psychiatry and Psychiatric Epidemiology, 48*, 1417–1430.

van Duijl, M., Nijenhuis, E., Komproe, I. H., Gernaat, H. B. P. E., & de Jong, J. T. (2010). Dissociative symptoms and reported trauma among patients with spirit possession and matched healthy controls in Uganda. *Culture, Medicine, and Psychiatry, 34*, 380–400.

van Pachterbeke, M., Keller, J., & Saroglou, V. (2012). Flexibility in existential beliefs and worldview: Introducing and measuring existential quest. *Journal of Individual Differences, 33*, 2–16.

Varnum, M. E. W., Grossmann, I., Kitayama, S., & Nisbett, R. E. (2010). The origin of cultural differences in cognition: Evidence for the social orientation hypothesis. *Current Directions in Psychological Science*, *19*(1), 9–13.

Vaughan, B. (2002). Cultured punishments: The promise of grid-group theory. *Theoretical Criminology*, *6*(4), 411–431.

Volk, T. (2002). *What is Death? A Scientist Looks at the Cycle of Life*. New York: Wiley.

Vygotsky, L. S. (1978). *Mind in Society: The Development of Higher Psychological Processes*. Cambridge, MA: Harvard University Press.

Walinga, P., Corveleyn, J., & van Saane, J. (2006). Guilt and religion: The influence of Orthodox Protestant and Orthodox Catholic conceptions of guilt on guilt experience. *Archive for the Psychology of Religion*, *27*, 113–135.

Ward, C. (1980). Spirit possession and mental health: A psycho-anthropological perspective. *Human Relations*, *33*, 149–163.

Watson, P. (2006). *Ideas: A History of Thought and Invention, from Fire to Freud*. New York: Harper Perennial.

(2014). *The Age of Nothing: How We Have Sought to Live since the Death of God*. London: Orion Publishing.

Weaver, A. P. (Ed.). (1996). *Mennonite Theology in Face of Modernity: Essays in Honor of Gordon D. Kaufman*. Newton, KS: Mennonite Press.

Weaver, J. D. (1997). *Keeping Salvation Ethical: Mennonite and Amish Atonement Theology in the Late Nineteenth Century*. Scottdale, PA: Herald Press.

Webb, E. J., Campbell, D. T., Schwartz, R. D., & Sechrest, L. (2000). *Unobtrusive Measures*. Thousand Oaks, CA: SAGE Publications, Inc.

Weber, M. (1946). *From Max Weber: Essays in Sociology*. New York: Oxford University Press.

(1951). *The Religion of China: Confucianism and Taoism* (H. H. Gerth, Trans.). New York: The Free Press.

(2009). *The Protestant Ethic and the Spirit of Capitalism* (S. Kalberg, Trans.). New York: Oxford University Press (Original work published 1904).

Wedel, C. (September 26, 2007). New growth. *Messenger of Truth*, *105*(20), 2–3.

Weems, C. F., Costa, N. M., Dehon, C., & Berman, S. L. (2004). Paul Tillich's theory of existential anxiety: A preliminary conceptual and empirical examination. *Anxiety, Stress, and Coping*, *17*, 383–399.

Westen, D. (1985). *Self and Society: Narcissism, Collectivism, and the Development of Morals*. Baltimore: Cambridge University Press.

(1998). The scientific legacy of Sigmund Freud: Toward a psychodynamically informed psychological science. *Psychological Bulletin*, *124*(3), 333–371.

Wheeler, M. A., Stuss, D. T., & Tulving, E. (1997). Toward a theory of episodic memory: The frontal lobes and autonoetic consciousness. *Psychological Bulletin*, *121*(3), 331–354.

White, S. S. (2010). Out of the rubble and towards a sustainable future: The "greening" of Greensburg, Kansas. *Sustainability*, *2*, 2302–2319.

Whitehouse, H., & Laidlaw, J. (Eds.). (2004). *Ritual and Memory: Toward a Comparative Anthropology of Religion*. Walnut Creek, CA: AltaMira Press.

Whiting, J. W. M., & Child, I. L. (1953). *Child Training and Personality*. New Haven, CT: Yale University Press.

Wieviorka, M. (2012). *Evil*. New York: Polity.

Wilkinson, I. (2009). *Risk, Vulnerability and Everyday Life*. London; New York: Routledge.

Williams, L. E., & Bargh, J. A. (2008). Experiencing physical warmth promotes interpersonal warmth. *Science*, *322*(5901), 606–607.

Willis, P. E. (1977). *Learning to Labour: How Working Class Kids Get Working Class Jobs*. Farnborough: Avebury.

Wittrock, B. (2012). The Axial Age in global history: Cultural crystallizations and societal transformations. In R. N. Bellah, & H. Joas (Eds.), *The Axial Age and Its Consequences* (pp. 102–125). Cambridge, MA: Belknap Press.

Wolfenstein, M. (1957). *Disaster: A Psychological Essay*. New York: Free Press.

Wong, P. T. P. (2006). Existential and humanistic theories. In J. C. Thomas, & D. L. Segal (Eds.), *Comprehensive Handbook of Personality and Psychopathology*. Hoboken, NJ: Wiley.

Woodburn, J. (1982). Egalitarian societies. *Man*, *17*(3), 431–451.

Young, M. J., & Morris, M. W. (2004). Existential meanings and cultural models: The interplay of personal and supernatural agency in American and Hindu ways of responding to uncertainty. In J. Greenberg, S. L. Koole, & T. Pyszczynski (Eds.), *Handbook of Experimental Existential Psychology* (pp. 215–230). New York: Guilford Press.

Zadro, L., Williams, K. D., & Richardson, R. (2004). How low can you go? Ostracism by a computer is sufficient to lower self-reported levels of belonging, control, self-esteem, and meaningful existence. *Journal of Experimental Social Psychology*, *40*(4), 560–567.

Zapffe, P. W. (1933/2004). The last messiah. *Philosophy Now: A Magazine of Ideas*, *45*, 35–39.

Zaumseil, M., Schwarz, S., Vacano, M. von, Sullivan, G. B., & Prawitasari-Hadiyono, J. E. (Eds.). (2013). *Cultural Psychology of Coping with Disasters: The Case of an Earthquake in Java, Indonesia*. New York: Springer.

Zhong, C.-B., & Liljenquist, K. (2006). Washing away your sins: Threatened morality and physical cleansing. *Science*, *313*(5792), 1451–1452.

Index